2

Complete First Certificate

Student's Book *with answers*

Guy Brook-Hart

CAMBRIDGE UNIVERSITY PRESS
Cambridge, New York, Melbourne, Madrid, Cape Town, Singapore, São Paulo, Delhi

Cambridge University Press
The Edinburgh Building, Cambridge CB2 8RU, UK

www.cambridge.org
Information on this title: www.cambridge.org/9780521698269

First published 2008

Printed in the United Kingdom at the University Press, Cambridge

A catalogue record for this publication is available from the British Library

ISBN 978-0-521-69825-2 Student's Book with CD-ROM
ISBN 978-0-521-69826-9 Student's Book with answers and CD-ROM
ISBN 978-0-521-69828-3 Teacher's Book
ISBN 978-0-521-69830-6 Class Audio CDs (3)
ISBN 978-0-521-69827-6 Student's Book Pack
ISBN 978-0-521-69831-3 Workbook with Audio CD
ISBN 978-0-521-69832-0 Workbook with answers and Audio CD

Contents

Map of the units

Unit title	Reading	Writing	Use of English
1 A family affair	Reading Part 2: How to live with teenagers	• Writing Part 1: Email replying to a request for information • Making suggestions	Use of English Part 2: Who should do the housework?
2 Leisure and pleasure	Reading Part 1: My first bike	Writing Part 2: Article about a free-time activity	Use of English Part 4: Questions practising comparison of adjectives and adverbs
Vocabulary and grammar review Units 1 and 2			
3 Happy holidays!	Reading Part 3: Memorable train journeys	• Writing Part 2: Story – It was a trip I'll never forget • Using past tenses • Paragraph planning	• Use of English Part 3 • Forming adjectives from nouns and verbs
4 Food, glorious food	• Reading Part 2: Learning about food • Identifying cohesive features	• Writing Part 2: Review of a restaurant • Using descriptive adjectives	Use of English Part 1: Moso Moso restaurant
Vocabulary and grammar review Units 3 and 4			
5 Studying abroad	• Reading Part 3: A year abroad • Studying the questions	• Writing Part 1: Letter of invitation • Common spelling mistakes	• Use of English Part 3: Learn Polish in Poland • Forming nouns from verbs
6 The planet in danger	Reading Part 2: A close encounter in Africa	• Writing Part 2: Essay on class discussion about protecting the environment • Linkers and sequencers	Use of English Part 1: Earth getting darker as sunlight decreases
Vocabulary and grammar review Units 5 and 6			
7 My first job	Reading Part 1: Lucy's first job	Writing Part 1: Letter of application for a holiday job	Use of English Part 2: Volunteering with Katimavik
8 High adventure	• Reading Part 2: Are you ready for an adventure race? • Using cohesive features	• Writing Part 2: Report on sports activities in your area • Formal and informal styles	Use of English Part 4: Questions practising comparison of adjectives and adverbs; infinitive and verb + *-ing*
Vocabulary and grammar review Units 7 and 8			
9 Star performances	Reading Part 3: Five young actors	Writing Part 2: Article about the best place to see films; article about being famous or successful	Use of English Part 1: Young people dream of fame
10 Secrets of the mind	Reading Part 1: The secrets of happiness	• Writing Part 2: Story – One of the happiest days of my life; A day I will never forget • Organising ideas	Use of English Part 4: Questions practising expressions + verb + *-ing*, modal verbs and reported speech
Vocabulary and grammar review Units 9 and 10			
11 Spend, spend, spend!	Reading Part 1: Help! My daughter's used my credit cards!	• Writing Part 2: Report on college improvements; report on improvements to your neighbourhood • Making suggestions and recommendations	Use of English Part 2: Bargain hunters
12 Staying healthy	Reading Part 2: Problem school changes diet	Writing Part 2: Essay about modern lifestyles and health; essay on health and fitness	• Use of English Part 3: Is there a doctor on board? • Negative prefixes
Vocabulary and grammar review Units 11 and 12			
13 Animal kingdom	Reading Part 3: Surviving an animal attack	• Writing Part 2: Letter of advice • Giving advice	Use of English Part 1: My sister's circus
14 House space	Reading Part 1: My new home in Venice, 1733	Writing Part 2: Article – My ideal home	Use of English Part 2: Living on a houseboat
Vocabulary and grammar review Units 13 and 14			
15 Fiesta!	Reading Part 2: The tomato fight fiesta	Writing Part 1: Email giving information, inviting and accepting	• Use of English Part 3: My local festival • Forming personal nouns • Forming nouns from verbs
16 Machine age	Reading Part 3: New products review	Writing Part 2: Review of a gadget	Use of English Part 4: Questions revising a variety of grammar and expressions
Vocabulary and grammar review Units 15 and 16			

Listening	Speaking	Vocabulary	Grammar
• Listening Part 1: Young people talking about their family lives • Two candidates doing Speaking Part 1	• Talking about one's family • Speaking Part 1: Giving personal information	• Adjectives describing character • Housework collocations • Collocations with *make* and *do*	• Present simple and continuous • Present perfect simple and continuous • Asking questions
• A young woman talking about an amazing experience • Listening Part 2: Video and computer games	• Comparing free-time activities • Speaking Part 2: Talking about free time and hobbies	Phrasal verbs	• Adjectives with *-ed* and *-ing* • Comparison of adjectives and adverbs
• Listening Part 3: Five young people talk about last year's holiday • Two candidates doing Speaking Part 3 • Five people talking about unforgettable journeys	• Talking about one's favourite type of holiday • Speaking Part 3: Deciding on an end-of-year trip • Turn-taking	• Types of holiday, holiday locations and activities • *Journey, trip, travel, way*	• Past simple, past continuous and *used to* • Past perfect simple and continuous
• Listening Part 4: The Slow Food Movement • Two candidates doing Speaking Part 4	• Talking about favourite dishes and healthy eating • Speaking Part 4: Supporting your opinions	*Food, dish, meal*	• *So* and *such* • *Too* and *enough*
• Listening Part 1: Young people talking about studying abroad • Two candidates doing Speaking Part 1	• Talking about reasons for studying abroad • Speaking Part 1: Talking about studying	• Words connected with studying • *Find out, get to know, know, learn, teach, study; attend, join, take part in, assist*	• Zero, first and second conditionals • Indirect questions
• Listening Part 2: Rainforest project, Costa Rica • Two candidates doing Speaking Part 2	• Talking about environmental threats • Talking about your area in 20 years' time • Speaking Part 2: Useful phrases and vocabulary	• Words connected with the environment • *Look, see, watch, listen, hear* • *Prevent, avoid, protect; reach, arrive, get (to)*	Ways of expressing the future
• Listening Part 3: Five people talking about first job • Two candidates doing Speaking Part 3	• Talking about suitable jobs for students • Speaking Part 3: Suggesting, agreeing and disagreeing, asking opinions • Working together as volunteers	*Work* or *job*; *possibility, occasion, opportunity*; *fun* or *funny*	• Countable and uncountable nouns • Articles
• Adventure racing • Listening Part 4: Learning to paraglide • Two candidates doing Speaking Part 4	• Talking about adventure sports • Talking about danger in sport • Speaking Part 4: Introducing an opinion, explanation, or example	Types of adventure sport	Infinitive and verb + *-ing*
• Listening Part 2: Participating in a quiz show • Two candidates doing Speaking Part 1	• Talking about TV tastes • Speaking Part 1: Talking about likes and dislikes	• Types of TV programme • *Play, performance, acting; audience, public, spectators; scene, stage*	• Reported speech 1 • Linking words for contrast
• Listening Part 1: Eight extracts on different subjects • Two candidates doing Speaking Part 3	• Talking about things which make you happy • Speaking Part 3: Speculating, using vocabulary	*Make, cause, have; stay, spend, pass*	Modal verbs to express certainty and possibility
• Listening Part 4: Redsands Park • Two candidates doing Speaking Part 2	• Talking with foreign visitors about shopping • Talking about teenage spending and pocket money • Who does the shopping? • Speaking Part 2 : Speculating	• Types of shop • Phrasal verbs • Words connected with money	• Modals expressing ability • *As* and *like* • *Look, seem, appear*
• Six people talk about being healthy • Listening Part 3: Five people talk about their visits to the doctor • Four candidates doing Speaking Part 4 • Young people talking about attitudes to health	• Talking about what it means to be healthy • Speaking Part 4: Discussing health issues	• Words connected with health • Parts of the body • Medical vocabulary	Relative pronouns and relative clauses
• Listening Part 1: Eight extracts on different subjects connected with animals • Two candidates doing Speaking Part 1	• Talking about the roles of animals in our lives • Talking about dangerous animals • Speaking Part 1: Talking about animals	*Named, called*	• Third conditional • *Wish, if only, hope*
• Listening Part 2: A haunted house • Five young people talking about staying with host families	• Talking about choosing where to live • Describing somewhere you have lived • Renovating a holiday home • Speaking Part 2: Different places to live	• Types of housing • *Space, place, room, area, location, square*	• Causative *have* • Expressing obligation and permission
• Listening Part 4: The Hat Fair • Two candidates doing Speaking Part 3	• Talking about festivals • Speaking Part 3: Turn-taking	Activities during festivals	• The passive • The passive with reporting verbs
• Listening Part 3: Five young people talk about their parents and computers • Two candidates doing Speaking Part 4	• Discussing uses of different devices • Speaking Part 4: Discussing new technology	• Types of machine or gadget • *Check, supervise, control*	• Linking words: *when, if, in case, even if, even though, whether* • Reported speech 2: reporting verbs

Introduction

Who this book is for

Complete First Certificate is a stimulating and thorough preparation course for students who wish to take the **First Certificate exam** from **Cambridge ESOL**. It teaches you the reading, writing, listening and speaking skills which are necessary for the exam as well as essential grammar and vocabulary. If you do not want to do the exam, the book teaches you skills and language at an upper-intermediate level (Common European Framework level B2).

What the book contains

In the **Student's Book** there are:

- **16 units for classroom study.** Each unit contains:
  - one part of each of the five papers in the First Certificate exam. The units provide language input and skills practice to help you to deal successfully with the tasks in each part.
  - essential information on what each part of the exam involves and the best way to approach each task.
  - a wide range of enjoyable and stimulating speaking activities designed to increase your fluency and your ability to express yourself.
  - a step-by-step approach to doing First Certificate Writing tasks.
  - grammar activities and exercises with the grammar you need to know for the exam. When you are doing grammar exercises you will sometimes see this symbol: ⊙. These are exercises which are based on research from the **Cambridge Learner Corpus** and they deal with areas which cause problems for many students when they do the exam.
  - vocabulary necessary for First Certificate. When you see this symbol ⊙ by a vocabulary exercise, the exercise focuses on words which First Certificate candidates often confuse or use wrongly in the exam.
- **Eight unit reviews.** These contain exercises which revise the grammar and vocabulary that you have studied during the previous two units.
- **Speaking and Writing reference sections.** These explain the possible tasks you may have to do in the Speaking and Writing papers, and they give you examples and advice on how best to approach them.
- A **Grammar reference section** which clearly explains all the main areas of grammar which you need to know for the First Certificate exam.
- A complete **First Certificate exam supplied by Cambridge ESOL** for you to practise with.
- A **CD-ROM** provides extra practice, with all extra exercises linked to the topics in the Student's Book.

Also available are:

- **Three audio CDs** containing listening material for the 16 units plus the recorded Listening Test supplied by Cambridge ESOL. The listening material is indicated by different coloured icons in the Student's Book as follows: CD1, CD2, CD3.
- A **Teacher's Book** containing:
  - **Step-by-step guidance** for handling all the activities in the Student's Book.
  - A large number of suggestions for **alternative treatments** of activities in the Student's Book and a large number of **suggestions for extending activities** beyond what is contained in the Student's Book.
  - **Extra photocopiable materials** for each unit of the Student's Book to practise and extend language abilities beyond the requirements of the First Certificate exam.
  - **Complete answer keys** including sample answers to Writing tasks.
  - **Complete recording scripts** for all the recorded material.
  - **Four photocopiable progress tests**, one for every four units of the book.
  - **16 photocopiable word lists** (one for each unit) containing vocabulary found in the units. Each vocabulary item in the word list is accompanied by a definition from the *Cambridge Advanced Learner's Dictionary*.
- A **Student's Workbook** to accompany the Student's Book, with four pages of exercises for each unit. These exercises practise the reading, writing and listening skills needed for the First Certificate exam. They also give further practice in grammar and vocabulary. The Student's Workbook is also accompanied by an **audio CD** containing listening material.

First Certificate content and overview

Part/timing	Content	Test focus
1 **READING** 1 hour	**Part 1** A text followed by eight multiple-choice questions. **Part 2** A text from which seven sentences have been removed and placed in a jumbled order, together with an additional sentence, after the text. **Part 3** A text or several short texts preceded by 15 multiple-matching questions.	Candidates are expected to show understanding of specific information, text organisation features, tone, text structure.
2 **WRITING** 1 hour 20 minutes	**Part 1** One compulsory question. **Part 2** Candidates choose one task from a choice of five questions (including the set text options).	Candidates are expected to be able to write non-specialised text types such as an article, an essay, a letter, an email, a report, a review or a short story, with a focus on advising, apologising, comparing, describing, explaining, expressing opinions, justifying, persuading, recommending, suggesting.
3 **USE OF ENGLISH** 45 minutes	**Part 1** A modified cloze test containing 12 gaps and followed by 12 multiple-choice items. **Part 2** A modified open cloze test containing 12 gaps. **Part 3** A text containing 10 gaps. Each gap corresponds to a word. The stems of the missing words are given beside the text and must be changed to form the missing word. **Part 4** Eight separate questions, each with a lead-in sentence and a gapped second sentence to be completed in two to five words, one of which is given a 'key word'.	Candidates are expected to demonstrate the ability to apply their knowledge of the language system by completing a number of tasks.
4 **LISTENING** Approximately 40 minutes	**Part 1** A series of eight short unrelated extracts from monologues or exchanges between interacting speakers. There is one multiple-choice question per extract. **Part 2** A monologue or text involving interacting speakers, with a sentence completion task which has 10 questions. **Part 3** Five short related monologues, with five multiple-matching questions. **Part 4** A monologue or text involving interacting speakers, with seven multiple-choice questions.	Candidates are expected to be able to show understanding of attitude, detail, function, genre, gist, main idea, opinion, place, purpose, situation, specific information, relationship, topic, agreement, etc.
5 **SPEAKING** 14 minutes	**Part 1** A conversation between the interlocutor and each candidate (spoken questions). **Part 2** An individual 'long turn' for each candidate, with a brief response from the second candidate (visual and written stimuli, with spoken instructions). **Part 3** A two-way conversation between candidates (visual and written stimuli, with spoken instructions). **Part 4** A discussion on topics related to Part 3 (spoken questions).	Candidates are expected to be able to respond to questions and to interact in conversational English.

Unit 1 A family affair

Starting off

Work in pairs. Are these sentences true for you? Give some details in your answers.

1 I'm an only child.
2 In my family we usually have our meals together.
3 My grandparents helped to look after me when I was small.
4 I help my family to do the housework.
5 When I'm at home, I prefer being in my own room.
6 I'd prefer to share a flat with my friends than live with my family.

Listening Part 1

You will hear part of an interview with four young people talking about their family lives.

1 Before you listen, describe the photos above.

- What does each photo show about family life?
- Which of these things do you do with your family?

2 (2) Now listen to the interview. Match the speakers to the photos.

	photo
Patrick	
Tracey	
Vicky	
Kostas	

3 (2) Now listen again and choose the best answer A, B or C for each speaker. Before you listen, read each question carefully.

1 In Patrick's opinion, why does his mother help him?
  A She enjoys it.
  B She worries about him.
  C She has plenty of time.

2 What is Tracey's family doing to the house at the moment?
  A extending it
  B cleaning it
  C painting it

3 How often do Vicky and her father take exercise together?
  A regularly, once a week
  B occasionally
  C only in the summer

4 How does Kostas feel about family celebrations?
  A bored
  B embarrassed
  C amused

Exam information

In Listening Part 1, you:

- listen to people talking in eight different situations
- choose A, B or C to answer one question for each situation
- hear each piece twice.

4 (3) **Correct the mistakes in questions 1–4 on the notepad. Then check by listening to the questions again.**

1 How much you help around the house?

2 How often are you all doing things together as a family?

3 You ever do sports with other people in your family?

4 Are you enjoy family celebrations?

5 ....?

6 ....?

7 ....?

8 ....?

5 Work in pairs. Add four more questions to the notepad to ask other members of the class about their family life.

You can ask about: family holidays, things they enjoy doing with their family, how the family spends weekends, which family member they are most similar to, etc.

6 Now ask your questions to another member of the class.

Grammar

Present simple and present continuous

1 Look at the underlined verbs in each of these sentences from the listening exercise. Which are present simple and which are present continuous?

1 I don't have a lot of free time these days because I'm studying for my exams. *present continuous*
2 We live in this really old house by the sea …
3 … it's looking nicer and nicer.
4 … my dad is a fitness fanatic, so he's always running or cycling or doing something energetic.
5 I do sporty things with him now and again, more often in the summer.
6 … he's probably doing something sporty right now.
7 Someone is always standing up and giving a speech or singing a song …

2 Which tense and which example is used to describe …?

1 a situation which is permanent
Tense: *present simple* Example: *sentence 2*
2 an activity happening at the present moment
Tense: Example:
3 an activity in progress, but not happening exactly now
Tense: Example:
4 something which happens frequently with *always*
Tense: Example:
5 an activity which happens regularly or occasionally
Tense: Example:
6 a situation which is changing or developing
Tense: Example:
7 an activity which irritates the speaker
Tense: Example:

page 153 *Grammar reference: Present simple and present continuous*

3 Put the verbs in brackets into the correct tenses (present simple or continuous) in these sentences.

1 Max has passed his driving test, so he ....*often gives*.... (often give) me a lift to school in the morning.
2 Sandra's dad and my dad .... (work) together. They joined the same firm 20 years ago.
3 I'd love to come out now, but I .... (work) on my English grammar – I .... (prepare) for a university entrance exam next month, you see.
4 Look! The sun .... (come out) so we should be able to go out for a walk this afternoon.
5 You .... (always interrupt) my private conversations! Can't you mind your own business?
6 Why do they have to phone me now, just when I .... (watch) my favourite programme?
7 I think winter .... (come); the days .... (get) cooler.
8 My mum .... (not do) much cooking because she .... (always bring) work home from the office.

Reading Part 2

1 **Work in pairs. You will read an article giving advice to parents. Before you read, write these adjectives in the most appropriate column below.**

~~critical~~ fussy hard-working lazy mature tactful polite quiet nervous relaxed responsible rude sensitive strict talkative tidy tactless

usually positive	usually negative	could be either
	critical	

2 **Add one of these prefixes *un-*, *im-*, *ir-*, *in-* to each of these words to make opposites, e.g. *critical* – *uncritical*.**

~~critical~~ uncritical mature polite responsible sensitive tidy

3 **Match each of these words with its opposite, e.g. *hard-working* – *lazy*.**

hard-working tactful polite quiet relaxed rude strict lazy tactless talkative

4 **Which of the adjectives above describe/described your parents' attitude to you as a teenager? Why? Which describe/described your attitude to your parents as a teenager? Why?**

5 **Work in small groups.**

- Make a list of things that parents sometimes say about their teenage children, e.g. *He's so untidy! He's always leaving his clothes on the bathroom floor! She's very hard-working. She spends hours studying in her room.*
- What do you think parents can do to live happily with their teenage children? For example, *Listen to what their children say.*

6 **Read the article quickly without paying attention to the gaps. Do you think Penny Palmano has a mostly positive or a mostly negative attitude to teenagers?**

How to live with teenagers

There have been countless books and television series on living with teenagers, yet parents don't seem to have discovered how to get their children to pick up their clothes from the bedroom floor, or even clean their room occasionally. It might be difficult to accept, but a new approach to dealing with rude or difficult teenagers is for parents to look at their own behaviour.

"The key to getting teenagers to respect you is to respect them first," says Penny Palmano, who has written a best-selling book on teenagers. "You can't continue to treat them the same way that you have been treating them for the previous 12 years: they have opinions that count. **1** H You'd be very upset. You'd never say that to an adult, because it shows a total lack of respect."

Palmano, who has a daughter aged 19 and a 16-year-old stepdaughter, has even allowed the children to hold several teenage parties at her home. They passed without problems. "I've found that if you have brought them up to do the right thing, and then trust them to do it, usually they'll behave well," she says. "I make them sandwiches and leave them alone. But I make it clear that they have to clear up any mess. **2** ____ "

She agrees that teenagers can be irritating: enjoying a world that is free of responsibility, yet desperate for independence. She doesn't think, however, that they are trying to annoy

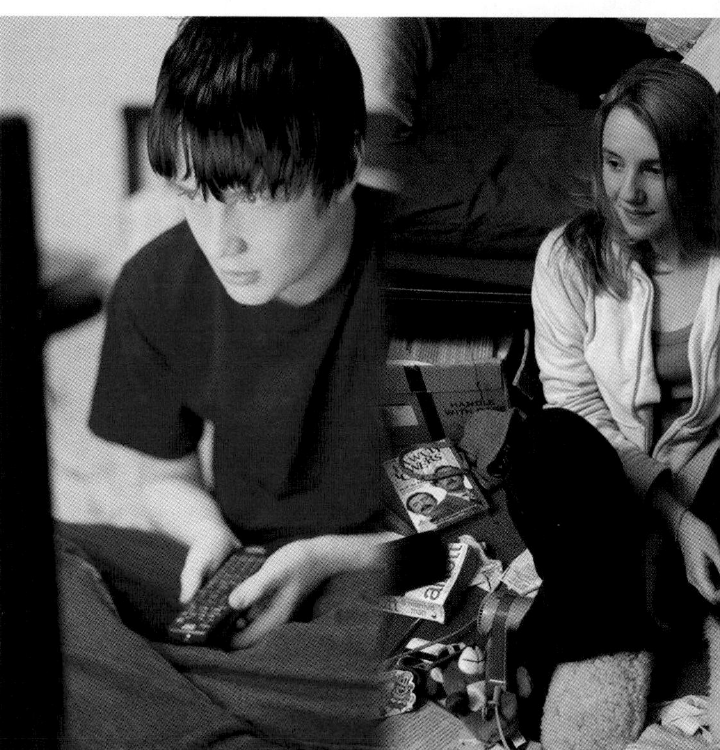

you. Until recently, scientists assumed that the brain finished growing at about the age of 13 and that teenage problems were a result of rising hormones and a desire for independence. **3** ______

"This would explain why many teenagers can't make good decisions, control their emotions, prioritise or concentrate on several different things at the same time. **4** ______ It means that they do not intentionally do the wrong thing just to annoy their parents," says Palmano.

The key to happiness for all, Palmano believes, is calm negotiation and compromise. If you want your teenagers to be home by 11 pm, explain why, but listen to their counter-arguments. If it's a Saturday, you might consider agreeing to midnight (rather than 1 am, which is what they had in mind). **5** ______ Instead, ask if they've had a problem with public transport and let it pass; they've almost managed what you asked.

She urges a bit of perspective about other things, too. "There have been times when my daughter's room has not been as tidy as I expected, but as she said once, 'I'm a teenager –what do you expect? **6** ______ ' "

"It's vital to choose your battles carefully: don't criticise teenagers for having an untidy room, then suddenly criticise them for other things. **7** ______ One minute, it's about an untidy room and the next, you're saying, 'And another thing ...' and criticising them for everything."

Adapted from *The Daily Telegraph*

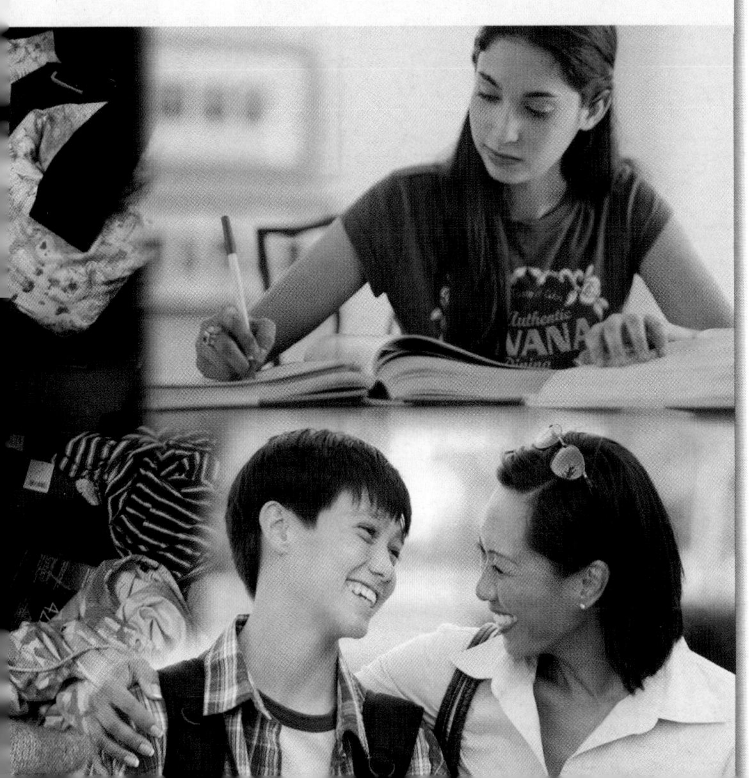

7 **Seven sentences have been removed from the article. Choose from the sentences A–H the one which fits each gap. There is one extra sentence which you do not need to use.**

A But it turns out that the region of the brain that controls judgement and emotions is not fully mature until the early twenties.

B If they are up to 20 minutes late, don't react angrily.

C For example, they may find it difficult to make the right decision between watching television, ringing a friend, or finishing their homework.

D I'm not turning into a criminal, it's just clothes on the floor.

E Parents often complain that teenagers can be charming to people outside the home but irritating to their family.

F I've never had a problem; in fact, the kitchen was sometimes cleaner than I'd left it.

G On these occasions, parents tend to mention all the other things that they may or may not have done wrong.

H Imagine if you'd spent two hours getting ready to go out for the evening and someone said, 'You're not going out looking like that, are you?'

Exam information

In Reading Part 2, the text contains seven gaps. Following the text there is a list of eight possible sentences to fill the gaps.

You must choose the correct sentence for each gap; there is one sentence you will not need.

This task tests your understanding of the structure of the text and how the argument is developed.

8 **Write down on a piece of paper three things teenagers do which their parents find annoying. Pass the paper to another student.**
Take turns to tell each other what parents should do to deal with the things that annoy them.

Grammar

Present perfect simple and continuous

1 Look at the pairs of sentences below and answer the questions.

1 a *... Penny Palmano, who has written a best-selling book on teenagers.*
  b *She's been writing books for more than 20 years ...*
  Which sentence ...
  1 talks about the result of an activity?
  2 talks about the length of an activity?

2 a *I've been learning how to do things like carpentry and so on.*
  b *I've phoned her more than six times, but she never answers the phone.*
  Which sentence ...
  1 talks about how many times something has been repeated?
  2 talks about changes or developments which are not finished?

3 a *I've been helping my mum while her secretary is on holiday.*
  b *We've lived in this house since I was a small child.*
  Which sentence ...
  1 talks about something which is temporary?
  2 talks about something which is permanent?

page 153 *Grammar reference: Present perfect simple and present perfect continuous*

2 Complete these sentences by putting the verb into either the present perfect simple or the present perfect continuous.

1 I've been visiting (visit) friends, so I haven't spoken to my parents yet today.
2 I .... (ask) him to tidy his room several times.
3 I .... (clean) the kitchen, so what would you like me to do next?
4 My neighbour .... (play) the violin for the last three hours and it's driving me mad!
5 Congratulations – you .... (pass) the exam with really high marks!
6 We can't leave Adrianna to run the shop – she .... (only work) here for a few days.
7 We .... (spend) every summer in Crete since I was a child, so it'll be sad if we don't go there this year.
8 I'm really tired because I .... (cook) all day!

Use of English Part 2

1 Work in pairs. You will read a text about housework in Britain. Before you read, match the verbs (1–8) with the nouns (a–h) to make word combinations for some common household chores.

1	do	a	the beds
2	do	b	the dinner ready
3	dust	c	the floor
4	get	d	the furniture
5	hang	e	the ironing
6	lay	f	the table
7	make	g	the washing out to dry
8	sweep	h	the washing-up

2 Discuss:

- Who does each of these chores in your family, and why? Example:
  My dad does the ironing because he has more time.
- Which of these chores do your parents enjoy doing, and which do they hate doing?
- Do you think men or women do more housework in your country? Why?

3 **Read the text quickly to find out if the text says who should do the housework: men or women?**

Who *should* do the housework?

Even in an age when most women (0) ....go.......... out to work, many of them full-time, they still find themselves doing most (1) .... the chores. Research shows that mothers spend, on average, three hours a day (2) .... housework and cooking, whereas fathers spend just 45 minutes. Men still expect women to do the housework. (3) .... men do things around the house, they act as though they are doing their partner a favour. They say things like: 'I've done the washing-up (4) .... you', instead of regarding it as something (5) .... benefits both of them.

Housework is (6) .... important that couples should discuss (7) .... along with all the other big issues when they are first deciding whether to marry or (8) .... Men give all sorts of excuses for not doing housework: 'I work long hours and I don't think my wife's work is as stressful as (9) ....', or: 'I would do more, but she's so much better (10) .... it than me.' But what a man really means by this (11) .... that he feels his job is ultimately (12) .... important than his partner's.

Adapted from *The Daily Mail*

4 **Read the text again more carefully. What four reasons do men give for doing less housework?**

5 **Complete the text by writing one word in each space. Make sure that you spell the word correctly.**

Exam information

In Use of English Part 2 there is a text with 12 gaps. You must write **one word** in each gap.

You are given an example (0).

You usually need 'grammar' words, e.g. articles (*a, the, an*), prepositions (*to, with, by*, etc.), auxiliary verbs (*do, did, have*, etc.), pronouns (*it, them, which*, etc.), conjunctions (*and, although, but*, etc.).

6 **When you have finished, look at the box which follows Exercise 7.**

7 **Work in groups. Imagine that you are going to share a flat together. Discuss and decide which of you will do each of the chores in Exercise 1.**

These are the words you need. Check them against your answers and make the changes you think are necessary.

at doing for if/when is it mine
more not of so that/which

Vocabulary

Collocations with *make* and *do*

A collocation is a combination of words formed when two or more words are frequently used together, e.g. *do an exam* not ~~*make an exam*~~. Recognising and using collocations is important for success at First Certificate.

1 **First Certificate candidates often confuse *make* and *do*. Circle the correct alternative in *italics* in the sentences below to form collocations with *make* and *do*.**

1 When men *make* / *do* things around the house, they act as though they are *making* / *doing* their partner a favour.

2 I always *make* / *do* my own bed in the morning but I don't *do* / *make* any other housework.

2 **Read the extract from the *Cambridge Advanced Learner's Dictionary* and the list of common collocations. Then complete the sentences on page 14 with the correct form of *make* or *do*.**

do or make?

Do usually means to perform an activity or job.

I should do more exercise.

~~*I should make more exercise.*~~

Make usually means to create or produce something.

Did you make the dress yourself?

~~*Did you do the dress yourself?*~~

Common collocations

Do business, a course, exercise, a favour, housework, homework, the shopping, work

Make an appointment, the bed, a decision, an effort, an excuse, friends, money, a noise, a phone call, a plan, a promise

1 Would you please stop ......making...... so much noise? I've got a lot of work to ....
2 My mum is .... me a cake for my birthday tomorrow.
3 Patsy likes being a teacher. She feels she's .... something useful.
4 If you want to go to university, you'll have to .... more effort and .... a lot more homework than you're doing at the moment.
5 I think the best film Stanley Kubrick ever .... was *Space Odyssey 2001*.
6 I joined the sports club partly to .... friends and partly to .... a bit of exercise.

Speaking Part 1

Exam information

The Speaking paper has four parts and you do it with a partner.

In Speaking Part 1 you will each be asked questions about yourself, your life, your work or studies, your plans for the future, your family and your interests.

1 Look at these two questions which the examiner may ask you in Speaking Part 1.

- *Where are you from?*
- *What do you like about the place where you live?*

1 Which question asks you to give your personal opinion and which asks you for personal information?
2 Which question can be answered with quite a short phrase and which question needs a longer answer?

2 (4) Listen to two students, Irene and Peter, answering the questions above. Note down their answers.

Irene: ....

....

Peter: ....

....

3 Who do you think gives the best answers? Why?

4 Work in pairs. Take turns to ask each other these questions:

1 Where are you from?
2 What do you like about the place where you live?
3 Do you come from a large family?
4 What do you like about being part of a large/small family?
5 Who does the housework in your family?
6 What things do you enjoy doing with your family?
7 Tell me about your friends.
8 What things do you enjoy doing with your friends?
9 Which are more important to you: your family or your friends?
10 Do you have similar interests to your parents?

page 178 *Speaking reference: Speaking Part 1*

Writing Part 1

Exam information

In Writing Part 1 there is one task you must do. You:

- read a short text (e.g. an email, a letter, an advertisement or an article) and some notes about it; there are **four** points **you must deal with** in your answer
- write a letter or email dealing with the four things
- must follow the instructions exactly.

You have to make enquiries, suggestions, requests, give reasons, etc.

You have about 40 minutes and you should write between 120 and 150 words.

1 Read the writing task below and <u>underline</u> the four points you must deal with in the first email on page 15.

An English friend of yours, Anne, is a student. She has written to you asking for advice. Read Anne's email and the notes you have made. Then write an email to Anne using all your notes.

2 Work in pairs. Make brief notes on:

- the best time of year to visit your country
- the best way to meet young people
- what clothes Anne and her friends should bring.

Hi!

I've got together with six of my friends from college and we're hoping to travel to your country for about two weeks for a holiday. Can you give us some help, please?

We'd like to know when is the best time of year to visit your country. Also, we want to meet people our own age (17 –18). What's the best way to do this?

We don't want to carry too much stuff, so can you tell us what clothes we should bring?

And while we're there, would you like to join our group and travel round with us? I think it would be great fun, don't you?

Many thanks and looking forward to hearing from you.

Anne

Tell her when and why

Suggest ...

Advise her

Thank her

3 Read Chiara's email to Anne.

1 Has she answered all four points?
2 Were her ideas the same as yours?

To: Anne Ryder
Subject: Holiday

Hi Anne,

Thanks for your email. It's very exciting to hear you're coming to Italy. Personally, I think the best time to come is in the spring before it gets too hot.

If you want to meet young people I suggest spending a few days at a school or college. How about coming to mine? I'm sure we can organise something with the teachers. Also, it would be a good idea to stay in a youth hostel.

In the spring the weather is usually quite changeable, so you should bring some light clothes for the daytime but a jersey and a jacket for the evenings.

Thanks also for your invitation to join the group. I'd love to do so if I'm free. I'll be able to show you some of the most interesting things in my area. Let me know when you're coming!

Best wishes,

Chiara

page 169 *Writing reference: Writing Part 1*

4 Read the email again and <u>underline</u> three suggestions Chiara makes.

5 Put the words in the sentences below into the correct order to form ways of making suggestions. The first and last words are given.

1 ~~How~~ to some school young my meet visiting about ~~people~~?
How ....about visiting my....
....school to meet some young....
people?

2 I in going clubs the cafés to suggest and evenings.
I ....
....
evenings.

3 It idea a club good contact be youth in to my would the area.
It ....
....
area.

6 Write your own answer to the writing task. Use the notes you made in Exercise 2. Write between 120 and 150 words.

Unit 2 Leisure and pleasure

Starting off

1 Work in pairs. Choose a word or phrase from the box for each of these photographs.

riding motorbikes playing computer games clubbing window shopping doing aerobics playing chess playing team sports

2 Answer the questions below.

1 Which of the activities in the photos have you done?
2 Which do you think is …?
  a the most enjoyable
  b the cheapest
  c the healthiest
  d the most relaxing
  e the least active
  f the best one to do with friends
3 Which would you like to try? Why?

Reading Part 1

You will read an extract from a book in which Scottish actor Ewan McGregor explains how he first became interested in motorbikes.

1 Before you read, work in pairs. What do you think people most enjoy about riding motorbikes?

2 Read the extract quickly to find out how Ewan McGregor became interested in motorbikes.

My first bike

Film star, Ewan McGregor, recently rode round the world on a motorbike. He talks about how he first took up riding motorbikes.

My biking beginnings can be summed up in two words: teenage love. My first girlfriend was small with short mousy blonde hair, and I was mad about her. Our romance came to an abrupt end, however, when she started going out with another guy in my hometown, Crieff. He rode a 50 cc road bike first and then a 125. And whereas I had always walked my girlfriend home, suddenly she was going back with this guy.

I was nearly sixteen by then and already heartbroken. Then one day, on the way back from a shopping trip to Perth with my mum, we passed Buchan's, the local bike shop. I urged my mother to stop the car. I got out, walked up the short hill to the shop and pressed my nose to the window. There was a light blue 50 cc bike on display right at the front of the shop. I didn't know what make it was, or if it was any good. Such trivialities were irrelevant to me. All I knew was that I could get it in three or four months' time when I was sixteen and allowed to ride it. Maybe I could even get my girlfriend back.

I'd ridden my first bike when I was about six. My father organised a tiny red Honda 50 cc and we headed off to a field that belonged to a family friend. I clambered on and shot off. I went all over the field. I thought it was just the best thing. I loved the smell of

it, the sound of it, the look of it, the rush of it, the high-pitched screaming of the engine. Best of all, there was a Land Rover parked next to two large piles of straw with about a metre and half between them. I knew that from where the adults were standing it looked as if there was no distance between them. Just one large heap of straw. I thought I would have a go. I came racing towards the adults, shot right through the gap in the straw. I was thrilled to hear the adults scream and elated that it had frightened them. It was my first time on a motorbike. It was exciting and I wanted more.

So when I looked through Buchan's window in Perth that day, it suddenly all made sense to me. It was what had to happen. I can't remember whether it was to win back my ex-girlfriend's heart or not, but more than anything else it meant that, instead of having to walk everywhere, I could ride my motorbike to school and the games fields at the bottom of Crieff and when I went out at weekends.

I started to fantasise about it. I spent all my waking hours thinking about getting on and starting up the bike, putting on the helmet and riding around Crieff. I couldn't sleep. Driven to desperation by my desire for a bike, I made a series of promises to my mum: I won't leave town. I'll be very safe. I won't take any risks. I won't do anything stupid. But, in fact I was making the promises up – I never thought about keeping them.

Crieff is built on a hill. It's a small town and my whole childhood was spent walking around the town, from my parents' house to school to friends' houses. It was great, but I was getting to that age when children become aware of the possibilities of venturing further afield. Crieff is smack in the middle of Scotland, no more than a day's drive from anywhere in the country. Unless, like us, you went everywhere by bicycle. With so many beautiful places nearby, the idea of getting a motorbike was too much to resist.

Adapted from *Long Way Round* by Ewan McGregor and Charley Boorman

3 For questions 1–8, choose the answer (A, B, C or D) which you think fits best according to the text.

1 Why did Ewan's relationship with his first girlfriend finish?
- **A** She didn't enjoy walking.
- **B** She met someone with a motorbike.
- **C** He was upset by her behaviour.
- **D** He made her angry.

2 What does 'such trivialities' refer to in line 17?
- **A** his mother's attitude to the bike
- **B** the bike's size and colour
- **C** the bike's price
- **D** the bike's quality and its manufacturer

3 Why didn't Ewan buy the bike immediately?
- **A** He couldn't afford it.
- **B** He wasn't old enough to ride it.
- **C** He hadn't learnt how to ride it.
- **D** He didn't know if his girlfriend would like it.

4 The adults were frightened the first time Ewan rode a motorbike because they thought
- **A** the bike was too noisy.
- **B** the bike was too fast.
- **C** he was going to have an accident.
- **D** the bike was too big for him.

5 What was Ewan's main reason for buying the motorbike?
- **A** It was less expensive than a car.
- **B** It would help his relationship with his girlfriend.
- **C** It was good for his image.
- **D** It was a useful means of transport.

6 How did Ewan's desire for the bike affect his behaviour?
- **A** He couldn't think about anything else.
- **B** He spent more time talking to his mother.
- **C** He invented reasons for buying the bike.
- **D** He spent a lot of time riding a friend's bike.

7 What does Ewan mean by 'venturing further afield' in line 53?
- **A** taking greater risks
- **B** becoming more independent
- **C** travelling to more distant places
- **D** living somewhere different

8 Who, according to the whole passage, was most against Ewan getting a motorbike?
- **A** his first girlfriend
- **B** his father
- **C** his mother
- **D** his friends

Exam information

In Reading Part 1, you must:

- read a text of 550–700 words
- answer eight questions about it by choosing A, B, C or D.

You have about 20 minutes to do this.

4 Work in pairs.

Student A: You are a teenager. You want to buy a motorbike, but you need your parents to help you by lending you some money. Think of reasons why you want a motorbike and then try to persuade your mother/father to lend you the money you need.

Student B: You are one of Student A's parents. You don't want him/her to buy a motorbike. Think of reasons why he/she shouldn't buy a motorbike and try to persuade him/her not to do so.

Vocabulary

Phrasal verbs

1 Match these phrasal verbs in the text (1–7) with their definitions from the *Cambridge Advanced Learner's Dictionary* (a–g).

1 take up (lines 2–3)
2 sum up (line 4)
3 go out with (line 7)
4 head off to (line 22)
5 shoot off (line 23)
6 start up (line 43)
7 make up (lines 47–48)

a describe the important facts about something briefly
b go to
c have a romantic relationship with someone
d invent something, such as an excuse or a story, often in order to deceive
e start doing a particular activity
f start moving very quickly
g start the engine of a bike or car

2 Write one of the phrasal verbs in the correct form in each space in these sentences.

1 After they had finished, they headed off to a café for a sandwich and a cup of coffee.
2 How would you .... her personality in just a few words?
3 Mark found it hard to .... his bike in the cold weather.
4 Sometimes when I arrive home late I .... an excuse to tell my parents why I am late.
5 The girl who he .... hopes to be a famous film star.
6 I need to get more exercise, so I'm thinking of .... jogging or aerobics.
7 When the meeting ended, she suddenly .... without saying a word to anyone.

Grammar

Adjectives with *-ed* and *-ing*

1 Look at these sentences from the reading text.

I was thrilled to hear the adults scream and elated that it had frightened them. It was my first time on a motorbike. It was exciting and I wanted more.

1 Which of the underlined words refer to how Ewan felt?
2 Which of the underlined words refer to what made him feel like that?

page 154 *Grammar reference: Adjectives with* -ed *and* -ing

2 First Certificate candidates often confuse adjectives with *-ed* and adjectives with *-ing*. Circle the correct adjective in *italics* in each of these sentences.

1 Visiting Disneyland, Paris was an *amused* / *amusing* experience.
2 It can be very *annoyed* / *annoying* if people are rude.
3 You will never get *bored* / *boring* at night in Taipei because the nightlife is wonderful.
4 I am very *confused* / *confusing* about what you are offering in your advertisement.
5 The situation was very *embarrassed* / *embarrassing* for me and I felt uncomfortable.
6 I was really *excited* / *exciting* and wanted to see as much of the city as possible.

3 **Use the word given in capitals at the end of the lines to form a word that fits in the gap.**

1 I was very ....surprised.... that you didn't phone me last night. **SURPRISE**
2 I thought the film was rather .... after all the publicity it had received. **DISAPPOINT**
3 She's an .... teacher and that's what makes her lessons so enjoyable. **INTEREST**
4 Anita looked quite .... when she left the police station. **WORRY**
5 Paul found climbing the mountain an .... experience. **EXHAUST**
6 Marie told me a rather .... story about her trip to the fashion show in Milan. **AMUSE**

4 (5) **You will hear a girl talking about one of the experiences listed below. Listen and decide which experience she is talking about.**

a I rode a motorbike for the first time.
b I was punished for something I didn't do.
c I had to study all weekend for an exam.
d I broke a bone.
e I was trapped in a lift.
f I won a competition.
g I did a parachute jump.

5 (5) **Listen again. Which adjectives did she use to describe each of these things?**

1 The whole experience: ....amazing....
2 How she felt after studying: ....
3 How she felt about her boyfriend's suggestion: ....
4 The thought of breaking a bone: ....
5 How she felt in the plane: ....
6 The jump itself: ....

6 **Work in pairs. Look at the experiences a–g in Exercise 4. Have you done any of these or have any of them happened to you? How did you feel about them? Take turns to describe your experience.**

Listening Part 2

1 **Work in small groups. You will hear a television interview in which a psychologist talks about playing video and computer games. Before you listen, discuss the questions below using the words in the box to help you. Example: *People who play video games are more creative in the way they think.***

1 What are the positive effects of computer games?
2 What criticisms do people sometimes make of video games?

creative	distract	educational	imagination
concentrate on	skills	solve problems	
unsociable	violent	waste of time	

Exam information

Listening Part 2 is an interview or talk.

- You must listen and complete ten sentences.
- For most spaces you will need between one and three words.
- Write words you actually hear.
- You hear the recording twice.

2 **Now read the sentences below and discuss what type of words (nouns, adjectives, verbs, etc.) you could use to complete the sentences.**

Some people think video and computer games make young people (1) ....

Computer games may cause a reduction in the number of (2) ....

According to some teachers, students do (3) .... than before.

Evidence suggests games players have (4) .... skills.

Playing games may improve old people's (5) ....

Gamers can follow up to (6) .... on the screen simultaneously.

Computer games might help (7) .... do their jobs better.

Some experts suggest video games are (8) .... than traditional classroom teaching.

Young people learn to (9) .... and think clearly.

They learn the value of making a consistent (10) .... when working.

3 (6) **Listen to an interview about video and computer gaming, and complete the sentences in Exercise 2.**

4 **Work in small groups. Which of the ideas expressed in the recording do you agree with, and which do you disagree with? Why?**

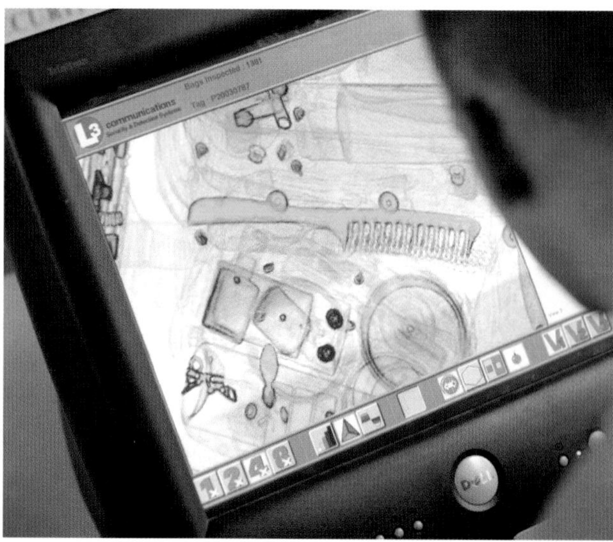

Grammar

Comparison of adjectives and adverbs

1 **Look at these sentences (many are from Listening Part 2). Then complete the rules below for comparison of adjectives and adverbs by writing examples from the sentences in the spaces.**

- ... video games and television programmes tend to make youngsters more violent.
- ... fewer crimes are being committed ...
- ... they do less homework than they used to ...
- ... certain games give people better visual skills ...
- It's one of the easiest games to play ...
- ... airport security staff might do their job better if they were trained with computer games.
- ... teachers are finding it harder to compete for their students' attention and enthusiasm.
- ... computer games can be more educational than a lot of the traditional activities that go on in the classroom.
- ... some of the most successful games are highly educational ...
- ... many computer games can be played on the cheapest computers.

Rules

Adjectives and adverbs with one syllable form comparatives and superlatives with -er and -est. Examples: (1) ...*fewer*... ; (2) ...., (3) ....

Adjectives ending in -*y* and -*ly* form comparatives and superlatives with *-er* and *-est*. Example: (4) ....

Adjectives and adverbs with two or more syllables form comparatives and superlatives with *more* and *most*. Examples: (5) .... (6) .... and (7) ....

Some adjectives and adverbs form irregular comparatives. Examples: *good*, (8) ...., *best; little*, (9) ...., *least; well*, (10) ...., *best*

page 154 *Grammar reference: Comparison of adjectives and adverbs*

2 **First Certificate candidates often make mistakes with comparisons of adjectives and adverbs. Correct the mistake in each of these sentences.**

1 There are lots of ways to keep fit, but I think ~~the healthier~~ of all is aerobics. *the healthiest*
2 Playing chess is more cheaper than gaming.
3 Clubbing is more sociable that biking because you meet and speak to a lot of people.
4 When you play chess, you have to think more hardly than when you're gaming.
5 I don't go window shopping as often than I used to.
6 For me, clubbing is the more enjoyable way to spend my free time.
7 Speaking for myself, I find team sports the less interesting.
8 Biking is more good than team sports.

Use of English Part 4

Exam information

In Use of English, Part 4 you must:

- complete eight sentences with between two and five words so that they mean the same as the sentences printed before them
- use a word given in **CAPITALS** without changing it in any way.

This part tests your knowledge of grammar and vocabulary.

1 **For questions 1–8, complete the second sentence so that it has a similar meaning to the first sentence, using the word given. Do not change the word given. You must use between two and five words, including the word given.**

1 He doesn't enjoy running as much as cycling.
MORE
He likes ....*cycling more than*.... running.

2 Lena enjoys reading more than any other free-time activity.
MOST
For Lena reading ....
free-time activity.

3 It is easier to learn the guitar than most other musical instruments.
ONE
The guitar is ....
musical instruments to learn.

4 Olivia finds watching TV more boring than reading.
NOT
For Olivia, watching TV is ....
.... reading.

5 Maria's brothers are better tennis players than her.
SO
Maria doesn't .... her brothers.

6 No one in the class works harder than Peter.
HARD-WORKING
Peter .... person in the class.

7 Sailing is more expensive than biking.
NOT
Sailing is .... biking.

8 It took Janusz longer to finish the game than Sarah.
MORE
Sarah finished the game ....
.... Janusz.

2 **Check your answers by looking at the clues for questions 2–8 below. Change your answers where necessary.**

Clues

2 Use the adjective of *enjoy*.
3 You need an adjective + *-est*.
4 Use *as* ... *as* or *so* ... *as*.
5 You need to use an adverb.
6 *Hard-working* is a three-syllable adjective.
7 Use *as* ... *as* or *so* ... *as*.
8 You will need to use an adverb.

Speaking Part 2

Exam information

In Speaking Part 2 the candidates take turns to:

- speak on their own for a minute
- compare two photographs which the examiner gives them
- answer a question connected with both photographs.

Work in pairs, either as Pair A or Pair B.

1 Study your question. You will have to answer it by talking to someone from the other pair. Work together and decide what you can say.

- Prepare to answer both parts of the question.
- Don't describe the photographs in detail, but compare the activities in general, e.g. why the people in the photographs might be doing them, which is most useful, enjoyable, etc. and why.
- Think of reasons and examples to back up the second part of the question.

2 Work with a partner from the other pair and take turns to speak for one minute about your photographs.

page 179 *Speaking reference: Speaking Part 2*

Pair A

Compare these photographs and say how you think people benefit from spending their free time in this way.

Pair B

Compare these photographs and say why you think it's important for people to have hobbies.

Writing Part 2 An article

1 Work in pairs. Look at the following writing task and underline the points you must write about.

You have seen this announcement in an English-language magazine.

> **A great way to spend your free time**
>
> Tell us about a leisure-time activity you really enjoy.
>
> → How did you get started?
>
> → Why do you enjoy it so much?
>
> We will publish the most interesting articles in next month's issue.

Write your **article**.

2 Work in pairs. Tell your partner about one of your free-time activities. While speaking, answer the questions in the writing task above.

3 The following article contains four paragraphs.

1 Put the paragraphs in the correct order by writing a number in each box.
2 In which paragraphs does the writer say how he/she got started?
3 In which paragraphs does the writer say why he/she enjoys it so much?

Cooking – it's creative and useful!

☐ **A** When we went back to school after the summer, I decided to do cookery lessons and now I think I'm quite a competent cook. When friends come round to my house I often cook them something because I find it really satisfying and relaxing. I find inventing new dishes fascinating and it's wonderful to see people enjoying a meal I've made.

☐ **B** I'd recommend it as a hobby because for me it's one of the most creative and useful free-time activities I can imagine.

☐ **C** I found I really liked it and was soon doing things which were more complicated. Not everything I cooked was as successful as my aunt's cooking. My younger brother and sister sometimes complained, but usually they ate the food quite happily.

☐ **D** I first got interested in cookery one summer holiday when I was about 12. I was staying with my aunt, who is a keen cook, and I wanted to try it for myself. She encouraged me by teaching me to do fairly easy dishes to start with.

 page 171 *Writing reference: Writing Part 2*

4 Find adjectives in the article which describe the following.

1 how the writer feels about cooking: satisfying
2 cooking as a hobby: ....
3 the writer's ability to cook: ....

5 Write your own article to answer the writing task in Exercise 1. Write 120–180 words.

Exam information

In Writing Part 2:

- you must answer one question from a choice of four: either an article, a letter, a report, an essay, a review, or a story
- the final question is based on a set book (reading the set book is optional)
- you must write between 120 and 180 words and you have about 40 minutes to do this.

Unit 1 *Vocabulary and grammar review*

Vocabulary

1 Complete the sentences below by writing an adjective in each space. Choose from the adjectives or their opposites in the exercises in Reading Part 2 on page 10. In some cases more than one answer is possible.

1 Juan's parents are very ......strict...... and don't allow him to do everything he wants.
2 You were rather .... inviting his ex-girlfriend to the same party as him.
3 Pascale is quite .... about what she eats; she doesn't like fish and she will only eat a few vegetables.
4 David is so .... that it's hard for anyone else to say very much.
5 Melanie tries to act confidently even when she's feeling very .... about things.
6 I wouldn't have criticised you if I had known how .... you were!
7 Helen is very young, but she behaves in a .... and responsible way.
8 I know my room is not very ...., but I've been very busy studying for exams!

2 Complete these sentences with a verb in the correct form.

1 When the washing machine finishes, could you ....hang out.... the clothes on the washing line to dry?
2 He had just .... the floor and put away the broom when she walked in wearing muddy boots.
3 I don't mind washing clothes, but I hate .... the ironing!
4 Have you .... the table yet? We're about to eat.
5 I worked in a London hotel for a couple of months, so I know how to .... beds!
6 I'll .... the washing-up while you relax!

3 Complete these sentences with the correct form of *make* or *do*.

1 Could you ....do.......... me a favour and let me copy your notes from the last class?
2 Do you mind if I use your phone? I've got to .... an urgent phone call.
3 I'll .... the shopping on my way home this evening.
4 I'm .... this English course because I'm hoping to study in the USA next year.
5 I've got so much homework to .... that I can't come out with you tonight.
6 Marco has .... a big effort with his students, so I'm afraid he's a bit disappointed with their results.
7 Sarah wasn't enjoying the party, so she .... an excuse and left.
8 We phoned the police because our neighbours were .... too much noise.

Grammar

4 Circle the best alternative in *italics* in each of these sentences.

1 *We just live* / *We're just living* with my grandparents while our house is being painted.
2 *He's doing* / *He does* this job for a couple of months before *he goes* / *he's going* to university.
3 Susie *learns* / *is learning* to drive.
4 The reason *I never phone* / *I'm never phoning* you is that my mum *always talks* / *is always talking* on the phone to her friends when *I get* / *I'm getting* home.
5 The roads *get* / *are getting* more and more crowded. Soon we won't be able to drive anywhere.
6 Andy *does not come* / *isn't coming* with me today because *he plays* / *he's playing* football every Saturday.

5 Write the verb in brackets in either the present perfect simple or present perfect continuous. In some cases, both forms are possible.

1 I'm celebrating because my team ....has won.......... (win) the league!
2 At last you .... (arrive) – we .... (expect) you for ages.
3 Of course I'm annoyed. I .... (spend) ages preparing for this party and no one .... (turn up) yet.
4 We .... (have) a really interesting time. Gavin .... (tell) us about his trip round the world. There are a few countries he still .... (not tell) us about, but I get the impression he .... (see) almost everything!
5 Kate .... (lose) a lot of weight since she got married. I don't think she .... (feel) very happy.

Unit 2 *Vocabulary and grammar review*

Vocabulary

1 Complete the sentences below by writing a phrasal verb from the box in the correct form in each of the spaces.

take up	sum up	~~go out with~~	head off to
shoot off	start up	make up	

1 When Andrea first ....went out with.... Carlos, her parents weren't too happy, but now they like him a lot.
2 She turned the key in the ignition and the engine .... immediately.
3 Mario is thinking of .... jogging as he doesn't feel he's getting enough exercise.
4 Instead of reading to the children, I think I'll just .... a story for their bedtime.
5 I'll .... the argument in just a few words to save time.
6 When the traffic light turned green, the taxi .... really quickly. It was an exciting journey!
7 After the match they all .... a local club to celebrate.

Grammar

2 Correct the mistakes in each of these sentences.

1 I wish you'd be ~~more quiet~~! quieter
2 Small towns are more safety to live in than large cities.
3 Today's the hotest day of the year so far.
4 She looks more relax than she did before the exam.
5 Patty is so smart – she's always dressed in the last fashion!
6 If you study more hardly, you'll get higher marks.
7 Everest is the higher mountain in the world.
8 His first day at school was the worse day of his life.
9 We need to eat more healthier food.
10 We should buy this sofa because it's definitely the comfortablest.

Word formation

3 Use the word given in capitals at the end of each sentence to form a word that fits in the gap.

1 What an ....amazing.... band! I never expected they'd be that good. AMAZE
2 They found the journey so .... that they fell asleep as soon as they arrived. EXHAUST
3 My problem at school was that I was .... with the lessons. BORE
4 Jake felt .... with his exam results. He had hoped to do better. DISAPPOINT
5 Why are the buses always late? It's .... to have to wait in the rain! ANNOY
6 I'm doing this course because I'm .... in studying architecture at university. INTEREST
7 Annette felt very .... that she hadn't been invited to the party. SURPRISE
8 I found driving a Formula 1 car a really .... experience. EXCITE

Unit 3 Happy holidays!

Starting off

1 **Work in pairs. Write the words and phrases in the box in the appropriate columns below.**

~~a camping holiday~~ ~~at a campsite~~
~~walking and climbing~~ at a luxury hotel
a beach holiday on a cruise ship
meeting new people sunbathing
a sightseeing holiday relaxing a cruise
at a youth hostel at sea in the mountains
backpacking visiting monuments in the city centre
at the seaside seeing new places

types of holiday	holiday places	holiday activities
a camping holiday	at a campsite	walking and climbing

2 **Now look at the photos and answer these questions using some of the words and phrases from the box.**

1 What type of holiday does each photo show?
2 What do people do on these holidays?
3 Why do people choose these holidays?
4 Which holiday would you enjoy most? And which least? Why?

Listing Part 3

1 You will hear five people talking about the holiday they took last year. Before you listen, work in pairs. Read each statement A–F below and discuss what type of holiday each speaker might talk about.

- **A** We ate good food and visited galleries.
- **B** We did something new but not dangerous.
- **C** We did very little during the day.
- **D** We got a lot of exercise in an unspoilt area.
- **E** We stayed in friendly places that didn't cost too much.
- **F** We travelled to different cities and islands in style and comfort.

2 Match the underlined words and phrases with words and phrases with similar meanings in the box, e.g. *something new – a complete novelty.*

a complete novelty	delicious meals	kind
in luxury	natural	physical activity
risky	sat around	

3 (7) Now listen and for questions 1–5 below, choose from the list (A–F) in Exercise 1 what each speaker says about their holiday. Use the letters only once. There is one extra letter which you do not need to use.

1 Francesca ☐
2 Mike ☐
3 Sally ☐
4 Paul ☐
5 Katie ☐

Exam information

In Listening Part 3:

- You listen to five different speakers talking about a related subject. You must match each speaker with one of six statements A–F. There is one extra statement you don't need.
- You hear each speaker twice.

4 Work in small groups.

- What do you like about holidays with your family?
- What do you like about holidays with your friends?

Vocabulary

Journey, trip, travel and *way*

1 First Certificate candidates often confuse the following words: *journey, trip, travel* and *way.* Look at these sentences from the recording script in Listening Part 3 and complete the extract below from the *Cambridge Advanced Learner's Dictionary* by writing *journey, trip, travel* or *way* in each space.

- I went on one of those **journeys** overland to Kenya …
- … during the day we just sat around by the pool and were really lazy, unless we made a **trip** to the beach, which was about 20 minutes away by bus.
- We had just climbed one of the really high peaks and we were on the **way** down when a storm came.
- I think that's one of the best things about foreign **travel** – meeting new people.

travel, journey, trip or way?

The noun (1) .... is a general word which means the activity of travelling.

Use (2) .... to talk about when you travel from one place to another.

A (3) .... is a journey in which you visit a place for a short time and come back again.

(4) .... refers only to the route that you take to get from one place to another.

2 Circle the correct alternative in *italics* in each of the following sentences.

1 She met plenty of interesting people during her weekend *travel / trip* to Montreal.
2 We stopped at the supermarket on the *way / trip* to the beach to pick up some cold drinks.
3 This August I've booked a *journey / trip* to Greece with my wife.
4 I realise that for you this is a business *journey / trip*, but I hope we'll have time to see each other.
5 People spend far more on foreign *travel / journey* than they did 50 years ago.
6 The *travel / journey* to my village will take about three hours.
7 Have a good *travel / trip* to Budapest – see you next week when you get back.
8 You can't get to work by bicycle if the *journey / way* is very long – over 30 kilometres, for example.
9 Excuse me, I'm a bit lost. Can you tell me the best *journey / way* to the bus station?

3 Work in small groups. Imagine you are planning a day trip together this weekend. Decide where you'll go, how you'll get there and what you'll do when you're there.

Grammar

Past simple, past continuous and *used to*

1 Read the grammar rules below. Then read the extracts from Listening Part 3 which follow and decide which sentence (a–e) is an example of each rule.

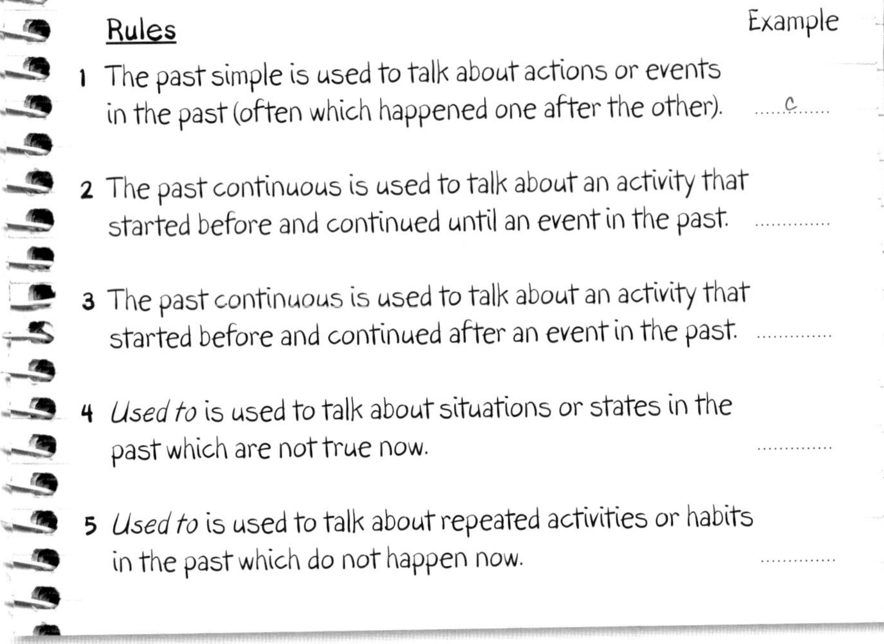

Rules	Example
1 The past simple is used to talk about actions or events in the past (often which happened one after the other).	c
2 The past continuous is used to talk about an activity that started before and continued until an event in the past.	....
3 The past continuous is used to talk about an activity that started before and continued after an event in the past.	....
4 *Used to* is used to talk about situations or states in the past which are not true now.	....
5 *Used to* is used to talk about repeated activities or habits in the past which do not happen now.	....

a My dad <u>used to be</u> a climber and when he was younger ...

b Still there was an upside to it, because that's when I met this Polish girl called Jolanta, while we <u>were walking</u> round one of the museums.

c ... so we <u>left</u> our parents to get on with things and <u>went</u> off for the day together. We <u>had</u> a really great time ...

d ... we took trains and buses everywhere and stayed in these really cheap places with lots of other young people from all over the world who <u>were doing</u> the same sort of thing as us.

e ... on my family holidays we always <u>used to go</u> to the same hotel and lie on the beach ...

page 155 *Grammar reference: Past simple, past continuous and* used to

2 Circle the correct alternative in *italics* in each of the following sentences.

1 When he *walked* / *was walking* home from work, he found a wallet which someone had dropped.

2 When I went to primary school, I *was doing* / *used to do* about one hour's homework a day.

3 As soon as Mandy *was getting* / *got* the message, she *was jumping* / *jumped* into her car and *was driving* / *drove* to the station.

4 When I was a child, we *used to spend* / *were spending* our holidays in my grandparents' village.

5 Luckily, we *walked* / *were walking* past a shopping centre when the storm *began* / *was beginning*.

6 I *used to visit* / *was visiting* many unusual places when I *was* / *was being* a tour guide.

Reading Part 3

1 Work in pairs. What are the advantages and disadvantages of travelling by train on holiday? Think about cost, meeting people, comfort, convenience, etc.

2 You are going to read about seven people's most memorable train journeys. Before you read what they say, read questions 1–15 carefully and <u>underline</u> the most important words in each question.

3 For questions 1–15, choose from the people (A–G). The people may be chosen more than once.

4 Work in small groups.

- Which of the train journeys on page 29 sounds the most exciting to you?
- Take turns to tell each other about a memorable journey you have made. Then decide which of you made the most interesting journey.

Exam information

In Reading Part 3, you must match 15 questions or statements with parts of a text or a number of short texts. This task tests your ability to read quickly and locate specific information.

My most memorable train journey

A **Rose:** I was 18 and I'd just left school when I went on holiday to Thailand. I stepped onto a train travelling to Chiang Mai from Bangkok, ready to endure many hours of discomfort. This, after all, was what travelling involved. I was really surprised when I saw how soft the seats were. Mine even converted into a bed and had a curtain in case I wanted privacy. The scenery was beautiful and delicious snacks were offered through my window at every station. I had a wonderful time and the curtain stayed open the whole way.

B **Kate:** My most memorable train journey took place quite recently. While we were sitting in our compartment, two women entered with screwdrivers and dismantled the wood panels on the wall. They then took fake designer watches out of a black holdall bag and they hid them in the walls. When we got to the border a guard came to check our compartment, tickets and passports. One of the watches had an alarm which fortunately went off when the guard had left our compartment.

C **Amy:** *Mon billet est tombé dans la mer!* (*My ticket fell in the sea!*) Careless, 17, and with very little money, I was leaning on the rails of the ship carrying me to France when a gust of wind snatched my ticket from the top of my open bag and dropped it in the sea. A wonderful ship's officer took pity on me and provided a handwritten letter explaining what had happened. With only the letter and the phrase 'Mon billet est tombé dans la mer!', I travelled the French railways for three weeks to the south and home again.

Which person

expected to have an unpleasant journey?	1	A	
lost something at the beginning of their journey?	2		
travelled with an animal?	3		
was asked to help solve a problem by people they met?	4		
travelled with people who seemed especially nervous?	5		
saw wildlife from the train?	6		
was entertained on the journey by another traveller?	7		
was happy to arrive despite a problem on the journey?	8		
travelled without all the correct documents?	9		
travelled through an area where few people live?	10		
didn't mind when the train didn't arrive on time?	11		
witnessed an illegal activity on the journey?	12		
was on a very crowded train?	13		
obtained food when the train stopped?	14		15

D **Dave and Jess:** Crossing Australia from Sydney to Perth on the 'Indian Pacific' is an adventure. You pass through time zones and areas where man and animals have adapted to the harsh environment over many centuries. You travel from mountains covered with eucalyptus trees to dry dusty plains and deserts. You see kangaroos, camels and wedge-tailed eagles. As we headed west, towns and villages became fewer and fewer. Finally we reached Cook, a place on the Nullarbor Plain. It only had four residents left and they invited us to become ill in order to prevent the local hospital from being closed.

E **Andy:** An epic journey down India's east coast from Calcutta to Chennai took two nights and almost three days. The bare, sweaty, second class carriage was packed full of people. During the journey a wise old man told me numerous stories which always ended with the proclamation 'that is the Indian way'. At the stations I had countless cups of sweet tea and omelettes delivered by boys from the platforms. And no one cared that the train had arrived four hours late.

F **Anna:** My most memorable train journey was on an overnight steam train from Mombasa to Nairobi. I spent the journey trying to rescue my pet monkey who had got trapped under the seat. When I greeted my mother at the bustling station, I was covered in dirt and had bites all over my hands. But I'd rescued my pet, so I was smiling!

G **William:** My most memorable rail trip must be the Regionalle train between Florence and Rome. The scenery was magnificent and it gave us a great opportunity to see the country and the people close up for the first time. In our compartment there was a man who got off at every station to make sure we hadn't arrived in Rome, and an older woman who, as we pulled out of every stop, took her bag down off the rack to check that nothing had been stolen.

Adapted from *The Times*

Grammar

Past perfect simple and continuous

1 Look at this sentence from Reading Part 3 B (Kate) and answer the questions.

> One of the watches had an alarm which fortunately went off when the guard had left our compartment.

1 Which of these actions happened first?
   a The alarm went off.
   b The guard left our compartment.
2 Which verb form is used to indicate that something happened before something else in the past?
3 Compare the sentence above with the one below. Why do you think *fortunately* is used in one sentence and *unfortunately* in the other?

> One of the watches had an alarm which unfortunately went off when the guard was leaving our compartment.

page 155 *Grammar reference: Past perfect tenses – past perfect simple*

2 Work in pairs. Find at least six other examples of the past perfect tense (*had been / had done*) in Reading Part 3.

Why is the past perfect used in each case, i.e. what is the event or situation in the past simple? Example: Reading Part 3 A (Rose) *I'd just left school:* She was on holiday in Thailand.

3 Put the verbs in brackets in the following sentences into either the past simple or past perfect.

1 We were feeling hungry although we ....*had eaten*......... (eat) lunch only an hour before.
2 I didn't know my way around the city because I .... (never be) there before.
3 The party, which our hosts .... (organise) before we arrived, was one of the most enjoyable parts of our trip.
4 When I .... (arrive) in Nairobi, I wasn't allowed into the country because I .... (lose) my passport.
5 I .... (recognise) her from the photograph although I .... (never speak) to her before.
6 He helped to raise money to repair homes which the hurricane .... (damage).

4 Look at the sentences below.

- Which sentence focuses on the length of time spent travelling?
- Is the underlined verb in the past perfect simple or past perfect continuous?
   a *Paul was tired because he'd been travelling all day.*
   b *Paul went to the information office because he'd never travelled in the region before.*

page 155 *Grammar reference: Past perfect tenses – past perfect continuous*

5 Put the verbs in brackets into the past simple, past perfect simple or past perfect continuous.

1 The storm damaged the house where she ...*had been living*... (live) since she left school.
2 We .... (walk) up the mountain for about three hours when suddenly it .... (begin) to rain.
3 I .... (already finish) the work when she .... (offer) to help me.
4 I .... (only speak) for 30 seconds when he interrupted me with a question.
5 I was tired and dirty when I .... (get) home because I .... (walk) in the country all afternoon.

page 168 *Grammar reference: Irregular verbs*

Use of English Part 3

1 Form adjectives from the following nouns and verbs.

noun (n) or verb (v)	adjective
nature (n)	natural
danger (n)	
friend (n)	
comfort (n + v)	
luxury (n)	
risk (n + v)	
nerve (n)	
crowd (n + v)	
disappoint (v)	
care (n + v)	
wonder (n + v)	
dust (n + v)	
memory (n)	
hunger (n)	
enjoy (v)	

2 Adjectives can be formed from nouns and verbs by adding these suffixes: -al, -ous, -ly, -able, -y, -ed, -ing, -ful, -less, -ive, -ic.
Form adjectives from the nouns and verbs in the box. In some cases more than one answer is possible.

educate	space	mass
dirt	use	care
thought	accept	mood
emotion	change	base

Exam information

In Use of English Part 3, there is a text with ten gaps. You must write the correct form of the word given in **CAPITALS** at the end of the line in the space.

This tests your knowledge of vocabulary and your ability to form words.

3 Read the text below. Use the word given in capitals at the end of some of the lines to form a word that fits in the gap in the same line. (In the exam the word will be any type: noun, adjective, adverb or verb.)

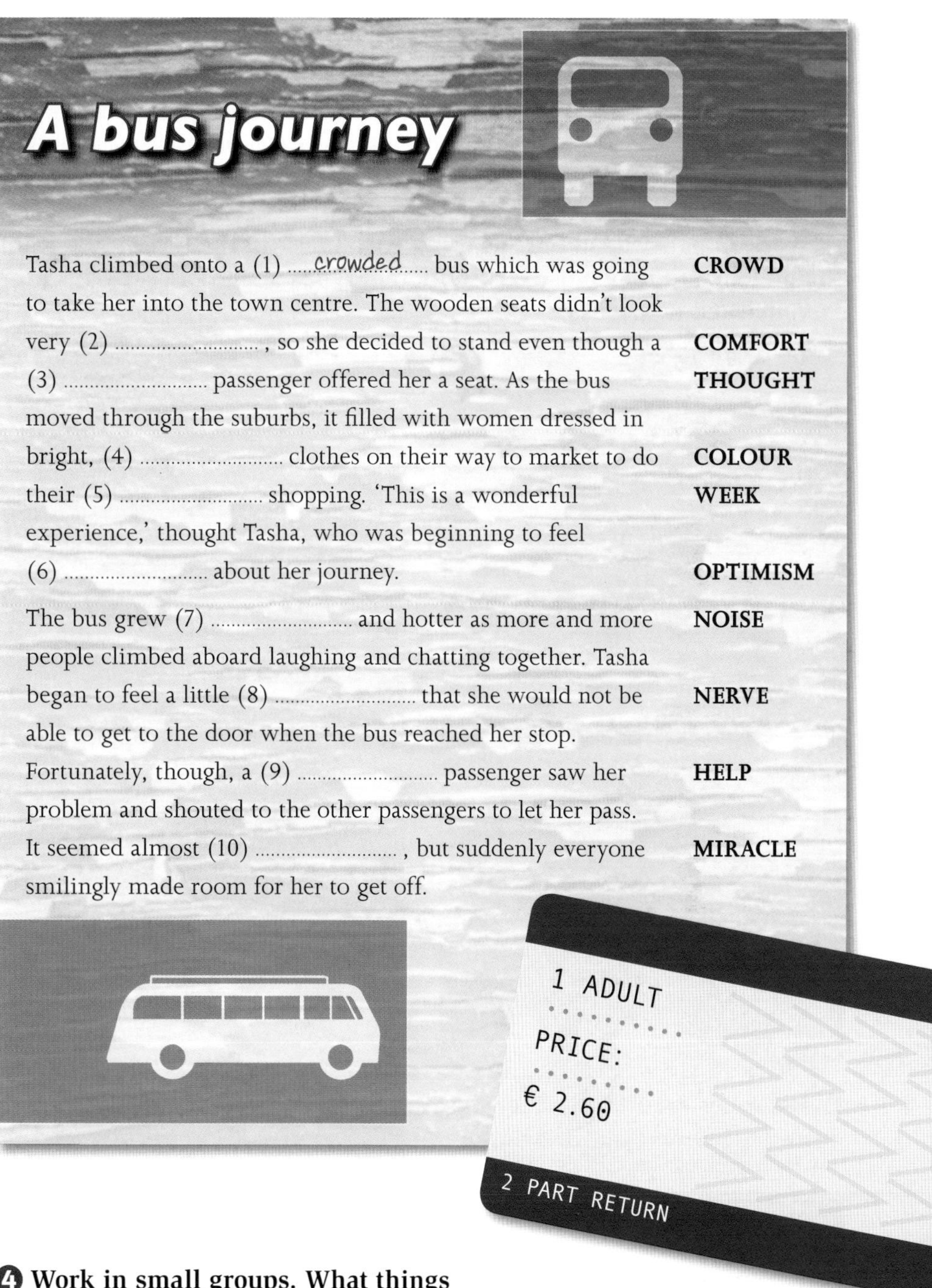

A bus journey

Tasha climbed onto a (1) ......crowded...... bus which was going **CROWD**
to take her into the town centre. The wooden seats didn't look
very (2) .... , so she decided to stand even though a **COMFORT**
(3) .... passenger offered her a seat. As the bus **THOUGHT**
moved through the suburbs, it filled with women dressed in
bright, (4) .... clothes on their way to market to do **COLOUR**
their (5) .... shopping. 'This is a wonderful **WEEK**
experience,' thought Tasha, who was beginning to feel
(6) .... about her journey. **OPTIMISM**

The bus grew (7) .... and hotter as more and more **NOISE**
people climbed aboard laughing and chatting together. Tasha
began to feel a little (8) .... that she would not be **NERVE**
able to get to the door when the bus reached her stop.
Fortunately, though, a (9) .... passenger saw her **HELP**
problem and shouted to the other passengers to let her pass.
It seemed almost (10) .... , but suddenly everyone **MIRACLE**
smilingly made room for her to get off.

4 Work in small groups. What things make you nervous when you're travelling?

Speaking Part 3

Exam information

In Speaking Part 3, the two candidates must discuss a situation or problem together and reach a decision. The examiner:

- gives you a page with a picture or several pictures showing different ideas or options
- tells you what your task is. He/She asks you to discuss the options and tells you what you should decide about. The questions are also printed on the prompt sheet.

This part of the exam takes about three minutes.

Imagine that your college is organising an end-of-year trip for its students. The photographs show some of the options.

- First talk together about how each of these trips could benefit the students.
- Then decide which one you think would be the most suitable.

1 Work in pairs. Read the Speaking Part 3 task in the box on the right and look at the photos. What different types of end-of-year trips are you asked to discuss?

2 (8) Listen to two First Certificate candidates beginning the task. Note down what benefits they mention for the first two photos.

3 (8) Complete these questions the students ask each other by writing one or two words in each space. Then listen again to check your answers.

- (1) ....*Shall*............ I start?
- How do you (2) .... a sightseeing holiday can benefit students?
- (3) .... this photo? It's an activity holiday in the mountains, (4) .... ?
- And the third photo? What about (5) .... ?

4 Now do the complete task yourselves.

- Ask each other questions as in Exercise 3.
- Talk about each of the photos in turn. Take about 1½ to 2 minutes to do this.
- Decide which trip would be most suitable. Take about 1 to 1½ minutes to do this.

page 180 *Speaking reference: Speaking Part 3*

Writing Part 2 A story

Exam information

In Writing Part 2, you may be asked to write a short story. This task usually gives you the words you must use to start or end your story. The task tests your ability to:

- structure your writing
- use a variety of tenses, grammatical structures and vocabulary.

1 Look at the following writing task and underline:

- the words you must use to start your story
- where the story will appear, so that you know who is going to read it.

> Your teacher has asked you to write a story for the English-language magazine at your college. The story must begin with the following words:
>
> *It was a trip I'll never forget.*
>
> Write your **story**.

2 (9) Now listen to five people talking about trips and journeys they will never forget. For questions 1–5 below, choose the trip or journey from the list (A–F). Use the letters only once. There is one extra letter which you do not need to use.

A A family excursion
B A first flight
C A school trip
D A frightening voyage
E A visit to a relative
F A long car journey

Jean	1	
Mark	2	
Maya	3	
Patrick	4	
Sarah	5	

3 Work in pairs.

- Which of the stories you heard do you think would make the most interesting contribution to the college magazine?

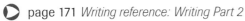

page 171 *Writing reference: Writing Part 2*

4 Read this story in a college magazine and circle the best alternative 1–10 in *italics*.

It was a trip I'll never forget. We (1) *were feeling / had felt* very excited as we climbed into a rather ancient bus. With 40 noisy children and three nervous teachers, it was very crowded. I was at primary school and our teachers (2) *had decided / were deciding* to organise an excursion to a wildlife park nearby.

We found the tour round the park fascinating because we were seeing animals we (3) *had only read / only read* about in books before, such as zebras and elephants. We were delighted to see them in real life.

Anyway, just after we (4) *had entered / were entering* the part where the monkeys lived, the bus (5) *had / was having* a puncture. While we (6) *were waiting / had waited* for the driver to change the wheel, a whole group of monkeys (7) *approached / had approached* the bus and started climbing all over it. We children (8) *had never felt / were never feeling* so thrilled in our lives and we (9) *started / were starting* laughing and shouting even more. I think the teachers felt relieved when the driver (10) *managed / had managed* to change the wheel and continue the tour. All in all, it was a very memorable trip.

5 Answer these questions in pairs.

1. How many paragraphs are there and what is the subject of each paragraph?
2. What adjectives does the writer use?
3. What things do you think made the journey memorable for the writer?

6 Write your own story for the college magazine in 120–180 words.

- Before you write, think about what you want to say and make a plan of what to include in each paragraph. Your story can be true or invented.
- When you write, think what tenses you can use, and try to use a variety.
- Include adjectives to describe your feelings.
- When you have finished, check your writing for mistakes.

Unit 4 Food, glorious food

Starting off

Work in pairs.

1. What is your favourite dish?
2. Do you prefer eating alone or with other people? Why?
3. Look at the photos. Which of these ways of eating do you most enjoy? Why?
4. Which photos show people eating in a healthy way? Which show people eating in a less healthy way? Why?

1

2

3

4

Reading Part 2

1 Work in small groups.

You will read about a school in California where the students grow, cook and eat their own food. How do you think students benefit from this?

2 Read the text quite quickly to find out how students benefit from growing, cooking and eating their own food.

Learning about food

A school in California finds a new way to teach students about healthy eating

Alice Waters – chef and restaurant owner – is sitting in the kitchen garden of the Martin Luther King School in Berkeley, California. The kitchen garden is called the Edible Schoolyard and students at this public school are preparing a vegetable bed as part of a lesson. Later, they will cook what they pick as part of their school lunch.

1 H Each student receives between 18 and 40 hours tuition a year in the Schoolyard and as a result what they eat at school has changed. A good part of the food grown here is used in the school's daily meals.

Waters has been fighting to improve children's diets for a decade, and in 1996 she started a campaign to raise funds for the Edible Schoolyard and the School Lunch Initiative. **2** ______ And Waters hopes that they will set an example for other parts of the country as well. "We have such a huge problem of bad eating habits in the United States that teaching about food cannot be left to parents," she says. "So many children generally are eating fast, cheap, easy food that something has to be done."

Marsha Guerrero, director of the School Lunch Initiative, explains how it all works. "This is mainly a teaching garden," she says. " **3** ____ " Nearby farms therefore also supply food as part of the regular lunches at the school. These are prepared using fresh organic ingredients when possible.

Typical classes in the Edible Schoolyard involve plenty of gardening activity. However, they are not a break from normal school work as academic projects are always attached. In one lesson the students are asked to choose one part of the garden as their personal spot for the entire year. They then observe and record in a journal what happens in this spot as time progresses. They record their observations of insect life, the soil and changes to the plants. **4** ____

Classes in the kitchen involve cooking lunch, but also link into classroom academic subjects. The food cooked here includes a range of dishes from pasta to stuffed vine leaves and delicious Italian omelettes filled with herbs and vegetables. The recipes are dictated by what vegetables are available. Science is taught through nutrition and cooking technique; geography through the effects of the seasons and eating habits around the world. **5** ____

Today's midday meal consists of home-made pesto and tomato sandwiches, with a big vegetable salad. Everyone is eating. Teo Hernandez, 13, says he has changed the way he eats. "I can now cook and grow things," he says. " **6** ____ I have changed my attitude to food; I like some herbs and lettuce and I use less salt. It's been fun, the teachers are nice – and there's no homework." Teo has been in the US for only three years, but his teachers say he has learned to speak perfect English in such a short time because he is so happy at school.

But has Alice Waters succeeded? Is the Edible Schoolyard model the way forward? **7** ____ "When kids become unhealthy due to bad diet, they become isolated," says Waters. "But eating such good food and picking, smelling and cooking the vegetables and fruit in this garden makes them care about what they eat – and it shows them that we care about them. Just seeing a child saying to another, 'Would you like some?' – that is the essential thing."

Adapted from *The Daily Telegraph*

3 Seven of the eight sentences below have been removed from the article. There is one extra sentence. Highlight or <u>underline</u> the words and phrases in the sentences which refer to something in another part of the article. (Sentences A–C have been done for you as an example.)

A I don't know yet if I will continue doing so in the future but I know I can.

B Judging by the happiness in this garden among a mixed bunch of ordinary children, the answer would have to be yes.

C Keeping notes in this way is viewed as an essential part of experimental learning.

D One lesson, on European diets in the Middle Ages, ends with the children cooking roasted vegetables with herbs and garlic.

E The problem, according to some critics, is that these projects may be just too expensive to run.

F These two projects aim to provide all 10,000 students in Berkeley's public schools with good food while also placing food at the heart of the curriculum.

G We couldn't possibly produce enough food in this small space to feed all 300 children.

H Lessons like this one take place in the garden and kitchen and they form part of the curriculum.

4 Choose from the sentences A–H the one which fits each gap (1–7). When you place a sentence, check what the words and phrases which you highlighted refer to.

Exam advice

- Read the text carefully before you look at the spaces, so you have an idea of what each paragraph contains.
- Read the sentences carefully; can you recognise where some sentences should go?
- When you finish, read the complete text again to check your answers.

5 Work in small groups.

- Do you think all schools should teach students cookery and healthy eating habits? Why (not)?
- Did you study cookery at school?
- How would you teach your children to have a healthy diet?

Vocabulary

Food, dish and *meal*

1 First Certificate candidates often confuse *food*, *dish* and *meal*. Read these extracts from the *Cambridge Advanced Learner's Dictionary*.

food *noun* [C or U] something that people and animals eat, or plants absorb, to keep them alive: *baby food* ∘ *There was lots of food and drink at the party.*

dish FOOD *noun* [C] food prepared in a particular way as part of a meal: *a chicken/vegetarian dish*

meal FOOD *noun* [C] an occasion when food is eaten, or the food which is eaten on such an occasion: *I have my main meal at midday.* ∘ *You must come round for a meal sometime.*

2 Look at these sentences from the Reading text and write the correct word in each space in the correct form. Then check your answers by looking at the text again.

- A good part of the (1) ....*food*.... grown here is used in the school's daily (2) ....
- The (3) .... cooked here includes a range of (4) .... from pasta to stuffed vine leaves and delicious Italian omelettes filled with herbs and vegetables.
- Today's midday (5) .... consists of home-made pesto and tomato sandwiches.

3 Each of the sentences below contains a word which is often used wrongly by First Certificate candidates. Cross out the wrong word and write the correct word.

1 I'm quite surprised but I'm really enjoying English ~~meal~~. *food*
2 Moussaka is one of the most delicious meals you can eat in my country.
3 The beef food is really tasty and looks quite healthy.
4 The meal in my country is delicious.
5 Too many people eat ready foods which they buy from supermarkets.
6 When I visit you I could cook a food that is from my country.
7 The cost of your holiday includes two dishes a day: breakfast and dinner.

4 Work in pairs.

- Do/Did you eat at school or college? If so, what is/was the food like?
- How many meals do you eat each day? Which is your favourite meal?
- Which is your favourite dish? Who prepares it for you?

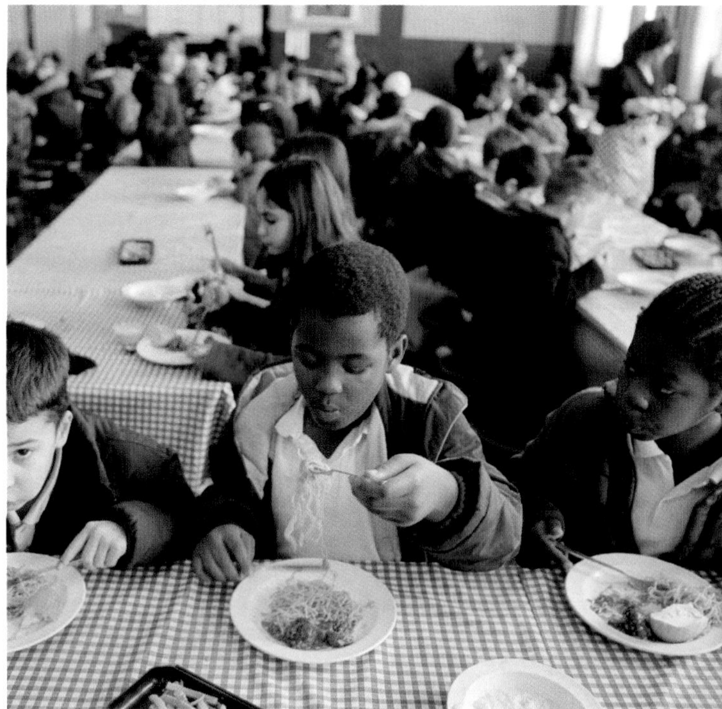

Grammar

So and *such*

❶ **Complete these sentences from the Reading text by writing *so*, *such* or *such a* in each space.**

- "We have (1) ......*such a*....... huge problem of bad eating habits in the United States that teaching about food cannot be left to parents," she says. "(2) .... many children generally are eating fast, cheap, easy food that something has to be done."
- Teo has been in the US for only three years, but his teachers say he has learned to speak perfect English in (3) .... short time because he is (4) .... happy at school.
- "But eating (5) .... good food … makes them care about what they eat …"

❷ **Complete the rules below by writing *so* or *such* in each space and the number of the example from Exercise 1 above.**

Rules

a .... + *a/an* + adjective + singular countable noun (+ *that* ...) Examples: ..*1*...... and ....

b .... + adjective + uncountable noun / plural noun (+ *that* ...) Example: ....

c .... + adjective / adverb (+ *that* ...) Example: ....

d .... + *much* / *many* / *little* / (+ noun) (+ *that* ...) Example: ....

page 155 *Grammar reference: So and such*

❸ **Write *so*, *such* or *such a(n)* in each space in the following sentences.**

1 I always enjoy visiting his house because he makes ....*such*....... lovely food.
2 There are .... many good restaurants in this town that I don't know which to choose.
3 I don't think going out for a meal is .... good idea – all the restaurants will be full.
4 It's difficult not to cook good food when the ingredients are .... fresh.
5 It was .... interesting conversation that I've been thinking about it all night.
6 I've got .... little food in the house that I think we'd better go out for a meal.

❹ **Most of the sentences below contain mistakes made by First Certificate candidates. However some of the sentences are correct. Find and correct the mistakes.**

1 I'll remember the meal for a long time because it was ~~such~~ delicious. *so*
2 I can't work in so much stressful conditions.
3 It was such fun for all of us to be together.
4 They're so nice, talkative, funny people.
5 I'm glad to see you after so long time.
6 It's difficult for animals to survive in such different climate.
7 It's a pity that there were so few spectators at the football match.
8 There are few hotels in this town with so comfortable beds.

Listening Part 4

❶ **You will hear an interview about Slow Food with Valerie Watson, a representative for an organisation called the Slow Food Movement. Before you listen, work in pairs.**

- What is fast food? Why is it called fast food?
- Do you think fast food is good for your health? Why (not)?
- What do you think *Slow Food* is?

❷ (10) **Listen to the interview once to find out what the purpose of the Slow Food Movement is.**

3 Read questions 1–7. Underline the important part of each question (but not the options A, B and C). The first has been done as an example.

1 The Slow Food Movement was originally started because
- **A** people wanted more time to enjoy cooking and eating.
- **B** a restaurant was opened in a historic location.
- **C** doctors warned that fast food was bad for people's health.

2 What, according to Valerie, is Slow Food?
- **A** food which is complicated to cook
- **B** food which takes a long time to eat
- **C** food of good quality

3 What does Valerie say is the problem with fast food companies?
- **A** They serve the same food all over the world.
- **B** They make traditional food producers disappear.
- **C** Their food is not as healthy as traditional food.

4 According to Valerie, the main aim of the Movement is to improve people's
- **A** diet.
- **B** health.
- **C** lifestyles.

5 What is the Salone del Gusto?
- **A** an event where food producers can show their products
- **B** an organisation which educates people about food
- **C** a company which sells traditional Italian food

6 What surprised Valerie about the Salone del Gusto?
- **A** the wide range of foods she saw there
- **B** the nationality of many of its visitors
- **C** the effect it has had on British food

7 Who does Valerie think will benefit most from the Slow Food Movement?
- **A** children
- **B** working parents
- **C** families in general

4 (10) Listen to the interview again and choose the best answer A, B or C.

Exam information

In Listening Part 4, there are seven questions and you choose one answer from three possible options. You hear the recording twice.

5 Work in small groups.

- Do you think Slow Food is a good idea?
- Should we spend more time cooking and eating food, or should we spend the time doing other things?

Salone del Gusto

Grammar

Too and *enough*

1 Read these sentences from Listening Part 4. Write either *too, too many, too much* or *enough* in each space.

- … people eat (1) too many hamburgers, (2) .... pizzas, and (3) .... fast food in general.
- We don't have (4) .... time to take care of ourselves, or enjoy our lives.
- … wherever you sit down for a meal, whether it's in Tokyo, Milan or Cape Town, the food you're given is (5) .... similar.
- There's just not (6) .... variety.
- … we'll be relaxed (7) .... to talk to each other more.

2 Complete these grammar rules by writing *too* or *enough* in each space.

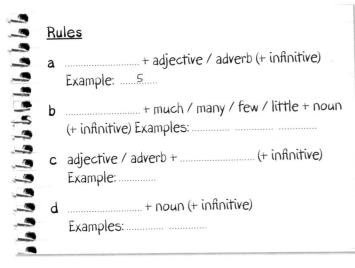

Rules

a .... + adjective / adverb (+ infinitive)
Example: ....5....

b .... + much / many / few / little + noun (+ infinitive) Examples: ....

c adjective / adverb + ... (+ infinitive)
Example: ....

d .... + noun (+ infinitive)
Examples: ....

page 155 *Grammar reference:* Too *and* enough

3 Complete these sentences with either *too, too many, too much* or *enough*.

1 School meals in Britain contain ....too many.... chips and not .... fresh vegetables to be really healthy.
2 Schools don't really spend .... time teaching students about nutrition.
3 Teachers don't take .... interest in their students' diets.
4 The canteen is .... small for all the students to eat lunch at the same time.
5 Most of us eat our meals .... quickly to really enjoy them.

4 Each of the following sentences contains a mistake made by First Certificate candidates with *too, too many, too much, enough* and *very*. Find the mistake and write the sentence correctly.

1 I liked the restaurant but ~~the food wasn't enough~~.
there wasn't enough food
2 Experts say that fast food is ~~not too much good for you~~. not very good for you
3 I don't have money enough to pay for your dinner.
4 We didn't like the hotel because it wasn't enough comfortable.
5 The food takes too much long to prepare so customers become impatient.
6 Some people suffer from doing too hard work.
7 It is too much cruel to keep animals in small cages.
8 It's not a sport too difficult, so I think you can learn it quite quickly.
9 The bed was not too much comfortable.
10 I'm afraid the meal was too much expensive.

5 Work in pairs. Imagine you have both been to a birthday party at a restaurant. Unfortunately, it was probably the worst restaurant either of you have ever been to. Discuss together how terrible the experience was, e.g. *The restaurant was too crowded. The service wasn't fast enough*, etc. You can talk about:

- the food
- the service
- the price
- how you felt.

Speaking Part 4

Exam information

In Speaking Part 4, the examiner:

- asks both candidates questions to find out their opinions on topics related to Part 3 (see page 32)
- may also ask you to react to opinions the other candidate expresses, so it's important to listen to what he/she says.

1 (11) You will hear two First Certificate candidates, Magda and Miguel, practising Speaking Part 4. Listen and decide which two questions below they are answering.

1 How can children and young people be encouraged to eat healthily?
2 Do you think young people should be taught how to cook at school? (Why / Why not?)
3 Do you think that fast food is bad for you? (Why / Why not?)
4 Do you think it is important for families to eat together? (Why / Why not?)
5 How important is it for people to be interested in the food they eat?
6 What, for you, is a healthy diet?

2 Work in pairs. True or false?

1 Magda and Miguel answer the questions with just two or three words.
2 They add ideas to support their opinions.
3 They don't just repeat the words of the questions, but use other vocabulary as well.

3 Work in pairs. Discuss the questions in Exercise 1 above.

page 181 *Speaking reference: Speaking Part 4*

Use of English Part 1

1 You will read a short review of a restaurant in Manchester. Read the review quickly to find out what the writer liked about the restaurant, e.g. the price.

Moso Moso

I (0) ....B.......... Moso Moso for the first time this month, and (1) .... that it was easily the best Chinese restaurant I've eaten in.

The surroundings were modern, yet it (2) .... felt airy and cosy. The waiters were very friendly and informative, and not (3) .... busy, as is often the (4) .... in some of the city's more popular restaurants.

As I was eating with a party of eight, we (5) .... to sample a good range of items on the menu, and between us couldn't find a single item that wasn't satisfying and delicious. Every (6) .... featured wonderful combinations of flavours. All the ingredients were clearly (7) .... and of the highest quality, and in my opinion, the seafood was particularly (8) .... We felt that we were given very good (9) .... for money, because the meal came to about £10 per person which we thought was very reasonable.

All of us would highly (10) .... this restaurant and, as it is located (11) .... a short walk from our workplace, we will no (12) .... be back for many more lunches!

Adapted from *Manchester Evening News*

2 For questions 1–12, read the text again and decide which answer (A, B, C or D) best fits each gap. There is an example at the beginning (0).

	A	B	C	D
0	A went	B (tried)	C tested	D proved
1	A revealed	B noticed	C found	D knew
2	A then	B already	C even	D still
3	A too	B much	C more	D enough
4	A reality	B case	C situation	D fact
5	A achieved	B succeeded	C managed	D reached
6	A plate	B dish	C food	D meal
7	A fresh	B new	C recent	D best
8	A tasteful	B tasty	C charming	D special
9	A price	B worth	C cost	D value
10	A recommend	B propose	C suggest	D advise
11	A hardly	B almost	C exactly	D just
12	A chance	B problem	C doubt	D likelihood

Exam information

In Use of English Part 1 you read a text with 12 gaps. You must choose the best alternative A, B, C or D for each gap. In the exam you will have about 10 minutes for this.

Part 1 tests your knowledge of the meanings of words, how they are used, and the grammar connected with particular words.

3 Work in pairs. Describe your perfect restaurant.

Writing Part 2

A review

Exam information

In Writing Part 2 you may be asked to write a review.

- Possible subjects of the review may include a book, film, theatre, restaurant or shop.
- This task tests your ability to express your opinions, describe things, make recommendations, etc.

1 Work in pairs. Read the writing task below and discuss the question which follows.

You have seen this announcement in your local English-language newspaper.

> Have you eaten at a local restaurant recently? If so, why not write a review for our *Food* section, telling other readers what the restaurant and its food is like?
>
> All reviews published will receive a free meal at the restaurant.

Write a **review**.

Which of these elements do you think a restaurant review should contain?

		yes / no / maybe
1	The type of restaurant	yes
2	The writer's general opinion of the restaurant	
3	A description of its design and surroundings	
4	A description of the food	
5	A description of the other customers	
6	A description of the service	
7	An explanation of how to get there	
8	A recommendation	
9	An indication of the price	
10	The location	

2 Read the review in Use of English Part 1 again. Which of these elements did the review contain? In which paragraph?

		yes / no	paragraph
1	The type of restaurant	yes	1
2	The writer's general opinion of the restaurant		
3	A description of its design and surroundings		
4	A description of the food		
5	A description of the other customers		
6	A description of the service		
7	An explanation of how to get there		
8	A recommendation		
9	An indication of the price		
10	The location		

3 A review is a good opportunity to show your range of vocabulary. Write each of the adjectives below in the appropriate column. You can write some adjectives in more than one column.

airy cosy ~~delicious~~ fresh friendly modern reasonable satisfying tasty wonderful informative

the waiters	the interior	the food	the price
		delicious	

4 Add two more adjectives of your own to each column.

5 Read the following writing task.

You have read this announcement in your college magazine.

> Do you have a favourite restaurant in town? If so, why not write a review for our *Free time* section, telling other readers what the establishment is like and giving us a recommendation?
>
> The three best reviews will receive a prize of 50.

Write a **review**. Write 120–180 words.

Write a plan for your review. Your plan could include:

Paragraph 1: Introduction: name and type of restaurant + where situated; your overall opinion of it
Paragraph 2: Particular dishes the restaurant serves + your opinion; the décor, service, etc.
Paragraph 3: Things you particularly like + price(s)
Paragraph 4: A general recommendation

6 Work in pairs. Discuss your ideas for your plans. Think of vocabulary you can each use.

7 Work alone and write your review.

page 171 *Writing reference: Writing Part 2*

Unit 3 *Vocabulary and grammar review*

Vocabulary

1 Circle the correct option in *italics* in each of these sentences.

1 Welcome to the Intercity Hotel. I hope you had a good *travel* / *journey*.
2 Sarah came back from her shopping *trip* / *journey* with lots of new clothes.
3 Among Brian's many interests, he lists foreign *journeys* / *travel* and climbing.
4 Do you know the *way* / *journey* to the cathedral?
5 Marco Polo's *trip* / *journey* to China took him several years.
6 I always stop for coffee at a café on my *journey* / *way* to work.
7 I made a *trip* / *travel* to Egypt this summer and really enjoyed it.
8 Many of our students have quite a long *trip* / *journey* to college each morning.

Word formation

2 Read the text below. Use the word given in capitals at the end of some of the lines to form a word that fits in the gap in the same line.

Paradise Hotel

Can you imagine a more (1) relaxing way to spend one's summer holiday than in a (2) .... hotel? The hotel which we had booked was beside a lake and surrounded by spectacular mountains. Imagine how (3) .... we felt when we arrived at the Paradise Hotel and found that we had been given a room with a view over the kitchens and not the (4) .... mountain scenery we had been expecting. Then when we went down for dinner the first evening feeling (5) .... after our long journey we found that a coach tour had arrived and the restaurant was so (6) .... that we had to wait for a table. It was really (7) .... with so many people talking and when we finally sat down for dinner the waitress was tired, irritable and generally (8) .... So the next day we decided to move to a smaller and (9) .... hotel just down the road. And fortunately we made the right decision because we had a thoroughly (10) .... stay there.

RELAX
COMFORT
APPOINT
NATURE
HUNGER
CROWD
NOISE
FRIEND
QUIET
ENJOY

Grammar

3 For questions 1–6, complete the second sentence so that it has a similar meaning to the first sentence, using the word given. Do not change the word given. You must use between two and five words, including the word given.

1 During my visit to London, I took hundreds of photos.
WHILE
I took hundreds of photos while I was visiting London.

2 I didn't notice that my passport was missing until I reached the immigration desk.
LOST
When I reached the immigration desk, I noticed that .... my passport.

3 I've given up using public transport to travel to work.
USED
I .... by public transport, but I've given it up.

4 She was still at university when she got married.
STUDYING
She got married .... at university.

5 Paola and Antonio met for the first time at the party yesterday.
NEVER
Paola and Antonio .... before the party yesterday.

6 Pablo is no longer as frightened of spiders as in the past.
USED
Pablo .... frightened of spiders than he is now.

Unit 4 *Vocabulary and grammar review*

Vocabulary

1 Complete the following text by writing *food*, *dish* or *meal* in the correct form in the spaces. In some spaces more than one answer is possible.

Last week, my boyfriend, Nigel, invited me out for a (1) ......meal...... in a restaurant. The (2) .... was not very good though. For my first course I chose a (3) .... called 'Chef's special', which turned out to be a kind of pizza. Generally, I'm not very keen on fast (4) .... , and this (5) .... was quite disappointing because it wasn't very special. Nigel didn't enjoy his (6) .... very much either. Personally, I think we would have enjoyed ourselves more if I'd cooked a (7) .... at home – after all, I had plenty of (8) .... in the fridge.

Word formation

2 Read the text below. Use the word given in capitals at the end of some of the lines to form a word that fits in the gap in the same line.

Changing diets

Even in quite (1) ...traditional... societies eating habits	TRADITION
are changing. In the past people used to prepare all	
their meals from fresh ingredients, but now	
(2) .... food and ready meals are becoming	CONVENIENT
increasingly popular. Experts suggest that eating	
too much fast food may not be very (3)	HEALTH
and so governments and other (4) .... now	ORGANISE
offer information about diet and nutrition in the	
hope that it will (5) .... people to eat more	COURAGE
fresh fruit and vegetables and have a generally more	
(6) .... diet.	BALANCE
On the other hand, some people argue that although	
many traditional dishes have (7) .... from	APPEAR
our menus, in general our diets are not as	
(8) .... as they used to be. There is a	REPEAT
much wider (9) .... of products available	CHOOSE
in supermarkets and other shops than there was 20	
years ago. Fresh fruit and vegetables are sold all the	
year round which means we can (10)	EASY
prepare meals which are good for us.	

Grammar

3 For questions 1–6, complete the second sentence so that it has a similar meaning to the first sentence, using the word given. Do not change the word given. You must use between two and five words, including the word given.

1 The food was so hot that we didn't really enjoy it.
TOO
The food was ...too hot for us to... really enjoy it.

2 The waitress spoke so quickly that we had difficulty understanding her.
ENOUGH
The waitress didn't speak .... understand her easily.

3 We didn't get a table at the restaurant because it was too full.
SO
The restaurant .... we couldn't get a table.

4 I asked for a second helping because the food was so delicious.
SUCH
It was .... I asked for a second helping.

5 Julio is not a very good cook so he won't get a job in that restaurant.
ENOUGH
Julio doesn't .... to get a job in that restaurant.

6 We ate very late because Phil spent too much time preparing the meal.
TIME
Phil spent .... preparing the meal that we ate very late.

Unit 5 Studying abroad

Starting off

1 Work in pairs. Find eight reasons for studying abroad by matching the beginning of each sentence (1–8) with its ending (a–h).

1	You live in and learn about	a	with other ways of thinking.
2	You get to know	b	new people.
3	You benefit	c	new friends.
4	You learn	d	more independent.
5	You become	e	after yourself.
6	You learn to look	f	from other approaches to studying.
7	You come in contact	g	to speak another language.
8	You make	h	another culture.

2 Which, for you, are the three best reasons for studying abroad?

3 Can you think of other reasons for studying abroad?

4 Have you studied abroad? If so, why? If not, would you like to? Why (not)?

Listening Part 1

1 You will hear people talking in five different situations connected with studying. Before you listen, match the following words connected with education to their definitions from the *Cambridge Advanced Learner's Dictionary*.

1	term	a	area of knowledge which is studied in school, college or university
2	subject	b	course of study at a college or university, or the qualification given to a student who has completed this
3	assignment	c	detailed study of an area of knowledge, especially in order to discover new information
4	course	d	information written on paper
5	tutor	e	number or letter which describes the quality of a piece of work done at school, college or university
6	research	f	one of the periods into which a year is divided at school, college or university
7	notes	g	piece of work given to someone as part of their studies
8	mark(s)	h	set of classes or plan of study on a particular area of knowledge, usually resulting in an exam or qualification
9	degree	i	teacher who works with one student or a small group at a British college or university

2 Now read the questions below and underline the main points in each question (but not the alternatives A, B or C).

1 You overhear a student talking about the course he has been doing. How does he feel about the course now?
   A frustrated
   B nervous
   C satisfied

2 You hear a student complaining about a problem she has had. Who caused the problem?
   A a teacher
   B a flatmate
   C a classmate

3 You hear a student at a language school in Japan. What does she like most about the experience?
   A attending language classes
   B doing other activities after class
   C meeting other language students

4 You hear an interview with a student who is thinking of studying abroad. What does she think will be the main benefit?
   A living in a different culture
   B living away from home
   C getting a better qualification

5 You overhear a teacher talking to his students. Why is he talking to them?
   A to explain something
   B to remind them of something
   C to cancel something

3 (12) Now listen and for questions 1–5 choose the best answer (A, B or C).

Exam advice

- Read the questions carefully, underlining the main ideas in the question as you read.
- The words you hear will be different from the words in the question; listen for the meaning rather than the actual words.

Vocabulary

Find out, get to know, know, learn, teach and *study*; *attend, join, take part* and *assist*

1 First Certificate candidates often confuse the words in *italics* above. Circle the correct alternative in each sentence.

1 I've been thinking of going to an Italian university and *learning* / *studying* international business for a year. (Speaker 4)

2 I was really embarrassed when I *found out* / *knew* what she'd done. (Speaker 2)

3 If I lived in Italy, I'd *learn* / *study* about how Italians live and think. (Speaker 4)

4 I *learn* / *know* Japanese from Japanese teachers. (Speaker 3)

5 I'm doing a karate course *learnt* / *taught* in Japanese. (Speaker 3)

6 ... I'm *knowing* / *getting to know* lots of Japanese people. (Speaker 3)

7 They also organise lots of other things for you to *assist* / *take part in* after you've finished your English lesson. (Speaker 3)

8 There are clubs you can *assist* / *join* if you're interested ... (Speaker 3)

9 You're expected to *join* / *attend* all your tutorials once a week ... (Speaker 5)

2 Now check your answers by reading these extracts from the *Cambridge Advanced Learner's Dictionary*.

assist *verb* [I or T] *formal*: to help: *You will be expected to assist the editor with the selection of illustrations for the book.*

attend BE PRESENT *verb slightly formal* [I or T]: to go to an event, place, etc.: *The meeting is on the fifth and we're hoping everyone will attend.*

get to know sb/sth: to spend time with someone or something so that you gradually learn more about them: *The first couple of meetings are for the doctor and patient to get to know each other.*

join BECOME A MEMBER *verb* [I or T]: to become a member of an organisation: *I felt so unfit after Christmas that I decided to join a gym.*

take part: to be involved in an activity with other people: *She doesn't usually take part in any of the class activities.*

Common Learner Error

know or find out?

If you **know** something, you already have the information.

Andy knows what time the train leaves.

If you **find** something **out**, you learn new information for the first time.

I'll ring the station to find out what time the train leaves.

~~*I'll ring the station to know what time the train leaves.*~~

learn, teach or study?

To **learn** is to get new knowledge or skills.

I want to learn how to drive.

When you **teach** someone, you give them new knowledge or skills.

My dad taught me how to drive.

~~*My dad learnt me how to drive.*~~

When you **study**, you go to classes, read books, etc. to try to understand new ideas and facts.

He is studying biology at university.

3 **Complete these sentences by using one of the words or phrases from the box in the correct form.**

assist	~~attend~~	find out
get to know	join	
know	learn	study
take part in	teach	

1 Dimitri has been ...attending... Spanish classes because he hopes to study in Seville next year.
2 I've .... a lot of interesting people from different countries while doing this course.
3 Maria hopes to .... chemistry when she goes to university.
4 While Karen was at summer camp, she .... how to windsurf.
5 The best way to .... the answer to this question is to look on the internet.
6 I'd like to ring Kevin but I don't .... his phone number.
7 I had a wonderful course tutor who .... me to speak Spanish really well.
8 The university has an accommodation officer who will .... students with finding somewhere to live.
9 Kostas .... a youth club because he wanted to meet people.
10 It was the first time he had .... a marathon, so people were surprised when he won.

Grammar

Zero, first and second conditionals

1 **Read the sentences (1–6) below. Which ...?**

a refer to something which the speaker thinks is possible
b refer to something which the speaker is imagining, thinks is improbable, or thinks is impossible
c refers to something which is generally true

1 *If you speak a bit of the language, it's much easier to make friends.*
2 *If I went, it might make it more difficult for me to get a good degree.*
3 *If for any reason you can't make it to a tutorial, try to let your tutor know.*
4 *If I lived in Italy, I'd learn about how Italians live and think.*
5 *If your tutor has to cancel a tutorial or put it off, he or she'll try to tell you the week beforehand.*
6 *Your tutors will organise you into groups and suggest research unless you prefer working alone.*

page 156 *Grammar reference: Zero, first and second conditionals*

2 **Match the beginning of each sentence with its ending.**

1 I won't mention your name
2 I'd travel round the world
3 We don't allow people to do the course
4 I'll have to buy the book
5 If I decide to study abroad,
6 If I see her,
7 If I wasn't so busy,
8 If I went to study in Australia,
9 I'd take a taxi
10 If students come to class regularly

a I won't see my girlfriend for several months.
b they usually get good results.
c I'd go to the cinema with you.
d I wouldn't come back.
e I'll tell her you called.
f if I had the money.
g unless I can find it in the library.
h unless you want me to.
i if I could afford one.
j unless they have the right qualifications.

3 **Work in pairs. Take turns to ask each other these questions.**

- If you could study anywhere in the world, where would you go?
- If you studied in a different country, what do you think would be your biggest problem?
- How will you celebrate if you pass all your exams this year?
- If you could change one thing in your life, what would it be?
- If, one day, you became famous, what do you think you'd be famous for?

Use of English Part 3

1 Form a noun from these verbs. Then look at extracts B, C and E in Reading Part 3 to check your answers.

verb	noun
qualify	1 qualification
confide	2
understand	3
improve	4
behave	5
advise	6
assist	7
know	8

2 Each of the nouns below has been formed from a verb. Write the verb next to each noun.

verb	noun
1 advertise	advertisement
2	entertainment
3	feeling
4	achievement
5	investigation
6	obedience
7	preference
8	sensation

3 Read the text on the right. Use the word given in capitals at the end of some of the lines to form a word that fits in the space in the same line.

Learn Polish in Poland

We run Polish language courses with small classes so that students receive individual (0) ...attention... from their teachers. During the course, you will gain a good working **ATTEND**
(1) .... of Polish as well as an **KNOW**
(2) .... of Polish culture. At the same time you **APPRECIATE**
will meet (3) .... people and have fun. **INTEREST**

While we realise that many people have some (4) .... **DIFFICULT**
learning Polish, we do our best to make it easy and
(5) .... Our language programme focuses on **ENJOY**
intensive classroom instruction of reading, writing, oral
(6) .... , grammar and vocabulary. Starting from **COMMUNICATE**
the most (7) .... situations, you will notice a **BASIS**
gradual (8) .... in your language skills until you **IMPROVE**
eventually master Polish.

To learn a language, one must interact with native speakers; our students are immersed in city life with the (9) .... of **ASSIST**
qualified teachers who are on hand to teach, and encourage students with the aim of increasing their (10) .... **CONFIDENT**
with Polish.

Adapted from *www.polishsummer.com*

Exam advice

- Read the text quickly to get a general idea of what it is about.
- Look at the space and decide what type of word you need (noun, verb, adjective or adverb).
- When you have finished, check your answers by reading the text carefully again.

4 Work in pairs.

Apart from going to classes, what other things can you do to improve your knowledge of a language you're learning?

Reading Part 3

1 **Work in pairs. The pictures below show problems students sometimes have when studying abroad.**

- What are the problems?
- How would you deal with each problem?

2 **You will read about five students' experiences of studying abroad. Before you read, underline the main ideas in each question.**

Which person

did better in their studies as a result of going abroad?	**1**	B
says other students made good progress with a foreign language?	**2**	
was entertained by a teacher?	**3**	
wanted to spend less time studying?	**4**	
overcame some initial difficulties with the academic system?	**5**	
particularly appreciated meeting people from many different countries?	**6**	
says some people are discouraged from studying abroad by problems they may have?	**7**	
felt homesick when first in the country?	**8**	
found communicating with other students difficult?	**9**	
thinks studying abroad is a unique experience?	**10**	
suggests that studying abroad may make you more attractive to future employers?	**11**	
was surprised by the country despite speaking the language?	**12**	
learnt a lot about people?	**13**	
were able to get practical working experience in the countries they studied in?	**14** ☐ **15**	

3 **Work in pairs. Read the questions again. Which questions:**

a are about the students' classmates?
b are about problems when the student arrived in the country?
c seem to be about positive aspects of their experiences?
d seem to be about negative aspects of their experiences?
e are not about studying?

Exam advice

Before reading the extracts:

- read the questions carefully first, underlining the main ideas
- think how the idea in each question may be expressed.

Then:

- read the first extract and find which questions it answers
- at the same time, underline the words in the extract which give you each answer
- deal with each extract in turn in this way.

4 **For questions 1–15, choose the person A–E from the extracts on page 49 and underline the words in the extracts which give you the answer. The people may be chosen more than once. For questions 14 and 15 you will need to choose two people.**

A year abroad

Have you ever thought of studying abroad? Read about five people who have done just that.

A Vanna studied in Australia

My first weeks were one of the worst experiences of my life. I felt extremely lonely and lost. In my country, students hardly ever live away from home when they are at university, so the first thing I had to do was to learn to look after myself. Then I had to face my second big challenge: the language. It was hard to listen to a foreign language 24 hours a day, and even harder to take notes during the lectures! I found the teachers quite easy to understand, as they generally spoke English very clearly. Unfortunately that was not always the case with my classmates. Coming to terms with a different teaching method was another surprise, but when I got used to working in groups and doing assignments, I began to feel more confident.

B Mandy studied in Finland

The hospital where I studied was small and friendly. I spent five weeks as a nursing assistant on an orthopaedic ward. My mentor had already worked in a London hospital, so she was familiar with the English hospital system. I also had a fantastic tutor who was incredibly helpful. She drove me to Helsinki several times to catch boats and buses and I spent many Sundays at her house enjoying her cooking and hospitality. I feel that my contact with patients and hospital staff has given me a much better understanding of human nature and human behaviour and <u>I've also noticed a marked improvement in my academic work</u>.

C Karl studied in the UK

London as a multicultural city gave me the feeling that I was at the centre of things. One of the best things was that as a university student I was able to get to know people from all over the world. Another thing I liked about studying in the UK was having the opportunity to change aspects of my studies if I wanted to. I was also lucky to take part in an internship programme, which enabled me to work in the British Parliament as a politician's assistant, so my studies were not just theoretical.

D Verina studied in Brazil

I spent my second year abroad in São Paolo. My mum's French and my dad's Portuguese, so being bilingual I already had the advantage of knowing the language well, but I was totally unprepared for the amazing experience of living in Brazil. I studied on average 38 hours a week, which I felt was too much, but it was fantastic mixing with other students. I had a great social life and managed to combine studying with everything else, like my day-to-day chores. Studying in a foreign university is a once-in-a-lifetime opportunity, but you have to make the most of it as the year flies by so quickly.

E Paul studied in Austria

Luckily, because my mother is German, I didn't come up against a language barrier, but I did meet lots of people from all over Europe with only a basic knowledge of German. After a few months they were all speaking with much more confidence. Many people have told me that if there was no language barrier, they would love to have this sort of experience. My advice is always go. If you do, by the end of the year you will be able to put on your CV that you have working knowledge of another language. But if studying in a foreign language really scares you, there is an option in many countries of studying in English and many of the textbooks are in English anyway.

5 Work in small groups. One of your mother's friends has received this letter. She has asked you for your opinions. Think about the experiences of the five students you have just read about and decide what Anna should do.

I'm interested in coming to your country for a few months to learn the language. I know a little of the language, but I'd like to speak it much better. I'm 17 years old and I think this would be a useful way to spend some time before I go to university next year. What do you think I should do? Should I look for a job or find somewhere to study?

I look forward to hearing your opinions.

Yours,

Anna

Speaking Part 1

1 Work in pairs. Ask each other these questions.

- Which is/was your favourite subject at school? Why?
- How do you think you'll use English in the future?
- Do you enjoy studying? Why (not)?

2 (13) Listen to how Nikolai and Magda answer questions.

1 What is Nikolai's favourite subject and what reasons does he give?
2 How will Magda use English in the future?

3 🎧13 **Now listen again and answer the questions below. True or false?**

	T	F
1 They answer the questions very briefly.		
2 They give reasons for their answers.		
3 They sound positive and enthusiastic when they are speaking.		

Exam advice

- Listen carefully to the question and make sure your answers are relevant.
- Answer the question and where possible:
  - give reasons for your answer, or
  - add a little extra information.

4 Work in pairs. Take turns to ask your partner the questions in the boxes.

Student A

- Can you describe the school you go to / went to?
- What would you like to study in the future if you had the chance? Why?
- How much homework do students in your country generally do?
- Can you tell me what you most enjoy about learning English?
- Tell me about the best teacher you've ever had.

Student B

- Do you prefer studying alone or with other people? Why?
- Can you remember your first day at school? Tell me about it.
- Would you like to study in a different country? Why (not)?
- How important are exams in your country?
- How important is learning English to you?

Writing Part 1

1 Work in pairs. Read the following writing task and discuss questions 1–4 below.

A Canadian friend, Matt, recently visited you and has just sent you a letter. Read Matt's letter and the notes you have made.

1. How long would you go to Canada for?
2. If you went to Canada, what would you study?
3. What do you think are the advantages of going to the Rocky Mountains?
4. What do you think are the advantages of sharing a flat with Matt's friends?

Thanks for having me to stay last month and showing me around your town. You mentioned when I was there that you would like to come to my town to study next year. It would be great to see you again. Please let me know how long you're thinking of coming for — Say how long for *and what you would like to study so I can find information for you.* — Explain what I want to do

Also, if you came in the summer we could do a trip together either to the Rocky Mountains or to Vancouver. Which would you prefer? — Rocky Mountains because ...

If you like, I could arrange for you to share a flat with some friends of mine. Would you be interested? — Yes, say why ...

Best wishes,

Matt

2 Read Pia's reply to Matt's letter. How does Pia answer questions 1–4 above? (You should ignore spelling mistakes for now.)

Dear Matt,

Thanks for your letter offering to find some information about corses for me. I'm hoping to come for two months from the begining of July to study English. Do you know if there's a language school or university in your town wich runs classes during the summer?

I think it's an excelent idea for us to go on a trip together in the summer. I'd preffer to go to the Rocky Mountains as I visited Vancouver two years ago and I'd like a completely new experence.

Thanks also for offering to organise accomodation for me. I'd really like to share a flat with your friends becaus this would give me an oportunity to make some friends myself and practise my English.

Many thanks for your help and I'm looking foward to hearing from you soon.

Best wishes,

Pia

3 **The letter contains ten spelling mistakes commonly made by First Certificate candidates. Find the mistakes and write the correct spelling** (e.g. ~~corses~~ – *courses*).

4 **Study these examples of direct and indirect questions. Decide whether questions 1–5 below are true or false.**

direct questions	indirect questions
a Is there a language school or university in your town which runs classes during the summer?	Do you know if there's a language school or university in your town which runs classes during the summer? (*from Pia's letter*)
b Where is the nearest airport?	Could you tell me where the nearest airport is?
c How much would it cost to rent a flat?	Can you give me an idea of how much it would cost to rent a flat?
d When do you expect to go to the mountains?	Let me know when you expect to go to the mountains.

1 In each pair of examples, the order of the words in the underlined part is the same. *False*
2 In indirect questions, the word order of the underlined part is the same as in a statement (a sentence which is not a question).
3 Example a is a *yes/no* question. In indirect *yes/no* questions you must use *if* or *whether.*
4 In example d, the auxiliary verb *do* is used in both the direct and indirect questions.
5 Indirect questions always need a question mark (?).

page 156 *Grammar reference: Indirect questions*

5 **Rewrite these questions which someone enquiring about studying in Canada might write in a letter, starting with the words given.**

Example: When does the course start?
Can you tell me when *the course starts?*

1 How much does it cost to rent a flat?
Can you tell me ....
2 What qualification would I get at the end of the course?
I would like to know ....
3 How far is the college from the city centre?
Do you know ....
4 Will I have to do a lot of homework?
I'd like to know ....
5 Does the college have sports facilities?
Can you tell me ....

6 **Do the writing task below and write a letter of between 120 and 150 words. Remember to use all the handwritten notes and try to use some of the question forms you have just practised.**

Your Australian friend, Caroline, has recently sent you this email. Read her email and the notes you have made on it. Then write an email to Caroline using all your notes.

I've just found out about an educational summer camp here in Australia and I immediately thought of you! Would you be interested in coming? — *Of course! What dates?*

There would be lots of people our age from all over the world. You can choose which subjects you want to study and there's also the opportunity to do lots of sports. — *Say which subjects I want and why*

It's not very expensive and afterwards we could do a trip together. — *How much?* Which would you prefer: to visit the Australian desert or the Great Barrier Reef? — *The Great Barrier Reef because ...* I'm enclosing a couple of photos of them to help you decide!

Let me know soon.

Love,

Caroline

Exam advice

- Make sure that you deal with all the points in the notes or you will lose marks.
- When you have finished, check what you have written, including the spelling.

Unit 6 The planet in danger

exhaust fumes from cars and lorries

Starting off

1 **Work in small groups. The photos show environmental problems. Use words and phrases from the box to label the pictures.**

~~exhaust fumes from cars and lorries~~	
water problems	rising sea levels
industrial pollution	climate change
endangered species / threats to wildlife	
destruction of rainforests	construction work

2 **Which of these environmental problems do you think are the most serious in your country? Why?**

3 **How do you think they will affect your country in the future?**

Reading Part 2

1 **Work in pairs. You will read an article by someone who went to see some gorillas in the wild. Before you read: why is it important to protect endangered species like gorillas?**

2 **Read the text quite quickly.**

- What were the gorillas doing?
- How did they react to the tourists' visit?

A close encounter in Africa

There are only 600 mountain gorillas left in the world, half of them in Uganda's Great Impenetrable Forest. Tim Adams joined a jungle adventure to visit this endangered species.

I realised why it was called the Great Impenetrable Forest after we had been climbing all morning through thick forest; our guide, Caleb, had to cut a path through the trees with a machete.

Less than 48 hours earlier, I had been in London running my finger over a map of this prehistoric green mountainside. **1** I Now I was beginning to feel near the heart of Africa.

During our climb, Caleb had told our little party that there were about 330 mountain gorillas in this forest, half of the world's population. **2** ____ The one we were following, group C, contained 23 members. As each adult needs to find and to eat 30 kg of vegetation a day, they must keep moving. **3** ____ He had brought

photographs of his hairy, sleepy friends from back home which he showed us while we rested and drank water.

There is something very exciting about scrambling through a rainforest in search of great apes. **4** Despite the climb, everyone was extremely watchful, studying the paths for footprints, sniffing the air, listening for any change in the birdsong, occasionally catching the movement of a red-tailed monkey high up in the trees.

Caleb had been doing this for ten years. **5** Despite taking tourist groups to see them every day, he still loved the job.

As we walked, Caleb talked quietly on a radio to fellow guides who had gone ahead to discover where group C had headed. He looked for some time until he finally crouched down in the undergrowth and gestured to us that the gorillas were nearby.

As he moved forward slowly, Caleb made a series of strange low noises to say hello. **6** Then, as the vegetation cleared, we saw a young male gorilla sitting in a tree about three metres away. The gorilla watched us idly while he ate leaves from the branches around him. **7** We followed him along a little path, while ahead of us we could hear the noise of breaking branches as the family ate their lunch.

Two youngsters were playing under a tree. The leader of the group wandered past them, listened to Caleb's noises for a moment and then disappeared into the darkness of the forest. **8** No one felt afraid, but we all felt a little strange. I squatted about two metres from a mother while she broke branches for her baby son to eat.

We watched the gorillas like this for maybe 45 minutes. The mother and son stared back at us, before they disappeared into the thicker bushes. We sat to eat while we compared impressions of what we had witnessed. Then we headed back down the mountain.

Adapted from *The Observer*

3 Eight sentences have been removed from the article. Read it again more carefully and <u>underline</u> words and phrases before and after the gaps which you think may connect to something in the missing sentences.

4 Now choose from the sentences A–I the one which fits each gap (1–8). There is one extra sentence which you do not need to use.

- **A** All around we could see the black eyes of the rest of his family looking at us through the low branches.
- **B** There were seven in my party, including a keeper from Chicago Zoo who looked after gorillas for a living but had never seen them in the wild.
- **C** They were divided into family groups, five of which were used to people watching them.
- **D** We followed rather cautiously, our heads full of King Kong.
- **E** When he first started, he had to sit in a clearing every day without moving and let the gorillas sniff around him until they accepted him.
- **F** When he had finished he slipped down to the ground, and then pulled the tree down behind him.
- **G** I was so close to him that I was able to reach out and touch him.
- **H** You've seen films of it but the idea of actually meeting wild gorillas makes you very alert.
- **I** After an overnight flight to Kampala, we had driven for ten hours to Bwindi in the remote south-west corner of Uganda.

Exam advice

- In the exam seven sentences are removed, not eight as here.
- Read before and after the gaps carefully to find clues to help you.
- Read the sentences in the list carefully too, looking for clues which will connect them with the text.

5 Work in small groups.

Would a trip like this interest you? Why (not)?

Vocabulary

Look, see, watch, listen and *hear*

1 **First Certificate candidates often confuse *look, see* and *watch*, and *listen* and *hear*. Complete these sentences from the reading text using *look, see, watch, listen* and *hear* in the correct form. When you have finished, check your answers by looking at Reading Part 2 again.**

1 … ahead of us we could ......hear...... the noise of breaking branches as the family ate their lunch.
2 The leader of the group wandered past them, ... to Caleb's noises for a moment and then disappeared into the darkness of the forest.
3 We .... the gorillas like this for maybe 45 minutes.
4 All around we could .... the black eyes of the rest of his family .... at us through the low branches.

2 **Read these two extracts from the *Cambridge Advanced Learner's Dictionary.* Then circle the correct alternative in *italics* in the sentences which follow.**

Common Learner Error

look, see or watch?

See means to notice people and things with your eyes.

She saw a big spider and screamed.

Look (at) is used when you are trying to see something or someone. If look is followed by an object, you must use a preposition. The usual preposition is 'at'.

I've looked everywhere, but can't find my keys. I looked at the map to find the road.

Watch means to look at something for a period of time, usually something which moves or changes.

He watched television all evening.

listen, listen to or hear?

Use hear when you want to say that sounds, music, etc. come to your ears. You can hear something without wanting to.

I could hear his music through the wall.

Use listen to say that you pay attention to sounds or try to hear something.

The audience listened carefully.

Use listen to when you want to say what it is that you are trying to hear.

The audience listened to the speaker.

1 I *looked at* / *watched* my watch and saw that it was time to leave.
2 I really enjoy *looking at* / *watching* horror films.
3 We live near a motorway and can *listen to* / *hear* the traffic non-stop.
4 I've been *looking at* / *watching* our holiday photos.
5 Did you *watch* / *see* Buckingham Palace when you were in London?
6 She knew the policeman was *looking* / *watching* what she did.
7 Jenny looks so relaxed when she's *listening to* / *hearing* music on her MP3 player.
8 Martin was in the kitchen so he didn't *listen to* / *hear* the telephone when it rang.

Listening Part 2

1 **You will hear part of a radio interview with Sylvia Welling, a student who is working on a rainforest project in Costa Rica. Before listening, work in pairs. Use the photos on the right to help you.**

- Why are rainforests being destroyed?
- Why is it important to preserve rainforests?

2 **Look at the sentences below. What type of information do you need to complete each space (e.g. a date, a number) and/or what type of word(s) do you need to complete each space (e.g. a verb, an adjective)?**

Rainforest Project, Costa Rica

Sylvia is spending her (1) .... working on the project.

The aim of the project is to (2) .... about the rainforest.

Sylvia is on the project because she wants to gain (3) .... experience.

One part of her job involves (4) .... in the forest.

She also works as a (5) .... for visitors.

She says rainforests are destroyed to make land available for (6) ....

She predicts that (7) .... of rainforests will have been destroyed by the year 2050.

As a result, the world will probably become (8) ....

She thinks that many species of animals will only be found (9) ....

She hopes visitors will be more careful about (10) .... when they go home.

3 (14) **Now listen and complete the sentences.**

Exam advice

- Before you listen look at the incomplete sentences, including any words which come after the space.
- Think about what type of information you need for each space (a date, a job etc.).
- Think about what type of word(s) you need for each space (a noun, adjective, etc.).
- For most spaces you will need between one and three words.
- You should write words you actually hear.

4 Work in pairs.

Would you prefer to work on a project like this or to visit it as a tourist?

Grammar

Ways of expressing the future

1 Complete the table below by writing the underlined verbs from Listening Part 2 in the column headed example(s). For one tense you will need two examples.

1 … by the year 2050, 70% of rainforests will have disappeared.
2 It's going to have really drastic consequences for the rest of the planet.
3 I'm going to work as a researcher when I finish my degree …
4 … in 40 or 50 years' time these animals will only be living in zoos.
5 They just won't exist in the wild …

name of tense	example(s)	uses
future simple	*won't exist*	*d*
future continuous		
future perfect		
'going to' future		

2 Write each of these ways future tenses are used (a–e) in the column above headed uses.

a Actions or events which will be finished at a time in the future
b For an event which will be in progress at a particular time or over a period of time in the future
c For actions in the future which we have already decided to do
d For things which we predict will happen in the future but are not the result of a decision
e Predictions about the future which are based on evidence in the present

page 157 *Grammar reference: Ways of expressing the future*

3 **Circle the correct alternative in *italics* in each of the sentences below.**

1. Isn't it hot? I think *I'll open* / *I'll be opening* the window to let in some fresh air if that's all right.
2. I have to leave class early tomorrow – *I'm going to take part in* / *I'll take part in* a debate on global warming.
3. *We're going to spend* / *We'll spend* our summer holidays in the south of France – I've booked the hotel already.
4. By the year 2050, global temperatures *will be rising* / *will have risen* by at least 1.5 degrees.
5. Sarah has decided that *she'll study* / *she's going to study* Earth Sciences at university, so she's been preparing really hard for her final school exams.
6. With global warming I think that the way we live *will change* / *will have changed* a lot over the next 50 years.
7. I hope people *will remember us* / *will be remembering us* for saving the earth from environmental disaster – not for destroying it.
8. What a lot of dust! *It's going to make* / *It'll be making* me sneeze!

4 **Work in small groups. Copy the questionnaire below into your notebooks, then complete it by discussing the questions.**

Questionnaire

What do you think the area where you live will be like in 20 years' time?

	Student 1:	Student 2:	Student 3: ....
Do you think there will be more people living in the area or fewer?			
How do you think the shops will have changed?			
What new buildings do you expect to see?			
Will the countryside have changed?			
What do you think people will be doing in their free time?			
What other changes do you think will happen?			
Do you think it will be a better area to live in or worse? Why?			

Use of English Part 1

1 **You will read a newspaper article about how less light is reaching the Earth from the sun. Before you read:**

- What may be causing this?
- What might happen as a result?

2 **Read the article without paying attention to the gaps and find the answers to the questions in Exercise 1.**

Earth getting darker as sunlight decreases

In a recent report, scientists (0) ..C........ that the Earth is getting darker because of pollution in the atmosphere. The reason for this (1) .... apparent in 2001 when flights in the US were grounded for a few days and scientists (2) .... that days were brighter and nights were cooler. It is thought that pollution is (3) .... for this. Sunlight is reflected back into space after hitting particles created by car fumes, aerosols and aeroplanes.

Scientists (4) .... that this phenomenon may have (5) .... the climate from becoming even warmer. They also believe that when anti-pollution laws (6) .... into effect, the speed at which the world's climate changes will (7) .... To the surprise of scientists (8) .... the world, hundreds of instruments recorded a drop of around ten per cent in the amount of sunshine which was (9) .... the surface of the Earth from the late 1950s to the early 1990s.

The (10) .... on agriculture could be very damaging, since even a one per cent reduction in sunlight is enough to reduce the growth of some crops. The factors that have led to the reduction in sunlight also cause various environmental problems, such as air pollution and acid rain. Some scientists believe that the reflection of heat has (11) .... the oceans cooler. As a result, less rain forms and this may have played a (12) .... in changing weather patterns in the last few years.

Adapted from *The Daily Mail*

3 **For questions 1–12, read the text again and decide which answer (A, B, C or D) best fits each gap. There is an example at the beginning (0).**

	A	B	C	D
0	A tell	B inform	C claim	D instruct
1	A came	B became	C got	D made
2	A noticed	B learned	C knew	D measured
3	A guilty	B accused	C suspicious	D responsible
4	A advise	B alert	C alarm	D warn
5	A prevented	B avoided	C controlled	D protected
6	A go	B arrive	C come	D become
7	A increase	B grow up	C develop	D hurry up
8	A over	B around	C in	D through
9	A arriving	B touching	C getting	D reaching
10	A effect	B result	C change	D consequence
11	A caused	B resulted	C made	D got
12	A piece	B part	C effect	D game

Exam advice

- Read the title and the text quickly to get a general idea of what it's about.
- Deal with the spaces one by one. Read carefully before and after the space.
- If you are not sure which alternative is correct, discard the alternatives you think are wrong and choose from the others.
- When you have finished, read the text again to check your answers.

Vocabulary

Prevent, avoid and *protect*; *reach, arrive* and *get (to)*

1 **First Certificate candidates often confuse the words in *italics* below. Circle the correct alternative.**

1 The government has opened a nature reserve to *prevent / avoid / protect* people from hunting endangered species.

2 We *reached / arrived / got* at the nature reserve at nightfall.

2 **Read the following extracts from the *Cambridge Advanced Learner's Dictionary*. Then write one of the words in blue in the correct form in each of sentences 1–7 below. In some cases more than one answer may be possible.**

prevent to stop something from happening or someone from doing something: *Label your suitcases to prevent confusion.*

avoid to stay away from someone or something: *We left early to avoid the traffic.*

protect to keep someone or something safe from injury, damage or loss: *It's important to protect your skin from the harmful effects of the sun.*

reach to arrive at a place, especially after spending a long time or a lot of effort travelling: *We finally reached the hotel just after midnight.* It is not normally followed by a preposition. It is not normally used with here or there.

arrive to reach a place, especially at the end of a journey. *It was dark by the time we arrived at the station.* You arrive at a building or part of a building: *We arrived at the theatre just as the play was starting.* You arrive in a town, city or country: *When did you arrive in London?* You arrive home/here/there: *We arrived home yesterday.*

get (+ to) to reach or arrive at a place: *If you get to the hotel before us, just wait at reception.* You get home/here/there: *What time does he normally get home?*

1 This cream is perfect for ....protecting.... you from insect bites.

2 The weather was so bad that they didn't manage to .... the top of the mountain until three days later.

3 She's driving home and she'll phone me when she .... there.

4 The new law .... people from building houses near the National Park.

5 When they .... at the hotel, they went straight to their rooms.

6 I think we should set out early to .... the worst of the traffic.

7 You ought to be wearing a hat to .... your head from the sun.

Speaking Part 2

1 **Work in pairs. Look at these photos. They show people doing things to protect the environment. Decide which of these words and phrases you could use about each photo.**

pollution	countryside	exhaust fumes
natural surroundings	noise	picking up rubbish
litter	public transport	

2 (15) **Listen to Magda answering this question:** ***Compare the photographs, and say how important these activities are for protecting the environment.*** **Which of the words and phrases in the box does she use?**

3 (15) **Listen again. Which of these phrases does Magda use? Tick (✓) the ones you hear.**

The first picture shows … ✓	I think they're probably …
It's essential to …	In the other picture we can see …
In the first picture I suppose …	It's important to …
I think that's what's happening in the second photo …	

4 **Take turns to give your answer to the question for each pair of photos.**

Student A: Compare the photographs in Exercise 1 on the left and say how important these activities are for protecting the environment.

Student B: Compare the photographs below and say how activities like these help to protect the environment.

Exam advice

- Don't describe the photographs in detail. Make general comparisons about what the photographs show.
- Answer the second part of the question with your opinion, giving reasons for your opinion and examples if possible.
- You should speak for one complete minute.

Writing Part 2 An essay

1 **Read the following writing task and underline the main points you should deal with.**

> You have had a class discussion on the environment and the future. Your teacher has now asked you to write an essay giving your opinion on the following statement:
>
> *Our children will live in a worse environment than we do.*
>
> Write your **essay**.

2 **Work in pairs.**

- Do you agree or disagree with the statement in the writing task? Why? Briefly note down the main reasons for your opinion.

3 **Complete this plan for the essay by writing in your ideas.**

Paragraph 1: The present situation and your opinion:
....
....

Paragraph 2: First reason for your opinion:
....
....

Paragraph 3: Second and third reasons for your opinion:
....
....

Paragraph 4: Action we can take; consequences if we don't take it: ....
....

4 **Work in pairs. Make a list of vocabulary connected with the environment that you could use when writing the essay.**

5 **Read the sample essay below without paying attention to the gaps.**

- Compare the plan for this essay with the plan you made.
- Add useful vocabulary from the essay to the list you have just made.

Environmentalists have been warning us for many years about the effects of human activity on the environment. (1) ..Despite.. being aware of the dangers, we continue to harm it, and for (2) .... I believe that our children will live in a worse world than we do.

I think there are two aspects of human activity which are especially dangerous. (3) .... is atmospheric pollution, which is caused by exhaust fumes and industry. This will lead to changes in the climate and make sea levels rise. As a (4) ...., our children will live in a warmer world and people living near the coast may have to leave their homes.

(5) .... is the destruction of our natural environment such as rainforests and countryside. (6) ...., we are damaging the habitats of many animals and plants that live there and these will become extinct.

(7) ...., urgent action is needed to protect the environment by reducing pollution and creating nature reserves. (8) ...., the world our children live in will be much less pleasant than ours.

6 **Complete the essay by writing a word or phrase from the box in each of the spaces.**

consequently	~~despite~~	this reason
in my opinion	result	the first
the second aspect	unless we do so	

7 **It's important to use linking words and phrases like those in Exercise 6 when you are writing an essay. Linking words and phrases organise your ideas clearly and this helps the reader to follow your argument. Copy the table below into your notebook, then complete it by writing these linking words and phrases in the correct column.**

~~The first is~~	~~Consequently~~	~~In my opinion~~	
As a result	Because of this	Finally	Firstly
For this reason	I believe	I feel	I think
In addition	Lastly	The second (aspect) is	

expressing consequences	introducing your opinion	organising ideas logically
Consequently	In my opinion	The first is

8 **Work in pairs. Read the following writing task and follow steps 1–4 above.**

You have had a class discussion on things you can do to protect the environment. Your teacher has asked you to write an essay giving your opinion on the following statement:

The environment we live in will change dramatically in the next 50 years.

Write your **essay** in 120–180 words.

9 **Write the essay following your plan.**

Exam advice

In Writing Part 2, one task may be an essay in which you are asked to give your opinion on a subject.

- Read the question carefully, underlining the points you must deal with.
- Make a plan with the main ideas for each paragraph.
- Think of vocabulary you want to use and note it down.
- Write following your plan.

Unit 5 *Vocabulary and grammar review*

Vocabulary

1 Complete the crossword with words connected with education.

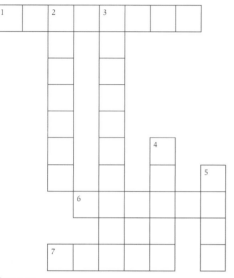

Across

1 During the course you do some .... to find out something new about the subject. (8)

6 He's hoping to study for a .... in history at university. (6)

7 I couldn't go to the last class, so can I borrow your .... so I can see what I missed? (5)

Down

2 What was your favourite .... at school? Mine was maths. (7)

3 My teacher has given me a really difficult .... to do this week. (10)

4 Sophie always gets high .... in her school exams. (5)

5 We don't do any exams here until the end of the second .... (4)

2 Circle the correct alternative in *italics* in each sentence.

1 Mario is thinking of taking driving lessons to *know* / *learn* how to drive.

2 Ludmila wants to *know* / *study* biology at university.

3 Sven is *teaching* / *learning* me how to ski.

4 If you *join* / *assist* this club, you will *know* / *get to know* people from all over the world.

5 You should *attend* / *assist* lessons every day if you want to get high marks.

6 Sayed decided to *assist* / *take part in* the debate on human rights.

Word formation

3 Write nouns for each of these verbs.

verb	noun
investigate	investigation
obey	
practise	
prefer	
achieve	
understand	
know	
qualify	

Grammar

4 Complete the second sentence so that it has a similar meaning to the first sentence, using the word given. Do not change the word given. You must use between two and five words, including the word given.

1 He won't pass the test because he doesn't work hard enough.
HARDER
If he worked ....harder, he would....... pass the test.

2 Studying abroad will make you more independent.
BECOME
If you .... more independent.

3 Sandra only goes to lessons because she wants to meet other students.
ATTEND
If Sandra didn't want to meet other students, ... lessons.

4 I'll lend you my book if you take care of it.
AFTER
If you .... , you can borrow it.

5 I can't tell you the answer because I don't know.
WOULD
If I .... tell you.

6 He's not very enthusiastic because he's tired.
SO
If .... , he'd be more enthusiastic.

Unit 6 *Vocabulary and grammar review*

Vocabulary

1 Complete these phrases connected with the causes and results of environmental problems by writing a word from the box in each space.

acid	change	destruction	extinct	~~fumes~~
habitats	pollution	rising	warming	

1 car exhaust ....fumes....
2 .... of the rainforests
3 industrial ....
4 destruction of animal ....
5 species of plants and animals becoming ....
6 global ....

....

...evels

...word A, B, C or D to complete

...... your house from thieves by

...n.

B protect
D avoid

...a door to .... talking to
...t like.

B prevent
D avoid

...d which .... him from

B missed
D avoided

...... until almost the end of

B arrive
D attend

... you want to .... to the bank before it closes.

A reach
B arrive
C get
D make

Grammar

3 Put the verbs in brackets into the correct future tense (future simple, future continuous, future perfect or *going to*) in the following sentences.

1 I read in the paper that they ....are going to build.... (build) a new road through these woods next year.
2 By the time I finish work tonight I think it .... (probably be) too late to go to the cinema.
3 By the year 2100 the global climate .... (change) completely.
4 I imagine that in the year 2050 some people .... (live) on the Moon.
5 When you come round this weekend, I .... (play) a game of tennis with you.
6 Don't call Jane before 8 o'clock because she .... (do) her homework.
7 What a beautiful red sunset! It .... (be) a beautiful sunny day tomorrow.
8 I firmly believe the world .... (be) a better place in 40 years' time.
9 Don't ask for your dinner before 8 o'clock because I .... (not cook) it by then.
10 Having problems? I .... (help) you if you like.

Unit 7 My first job

1 bank cashier

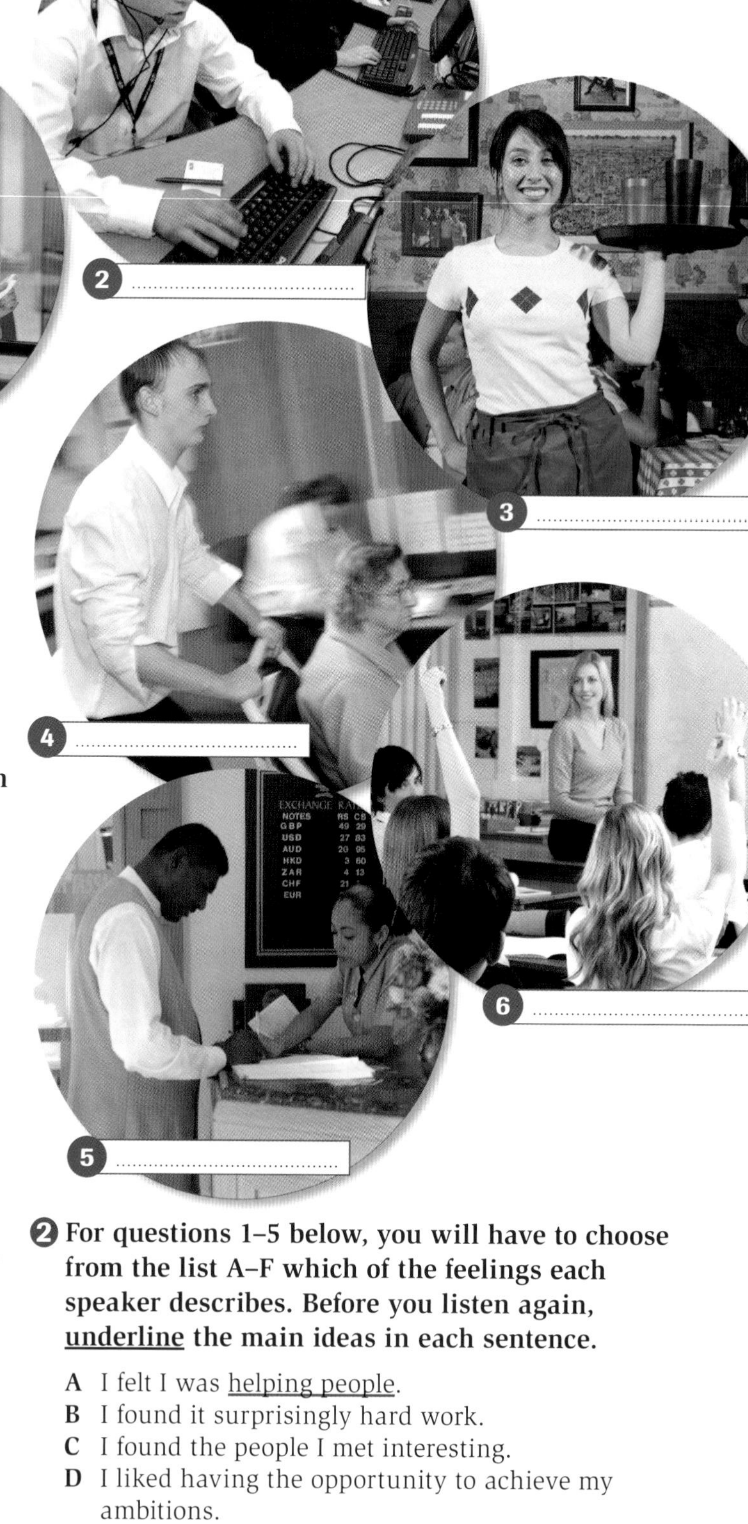

2 ....

3 ....

4 ....

5 ....

6 ....

Starting off

1 **Work in small groups. Match the job titles to the photos.**

teacher	~~bank cashier~~	call centre worker
waiter/waitress	hospital porter	hotel receptionist

2 **Which of the jobs do you think is the most difficult?**

3 **Which of the jobs would be suitable for students in their free time or in their holidays?**

4 **Which of the jobs would you prefer to do, and which would you prefer not to do? Why (not)?**

Listening Part 3

1 (16) **You will hear five people talking about their first job. Listen and decide:**

- which job from the list A–F each speaker is talking about (there is one job you will not need)
- if the speaker feels mainly positive or negative about the job.

	job	mainly positive or negative?
Speaker 1		
Speaker 2		
Speaker 3		
Speaker 4		
Speaker 5		

A bank cashier
B call centre worker
C waitress/waiter
D hospital porter
E hotel receptionist
F teacher

2 **For questions 1–5 below, you will have to choose from the list A–F which of the feelings each speaker describes. Before you listen again, underline the main ideas in each sentence.**

A I felt I was helping people.
B I found it surprisingly hard work.
C I found the people I met interesting.
D I liked having the opportunity to achieve my ambitions.
E I felt I was learning useful skills.
F I enjoyed some parts of the job more than others.

Speaker 1 ☐
Speaker 2 ☐
Speaker 3 ☐
Speaker 4 ☐
Speaker 5 ☐

3 (16) **Listen again and match the speakers with how they felt. Use the letters only once. There is one extra letter which you do not need to use.**

Exam advice

- Before you listen, read each alternative carefully, underlining the key words.
- Listen for the general idea of what each speaker is saying.
- Remember that the speakers may talk about something connected with other sentences but there is only one correct sentence for each speaker.

4 **Work in small groups. Take turns to describe a job to the other members of your group without mentioning its name. The others should guess what job you are describing.**

Vocabulary

Work or *job*; *possibility, occasion* or *opportunity*; *fun* or *funny*

1 **Read these sentences from the listening exercise. First Certificate candidates often confuse the words in *italics*. Circle the correct word.**

***Work* or *job*?**

1 ... it was hard physical *job* / *work*, you know, lifting people and helping them into wheelchairs and pushing them.
2 I got my first *job* / *work* as an assistant receptionist in a hotel when I was just 18.
3 It wasn't a very well-paid *job* / *work*, but then first *jobs* / *works* often aren't.

***Possibility, occasion* or *opportunity*?**

4 ... I thought it was a great *opportunity* / *occasion* / *possibility* to get some work experience.
5 And on some *opportunities* / *possibilities* / *occasions* I was left on my own as the person in charge of the whole of this enormous hotel.

***Fun* or *funny*?**

6 I have to say though that I found teaching *fun* / *funny* and challenging.
7 Students prefer it if you have a sense of humour and say something *fun* / *funny* from time to time, you know, make a joke.

2 **Read these extracts from the *Cambridge Advanced Learner's Dictionary* to see why each answer is correct. Then circle the correct alternative in *italics* in sentences 1–8.**

Common Learner Error

fun or **funny**?

If something is **fun**, you enjoy doing it.

I really liked the skating – it was such fun.

1 If something is **funny**, it makes you laugh.

It's a very funny film.

2 If something is **funny**, it is strange, surprising, unexpected or difficult to explain or understand

The washing machine is making a funny noise again.

---

possibility, **occasion** or **opportunity**?

A **possibility** is a chance that something may happen or be true. **Possibility** cannot be followed by an infinitive.

Is there a possibility of getting a job in your organisation?

An **occasion** is an event, or a time when something happens. **Occasion** does not mean 'chance' or 'opportunity'.

Birthdays are always special occasions.

An **opportunity** is a possibility of doing something, or a situation which gives you the possibility of doing something.

The trip to Paris gave me an opportunity to speak French.

I have more opportunity to travel than my parents did.

~~*I have more possibility to travel than my parents did.*~~

---

work or **job**?

Work is something you do to earn money. This noun is uncountable.

She enjoys her work in the hospital.

~~*He's looking for a work.*~~

Job is used to talk about the particular type of work activity which you do.

He's looking for a job in computer programming.

~~*Teaching must be an interesting work.*~~

---

1 I know he was trying to be *fun* / *funny* but none of his jokes made us laugh.
2 The trip was *fun* / *funny* – we should do it again sometime.
3 I don't think there's much *possibility* / *opportunity* of us choosing him for the job.
4 I only wear this suit on special *occasions* / *opportunities*.
5 Did you get a(n) *possibility* / *opportunity* to speak to Matt yesterday?
6 She's just written to our company applying for a *work* / *job*.
7 I'm a qualified engineer, so my aim is to find *work* / *job* in that field if I can.
8 One of my *works* / *jobs* was to count the money at the end of the day.

Grammar

Countable and uncountable nouns

1 The words <u>underlined</u> in the sentences below are either countable [C] or uncountable [U]. Look at the examples from the listening exercise and complete the rules 1–7 below by writing *countable* or *uncountable* in the gaps.

- My first job was when I was <u>a student</u>. [**C**]
- It was hard physical <u>work</u>. [**U**]
- I had to fetch <u>patients</u> [**C**] and wheel them to different hospital departments for treatment.
- I didn't have <u>much self-confidence</u> … [**U**]
- On <u>some occasions</u> [**C**] I was left on my own as the only person in charge …
- Sometimes all they wanted was <u>some information</u> … [**U**]
- Usually just a <u>few simple instructions</u> [**C**] over the phone were enough …
- I always had <u>a great deal of homework</u> [**U**] to correct …

Rules

1. ..*Countable*... nouns can use *a* or *an* in the singular.
2. .... nouns can be made plural.
3. .... nouns only have a singular form; they cannot be made plural.
4. .... nouns do not use *a* or *an*.
5. You can use *some* or *any* with uncountable nouns and with .... nouns in the plural.
6. You can use *few, a few, many* and *a large number of* with .... nouns in the plural.
7. You can use *little, a little, much, a great deal of* and *a large amount of* with .... nouns.

page 158 *Grammar reference: Countable and uncountable nouns*

2 Write these nouns in the correct column: countable or uncountable. If necessary, use a dictionary to check your answers.

~~accident~~	~~accommodation~~	advice	bed	
bus	damage	dish	equipment	food
furniture	homework	hotel	information	
instrument	knowledge	luggage	meal	
news	service	software	suggestion	
suitcase	task	tool	transport	

countable	uncountable
accident	*accommodation*

3 Most of the sentences below contain mistakes which are often made by First Certificate candidates. However, two of the sentences are correct. Correct the mistakes.

1. Could you please send me some ~~informations~~ about the job? *information*
2. I hope you don't mind if I give you an advice about how to apply for the job.
3. She's just found a work as an ambulance driver.
4. Public transport is still the best way to get around the city.
5. The hotel also provides accommodations for its employees.
6. Congratulations! The news about your job is very good.
7. He works in a shop selling furnitures.
8. Sorry to hear about the accident. Did it do many damages?

4 Complete these sentences by writing a word from the box. In some cases more than one answer is possible.

piece / bit	deal	number

1. Can I give you a ..*piece / bit*.. of advice about shopping in this town?
2. During the storm quite a large .... of trees were blown down.
3. Have you brought that .... of equipment I asked for? The amplifier, I mean.
4. I've got a wonderful .... of news to give you – I'm getting married!
5. They put a great .... of effort into arranging the party.

Reading Part 1

1 **You are going to read an extract from an autobiography by Lucy Irvine, who worked in her father's hotel. Before you read, work in small groups. What do you think are the advantages and disadvantages of working for your parents?**

2 **Read the text quickly to answer these questions.**

1 What was her job?
2 What part of her job was creative?

3 **Read questions 1–7 below and underline the words in the text which provide the answers.**

1 What did the people working at the hotel have in common?
2 How was Lucy's working day organised, and why?
3 What does the writer mean by *daunting* in line 22?
4 What did Lucy do while she walked from the kitchen to the dining room?
5 Why did Lucy enjoy serving breakfasts more than dinners?
6 How did Lucy's father improve her position in the hotel?
7 What was special about Lucy's Sweet Trolley?

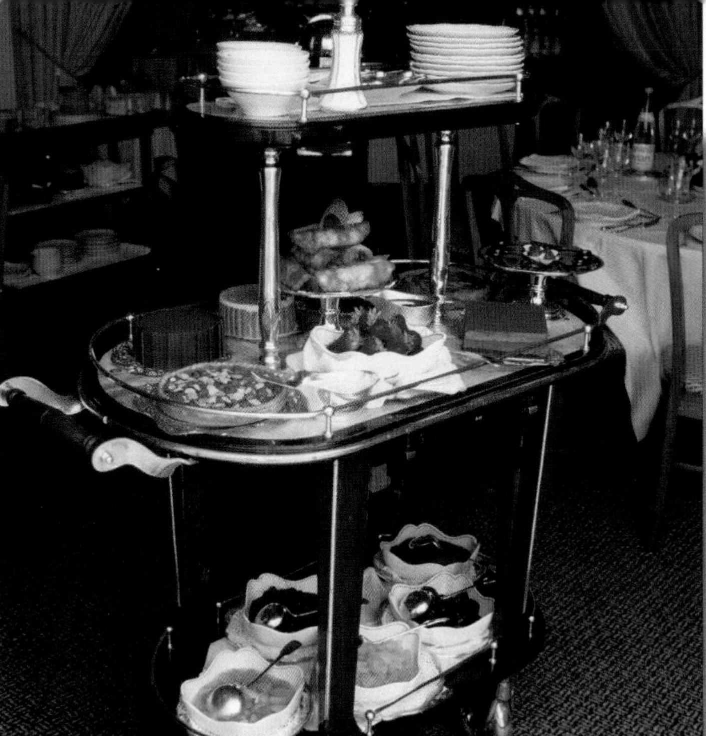

Lucy's first job

When I was just sixteen, my father bought an old guesthouse in the village where we lived and decided to turn it into a luxury hotel. At the early stages of the hotel, he experimented with everything. None of us had ever worked in a hotel before, but my dad had a vision of what guests wanted. His standards were extremely high and he believed that to reach those standards the most important thing was work.

For a month that summer I worked as a waitress at breakfast and dinner. As part of the job I had to lay the tables in the dining room beforehand and clean up afterwards. This gave me the middle of the day free for studying because my school report predictably had not lived up to my father's high expectations.

Like all the other waitresses, I was equipped with a neat uniform and told to treat the guests as though they were special visitors in my own home. Although I felt more like a stranger in theirs, I did not express my feelings. Instead I concentrated on doing the job as well as, if not better than, the older girls.

In the kitchen I learned how to deal with Gordon, the chef, who I found rather daunting. He had an impressive chef's hat and a terrifying ability to lose his temper and get violent for no clear reason. I avoided close contact with him and always grabbed the dishes he gave me with a cold look on my face. Then, as I walked from the kitchen to the dining room, my cold expression used to change into a charming smile.

I found waiting at breakfast was more enjoyable than at dinner. The guests came wandering into the dining room from seven-thirty onwards, staring with pleasure at the view of the sea and the islands through the dining room window. I always made sure that everyone got their order quickly and I enjoyed getting on well with the people at each table.

In the evenings it was funny how differently people behaved; they talked with louder, less friendly voices, and did not always return my smile. However, that all changed when Dad created a special role for me which improved my status considerably.

I started by making simple cakes for guests' picnics and soon progressed to more elaborate cakes for afternoon teas. I found that recipes were easy to follow and it was amusing to improvise. This led to a nightly event known as Lucy's Sweet Trolley. I used to enter the dining room every evening pushing a trolley carrying an extraordinary collection of puddings, cakes and other desserts. Most of them were of my own invention, I had cooked them all myself, and some were undeniably strange.

Adapted from *Runaway* by Lucy Irvine

4 For questions 1–8, choose the answer (A, B, C or D) which you think fits best according to the text.

1 What did the people working at the hotel have in common?
  A They knew what the guests expected.
  B They shared all the jobs.
  C They lacked experience.
  D They enjoyed the work.

2 Lucy's working day was organised in order to give her
  A time for her school work.
  B working experience.
  C time at midday to relax.
  D time to have lunch with her father.

3 What does the writer mean by *daunting* in line 22?
  A disgusting
  B frightening
  C interesting
  D strange

4 What did Lucy do while she walked from the kitchen to the dining room?
  A She smiled at Gordon in a friendly way.
  B She avoided touching Gordon.
  C She checked the food Gordon gave her.
  D She started to look more friendly.

5 Why did Lucy enjoy serving breakfasts more than dinners?
  A She enjoyed the view from the dining room while working.
  B She had a better relationship with the guests.
  C The guests were more punctual than at dinner.
  D She worked more efficiently at breakfast.

6 How did Lucy's father improve her position in the hotel?
  A He put her in charge of the restaurant.
  B He asked her to provide entertainment for the guests.
  C He made her responsible for part of dinner.
  D He gave her a special uniform.

7 What was special about the food on Lucy's Sweet Trolley?
  A Lucy made it following traditional recipes.
  B Lucy made the same food for picnics.
  C Lucy and Gordon made it together.
  D Lucy made most of it without following recipes.

8 What impression does Lucy give of her job throughout the passage?
  A It brought her closer to her father.
  B It was sometimes uncomfortable.
  C It was always enjoyable.
  D It was quite easy to do.

Exam advice

- First read the text quickly to get a general idea of what it is about.
- Read the first question, find where it is answered in the text and underline the words in the text which answer the question.
- Read each of the alternatives A, B, C and D carefully and choose the one which matches what the text says.

5 Work in pairs.

- Would you enjoy doing a job like Lucy's? Why (not)?
- What do you think are ideal holiday jobs for teenagers?

Grammar

Articles

1 Look at the underlined examples from the reading text in extracts 1–6. Then match them with the rules for articles (*a*, *an*, *the*) a–f.

1 When I was just sixteen, my father bought an old guesthouse (lines 1–2)
2 … my father bought an old guesthouse in the village where we lived (line 2)
3 At the early stages of the hotel, he experimented (line 4)
4 … my dad had a vision of what guests wanted (line 6)
5 … the most important thing was work (line 8)
6 the most important thing was work (line 8)

a No article is used when using uncountable nouns in the singular.
b *A* and *an* are used with singular, countable nouns mentioned for the first time.
c *The* is used when it's clear who or what we are referring to from the context.
d No article is used when talking in general and in the plural.
e *The* is used with superlative adjectives and adverbs.
f *The* is used with things mentioned before.

page 158 *Grammar reference: Articles*

2 Complete the spaces in the following text using *a*, *an*, *the* or – if no article is needed.

I was just 18 and it was (1) ..the.... first time I had worked in (2) .... office. It was (3) .... summer holidays and I had just finished (4) .... school. I thought it would be (5) .... good way of earning (6) .... bit of money before I went to (7) .... university in (8) .... autumn. I spent most of (9) .... day keying (10) .... information into the company's database. Although I found (11) .... job rather boring, I earned (12) .... good salary.

3 Sentences 1–12 below contain mistakes with articles made by First Certificate candidates. Correct the mistakes. Some sentences contain more than one mistake.

1 Have you heard ~~a~~ latest news about Bayern Munich in the Champions' League? *the*
2 I bought my first motorcycle at my age of 16.
3 I'm hoping to visit your town the next year.
4 She found a lot of useful information on internet.
5 You'll have difficulty parking in city centre on Saturday.
6 I think that bicycles are most effective means of transport.
7 The money can cause a lot of problems.
8 I really enjoy listening to the music, especially on radio.
9 When I visit the foreign cities, I really like the shopping for clothes.
10 I'm having wonderful time with my friends.
11 I've got a plenty of spare time at this moment, so we can have a dinner together if you like.
12 We can provide an accommodation for you in a comfortable hotel.

Speaking Part 3

1 Read the instructions for the speaking task below.

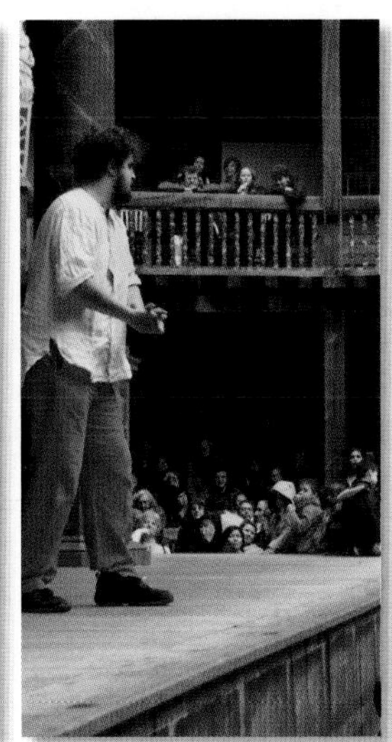

I'd like you to imagine that your college has invited some people with glamorous and exciting jobs to come and talk to students. They are jobs which many people dream of having.

- First, talk to each other about why people dream of doing these jobs.
- Then decide which two jobs it would be the most interesting to hear about.

(17) Now listen to two candidates practising this speaking task. Which of the things below do the candidates do?

1 They deal with both questions. ☑
2 They talk about just a few of the jobs. ☐
3 They listen to each other and respond to what the other person says. ☐
4 They ask each other's opinion. ☐
5 They interrupt each other. ☐
6 They reach a decision. ☐
7 One candidate speaks much more than the other. ☐

2 Copy the table below into your notebook and then write each of these phrases in the correct column.

~~Yes, and~~ … What about you? Do you agree? Perhaps people think that if they do this job, they'll… I'm not sure. I think … I think you're right. No, but … People may/might think a job like this is … What do you think? … don't you think? Sure. That's true. Maybe … Possibly … Why's that?

suggesting ideas	asking your partner's opinion	agreeing	disagreeing
		Yes, and …	

3 **Now work in pairs. Do the same task yourselves, but using the photos below.**

Exam advice

When you discuss the first part of the task:

- talk about each of the things shown in the pictures
- make suggestions, ask your partner's opinion and respond to your partner's ideas.

When you discuss the second part of the task:

- discuss several of the options and give reasons for your opinions
- try to reach a decision.

Use of English Part 2

1 **Work in small groups.**

You will read a short article about working as a volunteer in Canada. Why do people work as volunteers?

2 **Read the article without paying attention to the gaps.**

According to the article, what can young people gain from working as volunteers?

3 **For questions 1–12, read the text again and think of the word which best fits each gap. Use only one word in each gap. There is an example at the beginning (0).**

Exam advice

- Read the text quite quickly to get a general idea what it is about.
- Look at the words before and after the space and decide what type of word you need (an article, pronoun, preposition, etc.).
- Try different words in the space to see which word fits best.
- Words may be part of fixed phrases, e.g. *in order to, as far as I know*, etc.

Volunteering with Katimavik

Katimavik, the Canadian community service and volunteer programme is the perfect way (0) ......to...... give young people (1) .... experience they need. Volunteers (2) .... six months working in three different provinces. While they are (3) .... , they work between 35 and 40 hours a week and (4) .... valuable and necessary work for an organisation that really needs it.

The jobs range from database design to painting the walls of a recreation centre, and are all rewarding and interesting. Volunteers learn organisation and communication skills, as (5) .... as gaining experience working in (6) .... team environment. People gain a great (7) .... of self-confidence from the programme and this helps them when applying (8) .... other jobs afterwards.

It isn't like going to school (9) .... going to work. Volunteers choose (10) .... they want to learn and then they do it. They become responsible for themselves and the (11) .... team members, as they share household duties (12) .... as cooking and cleaning. Katimavik gets young people ready for life.

4 **The 12 words you needed to complete the text are among the words in the box below. Check your answers by looking at the box.**

a	but	deal	do	doing
far	for	lot	make	
more	much	one	or	
other	pass	spend	such	
the	there	this	~~to~~	well
what	with	your		

5 **Work in small groups. You have decided to spend a week of your holiday working together as volunteers. Decide what job you would all like to do together.**

Writing Part 1

1 Work in pairs. Look at the writing task below. Do you think this is an interesting job for a student? Why (not)?

You have seen this advertisement on the internet and you have decided to apply for a job. Read the advertisement and the notes you have made. Then write a letter to Mrs Macfane, using all your notes. Write your answer in 120–150 words in an appropriate style.

Forest Country Hotel

Job location: Galway, Ireland

Job description: Get work experience doing a variety of jobs in a friendly family-run hotel, e.g. waiter, chambermaid, receptionist, kitchen assistant, gardener — *Say which job I want to apply for*

Employment type: Temporary summer job – July/ August

Minimum experience required: Would suit student who speaks some English and wants to improve it while earning — *Explain why I want the job*

Minimum age required: 16

Salary: Depending on position — *Ask how much*

Benefits: Room and meals provided, great location, time off to explore the West of Ireland

Applications to: Mrs Patsy Macfane, Forest Country Hotel, Galway — *Describe myself briefly*

2 Work in pairs and write a plan for the letter. How many paragraphs do you think the letter should have and what would you write in each paragraph?

3 Read the letter below and compare your plan with the contents of this letter.

Dear Mrs Macfane,

I have seen your advertisement on the internet and I am writing to apply for a summer job as a waitress in your hotel.

I am an 18-year-old student from Denmark. I have just finished school, where I had a reputation among my teachers for being hard-working and reliable. In September I will be starting a degree at the University of Copenhagen. I have an upper-intermediate level of English and have just taken the Cambridge First Certificate exam.

I am interested in doing this job because I would like to gain some work experience in an English-speaking country. This will give me the opportunity to improve my English while also earning some money. I would also like the chance to travel round Ireland.

Could you please tell me what salary you are offering for this job?

I look forward to hearing from you.

Yours sincerely,

Lise Larsen

4 Underline any words or phrases in the letter which you think would be useful when you write a letter of application.

5 Now do the writing task below. Use the letter above as a model.

Children's Summer Camp

Job location: Fife, Scotland

Job description: Get work experience doing a variety of jobs at an international summer camp for 10–14-year-old children. We need young people to work as sports supervisors, activities supervisors, kitchen helpers and office administrators. — *Say which job I want to apply for*

Employment type: Temporary summer job for July and August

Minimum experience required: Would suit student who speaks some English and enjoys working with children — *Explain why I want the job*

Minimum age required: 16

Salary: Depending on position

Benefits: Accommodation and meals provided, great location, plenty of time off to explore Scotland — *Ask how much*

Applications to: — *Describe myself briefly*
Alan Reid
The International Camp, Fife, Scotland

Exam advice

- Read the text carefully, underlining the relevant points.
- Make a detailed plan with what you want to write in each paragraph.
- Make sure you cover all four sets of handwritten notes.
- Write following your plan.

Unit 8 High adventure

1 mountain biking
2 ....
3 ....
4 ....
5 ....

Starting off

❶ **Work in small groups. Match the names of the sports with the photos.**

athletics	canoeing / kayaking	cross-country running
karate	~~mountain biking~~	paragliding
windsurfing		

❷ **Which do you think are adventure sports?**

❸ **What other adventure sports can you think of?**

❹ **Which have you tried? Which would you like to try? Why (not)?**

6 ....
7 ....

Reading Part 2

❶ **Work in pairs. Before you read, look again at the pictures in Starting off. Which activities do you think might form part of an adventure race?**

❷ 18 **You will hear part of a radio interview in which Gary Peters, an adventure racer, talks about the sport. Listen and for questions 1–4, choose the best answer A, B or C.**

1 In adventure races, competitors race
A individually.
B in pairs.
C in groups.

2 Races usually take place in
A remote places.
B sports stadiums.
C large cities.

3 One of the main challenges of adventure races mentioned by Gary is lack of
A food.
B sleep.
C water.

4 For professional athletes, one of the attractions of adventure races is that they
A learn different skills.
B compete in different surroundings.
C compete as part of a group.

❸ **Work in small groups.**

- What do you think are the advantages of racing in teams?
- What are the main difficulties of adventure racing?

❹ **Read the following article quickly without paying attention to the gaps. Did Rebecca's team win the race in Australia?**

Are you ready for an adventure race?

Rebecca Rusch has competed in several Eco-Challenge races, where teams of four men and women race non-stop over a 500 km course which includes trekking, canoeing, horse riding, scuba diving, mountaineering and mountain biking.

Obviously, I did not feel so ready for the early races in my career as the races we've done recently. There is a lot to be said for just gaining experience. Just getting out there and getting your feet wet teaches you the right skills and attitude.

It's often not the most physically prepared or the fittest teams that win. The ones who come first are the teams who race intelligently and adapt to unexpected situations. **1** ____ The only way to develop those qualities is to get out and race or do long training trips with your team-mates and friends.

Adventure races are such a huge challenge that when you enter a race you always think, "Am I ready? Did I train enough? Did I forget something?" I remember one race in particular, my very first Eco-Challenge and only my second race ever. **2** ____ A 24-hour race seemed like an eternity to me. My background was cross-country running in high school and college where a two- or three-mile race seemed long.

Most of my fear was due to lack of experience and knowledge. I really had no idea what I was getting in to because I had never done a 24-hour race before. **3** ____

In preparation for Australia, I tried to approach my training in a methodical way. Looking back, I wasn't methodical at all. **4** ____ I was also working at the same time. In reality, I was training a couple of hours a day during the week and at weekends training with the team for perhaps four hours. **5** ____ I spent the rest of the time worrying about how slow I was.

So, we went to Australia and entered the race. We didn't plan a strategy at all, but just ran as fast as possible from the start. I just tried to keep up with my team-mates, who were more experienced than I was. **6** ____ It was a furious 36 hours. We arrived at a few of the check points in first place and were among the top five. I knew we didn't belong there.

To cut a long story short, two of my team-mates decided not to continue the race after just a day and a half. One was suffering hallucinations and feeling ill. He was just too tired to carry on. **7** ____ We had been going so fast that he felt uncomfortable asking us to stop so he could take care of his blisters. The other two of us, feeling fresh still, had to drop out with the rest of our team. **8** ____ I knew that our team had not been prepared or realistic about the pace we could keep, but not finishing that race was the most valuable lesson I could have learned.

I promised then to come back one day and finish the race. That was seven years (and thousands of race miles) ago.

Adapted from *Adventure Sports Journal*

5 Eight sentences have been removed from the article. Choose from the sentences A–I the one which fits each gap (1–8). There is one extra sentence which you do not need to use.

For each of the eight missing sentences, you will find clues which have been underlined. Use these underlined clues in the article and in the sentences A–I below, to help you choose the right answer.

Exam advice

- Pay attention to pronouns (*we*, *that*, *it*, etc.) and adverbs (*however*, *even so*, etc.) in the sentences which have been removed. What do they refer to in the text?
- In the exam, there is no example and no words are underlined.

A Another had severe problems with his feet.

B Four days later, we watched in disappointment as the winners crossed the finishing line.

C I kept my mouth shut and followed them.

D We won it even so, and were invited to compete in the Eco-Challenge in Australia.

E What I did was simply run, bike and paddle a kayak as much and as hard as I could.

F His encouragement helped me to complete it.

G That was how much I had prepared.

H When I did it, I felt totally afraid and unprepared.

I To achieve this you have to be flexible and patient.

6 Work in pairs.

- Would you like to try adventure racing? Why (not)?
- What do you think would be the hardest part of adventure racing for you?
- What is the hardest sporting experience you have ever had?

Grammar

Infinitive and verb + *-ing*

1 The following sentences are examples of when to use the infinitive and when to use the verb + *-ing* form. Decide which sentence (a–i) is an example (1–11) for each of the rules on this page. You can use some of the sentences as examples for more than one rule.

a **Not finishing** that race was the most valuable lesson I could have learned.
b I promised then **to come back** one day and finish an adventure race.
c My approach involved simply **running, biking and canoeing** as much and as hard as I could.
d There is a lot to be said for just **gaining** experience.
e I trained several hours a day **to get fit** for the race.
f There are medical teams **to take care of** injured runners.
g He was just too tired **to carry on**.
h It's no use **entering** a race if you haven't prepared properly.
i Two of my team-mates decided **not to continue** the race after just a day and a half.

Rules

The infinitive is used:

- to say why you do something (example: 1 .e..........)
- to say why something exists (example: 2 ....)
- after too and enough (example: 3 ....)
- after these verbs (there is a more complete list on page 159): *agree, appear, ask, arrange, decide, expect, fail, help, promise* (examples: 4 .... and 5 ....)

The negative is formed by placing *not* before the infinitive (example: 6 ....)

The verb + *-ing* is used:

- after prepositions (example: 7 ....)
- as subjects or objects of a verb (example: 8 ....)
- after these verbs (there is a more complete list on page 159): *admit, enjoy, finish, involve, mind, postpone, risk, suggest* (example: 9 ....)
- after these expressions *it's no good, it's not worth, it's no use, it's a waste of time, spend time, can't help* (example: 10 ....)

The negative is formed by placing *not* before the verb + *-ing* (example: 11 ....)

page 159 *Grammar reference: Infinitives and verb +* -ing *forms*

2 Complete these sentences by putting the verbs in brackets in the correct form.

1 Carlos has suggested ....starting..... (start) a five-a-side football team. What do you think?
2 I don't think the weather is good enough .... (go) sailing this afternoon.
3 We've decided .... (hold) the race early in the morning before it gets too hot.
4 .... (train) is essential if you want to perform well.
5 I've joined a gym .... (get) myself fitter.
6 If you train too hard, you risk .... (injure) yourself before the race.
7 It's no good .... (run) in a marathon if you're not wearing the right shoes.
8 She was disqualified from the race for .... (push) an opponent.

3 Circle the correct form in *italics* in each of these questions.

1 What sport would you advise someone *to take up* / *taking up* in order to make friends?
2 What sport would you choose *to learn* / *learning* if you had plenty of time and money?
3 If someone needed to get fit, what sport would you suggest *to do* / *doing*?
4 What sports do you avoid to *take part in* / *taking part in* and why?

Work in pairs. Ask and answer the questions giving your opinions.

4 The sentences below contain mistakes made by First Certificate candidates with the infinitive and verb + *-ing*. However, two of the sentences are correct. Correct the mistakes.

1 I hope you'll enjoy ~~to stay~~ in my town. staying
2 I recommend to learn a little Spanish before you arrive.
3 I suggest to wear casual clothes for the journey.
4 I would appreciate having more information about your courses.
5 I'd like introduce you to my friends.
6 I'm hoping meeting her after the match.
7 She succeeded in getting into university.
8 She's thinking about to get a job before going to college.

Listening Part 4

1 You will hear an interview with someone who went on a paragliding course. Before you listen, work in pairs.

- Do you think paragliding is a risky sport?
- Would you like to try it? Why (not)?

2 Read the questions below and underline the main idea in each question.

1 Why did Andrew want to try paragliding?
 A He had seen other people doing it.
 B He wanted to write an article about it.
 C He was bored with the sport he was doing.

2 Why did Andrew choose to do a paragliding course in France?
 A The location was safer.
 B The course was cheaper.
 C The weather was better.

3 What is the advantage of learning to paraglide from a sand dune?
 A You can land safely in the sea.
 B You can land safely on the sand.
 C You cannot fall too far.

4 How did Andrew spend the first morning of his course?
 A He learned to lift his paraglider.
 B He flew to the bottom of the dune.
 C He watched other people paragliding.

5 When he started flying, how did he receive instructions?
 A The instructor shouted at him from the ground.
 B The instructor talked to him over the radio.
 C The instructor flew with him.

6 When you land after paragliding, it feels like
 A jumping off a low wall.
 B falling from a horse.
 C falling onto a bed.

7 What, for Andrew, is the best reason to go paragliding?
 A It's more interesting than golf.
 B It isn't as dangerous as people think.
 C It's a very peaceful activity.

3 19 Now, for questions 1–7, listen and choose the best answer (A, B or C).

Exam advice

- Before you listen, underline the main idea in each question (not the alternatives), so that while you are listening you can quickly remember what it's about.
- When you listen, wait until the speaker has finished talking about an idea before you choose your answer.
- Listen for the same idea to be expressed, not the same words.

4 **Work in small groups. Number these sports from most dangerous (1) to least dangerous (5) in your opinion. Then number them from most enjoyable (1) to least enjoyable (5) in your opinion.**

	dangerous	enjoyable
paragliding		
climbing		
motorcycle racing		
scuba diving		
snowboarding		

Did you find any relation between danger and enjoyment?

Use of English Part 4

1 **In Use of English Part 4 you should complete the second sentence in each question so that it has a similar meaning to the first sentence, using the word given in capitals. You must use between two and five words including the word given. You must not change the word given.**

Example:
Swimming is Carol's favourite sport.
MORE
Carol enjoys .... other sport.

The gap can be filled by the words *swimming more than any*, so you write:

Carol enjoys ......*swimming more than any*...... other sport.

Work in pairs. For questions 1 and 2, choose the correct answer A–D. Why are the other answers incorrect?

1 Why don't we start jogging if we want some exercise?
TAKING
He suggested .... in order to get some exercise.

- **A** He suggested *that they should take up jogging* in order to get some exercise.
- **B** He suggested *taking up jogging* in order to get some exercise.
- **C** He suggested *to take up jogging* in order to get some exercise.
- **D** He suggested *going jogging* in order to get some exercise.

2 She won the match without difficulty.
EASY
She found .... the match.

- **A** She found *it easy to win* the match.
- **B** She found *that it was easy to win* the match.
- **C** She found *she could easily win* the match.
- **D** She found *it simple to win* the match.

2 **Now do these questions. Use the questions below to help you.**

1 Marianne prepared for the race by training every evening.
READY
Marianne trained every evening .... for the race.

- Can you think of an expression with *ready* which means *prepare*?
- Why did Marianne train every evening?
- Do you use the verb + *-ing* or an infinitive to say why she trained every evening?

2 It's against the rules to touch the ball with your hand.
ALLOWED
You .... the ball with your hand.

- How do you use *allowed* to mean *it's against the rules*?
- Do you use the verb + *-ing* or an infinitive after *allowed*?

3 **Now do these questions.**

1 We'd like all our students to participate in the sports programme.
PART
We are keen on all our students .... the sports programme.

2 Buying the equipment for this sport is cheaper than hiring it.
MORE
It's .... the equipment for this sport than to buy it.

3 You should have phoned her to tell her the game was cancelled.
GIVE
You were supposed .... to tell her the game was cancelled.

4 Playing rugby is more dangerous than playing football.
SAFE
Playing rugby .... as playing football.

5 'I'll never get angry with the referee again,' said Martin.
TEMPER
Martin promised never ....
.... with the referee again.

Exam advice

- Make sure your answer has the same meaning as the original sentence.
- Use the word in **CAPITALS** without changing it.
- Count the words. Contractions (*isn't*, *don't*, etc.) count as two words.

4 Check your answers by looking at these clues for each of the questions in Exercise 3.

1 Did you use an expression which means *participate*?
2 Have you used an opposite of *cheap*? Did you use an infinitive or a verb + *-ing*?
3 Did you use an expression which means *phone* (*give her a* ...)?
4 *Safe* means the opposite of *dangerous*, so did you use *not* in your answer?
5 Can you remember an expression with *temper* which means *become angry*?

Speaking Part 4

1 (20) Listen to two First Certificate candidates, Antonia and Magda, answering these questions in Speaking Part 4 and briefly note down their opinions.

Question: Do you think young people should be encouraged to do adventure sports?
Antonia: No, because ....
....

Question: Do you think that people generally do enough sport nowadays?
Magda: ....
....

2 (20) Write these phrases which Antonia and Magda used in the correct column below. Then listen again.

for instance ... ~~I believe~~ I mean ...
I'm not sure. I think ... No, I don't think so because ...
such as ... You see ...

introducing an opinion	adding an explanation	introducing an example
I believe		

Exam advice

The examiners want to hear how well you speak, so answer the questions by giving your opinion and explaining the reasons for your opinion.

You can also, where possible:

- add an extra idea or explanation (*You see* ..., *I mean* ...)
- give an example.

3 Work in pairs. Take turns to ask your partners the questions in your box. While you speak, try to use some phrases from Exercise 2 above.

Student A

- Some people would like to make all students do sports at school. Do you agree with this idea?
- Tell us about a sport you have never done which you would like to try.
- Which do you prefer: taking part in sports or watching them? Why?

Student B

- Which sport did you most enjoy as a child and why?
- Many people think that too much sport is shown on television. Do you agree?
- Some people say that doing sport improves our quality of life. Do you agree?

Writing Part 2 A report

❶ **Work in pairs. When you write, you should decide whether to write in a formal or an informal style. Would you use a formal (F) or an informal (I) style for each of these readers? Write F or I by each.**

1 a school director ....F......
2 classmates ....
3 friends ....
4 people much older than you ....
5 relatives ....
6 someone working in an office ....

❷ **Would you use a formal (F) or an informal (I) style for each of these tasks? Write F or I by each.**

1 a letter or email to a friend: ......I......
2 an article in your college magazine: ....
3 a letter or email to a Tourist Information office: ....
4 a report for the director of your college: ....
5 an essay for your teacher or college tutor: ....
6 a review of a film in an international magazine: ....
7 a story for a class competition: ....

❸ **In each pair below, decide which is generally a characteristic of formal (F) or informal (I) language. Write F or I by each.**

1 a Contractions (*it won't …, she's been …*): ......I......
b No contractions (*it will not …, she has been …*): ......F......

2 a Long words (*apologise, frequently, unfortunately*): ....
b Short words (*sorry, often, sadly*): ....

3 a Common words (*difficult, play*): ....
b Less common words (*complicated, perform*): ....

4 a Phrasal verbs (*fill in, ask for*): ....
b Other types of verb (*complete, order*): ....

5 a Complete sentences (*I was delighted to receive your letter*): ....
b Incomplete sentences (*Great to hear from you again*): ....

6 a Abbreviations (*Sept*): ....
b No abbreviations (*September*): ....

❹ **Read the writing task below and <u>underline</u> the two things you must deal with in your report.**

> Your town wants to spend a large amount of money encouraging young people to participate in more sports activities during their holidays. You have been asked to write a report for the town council saying what types of sporting activities the town should encourage and how doing these activities would benefit young people.
>
> Write your **report**.

❺ **Work in pairs. Answer the following questions about the writing task above.**

1 Who is going to read the report?
2 Should you use a formal or informal style? Why?
3 What types of sporting activities do you think your town should encourage?
4 How would they benefit young people (e.g. people might make new friends)?

❻ **Decide which ideas you would like to include in your report.**

❼ **Read the following report and circle the more formal option in *italics* in each case.**

Report on sports activities for young people

Introduction

The aim of this report is to (**1**) *suggest* / *come up with* (**2**) *a number of* / *some* sports activities which (**3**) *kids* / *young people* in this town could do during their holidays and to (**4**) *outline* / *sum up* (**5**) *the benefits of* / *what they'll get out of* these (**6**) *things* / *activities.*

Which sports?

The town (**7**) *is situated* / *is* between the coast and the mountains, and young people would (**8**) *have a good time doing* / *enjoy* sports which take place in these areas. (**9**) *Activities on the coast could include* / *We could do several things on the coast such as* windsurfing, swimming and diving which a local water-sports school could (**10**) *set up* / *organise.* (**11**) *Similarly* / *Also,* (**12**) *we could pay a local mountaineering club* / *a local mountaineering club could be employed* to run sports such as hiking and climbing.

Benefits to youngsters

Doing these activities would (**13**) *be good for* / *benefit* local young people by making them more independent, (**14**) *encouraging* / *building up* team spirit and giving them a sense of adventure. At the same time (**15**) *they'd get* / *they would become* fitter.

Conclusion

(**16**) *I recommend* / *I'm in favour of* organising these activities with the water-sports school and the mountaineering club. Young people would find that the sports are an interesting, (**17**) *enjoyable* / *fun* and healthy way to spend the holidays. The activities would also help them to (**18**) *grow* / *develop* physically and mentally.

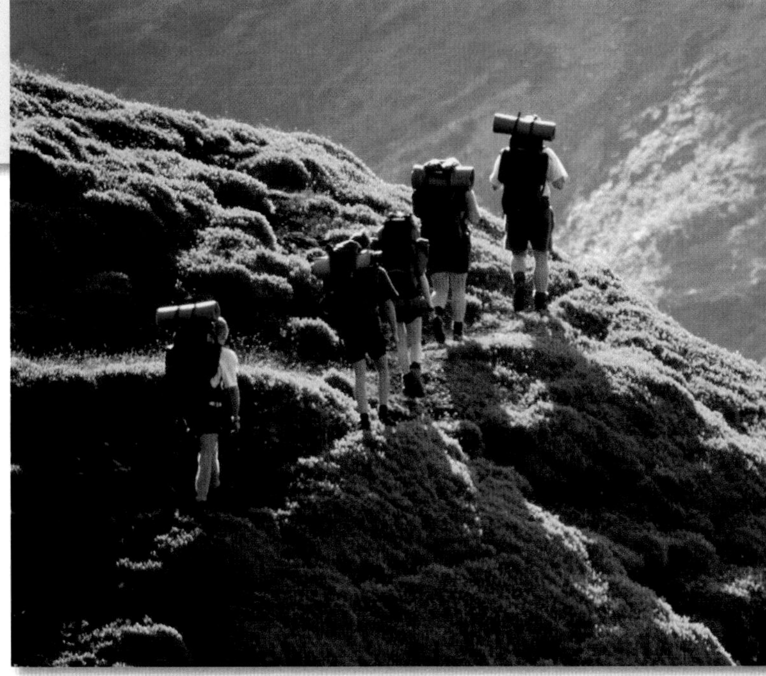

8 Read the report again and answer the following questions.

1. Does the report have a title?
2. How many sections does the report have? How do you know the subject of each section?
3. What is the purpose of the first section?
4. How many suggestions for sporting activities does the writer make in the second section?
5. How many benefits are mentioned in the third section?
6. What is the purpose of the conclusion?
7. Is the style of the report formal or informal?

9 Do the following writing task. Write between 120 and 180 words.

Your local sports club wants to organise a number of adventure sports to encourage young people to join the club. The organisers of the club have asked you to write a report saying which adventure sports you think would interest young people and how they would benefit from doing these sports.

Write your **report**.

Exam advice

When writing a report, remember these tips.

- Give the report a title.
- Divide it into sections and give each section a heading (the first and last sections could be *Introduction* and *Conclusion*).
- If appropriate, make suggestions and recommendations.
- Make sure that you answer all parts of the question.

Unit 7 *Vocabulary and grammar review*

Vocabulary

1 Complete the sentences below by writing a word from the box in each space.

fun	funny	job	~~occasion~~	occasion
opportunity	possibility	work		

1 Andrea's birthday was a great ...occasion... ! I won't forget it for a long time.
2 Excuse me! I have to get to .... and I'm already late.
3 Helena, you did an excellent .... arranging the meeting so efficiently!
4 My boss has lost his temper on only one .... as far as I can remember.
5 I didn't find working in the office much .... because my colleagues weren't very friendly.
6 Olga sees her part in this film as a great .... to show she can act in English as well as in Russian.
7 Polly took us to see a very .... film which made us laugh a lot.
8 You have no .... of getting a more responsible job with your qualifications.

Grammar

2 Countable and uncountable nouns. Circle the correct alternative in *italics* in each of the following sentences.

- He was looking for (1) *accommodation / accommodations* in a five-star hotel, but (2) *there were no rooms / there was no room* with a view available.
- Her (3) *luggage / luggages* consisted of seven heavy suitcases and some medical (4) *equipment / equipments*.
- If I could give you some (5) *advice / advices*, avoid using public (6) *transport / transports* in this city.
- Kuldip has to learn and remember a lot of (7) *fact / facts* of general (8) *knowledge / knowledges* for an international students' competition in the USA next month. He has looked on the internet, but he takes most of his (9) *information / informations* from his encyclopedia.
- Vanessa loves good (10) *food / foods* – in fact the (11) *meal she cooks is / meals she cooks are* amongst the best you'll ever eat.
- The government needs to create (12) *work / works* for nearly half a million people who are without (13) *job / jobs*.
- Patty wants to change all the (14) *furniture / furnitures* in her sitting room.
- Have you heard the latest news? (15) *It is / They are* really exciting!

3 Complete these sentences by writing one word in each space. In several sentences more than one word is possible.

1 Drive carefully! I paid a great ...deal... of money for that car.
2 I heard an interesting .... of news on the radio this morning – they're giving us a day's holiday next month.
3 I'd like to offer you a little .... of advice: don't go up to the castle at midday as it gets very hot.
4 That's a really useless .... of equipment – you should throw it away!
5 There are a large .... of shops in the town centre where you can buy souvenirs.

4 Complete this story by writing *a*, *an*, *the* or – if you think no article is needed.

I was travelling around Europe by (1) ...–... train one summer when I was about 18 years old and I arrived in (2) .... city (I can't remember (3) .... name) just as it was getting dark. I went looking for somewhere to stay such as (4) .... youth hostel, but the only one I found was full and they couldn't recommend anywhere else for (5) .... cheap accommodation. As usual, I had (6) .... problem with (7) .... money: I didn't have enough for (8) .... hotel. I wandered round (9) .... city looking for (10) .... park to sleep in. It was very dark when I came to (11) .... pair of (12) .... imposing gates leading into what looked like (13) .... park. I went inside, and fortunately I had (14) .... excellent sleeping bag, which I unrolled and climbed inside. Then I ate some bread, which was (15) .... only food I had. Halfway through (16) .... night it started to rain, and (17) .... rain continued until (18) .... early morning when I woke up and looked around me. I had (19) .... enormous surprise when I saw I had been sleeping in (20) .... someone's back garden!

Unit 8 *Vocabulary and grammar review*

Word formation

1 Read the text below. Use the word given in capitals at the end of each line to form a word that fits in the space in the same line.

Adventure racing

The teams that come first are the ones who race	
(1) intelligently and adapt to unexpected situations.	INTELLIGENT
Maintaining flexibility and (2) .... is the	PATIENT
key. (3) .... , in preparation for the race in	FORTUNE
Australia I didn't approach my (4) .... in a	TRAIN
methodical way. In fact I had so little experience that	
I (5) .... ran and cycled as much and as	SIMPLE
hard as I could. When we (6) .... did	ACTUAL
the race, one of my team-mates became just too	
(7) .... to continue. We had been going	TIRE
really fast without taking any rests and he had felt	
(8) .... about asking us to stop. I knew that	COMFORT
our team had not been prepared or (9)	REAL
about the pace we could keep. Not finishing that race	
was the most (10) .... lesson I could have	VALUE
learned.	

Grammar

2 Put the verbs in brackets into the correct form: infinitive or verb + *-ing*.

1 Can I suggest taking (take) a break in about ten minutes?
2 Did you manage .... (get) in touch with her?
3 Do you want me .... (invite) her?
4 He's considering .... (change) his course of studies.
5 He absolutely refuses .... (have) anything to do with them.
6 He admitted .... (steal) the money.
7 He persuaded them .... (finish) the job.
8 I expect .... (become) very rich one day.
9 I really don't mind .... (work) at weekends.
10 It's no good .... (ask) him anything. He's really unhelpful.
11 Toya enjoys .... (work) in an internet café.
12 You know it's not worth .... (spend) so much money on a meal like that.

3 Complete the second sentence in each question so that it has a similar meaning to the first sentence, using the word given in capitals. Do not change the word given. You must use between two and five words, including the word given.

1 Finding our way down the mountain in the dark wasn't easy.
DIFFICULT
We found it difficult to find our way down the mountain in the dark.

2 You can't go skydiving until you're 18 years old.
ALLOWED
People under 18 .... skydiving.

3 He didn't want to get sunburnt, so he stayed in the shade.
AVOID
He stayed in the shade .... sunburnt.

4 Paola hates windsurfing when the weather is cold.
BEAR
Paola .... when the weather is cold.

5 Could you please turn your mobile phone off?
MIND
Would .... your mobile phone off?

6 I asked Ana if she wanted to play tennis with me this afternoon.
INVITED
I .... tennis with me this afternoon.

7 You might have an accident if you don't take all the safety precautions.
RISK
If you don't take all the safety precautions, ... an accident.

8 The weather is so wet that it's not worth going for a walk today.
POINT
The weather is so wet that there's .... for a walk today.

Unit 9 Star performances

Starting off

1 Work in pairs. Look at the different types of television programme in the box below.

- Which types of television programme do you enjoy? Why?
- How much time do you spend each week watching them?
- Which types of programme do you never watch? Why not?
- Have you ever been on television? Do you know anyone who has?
- If you could appear on television, what sort of programme would you prefer to be in?

documentaries dramas cartoons
the news chat shows quiz shows
reality shows soap operas comedies films

Listening Part 2

1 Work in pairs. You will hear a conversation between two friends, Dan and Julie, talking about the time Julie's father was on a television quiz show. Before you listen, read the sentences in the box on the right and decide:

- what sort of information you need in each space (a person, a number, type of transport, etc.)
- what sort of word(s) could go in each space (noun, adjective, verb, etc.).

Participating in a quiz show

At first the TV producer had wanted Julie's (1) .... to go on the quiz show.

She didn't go because she was worried that she would be far (2) .... to speak or answer any questions.

Julie's father went to the show in a (3) ....

When he went to the show, he forgot to take a (4) ....

He prepared for the show by (5) ....

Before the show the contestants waited in (6) ....

He competed against a (7) .... and a bus driver.

During the show he had to answer (8) .... questions.

The show's presenter was very (9) .... during the show.

Julie's father won a (10) .... and a toy elephant.

2 (21) **Now listen and complete the sentences.**

Exam information

- Be careful to choose the right information from what you hear. Other ideas which are not correct may be mentioned.
- Read the completed sentences to make sure the words fit grammatically.
- Answer every question, even if you're not sure.

3 Work in small groups.

- How would you feel if you were invited to take part in a quiz programme?
- What would you like to win?
- Have you ever won anything in a competition?

Grammar

Reported speech 1

1 Look at these two sentences from the listening exercise. What do you think Julie's aunt's and sister's exact words were?

1 She said she was afraid she'd get too nervous and be unable to speak when they asked her questions!
 a 'I'm afraid I'll get too nervous and be unable to speak when they ask me questions!'
 b 'I'm afraid I got too nervous and was unable to speak when they asked me questions!'

2 My elder sister, who was only eleven at the time, told her she should go because it was the chance of a lifetime.
 a 'You'll go because it's the chance of a lifetime.'
 b 'You should go because it's the chance of a lifetime.'

page 160 *Grammar reference: Reported speech 1*

2 Complete these revision notes made by a First Certificate candidate. For questions 1–3 you should write two words in each gap. For questions 4–10, you should write one word in each gap.

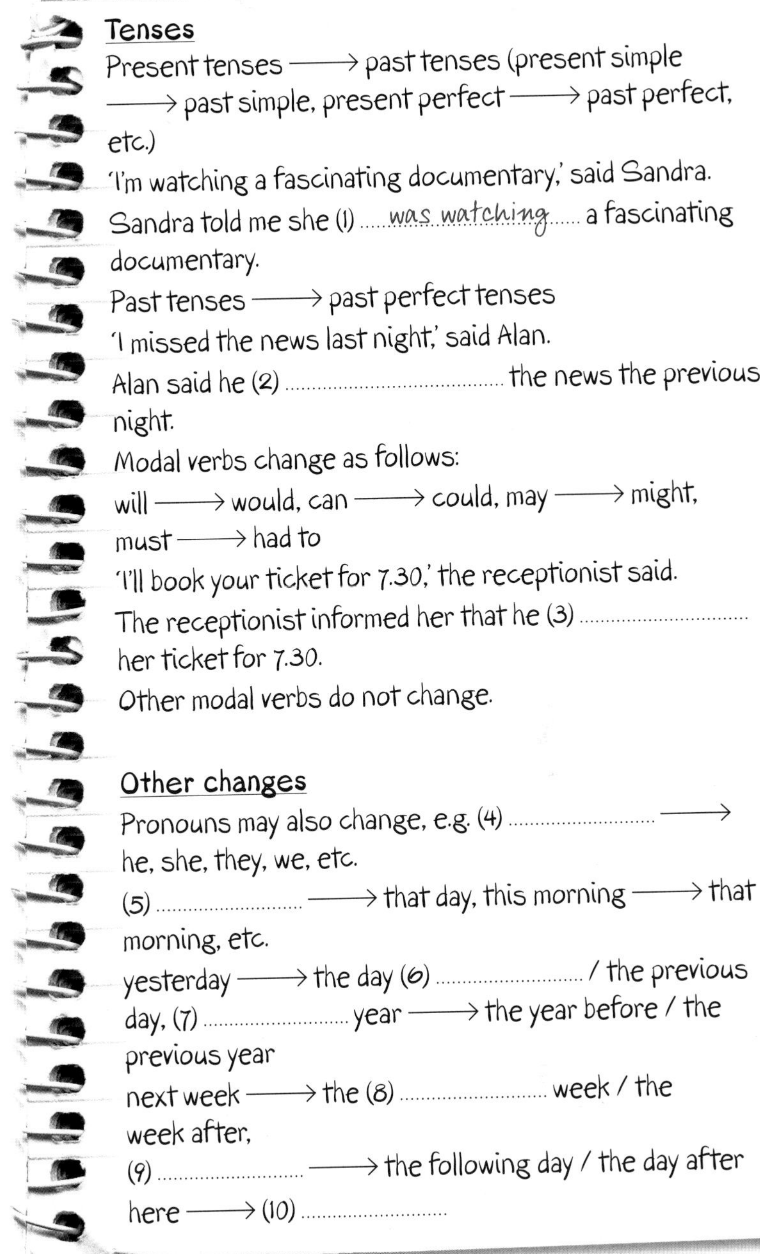

Tenses

Present tenses ⟶ past tenses (present simple ⟶ past simple, present perfect ⟶ past perfect, etc.)

'I'm watching a fascinating documentary,' said Sandra.

Sandra told me she (1) ....was watching.... a fascinating documentary.

Past tenses ⟶ past perfect tenses

'I missed the news last night,' said Alan.

Alan said he (2) .... the news the previous night.

Modal verbs change as follows:

will ⟶ would, can ⟶ could, may ⟶ might, must ⟶ had to

'I'll book your ticket for 7.30,' the receptionist said.

The receptionist informed her that he (3) .... her ticket for 7.30.

Other modal verbs do not change.

Other changes

Pronouns may also change, e.g. (4) .... ⟶ he, she, they, we, etc.

(5) .... ⟶ that day, this morning ⟶ that morning, etc.

yesterday ⟶ the day (6) .... / the previous day, (7) .... year ⟶ the year before / the previous year

next week ⟶ the (8) .... week / the week after,

(9) .... ⟶ the following day / the day after

here ⟶ (10) ....

3 For questions 1–6 complete the second sentence so that it has a similar meaning to the first sentence, using the word given. Do not change the word given. You must use between two and five words, including the word given.

1 'Last night I saw a fantastic film,' said Phil.
BEFORE
Phil told me that the ....night before he had seen.... a fantastic film.

2 'I'll return quite late from the theatre tonight,' said Elena.
BACK
Elena warned me that ....
.... quite late from the theatre that night.

3 'I won't be late for the show,' said Lucy.
ARRIVE
Lucy promised that she .... time for the show.

4 'You can't borrow my camera, Mike,' said his father.
ALLOWED
Mike's father told him he .... his camera.

5 'I know I got several answers wrong in this exercise,' Hannah said.
MISTAKES
Hannah admitted that she .... in the exercise.

6 'I really enjoyed the play,' Katie told George.
FOUND
Katie told George that she .... very enjoyable.

Reading Part 3

1 You will read a newspaper article about five actors at the beginning of their careers. Before you read, work in pairs.

What are the advantages and disadvantages of working as an actor?

2 Read questions 1–15 and underline the key idea in each question.

Which actor

1 believes actors must be ready to accept negative comments?
2 feels that they have learnt a lot from people already working in the theatre and TV?
3 says that listening to other people's suggestions improves their acting?
4 has always been excited by having people watching their performance?
5 had planned to enter a different profession before training to become an actor?
6 has already been invited to join a theatre company?
7 prefers working in theatre rather than in cinema or television?
8 did not want to work outside the theatre initially?
9 thinks it may be necessary to travel to find work?
10 thinks it is probably unnecessary to leave Scotland to find work?
11 feels worried about performing in front of some important people?
12 would be happy to work outside Scotland?
13 was motivated by the possibility of becoming well-known?
14 originally tried to train as an actor somewhere else?
15 wasn't so interested in working in the theatre initially?

3 Now read the newspaper article. For questions 1–15, choose from the people A–E.

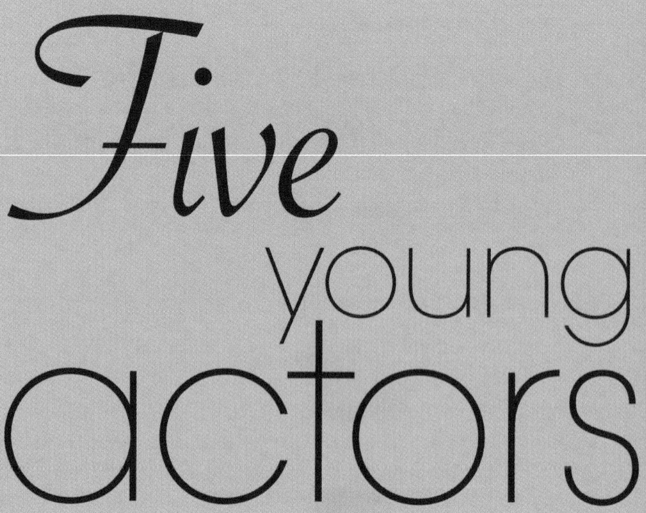

Five young actors

The curtains open in the theatre as a group of young actors make their way on to the stage. These are some young Edinburgh-based actors doing the final performance of their drama course.

A Scott Hoatson

22-year-old Scott is already a step ahead of his classmates as he has been offered a year-long contract with the National Theatre of Scotland's under-26 theatre group. He was discovered by someone from the theatre while performing in plays in Edinburgh and St Andrews, but he admits the students' final performance in front of directors and agents is still nerve-wracking. "It's so important for all of us. The fact that there are artistic directors from the big theatres who come to watch makes it such a big opportunity. There's so much happening in Scotland at the moment. There are a lot of opportunities up here, so it makes sense to stay closer to home. When I started the course, I thought that stage acting was the only thing I wanted to do, but now I want to do everything I can – whether it's on stage, TV, film or radio."

B Kim Gerard

21-year-old Kim got her first taste of performing as a ballet dancer when she was just two and has been hooked on performing ever since. Although her ballet days are now behind her, she admits that it gave her a great introduction to the profession. "It was just so exhilarating

drama schools down in London, but after being rejected by them I took a year out to go travelling. This course has given us so many useful skills and brought us into contact with so many actors and directors who have told us all about the industry. And we've been able to get some experience with TV as well as stage acting, which has been great. When it comes down to finding work, if it's in Scotland, that's great, but I'd love to travel around too."

to get up on stage and perform in front of an audience. Acting is the only thing that I have ever really wanted to do and this course has let me do my training close to home. Even though I'd done some theatre before, I always wanted to get into TV. I really liked the idea of being a famous, well-paid TV star in a drama series. But now, I've realised acting on stage is just as good."

C Allan Scott-Douglas

Although 23-year-old Allan has been interested in performing since his early teens, it was only in his second year of a primary teaching degree at Edinburgh University that he decided to pursue it as a career. "I kind of got into acting by accident," he admits. "I was more of a singer, but I ended up doing musical theatre and absolutely loved it. I'm pretty much open to anything. I suppose my heart will always belong to theatre, as there's a live audience there in front of you, but the film and TV work we've done has been great fun too, so I'd love to do some more. As a young actor, you've got to go where the work is. If I'm offered something down in London there's no way I'd ever be able to turn it down."

D Romana Abercromby

26-year-old Romana says she got involved with a lot of drama productions when she was still at school. "When I left school, I realised that it was the only thing I wanted to do. I tried applying to

E Neil Thomas

20-year-old Neil was just seven years old when he joined an after-school youth theatre company, which gave him his first taste of acting on stage. "I went once or twice a week and adored it," he says. "I was always keen to show off at school so it was the perfect outlet for me to perform properly. I've had the chance to do a lot of different types of acting and the training has been invaluable. It's intense, but everyone knows that's the nature of the career and you have to be prepared. People will give you all sorts of advice about your acting, which helps you to strip away your bad habits. In our profession you have to be prepared for brutal criticism, because that's what you'll expect when you start working."

Adapted from *The Scotsman*

Exam advice

- Many of the extracts may say quite similar things. You will have to read carefully to decide which extract answers the question exactly.
- Guess difficult words when you think it will help you to answer a question.

4 Work in small groups.

- Have you ever performed in public (e.g. acting, speaking in public, dancing, doing a sport)?
- How did you feel about the experience? What did you enjoy about it? What did you dislike?

Vocabulary

Play, performance and *acting*; *audience, public* and *spectators*; *scene* and *stage*

1 First Certificate candidates often confuse these words: *play, performance* and *acting*; *audience, the public* and *spectators*; *scene* and *stage*. Circle the correct alternative in *italics* in each of the sentences below. Then check by looking at the text in Reading Part 3 again.

- He was discovered by someone from the theatre while performing in **(1)** *plays / performances* in Edinburgh and St Andrews, but he admits the students' final **(2)** *acting / performance* in front of directors and agents is still nerve-wracking.
- When I started the course, I thought that stage **(3)** *acting / playing* was the only thing I wanted to do.
- It was just so exhilarating to get up on **(4)** *stage / scene* and perform in front of **(5)** *a public / an audience*.

2 Read the extracts below from the *Cambridge Advanced Learner's Dictionary*. Then complete each of the sentences which follow by writing one of the words or phrases in each gap. Use each word only once.

acting *noun* [U] the job of performing in films or plays: *He wants to get into acting.*

audience *group noun* [C] the group of people gathered in one place to watch or listen to a play, film, someone speaking, etc., or the (number of) people watching or listening to a particular television or radio programme, or reading a particular book

performance *noun* [C] the action of entertaining other people by dancing, singing, acting or playing music

play *noun* [C] a piece of writing that is intended to be acted in a theatre or on radio or television

scene *noun* [C] a part of a play or film in which the action stays in one place for a continuous period of time

spectator *noun* [C] a person who watches an activity, especially a sports event, without taking part

stage *noun* [C] the area in a theatre which is often raised above ground level and on which actors or entertainers perform

the public *group noun* [S] all ordinary people: *Members of the public were asked about their shopping habits.*

1 The garden in all its glory is now open to ...the public... .
2 He wrote his latest .... in under six weeks.
3 The thing I enjoy most about .... is the chance to work in other countries.
4 She gave a superb .... as Lady Macbeth.
5 The .... were clearly delighted with the performance.
6 The actor forgot what he was supposed to say in the third ....
7 The show ended with all the performers singing on.......................... together.
8 They won the football match 4–0 in front of over 40,000 cheering ....

Use of English Part 1

1 You will read an article about British teenagers and fame. Before you read, work in pairs.

Would you like to be famous? If so, what would you like to be famous as?

2 Read the article quickly without paying attention to the gaps. According to the article, what do British teenagers think are the main advantages of being famous?

Young people dream of fame

British teenagers are so keen to become celebrities that almost one in ten would (0) ...abandon... their education if they had the opportunity to (1) .... on television. Footballers and Hollywood stars were among their role models. Nine per cent of British teenagers believed that becoming famous was a great (2) .... to become wealthy without (3) .... or qualifications and a further 11 per cent said that they were 'waiting to be discovered'.

Daryll Rose, who is 16, is (4) .... of becoming rich and famous – (5) .... as a footballer but if not then as a model or an actor. Daryll, whose heroes are the footballer Thierry Henry and the actor Denzel Washington, said he would happily (6) .... of school if he was offered the (7) .... to go on a television show that would (8) .... his dreams. 'I would love to be rich,' he said. 'Everything seems easy when you are famous. I think I am going to be famous. I have got a lot of ambition and I work hard.'

Daryll (9) .... the importance of education but does not believe that education and a steady career will ever (10) .... him with the lifestyle that he (11) .... of. 'I would not like to go to the same job every day. I do not think you can become really rich with a normal job – I think you can be comfortable. When you are really rich you can do (12) .... you want. Being comfortable is not the same thing.'

3 For questions 1–12, read the text again and decide which answer (A, B, C or D) best fits each gap.

0 A neglect B abandon C get out of D depart

1 A appear B become C show D broadcast
Clue: The correct alternative means 'to be seen'.

2 A method B manner C means D way
Clue: Only one of these alternatives can be followed by the infinitive. The others are followed by 'of'.

3 A knowledge B skills C information D capabilities
Clue: You need a word which means: 'an ability to do an activity or job well, especially because you have practised it'.

4 A sure B confident C positive D convinced
Clue: All of these alternatives can be followed by 'that …'. One of them can be followed by 'of' in this context.

5 A ideally B suitably C well D excellently
Clue: Being a footballer would be the perfect job for Daryll.

6 A run out B give up C drop out D turn down
Clue: Look at the preposition which follows the gap. The correct answer means 'stop going to classes'.

7 A chance B opening C possibility D occasion
Clue: This word means 'opportunity'. Notice it is followed by an infinitive.

8 A extend B further C widen D progress
Clue: This means 'to make his dreams advance'. Two of the alternatives have the wrong meaning. Another cannot be followed by an object.

9 A agrees B believes C accepts D approves
Clue: Three of the alternatives are followed by prepositions: 'of', 'in' and 'with'.

10 A prepare B offer C provide D give
Clue: Notice the preposition later in the sentence. Which of the alternatives needs this preposition?

11 A hopes B longs C wishes D dreams
Clue: Three of these verbs are followed by the preposition 'for'.

12 A all B whatever C that D like
Clue: You need an alternative which means 'anything'.

Exam advice

- Think about the meanings of the different alternatives; is there one word which is usually used in the context?
- Is there a dependent preposition or other grammatical construction which will only go with one of the alternatives?

4 Work in small groups.

- Do you think Daryll is being realistic? Why (not)?
- What do you think is the easiest way to become a celebrity?
- What type of television programme do you think is best for someone who wants to be a celebrity?

Speaking Part 1

1 Complete the sentences below by putting the verb in brackets into the correct form: verb + infinitive (with or without *to*) or verb + *-ing*.

- **I really enjoy** (1) ...watching... (watch) quiz programmes – I think you learn a lot from them.
- **I can't stand** (2) .... (listen) to the news because I find it all so depressing.
- **I'm not too keen on** (3) .... (watch) cartoons. **I'd rather** (4) .... (watch) real actors acting …
- **I love** (5) .... (go) to the theatre and (6) .... (see) plays. I like seeing live performances.
- **I prefer** (7) .... (watch) films in the cinema because I think they're more entertaining when there's an audience.
- **I don't mind** (8) .... (watch) music programmes, but **I'm not too interested in** television in general. **I prefer** (9) .... (go) out with my friends.
- **I really hate** (10) .... (watch) series about doctors and hospitals because I think the plots and the characters are very unrealistic.

2 (22) Check your answers by listening to three candidates practising Speaking Part 1.

3 Copy the table below into your notebooks and write the words in bold above in the correct column.

likes	dislikes	neither likes nor dislikes
I really enjoy		

4 **Now change the sentences in Exercise 1 so that they are true for you. Compare your sentences with a partner.**

Example: *I can't stand watching horror movies because I find them too frightening.*

5 (22) **Listen to the candidates practising Speaking Part 1 again.**

1 What did Antonia say when she didn't understand the question?
2 When Peter noticed that he had made a mistake, did he correct it or not?
3 What did Miguel say when he didn't understand a question?

6 **Work in pairs. Take turns to ask and answer these questions.**

- Do you watch much television? What sort of TV programme do you like most?
- What sort of TV programmes do you find really boring?
- Which do you prefer: watching films on television or the cinema? What sorts of films do you prefer?
- Are there any types of film you don't like?
- What sort of entertainment do you enjoy most in your free time?
- Do you go to the theatre or cinema often?

Exam advice

- If you notice you make a mistake when speaking, correct yourself.
- If you don't understand a question, ask the examiner to repeat it.
- When you speak about things you enjoy, sound enthusiastic!

Writing Part 2 An article

1 **Read the writing task below and underline the points you must deal with in your answer.**

You see the following notice on your college noticeboard.

> **See your name in print!**
>
> The editors of the college magazine would like contributions to the magazine on the following subject:
>
> - Where do you prefer to see films: in the cinema or at home on TV or DVD?
>
> The writer of the best article will receive ten tickets to the local cinema.

Write your **article**.

2 **Work in small groups. Brainstorm a list of advantages of:**

- seeing films in the cinema
- seeing films at home on TV or DVD.

Which ideas would you use in your article?

3 **Read the article below.**

- Which way of seeing films does the writer prefer: in the cinema or on television?
- Which of the ideas you thought of are mentioned?

The best place to see films

In the past, before television was invented, people used to go to the cinema once or twice a week. They loved going because they could escape into a different world with exciting stories. Also they could see wonderful actors and strange places which they could never visit.

Although films are no longer something new, going to the cinema is still a magical experience. It's just not the same watching films on television. In the cinema, you're surrounded by the rest of the audience. You sit in front of a large screen and share the feelings of fear, sadness or happiness with many other people.

On the other hand, it's certainly cheaper to watch films on television. It has the added advantage that you can talk and discuss the film with your family while it's happening. However, it isn't as exciting as going out and doing something special. Without doubt, the films I remember and enjoyed the most are the ones I watched in the cinema. So, despite the cost, I prefer seeing films in the cinema.

4 **Look at the structure of the article. Which paragraph in the article deals with these points?**

1 What the writer prefers most: cinema or television
2 Why cinema is popular today
3 Why cinema was popular in the past

5 **Read the article again and decide how these linking words are used to contrast ideas: *although, however, despite*. Write each word in the correct space in the rules below.**

Rules

1 .... contrasts two facts or ideas and is followed by a noun or verb + *-ing*. It can go at the beginning or in the middle of the sentence.

2 .... joins two sentences with contrasting ideas. It can go at the beginning or in the middle of the sentence.

3 .... starts a new sentence and contrasts it with the previous sentence.

page 160 *Grammar reference: Linking words for contrast*

6 **Write *although, however* or *despite* in the spaces below.**

1 ..Although... the cinema is expensive, I try to go every week.
2 .... being given tickets to the football match, we decided to watch it on TV.
3 I wanted to go to the theatre. .... , I had to stay at home and study.
4 He was very easy to talk to .... being a famous film star.
5 Ten per cent of British teenagers dream of becoming famous. .... , the chances of becoming a celebrity are about one in 30 million.
6 I didn't enjoy the film .... I thought the action scenes were very exciting.

7 **Work in pairs. Read the writing task below and follow these steps.**

- Brainstorm ideas in favour of being famous, and ideas in favour of being successful but not so well known.
- Discuss which you would prefer.
- Write a plan for your article, i.e. what ideas you will express in each paragraph.
- Decide on a heading for the article.

You see the following announcement in an English-language magazine.

Dreams of fame?

Many people dream of being famous. Which would you prefer: to be famous, or to be successful but not so well-known?

The writer of the best article will be invited to appear on the TV programme: *The Next Millionaire.*

Write your **article**.

8 **Work alone and write the article using the plan you made with your partner.**

Exam advice

- Write a plan before you start writing the article.
- Organise your ideas into paragraphs, and use linking words such as: *however, despite, in addition, for example* and *on the other hand.*

Unit 10 Secrets of the mind

Starting off

1 **Work in pairs. Find ten different things which make people happy by matching the words and phrases below.**

1	being admired	a	a loving family
2	being part of	b	at school or university
3	doing really well	c	by the people around you
4	falling	d	do what you feel like
5	having enough money to	e	friends
6	having lots of	f	in a nice neighbourhood
7	having lots of time to spend	g	in love
8	living	h	on your hobbies
9	not having to	i	sports
10	winning at	j	work too hard

2 **Which of these do you think are essential for happiness? Which do you think are not so important?**

3 **Are there any other important things which make people happy?**

Reading Part 1

1 **You will read an article by a psychologist about happiness. Read the article quickly to find out what he thinks makes people happy.**

The secrets of happiness

Mihaly Csikszentmihalyi has devoted his life to studying happiness. He believes he has found the key.

I've been fascinated by happiness most of my life. When I was a small boy, I noticed that though many of the adults around me were wealthy and educated, they were not always happy and this sometimes led them to behave in ways which I, as a child, thought strange. As a result of this, I decided to understand what happiness was and how best to achieve it. It was not surprising, then, that I decided to study psychology.

On arrival at the University of Chicago fifty years ago, I was disappointed to find that academic psychologists were trying to understand human behaviour by studying rats in a laboratory. I felt that there must be other more useful ways of learning how we think and feel. Although my original aim had been to achieve happiness for myself, I became more ambitious. I decided to build my career on trying to discover what made others happy also. I started out by studying creative people such as musicians, artists and athletes because they were people who devoted their lives to doing what they wanted to do, rather than things that just brought them financial rewards.

Later, I expanded the study by inventing a system called 'the experience sampling method'. Ordinary people were asked to keep an electronic pager for a week which gave out a beeping sound eight times a day. Every time it did so, they wrote down where they were, what they were doing, how they felt and how much they were concentrating. This system has now been used on more than 10,000 people and the answers are consistent: as with creative people, ordinary people are happiest when concentrating hard.

After carrying out thirty years of

research and writing eighteen books, I believe I have proved that happiness is quite different from what most people imagine. It is not something that can be bought or collected. People need more than just wealth and comfort in order to lead happy lives. I discovered that people who earn less than £10,000 are not generally as happy as people whose incomes are above that level. This suggests that there is a minimum amount of money we need to earn to make us happy. But below and above that dividing line, people's happiness has very little to do with how much poorer or richer they are. Multi-millionaires turn out to be only slightly happier than other people who are not so rich. What is more, people living in poverty are often quite happy.

I found that the most obvious cause of happiness is intense concentration. This must be the main reason why activities such as music, art, literature, sports and other forms of leisure have survived. In order to concentrate, whether you're reading a poem or building a sandcastle, what you need is a challenge that matches your ability. The way to remain continually happy therefore, is to keep finding new opportunities to improve your skills. This may mean learning to do your job better or faster, or doing other more difficult jobs. As you grow older you have to find new challenges which are more appropriate to your age.

I have spent my life studying happiness and now, as I look back, I wonder if I have achieved it. Overall, I think I have and my belief that I have found the keys to its secret has increased my happiness immeasurably.

Adapted from *The Times*

2 For questions 1–3, the sentences in the article which give you the answers have been underlined. Read the questions and the underlined sentences. Then choose the answer (A, B, C or D) which you think fits best according to the underlined sentences.

1 What does 'this' in line 12 refer to?
- **A** the writer's decision to study psychology
- **B** the writer's interest in happiness
- **C** the writer's observations of adults
- **D** the writer's unhappy childhood

2 What did he consider was wrong with psychology 50 years ago?
- **A** Psychologists were trying to achieve the wrong objectives.
- **B** Psychologists were using the wrong scientific methods.
- **C** Psychologists were not making sufficient progress with their experiments.
- **D** Psychologists were carrying out experiments on animals.

3 Why did he concentrate on creative people to begin with?
- **A** They were obviously happier than other people.
- **B** They had greater freedom than other people.
- **C** They had clear aims in life.
- **D** They did not try to become happy by making money.

3 Now, for questions 4–8, choose the answer (A, B, C or D) which you think fits best according to the text.

4 The 'experience sampling method' showed in general that
- **A** creative people are happier than ordinary people.
- **B** ordinary people and creative people are equally happy.
- **C** people's happiness depends on who they are with.
- **D** people are happier when they are very focused on an activity.

5 What does the writer say about money and happiness?
- **A** Below a certain level of income, people are not so happy.
- **B** Poor people are often happier than rich people.
- **C** There is no relationship between money and happiness.
- **D** It is necessary to have money in order to be happy.

6 What is *that dividing line* in line 59?
- **A** a level below which people do not live so comfortably
- **B** a line dividing poor countries from rich ones
- **C** a line which divides happy people from unhappy people
- **D** a line dividing millionaires from poor people

7 According to the writer, people concentrate more when they are doing
- **A** something which they find easy.
- **B** something which they find difficult but possible.
- **C** something which they find too difficult.
- **D** more and more things all the time.

8 What impression do you have of the writer of the text?
- **A** He has become happier by studying happiness.
- **B** He has been unhappy most of his life.
- **C** He has always been a happy person.
- **D** He has only been happy for short times.

Exam advice

- Find where the question is answered in the text and read that section carefully.
- Then read each of the four alternatives with the question.
- Underline the words in the text which gave you the answer.

4 **Work in small groups.**

- Do you agree with the writer about what makes people happy?
- Do you think that being happy is the most important thing in life, or are there other more important things? If so, what?

Vocabulary

Stay, spend and *pass*; *make, cause* and *have*

1 **First Certificate candidates often confuse these words: *stay, spend* and *pass; make, cause* and *have*. Read the following sentences and circle the correct alternative in *italics*. Then check your answers by reading the extracts from the *Cambridge Advanced Learner's Dictionary*.**

1 Remember, your behaviour will *have* / *cause* an effect on other people.
2 I'm very sorry if I've *made* / *caused* you any problems.
3 I have *passed* / *spent* my life studying happiness.
4 Yesterday I *spent* / *stayed* two hours listening to the radio.
5 I really enjoy late-night films on TV when I can *stay* / *be* awake.

stay to continue doing something, or to continue to be in a particular state: *He's decided not to stay in teaching. The shops stay open until 9 o'clock.*

spend to use time doing something or being somewhere: *My sister always spends ages in the bathroom.*

pass if you pass time, you do something to stop yourself being bored during that period: *The visitors pass their days swimming, windsurfing and playing volleyball.*

make (+ noun/adjective) to cause to be, to become or to appear as: *It's the good weather that makes Spain such a popular tourist destination. Don't stand over me all the time – it makes me nervous.*

cause to make something happen, especially something bad: *The difficult driving conditions caused several accidents.*

Some common collocations with *cause*:
cause trouble, cause problems, cause damage, cause traffic jams, cause stress, cause pollution.

Note, however, these collocations:

have an effect: *The radiation leak **has had** a disastrous **effect** on/upon the environment.*

have/make an impact: *The anti-smoking campaign had/made quite an impact on young people.*

2 **Now complete each of these sentences using *stay, spend, pass, make, cause* or *have* in the correct form.**

1 I decided to ...spend... all day in camp.
2 Colin did a crossword to .... the time while he was waiting for the train.
3 We should be able to go camping because they say the weather will .... good for the rest of the week.
4 Do you think the disaster will .... any impact on the environment?
5 How did you .... your summer holidays? Did you enjoy yourself?
6 I .... two hours today trying to finish my homework.
7 I hope the children haven't been .... you problems again, Mrs Turner.
8 The bad sound quality .... the film very difficult to understand.
9 The new law should .... a dramatic effect on the number of traffic accidents.
10 Your jokes .... us all very happy.

Listening Part 1

1 **You will hear people talking in eight different situations. Before you listen, work in small groups. Discuss whether you agree with these statements or not.**

- When you meet someone for the first time, you form your first opinions of them from the things they say to you (not, for example, from their looks or their clothes).

- In general, people marry someone quite similar to them rather than someone very different.

- Young people nowadays are generally more intelligent than their grandparents were.

- Few people are afraid of flying in planes and getting in lifts. More people are afraid of heights.

- Everyone sometimes has a dream where they're flying, falling or running.

2 Now work in pairs. Read questions 1 and 2 and match the words and phrases in the box with each of the alternatives A, B and C in the two questions. (For some alternatives there may be more than one word or phrase.)

actual words	body language	character
things in common	gestures	hobbies
intonation	people we like	appearance

1 You hear an expert on a television programme giving advice about meeting people for the first time. What has the most impact?
A how you speak
B how you look
C what you say

2 You hear a man and a woman talking about successful marriages. What does the man think is the most important factor in a successful marriage?
A similar personalities
B the same friends
C similar interests

3 (2) Now listen and for questions 1 and 2, choose the best answer (A, B or C). Which of the words and phrases from the box above did you hear?

4 (3) Listen and for questions 3–8, choose the best answer (A, B or C).

3 You hear a radio programme in which a psychologist is talking about intelligence. What does she say is improving?
A our ability to do certain tests
B our intelligence
C our performance in exams

4 You overhear a student telling a friend about a project on what makes people happy. What does he say makes people happiest?
A becoming rich
B getting married
C having children

5 You overhear a man talking about things which frighten people. What frightens him?
A flying
B heights
C lifts

6 You hear a girl talking to a friend about her dreams. What does she dream?
A She's flying.
B She's falling.
C She's running.

7 You overhear two students talking about a friend. Why do they think she is stressed?
A She hasn't been sleeping well.
B She's been working too hard.
C She's been having problems with a relationship.

8 You hear a man and a woman talking about the man's free-time activities. What do they show about his personality?
A He's friendly and sociable.
B He's shy and prefers being alone.
C He's creative and adventurous.

Exam advice

- Listen to the whole piece before you choose: the answer may depend on the general idea rather than a few words.
- If you are not sure about the answer after listening the first time, try to discard answers you don't think are possible before you listen the second time.

5 Work in pairs.

- When you feel stressed, what do you do to relax?
- Talk about someone in your family. What do their free-time activities show about their personality?

Grammar

Modal verbs to express certainty and possibility

1 Read the following extracts from Listening Part 1 and look at the underlined modal verbs. Then answer the questions which follow.

- Do you know how you got this phobia, this thing which frightens you so much? – I think it <u>must</u> be because I got trapped in one when I was a child and there was a power cut. I <u>can't</u> have been alone in it for more than ten minutes, but it seemed like an hour.
- Well, I've heard that when you fall in your dreams it's because you <u>may</u> feel you've failed in some way, or you <u>might</u> just be afraid of failure. And the ones where you're running to get away from someone are because something or someone <u>could</u> be threatening you in your real life.

1 Which of the underlined verbs do we use:
- when we are certain something is true? (1) ......*must*......
- when we are certain something is not true? (2) ....
- when we think something is possibly true? (3) ...., (4) .... and (5) ....

2 Do the five underlined verbs refer to the present or the past?

page 161 *Grammar reference: Modal verbs to express certainty and possibility*

2 Complete the sentences below about the woman in the photo using a suitable verb and ideas from the box. Several answers may be possible.

~~a film star~~	French	going shopping	about 30
a politician	at the opening of a new film		famous

1 She must ......*be a film star.*......
2 She can't ....
3 She might ....
4 She could ....
5 She must ....
6 She may ....

3 Four of the following sentences contain mistakes made with modal verbs. However, one is correct. Find and correct the mistakes.

1 I think the school you go to looks lovely. You ~~may~~ really enjoy it! *must*
2 He's had a really good sleep, so he mustn't be tired any more.
3 The roads are very busy today, so drive carefully or you can have an accident.
4 I have a lot of work to do, so I may arrive home late.
5 She's got a really responsible job, so she can't be earning a lot of money.

4 Read these extracts from Listening Part 1 and complete the rules which follow by writing one of the underlined phrases in each space.

- Well, she had a maths exam last week, so she must have studied hard for it. But she's always been pretty hard-working, so she can't have got stressed by it. Anyway, she finds maths easy.
- I suppose she may have had a row with her boyfriend of hers – he can be a bit difficult sometimes, don't you think?

Rules

When we talk about the past:

- We use (1) .... + past participle (done, studied, eaten, etc.) when we are certain something is true about the past.
- We use (2) .... + past participle when we are certain something is not true about the past.
- We use (3) .... , might have and could have + past participle when we think something is possibly true.

5 Complete the following sentences by writing a modal verb in the gap and putting the verb in brackets into the correct form for the past or present. In some cases more than one answer is possible.

1 Everyone in the class ....must have worked.... (work) incredibly hard if you all passed the exam!
2 I think she .... (be) a really happy person because she's always smiling and laughing.
3 Jamie woke up in the night screaming. He .... (have) a bad dream.
4 I don't know why Patsy hasn't arrived yet. She .... (have to) stay on late at work, or she .... (stop) on the way to do some shopping.
5 I don't know how old the teacher is, but he looks young, so he .... (be) more than 30.
6 They say it .... (rain) at the weekend, in which case we won't be able to play football.
7 I can't find my keys. I suppose I .... (leave) them on the train but I don't know.
8 Don't do anything for my supper because I .... (go) out to a restaurant with a friend.

Use of English Part 4

For questions 1–8, complete the second sentence so that it has a similar meaning to the first sentence, using the word given. Do not change the word given. You must use between two and five words, including the word given.

1 Stella hates it when people smoke in her house.
STAND
Stella ....can't stand people smoking.... in her house.

2 'I spoke to Maria yesterday,' Paola said.
HAD
Paola said she .... previous day.

3 'Don't forget to lock the front door, Karl,' said his wife.
REMINDED
Karl's wife .... the front door.

4 Sven went skiing despite feeling ill.
WELL
Although Sven .... , he went skiing.

5 Although the music outside was loud, we managed to sleep.
DESPITE
We managed to sleep .... outside.

6 I'm sure Annabel wasn't in London all weekend.
HAVE
Annabel .... in London the whole weekend.

7 It's possible that my parents have discovered what we did at the weekend.
MAY
My parents .... out what we did at the weekend.

8 How long did it take you to write the essay?
SPEND
How long .... the essay?

Exam advice

Read the original sentence, the word given and the sentence with the gap. Think about:

- whether you need an expression, e.g. *he changed his mind*
- whether you need a phrasal verb, e.g. *give up*
- what grammar you will need, e.g. do you need to change from active to passive or put something into reported speech?

Speaking Part 3

1 Work in pairs.

Some people believe that the things people do in their free time tell us things about their personality. What activities do you enjoy doing? What do you think the activities might say about your personality?

2 Look at the pictures.

What kind of personality do you need to enjoy each of the activities shown in the pictures below? Match the personality adjectives in the box to the type of person shown in each picture. Some adjectives can match more than one picture.

adventurous	caring	creative	easy-going
friendly	good at working with other people		
hard-working	interested in other people		
responsible	sociable	solitary	thoughtful
unselfish	well-organised		

- What sort of personality does each of these people have?
- Which two people might be best for the job?

3 Think of other adjectives you can add to the list in Exercise 2.

4 (4) Work in pairs. Listen to the teacher giving instructions to candidates in Speaking Part 3 and two candidates starting the task shown here. Which of these things do the candidates do?

1. Each person talks about a different picture. *no*
2. They describe what the person is doing in one of the pictures.
3. They each speak for a long time.
4. They use a range of adjectives to describe the person's personality.
5. They use modal verbs to express certainty and possibility.

5 (5) Listen to the teacher's instructions again and do the Speaking task in pairs.

Exam advice

- Briefly describe the activities in each picture.
- Show how much you know by using different vocabulary for each picture.
- Use modal verbs (*may, might, must, can't*) when appropriate – not just *maybe* and *perhaps*.

Writing Part 2 A story

1 Look at the writing task below and think about a really happy day in your life. What made it happy? Here are some suggestions:

- you met someone special
- you were successful at something (passing an important exam, winning a competition, etc.)
- you spent the day with someone special
- you did something really enjoyable.

> You have decided to enter a short story competition in an English-language magazine. The competition rules say that the story must **begin** with these words:
>
> *I will always remember that day as one of the happiest days of my life.*
>
> Write your **story**.

2 **Work in pairs. Take turns to tell each other about your really happy day. When you tell your story, describe:**

- how you feel about that day now
- events just before the day
- what happened on the day and why it was so happy
- some details about people and places.

3 **The following answer to the writing task contains ten spelling errors (in addition to the example) which are often made by First Certificate candidates. Find and correct the errors.**

> I will always remember that day as one of the happiest days of my life. I had been ~~studing~~ studying English in London and I was flying home. Although living in London had been a marvelous experence, it was the summer holidays and I missed my family.
>
> The had all been staying at a confortable hotel in the mountains and having fun together while I was at school, so I fell a little envious. I knew that when I arrived at the airport I would have to take a long bus journey back home to my town.
>
> I got off the airplane and walked through the airport thinking about the rest of the journey I would have to make alone. Imagine my surprise, though, when I walked trough the arrivals gate to find my parents waitting there to meet me! When my mother had kissed me, she told me the exiting news that we were returning to the hotel together for another two weeks' holiday because they had missed me as well. For me, that was a very especial day.

4 **You can make a story more interesting for your reader by using a variety of tenses. Read the sample answer again and find examples of:**

- the past perfect tense (*had done / had been doing*)
- the past continuous tense (*was doing*).

Look at page 155 to check when these tenses are used.

5 **Read the writing task below and think about what meeting you can write about. Here are some ideas:**

- meeting a famous person
- meeting a friend or relative you hadn't seen for a long time
- meeting someone new who became a special friend.

> You have decided to enter a short story competition in an English-language magazine. The competition rules say that the story must **end** with these words:
>
> *That one meeting made it a day I will never forget.*
>
> Write your **story**.

6 **Work in pairs. Take turns to tell each other about the meeting. When you tell your story:**

- say how you feel about the meeting now
- describe the situation before the meeting and how it happened
- who you met and what you did
- briefly describe the person you met
- explain why the day was unforgettable.

7 **Do the writing task following the steps below. Write between 120–180 words.**

- Think about what you will say and make notes.
- Plan your story: how many paragraphs and what will you put in each paragraph?
- Write your story following your plan.
- Check what you have written for mistakes.

Exam advice

When you have finished writing, follow these tips.

- Check what mistakes you have made in the other writing tasks you have done during this course. Are there any mistakes which you have repeated? Check you're not making them again.
- Use a dictionary to check spellings and prepositions.
- Write down your important mistakes in your notebook. Before you do the exam, check what mistakes you've been making and avoid them!

Unit 9 *Vocabulary and grammar review*

Vocabulary

1 Choose the best word A, B, C or D for each space.

1 The flying display attracted about 50,000 .... despite the rain.
A public **B** assistants **C** spectators **D** audience

2 As a police officer, I get a lot of questions from members of the .... asking how to get to one place or another.
A people **B** public **C** audience **D** spectators

3 During the musical, the .... clapped at the end of every single song.
A audience **B** spectators **C** public **D** attendants

4 British actress Amanda Haslett gave a superb .... as Lady Macbeth at the Globe Theatre last night.
A play **B** act **C** performance **D** acting

5 If you're interested in a career in .... , you must be prepared to work hard for little money.
A acting **B** playing **C** performance **D** stage

6 That play is much better on the .... than in the film version.
A theatre **B** play **C** scene **D** stage

2 Complete each of the sentences below by writing a word or phrase from the box. In some cases more than one answer is possible. You can use the words and phrases more than once.

although	despite	even though	however	in spite of
whereas	while			

1 ...Although... Eva wanted to pursue a career in acting, she couldn't find a job.
2 Max gave a wonderful performance in the school concert .... his headache.
3 .... Jason dreams of being a footballer, Eva wants to work in the theatre.
4 .... not being very talented, she became a highly successful Hollywood star.
5 They spent millions on the film. .... , not many people were interested in going to see it.
6 I enjoy watching documentaries .... my brother prefers soap operas.
7 He insisted on playing loud music .... it was nearly 2 o'clock in the morning.
8 People of all ages go to rock concerts .... classical music concerts are mainly attended by people over 50.

Grammar

3 For questions 1–6, complete the second sentence so that it has a similar meaning to the first sentence, using the word given. Do not change the word given. You must use between two and five words, including the word given.

1 Although it was dangerous, she went swimming.
THE
In spite ....of the danger.............. she went swimming.

2 The theatre was full despite the high price of the tickets.
EXPENSIVE
Although ....
the theatre was full.

3 Although he felt ill, he went to work.
DESPITE
He went to work ....
.... well.

4 She enjoys her job in spite of her low salary.
EVEN
She finds her job enjoyable ....
.... low.

5 'I've been asleep all afternoon.'
SPENT
Helen admitted that ....
.... sleeping.

6 'I'll phone when the concert finishes.'
CALL
Martin said he ....
.... end of the concert.

Unit 10 *Vocabulary and grammar review*

Vocabulary

1 Complete each of the sentences below by writing a word or phrase from the box.

adventurous	creative	sociable	~~solitary~~
thoughtful	responsible	well-organised	
easy-going			

1 He's quite a ......solitary...... person and doesn't like spending much time with other people.
2 You can't be very .... , otherwise you wouldn't have left the plane tickets at home.
3 I'm looking for someone .... to go backpacking with me in Alaska.
4 It was very .... of you to offer to give me a lift when my car broke down.
5 Katrina is a very .... person, so you needn't worry at all about employing her as a baby-sitter.
6 Terry is very .... in his free time – he does a lot of sculpture and painting and things like that.
7 There are few people as .... as my Uncle Jack. He never seems to get worried or upset about anything.
8 They're a very .... couple and always holding parties or going to parties.

2 Circle the best alternative from the words in *italics*.

1 Sheila *spent* / *passed* her summer holiday painting the children's bedroom.
2 Do you think the new law will *cause* / *have* any impact on the way people drive?
3 There's no doubt that air travel *causes* / *makes* a lot of pollution.
4 I'm only doing this crossword to *spend* / *pass* the time – I'm not really interested in it.
5 Patricia studied really hard all weekend but it *had* / *caused* no effect on her final result in the exam.
6 I had such a good time at Sandra's party that it *caused* / *made* me happy for the rest of the week.
7 I *stayed* / *spent* six hours in a traffic jam last weekend.
8 The accident was *made* / *caused* by a driver who was speaking on his mobile phone.

Grammar

3 Complete this dialogue between two friends by putting the verbs in brackets into the correct form.

Andy: Why won't Stephen answer his mobile phone?
Nigel: He (1) ......must have switched...... (must / switch) it off while he was in class and forgotten to turn it back on again.
Andy: He (2) .... (can't / turn) it off because he didn't have a class today – his teacher is ill.
Nigel: Well he (3) .... (may not / hear) it, or he (4) .... (could / leave) it at home. Try ringing again. He (5) .... (might / answer) this time. Anyway, why do you want to call him?
Andy: I want to remind him about the party we're going to tonight. He (6) .... (might / forget) – you know what he's like.
Nigel: He (7) .... (can't / forget) – he was talking about it all yesterday and he was so excited!
Andy: Stephen excited? Why?
Nigel: He thinks he (8) .... (might / see) that attractive Mexican girl there. He's been talking about her a lot since he met her.
Andy: In that case I won't need to ring him – he's obviously not forgotten!

Unit 11 Spend, spend, spend!

Starting off

❶ **Work in small groups. Label each of the photographs with the type of shop listed in the box below.**

bookshop	delicatessen	~~department store~~
fashion boutique	market stall	supermarket

❷ **Discuss these questions:**

- Why might you visit each of the shops in the photos?
- Which type of shop do you think a foreign visitor to your country would find most interesting?

❸ **Do you enjoy shopping? What do you enjoy buying?**

1 *department store*

2 ....

3 ....

4 ....

5 ....

6 ....

Listening Part 4

❶ **Work in pairs. You will hear an interview with Will Payne, an architect who has designed a shopping centre called Redsands Park. Before you listen: what are the advantages and disadvantages of shopping in shopping centres?**

❷ (6) **Now write down the three most important advantages. Then listen to the interview once: how many of your ideas did Will Payne discuss?**

3 Read the questions 1–7. How many can you answer already?

1 Where is Redsands Park situated?
  A In the city centre.
  B In the city, but not near the centre.
  C Outside the city in the countryside.

2 The location was chosen because
  A it would not harm the environment.
  B it was easy to get permission to build there.
  C it was easy for people to reach.

3 What is the main attraction of Redsands Park?
  A It's a convenient place to do the shopping.
  B It's entertaining for the whole family.
  C It offers high-quality goods at low prices.

4 When Will visited shopping centres in the United States, he was impressed by
  A their luxury.
  B their security.
  C their friendliness.

5 Will says families argue when they go shopping because
  A they don't enjoy the same things.
  B they can't agree on what to buy.
  C they also argue at home.

6 How are the shops at Redsands organised?
  A Each shop chooses its own location.
  B Each section has a variety of shops.
  C Similar shops are located in the same section.

7 What does Will plan as the next development at Redsands?
  A electric vehicles
  B moving walkways
  C automatic delivery systems

4 (6) Listen again. For questions 1–7, choose the best answer (A, B or C).

Exam advice

You have one minute to read the questions before listening.

- Read the main part of each question carefully first.
- If you have time, go back and read the alternatives for each question **with** the question.

5 Work in pairs.

Do you enjoy shopping with your family? Why (not)?

Vocabulary

Phrasal verbs

1 Match these phrasal verbs from Listening Part 4 with their definitions from the *Cambridge Advanced Learner's Dictionary*.

1 take over	**a** attract
2 pull in	**b** collect, or to go and get, someone or something
3 cater for	**c** do less of something or use something in smaller amounts
4 hang around with	**d** go into or visit for a short time
5 pop into	**e** have to deal with a problem
6 cut down (on)	**f** make someone extremely tired
7 wear out	**g** provide what is wanted or needed by someone or something
8 come up against	**h** spend time with someone
9 come up with	**i** suggest or think of an idea or plan
10 pick up	**j** take control of / occupy

2 Use one of the phrasal verbs above in the correct form in sentences 1–10 below.

1 Chantal ......came up with...... the brilliant idea of selling her old clothes in the market on Saturday.
2 I'm spending far more than I can afford. I'll really have to .... something.
3 If you're in town, could you .... the post office and post this parcel for me?
4 It's an enormous music shop which .... all musical tastes from classical music to heavy metal.
5 Melanie doesn't like .... with her parents, so she's gone shopping on her own.
6 Shopping in Oxford Street .... us .... , so we decided to take a taxi back to the hotel.
7 This new film is so popular that it has been .... huge audiences.
8 We have .... an old building in the city centre to open our new shop.
9 I never expected to .... so many problems trying to get my mobile phone repaired.
10 Do you want to come to the shopping centre with me? I'm going to .... those red shoes I ordered.

Grammar

Modals expressing ability

1 Look at these sentences from Listening Part 4 and answer the questions which follow.

a We could have put the shopping centre out in the country … but the area we've chosen has got its own underground station and it's also close to the motorway …

b … getting permission took quite a long time. We were able to get it in the end though, as you can see.

c Then they started building them among green fields where everyone could go by car and park easily.

d From where I'm standing I can see trees …

In which sentence do the underlined words or phrases mean …?

1 It is possible to: ......d.....
2 It was generally possible to: ....
3 It was possible but it didn't happen: ....
4 We managed to, we succeeded in: ....

page 162 *Grammar reference: Expressing ability*

2 Circle the correct alternative in *italics* in each of the following sentences.

1 We walked all day and at 5 o'clock *we could* / *were able to* reach the top of the mountain.
2 I was so worried that I *couldn't sleep* / *couldn't have slept* and I lay awake all night.
3 When I was a small child, I *could* / *was able to* sing beautifully, but my voice isn't so good now.
4 *Can you* / *Are you able to* hear the neighbours' television? It's far too loud!
5 He was lucky to survive. He drove through a red light and *could be* / *could have been* killed.
6 Although the shop was very crowded, we *could do* / *were able to do* the shopping quite quickly.

3 First Certificate candidates often confuse *can*, *could* and *able to*. Correct the mistakes in the sentences below. One of the sentences is correct.

1 I ~~can't~~ carry everything so I had to leave some things behind. couldn't
2 I was very happy that I could meet all your friends when I visited you last month.
3 I'd be grateful if you can advise me about which book to buy.
4 I'm really pleased to hear that you could come to visit me next month.
5 It would be much easier if we can find the information on the internet.
6 The thieves' car broke down, so the police could arrest them.
7 We hope you'll be able to offer us a discount if we stay in the hotel for two weeks.
8 We should take a trip to London and visit the many shops that could be found there.

Use of English Part 2

1 Work in small groups. You will read a text about the differences between how men and women shop. Before you read, discuss these questions.

- Who does the shopping in your family? Why?
- How much time do you spend shopping each week?
- Do you think there are any differences between the way men and women shop? If so, why do you think they shop in different ways?

2 Read the text below in about one minute without paying attention to the gaps. What does the writer say are the differences? What reasons are given?

Bargain hunters

A study of 2,000 shoppers reveals (0) ....that........ men and women fall into two distinct categories (1) .... it comes to shopping and these go back to our origins as hunters and gatherers. Four out of five women behave (2) .... gatherers when they shop, taking time to search (3) .... they see the right item at the right price. They regard shopping (4) .... a leisure activity in itself, and are happy just to wander through shops looking at things. On the other (5) .... , men see shopping as a hunting mission. They know (6) .... they want to buy and go directly to a store they know sells (7) .... They will rarely shop around and compare prices. As a (8) .... , they will spend an average of 10 per cent more than a woman (9) .... comparable items. The difference in shopping styles can lead to arguments, (10) .... to researchers at Exeter University.

The research also reveals that the things people consider as bargains are (11) .... necessarily reduced in price. People in fact see the item as good value for money and they pay the normal price for many of the things (12) .... are rated as 'bargains'.

3 **Work alone. Decide which word best fits each space. When you have finished, compare your ideas with the rest of the group.**

Exam advice

- Answer the questions you find easy first. Go back to the more difficult questions later.
- Don't leave any spaces blank. If you can't decide what word to write, guess.
- When you have finished, check your answers by reading the completed text again.

4 **Work in small groups.**

- Do you agree with the main idea of the article that women shop like gatherers and men like hunters? Is internet shopping more like hunting or gathering?
- Do people enjoy shopping for food as much as shopping for clothes or CDs?

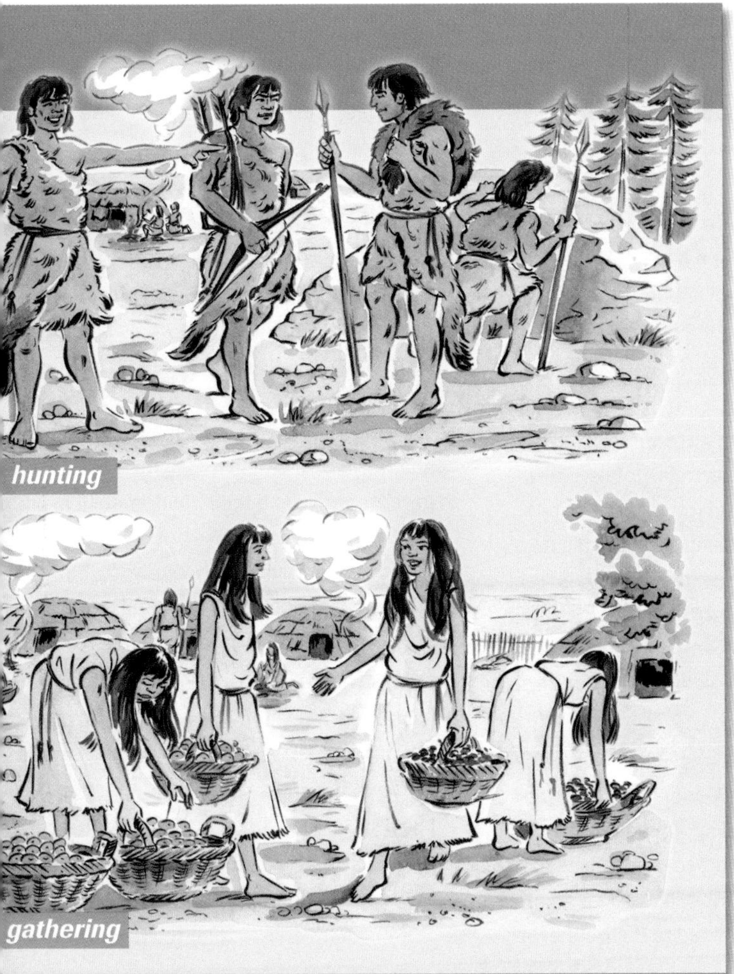

Grammar

As and *like*

1 **Look at the underlined phrases in the sentences below and answer the questions which follow.**

a Tom has two jobs: he's a teacher and a football referee. As a teacher he's very easy-going, but as a referee he's really strict.

b Mark is a social worker, but he spends so much time with young people that sometimes he feels like a teacher.

Which underlined phrase means …?

1 he is a teacher
2 he is similar to a teacher

page 162 *Grammar reference: As and* like

2 **Complete these sentences by writing *as* or *like* in each space.**

1 He has a weekend job ....as.... a shop assistant.
2 He was considered by his teachers .... the most brilliant student they had ever taught.
3 How embarrassing! Donna came to class wearing exactly the same clothes .... me!
4 I find certain subjects .... physics and chemistry very difficult to study.
5 I shall be on holiday next week .... you know.
6 I'm afraid I don't study .... much .... I should.
7 I'm speaking to you .... a friend.
8 My English teacher is lovely. She's .... a mother to me!
9 Several cities in Switzerland, such .... Zurich and Berne, have reputations .... excellent places to live.
10 Tanya's father gave her a car for her 18th birthday .... she'd done so well in her exams.

Reading Part 1

1 You will read an article about parents, teenagers and pocket money. Before you read, match these words and phrases which you will find in the article with their definitions from the *Cambridge Advanced Learner's Dictionary*.

1	pocket money	a	to be able to live with difficulty by having just enough money
2	credit card	b	small amount of money which parents regularly give to their child
3	to get by	c	larger amount of money that young people are given regularly, usually by parents
4	to debit	d	money that you pay for a journey on a vehicle such as a bus or train
5	fare	e	to take money out of a bank account
6	allowance	f	small plastic card which can be used as a method of payment

2 Work in small groups.

- How much pocket money should parents give their children at the following ages? Why?
  13 15 18
- What sort of things do teenagers typically spend their money on? What do/did you spend money on as a teenager?
- Is there anything you would like to have but can't afford to buy?
- What is the best age for young people to have their own bank account? When should they have their own credit card?
- Should young people be encouraged to save? Why? What for?

3 Read the article quite quickly to find out why the writer asks for help and what he can do about the problem.

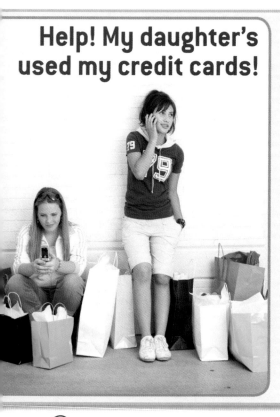

Help! My daughter's used my credit cards!

A few weeks after my daughter's 13th birthday, I glanced over a bank statement and saw a couple of suspicious items. I had been debited nearly £10 by iTunes, the Apple music download website, although I have never downloaded music.

I checked my credit card statement and found another £10 debited to Virgin Mobile. My wife examined her cards and found more things paid for without her permission. Suspicion fell on Emily, who denied it, even though the evidence pointed straight in her direction (she later confessed). Teenage spending had arrived; our wallets would never be our own again.

Little more than a year ago, Emily was getting by on just £1.20 a week pocket money – we had started out by giving 10p for every year of her age – when she discovered she was being given less than most of her classmates. The weekly sum was raised to £3, but her desire to spend money increased and she was soon asking for money from both of us at every opportunity – new shoes this week clothes the next, visits to the cinema, pizza restaurants, mobile top-ups, CDs, cosmetic accessories, large numbers of magazines. If we refused we risked being met with verbal abuse, angry expressions and a slammed d

It's a familiar situation to Canadian clinical psychologist Maggie Mamen. 'Every parent wants their child to be happy; they don't wa them to be the only one without a mobile phone – they don't want them to have less,' she says. 'But the more parents give their children, the more having all the things they want starts to be seen as a right, rather tha something special.'

In the end, we decided to tackle the incessa demands for money by giving her an allowan After consulting her friends' parents, Emily now gets £50 a month to cover most of her clothes, cosmetics and entertainment, plus £10 top-up on her mobile, two DVD rentals and one cinema trip each month. 'Ordinary' clothes, such as winter coats and underwea are still paid for by us, as well as her essenti toiletries. And train or bus fares. And lunch if she is out for the day.

Clare Brooks, a writer, also has a 13-year-old girl, Laura. She says: 'We decided to give her an allowance because of the amount we fou ourselves paying out every month. We aske her to write down how she would spend £40 a month; now it covers all her extras.' The advantage of an allowance, says Brooks, is that 'I can now say "no", because she knows she wants it, she has to pay for it herself.' Mo parents would like their children to help arou the house, but as Brooks puts it: 'Occasionall we do pay her for extra housework, but I say give you £2 to hoover the sitting room, and s says: "You must be joking, I want five".'

For parents, there are two issues. First, how to cope with the demands of children and teenagers who want to spend money as if th were adults, and second a concern that their children are growing up expecting money to always given to them, and not prepared to sa or wait for something they really want.

Adapted from *The Obser*

4 For questions 1–8, choose the answer (A, B, C or D) which you think fits best according to the text.

1 What had Emily been doing which upset her parents?
  A spending money on things she didn't need
  B spending money that wasn't hers
  C spending more than she was allowed
  D spending more than she had in her bank account

2 Why was her pocket money raised to £3?
  A She had more expenses than most teenagers.
  B She was receiving less than other people her age.
  C She became annoyed if she was given less.
  D She had to buy her own clothes.

3 According to Maggie Mamen, what is the problem with giving children too much pocket money?
  A They believe they should be allowed everything they want.
  B They're not happier as a result.
  C They have more things than other children their age.
  D They don't spend all the money they're given.

4 What things does Emily pay for from her allowance?
  A all her expenses
  B all her clothes, cosmetics and entertainment
  C some of her clothes, cosmetics and entertainment
  D her clothes, cosmetics, entertainment and mobile phone

5 Why did Clare Brooks start giving Laura an allowance?
  A to make her work if she wants something extra
  B to avoid arguments with her
  C to limit the money she gives her
  D to ensure she has everything she needs

6 What is Laura's attitude to housework?
  A She finds it amusing.
  B She's always ready to help.
  C She welcomes the extra money she earns doing it.
  D She'll only do it if it's well paid.

7 Apart from the amount their children spend, what is the other thing which worries parents?
  A Children do not learn good financial management.
  B Children are not grateful for what their parents do for them.
  C Children believe their parents' money is their own.
  D Children are likely to spend more money than they have.

8 Which of the following best summarises the writer's attitude to teenage spending throughout the passage?
  A Teenagers should receive more money from their parents.
  B Teenagers should earn the money they need.
  C Teenagers should spend less money than they do.
  D Teenagers should be more responsible about money.

Exam advice

- The answers to the questions come in the same order in the text, so, for example, you will locate the answer to question 2 after question 1.
- When you locate the relevant section of text, read it carefully.
- Make sure that you understand what the text says before you look at the alternatives (A, B, C or D).

5 Work in small groups.

- Which of these things do you think young people should pay for from their pocket money or allowance and which should parents pay for as extras? Tick (✓) the appropriate boxes.

	pay from pocket money	parents should pay
Shoes		
Essential clothes		
Fashion clothes		
Cinema tickets		
Music		
Cosmetics		
Magazines		
Mobile phone costs		
Travelling expenses		
Meals out		

- Do you think teenagers should earn some of the money they need by doing housework or taking a part-time job? Why (not)?

Speaking Part 2

1 (7) Look at the task for Speaking Part 2.

What are the people feeling?

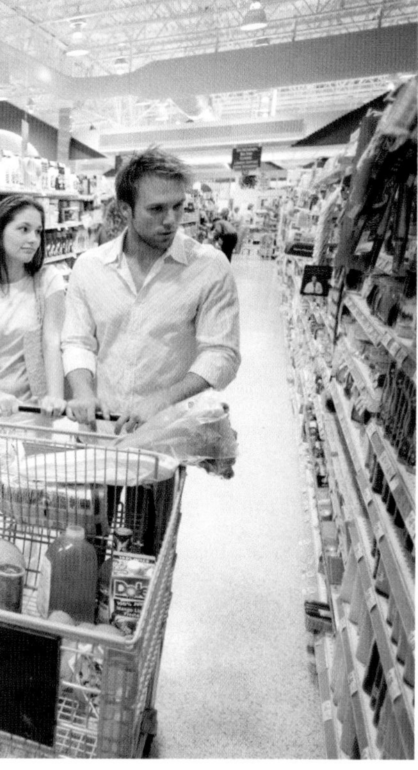

> Teacher: The photographs show people shopping. I'd like you to compare the photographs and say what you think the people are feeling.

Listen to Magda practising this part of the Speaking test and match the two halves of the sentences below according to what she says.

1	They look as if	a	having a good time.
2	They seem to be	b	quite happy.
3	They both look	c	quite relaxed.
4	They don't appear to be	d	rather tired.
5	The man looks	e	so happy.
6	The two girls seem	f	they're shopping for music.

page 162 *Grammar reference:* Look, seem *and* appear

2 (7) Listen again. Which of these ways of introducing a comparison did the candidate use?

in contrast   *whereas*   *on the other hand*

3 Now write three sentences of your own about the man in the second photo using *looks, seems* and *appears*.

4 Work in pairs. Take turns to do Speaking Part 2.

Student A

The photos show young people earning money. I'd like you to compare the photographs and say which you think is the best way for young people to earn money.

Student B

The photos show different places to go shopping. I'd like you to compare the photographs and say why people choose to shop in places like these.

Exam advice

When you're not sure what the photo shows, you can use:

- phrases like *she looks, she seems, she appears*
- modal verbs like *must, can't, may, might, could*
- words like *perhaps, maybe.*

Writing Part 2 A report

1 Work in pairs. Read the following writing task, underlining the things you must deal with in your answer. Which do you think the money should be spent on?

The college where you study has been given a large amount of money to spend either on improving the classrooms or on students' social activities. The director of your college has asked you to write a report describing the benefits of both ideas and saying which one you think should be chosen and why.

Write your **report**.

2 Answer the questions below.

1 Who will read your report?
2 Should you write in an informal or formal style?
3 What things must you include in your report?

3 Read the report below. Write one verb from the box in the correct form in each space.

benefit	contain	~~discuss~~	find	improve	
make	participate	recommend	reduce	spend	

Our College Money

Introduction

The purpose of this report is to (1) ......discuss...... whether the money which has been given to the college should be (2) .... on improving the classrooms or on students' social activities and to (3) .... a recommendation.

The classrooms

The college classrooms are well-equipped with the latest technologies. Each classroom already (4) .... computers with internet connections and an interactive whiteboard. However, the furniture needs replacing because students who attend class all day (5) .... it uncomfortable and this affects their concentration. Furthermore, the classrooms would (6) .... from an air-conditioning system, and this would also (7) .... the quality of students' work.

Social activities

The college already has a social programme with a wide range of activities for students to (8) .... in. If money was spent on this, it would (9) .... the cost of the activities for the students and they would be able to take part in more of them.

Recommendation

I (10) .... spending the money on new furniture and an air-conditioning system as this would have a beneficial effect on students' work in class.

4 Work in pairs.

1 What recommendation does the writer make to the college director?
2 How can the college director find things quickly in the report if he/she doesn't have much time?
3 Has the report dealt with everything in the writing task question?
4 What is the purpose of each section?
5 Which tenses are used? Why?
6 Does the report use contractions (*it's*, *we'll*)? Why (not)?

5 Complete these ways of making recommendations and suggestions by putting the verb in brackets into the correct form.

1 I recommend ...installing... (install) a new air-conditioning system.
2 I suggest .... (spend) money on improving the social programme.
3 I suggest that the college should .... (buy) new furniture for the classrooms.
4 It would be a good idea .... (equip) all the classrooms with computers.

6 Work in pairs. Write four more sentences making recommendations or suggestions for your own college or language school.

7 Work in pairs. Read the following writing task. How do you think the money should be spent?

Your town has a large amount of money available to spend on improving the neighbourhood where you live. You have been asked to write a report for the town council making recommendations.

Write your **report**.

8 Do the writing task. Write between 120 and 180 words. Follow these steps:

- Underline the points you must deal with in your report.
- Think and write a plan for your report. This should include sections and section headings.
- Write your report following your plan and using the report above as a model.
- When you have finished, check it for mistakes.

Exam advice

- Think about who will read the report and if you need a formal or informal style.
- Decide what sections you need and what section headings.
- Start the report by saying what the aim of the report is.
- Finish with your conclusions and, if the question asks for them, your recommendations.

Unit 12 Staying healthy

Starting off

❶ **Work in pairs. Read what each of these people says about their health and complete the spaces by writing the words from the box.**

~~active~~ check-up illness infection intake putting on treatment workout get over

'Here I am, in my 80s and still quite (1) ......*active*...... – I mean I go shopping, visit my friends and go to the cinema when I want to. What more can you ask for?'

'I do an hour's (2) .... in the morning before going to college, and in the evening I usually have time for a couple of hours' sport, so I really think I'm very fit.'

'I do get the occasional cold or other (3) .... You really can't avoid them in my job, but I (4) .... them pretty quickly and they don't usually stop me going to work.'

'I go to the doctor regularly once a year for a (5) .... Once or twice I've needed (6) .... for something she's found, but I think I can expect to live for quite a long time.'

'I never go to the doctor and in fact I don't even know my doctor's name. I'm lucky, I've never had a day's (7) .... in my life.'

'I'm very careful about what I eat – very little meat, a high daily (8) .... of fresh fruit and vegetables – and I'm careful about not (9) .... weight, so I take a moderate amount of exercise as well.'

❷ 🎧8 **Listen to the speakers and check your answers.**

❸ **Which speaker do you think has the healthiest lifestyle? Which speaker's description do you think is true for you? Why?**

Reading Part 2

❶ **Work in pairs.**

Which of these things do you think is the most important cause of bad behaviour in schools? Do you think there are any other important causes?

boring lessons badly-behaved parents neighbourhoods with social problems influence of friends diet personality stress teachers who can't control students

❷ **You will read an article about healthy diets in schools. Read it quickly to find out how the students have changed as a result of eating a healthy diet.**

❸ **Now read it again carefully, paying attention to the information before and after each gap.**

roblem school changes diet

Problems with school discipline? A healthy diet could be the solution, says Marco Visscher.

At first glance there seems nothing special about the students at Appleton Central High School in Wisconsin. They appear calm, interact comfortably with one another, are focused on their schoolwork and do not seem to misbehave.

And yet a couple of years ago, this school had a police officer patrolling its halls. Moreover, many of the students who attended the school were known to be troublemakers. **1** ____

Greg Bretthauer, who is a school counsellor, remembers when he first came to the school some years ago for a job interview. **2** ____ As a result, he felt no desire to work with them and when he was offered the job, he turned it down.

Several years later however, Bretthauer changed his mind and accepted the job after seeing that the atmosphere at the school had changed profoundly. **3** ____ Fights and offensive behaviour are extremely rare and the police officer is no longer needed.

What happened? A glance through the halls at Appleton Central High School provides the answer. The first change was getting rid of the vending machines which used to sell a selection of soft drinks and colas. They were replaced by water dispensers. **4** ____

The School Director LuAnn Coenen is still surprised when she speaks of the 'astonishing' changes that have occurred at the school since she took these drastic decisions eight years ago. In a school whose reputation was for violence there is no longer any vandalism, students do not drop litter and the teachers no longer fear attacks in the classrooms. **5** ____

The brain is a highly active organ. While it only accounts for two per cent of our body weight, it uses a massive 20 per cent of our energy. In order to generate that energy, we need a broad range of nutrients that we get from balanced and varied meals. The question is: does eating junk food really have such an extreme effect on people's behaviour? **6** ____

'Fast food' has become a term that covers all sorts of frozen meals, microwaved food and food which can only be described as junk food. The ingredients of the average meal have been transported thousands of kilometres before landing on our plates, so it's not hard to believe that some nutritional quality is lost in the process.

Do examples like the high school in Wisconsin point to a direct connection between nutrition and behaviour? **7** ____

He has proven that reducing the sugar and fat intake in our daily diets leads to higher IQs and better grades in school. When he supervised a change in meals served at 803 schools in low-income neighbourhoods in New York City, the number of students that passed final exams rose from 11 per cent below the national average to five per cent above. A study of one of the schools where these changes were made showed that the number of instances of bad behaviour fell by 37 per cent when vending machines were removed and canned food in the cafeteria was replaced by fresh alternatives.

Adapted from *ODE Magazine*

4 Seven sentences have been removed from the article. Read each sentence carefully and underline words and phrases which might connect with something in the article.

A Although she expresses amazement, the idea that food can affect the way our brains work and thus our behaviour is not so radical.

B It is certainly true that our eating habits have dramatically changed over the past 30 years.

C Stephen Schoenthaler, a law professor at California State University, has been researching exactly this relationship for more than 20 years.

D The next step was to take hamburgers and chips off the menu in the school restaurant, making room for fresh vegetables and fruits, wholegrain bread and a salad bar.

E It soon became evident that little academic work was possible in this school.

F They caused frequent problems including attacks on teachers and some of them even carried weapons.

G Today he describes the students as calm and well-behaved.

H While he was there, the students he met were rude, unpleasant and badly behaved.

5 **Choose from the sentences A–H the one which fits each gap (1–7). There is one extra sentence which you do not need to use.**

Exam advice

- Read the text looking carefully at the information before and after each gap.
- Read the sentences which have been removed looking for words and phrases which connect with information in the text.
- When you have finished, remember to read the text again to check your answers.

6 **Work in small groups.**

- Do you agree that diet affects the way we behave?
- What else can schools do to make sure that students behave well? Which things are most effective?

Vocabulary

Parts of the body

1 **Label the illustration using the words in the box.**

back	chest	chin	elbow	~~forehead~~	heel
hip	knee	neck	shoulder	thigh	wrist

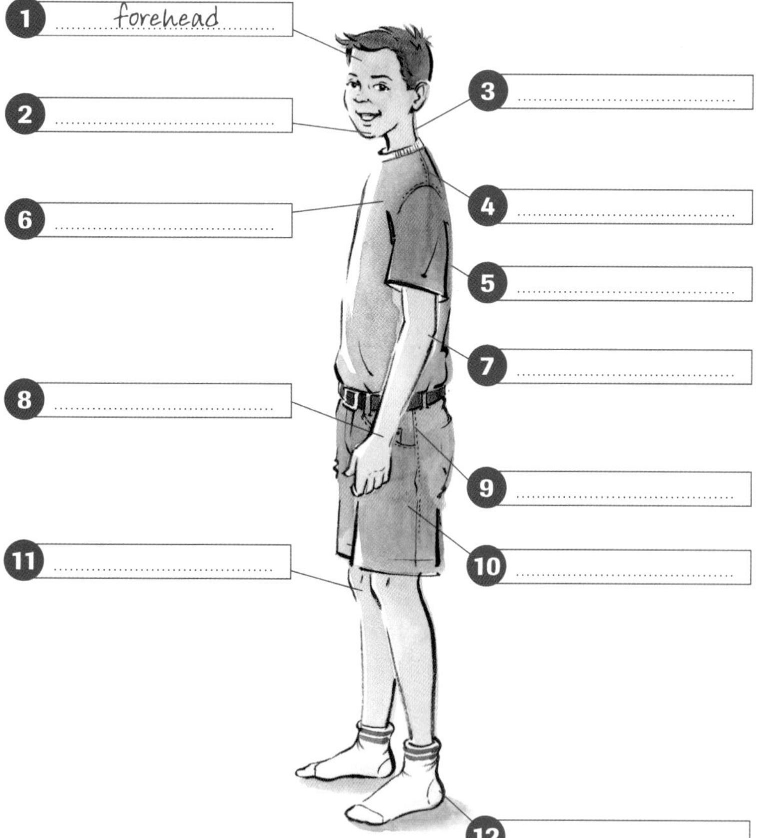

2 **Work in pairs. Make a list of five other parts of the body which you think other students may not know. Read your list to another pair of students and ask them to label the picture with your words.**

Grammar

Relative pronouns and relative clauses

1 **Complete these sentences from Reading Part 2 by writing one word in each gap. In some sentences more than one answer is possible.**

1. Greg Bretthauer, ...*who*.... is a school counsellor, remembers when he first came to the school some years ago for a job interview.
2. Many of the students .... attended the school were known to be troublemakers.
3. The first change was getting rid of the vending machines .... used to sell a selection of soft drinks and colas.
4. In a school .... reputation was for violence there is no longer any vandalism.
5. A study of one of the schools .... these changes were made showed that the number of instances of bad behaviour fell by 37 per cent.

page 163 *Grammar reference: Relative pronouns and relative clauses*

2 **Read the sentences below. Which contain defining relative clauses and which contain non-defining relative clauses? Write *defining* or *non-defining* after each.**

1. The village where I go for my holidays has a very healthy climate. ....*defining*....
2. Mrs Altmeyer, who you met on the train, is a nurse. ....
3. The children who you've been talking to all go to the same school. ....
4. Have you still got the book which I lent you? ....
5. My physical education teacher, who was an Olympic champion, says that exercise is essential for good health. ....
6. Students who eat a good breakfast often do better at school. ....

3 **In which of sentences 1–6 above could you use *that* instead of *which* or *who*?**

4 **In which sentences could you omit *who* or *which*?**

5 First Certificate candidates often make mistakes with relative pronouns. Each of the following sentences contains one wrong word or one extra word. Correct the mistakes.

1 Judy goes to the swimming club ~~it's~~ near the central station. *which is*
2 Frank has a brother his wife is in hospital with a broken leg.
3 She's a student of yoga, that is done by thousands of people in this country.
4 Can I read that essay which you wrote it last week?
5 Mandy supports the football team which it won the league last year.
6 I'm afraid I can't understand that you are saying.
7 Aziz lives in a large house which it has a view of the sea.
8 Gaby's friends, who you met them this morning, are going to the beach this afternoon if you want to come.

6 Join these sentences using a relative clause.

1 Did you see the film? They broadcast it on television last night.
Did you see the film which they broadcast on television last night? or
Did you see the film they broadcast on television last night?
2 He studied hard for his maths exam. He found it quite easy.
3 The man is a taxi driver. They sold the car to him.
4 Could you give me the newspaper? You were reading it earlier.
5 That white house over there is the house. He was born there.
6 Where's the envelope? I put the money in it.
7 Every morning I go running in the park with Patricia. You know her brother.
8 Karen and Teresa are on holiday in the Caribbean at the moment. We're looking after their dog.

Listening Part 3

1 Work in pairs. You will hear five people talking about a visit to their family doctors. Before you listen, match the words and phrases on the left with their definitions from the *Cambridge Advanced Learner's Dictionary*.

1 check-up
2 diagnose
3 examination
4 infection
5 prescription
6 sick note
7 treat
8 vaccination

a disease caused by bacteria or a virus
b injection to prevent someone getting a disease
c medical examination to test your general state of health
d piece of paper on which a doctor writes that a patient is ill and has permission not to go to work
e piece of paper on which a doctor writes the details of the medicine or drugs that someone needs
f recognise and name the exact character of a disease or a problem, by making an examination
g use drugs, exercises, etc. to cure a person of a disease or heal an injury
h when a doctor looks at a patient carefully in order to discover the problem

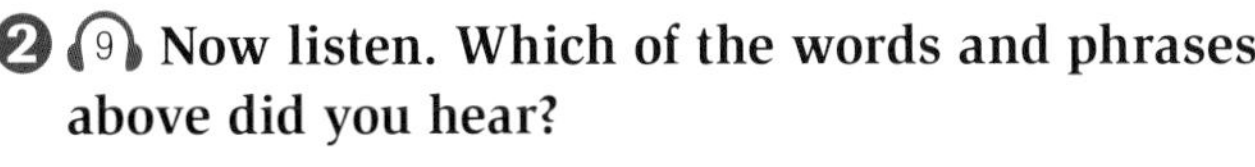

2 Now listen. Which of the words and phrases above did you hear?

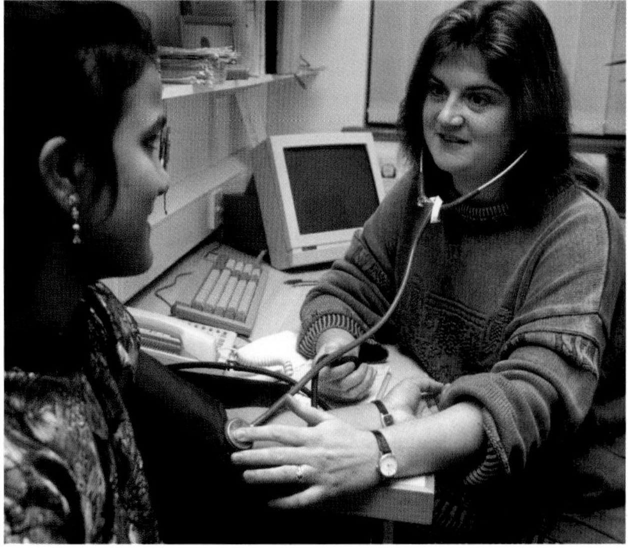

3 (9) **Listen again. For questions 1–5, choose from the list (A–F) what each speaker says about their visit. Use the letters only once. There is one extra letter which you do not need to use.**

A I wasn't given enough attention by the doctor at first.
B I was told by the doctor that I needed to relax.
C I was surprised by what the doctor said.
D I liked the way the doctor talked to me.
E I asked for a specialist to deal with my problem.
F I agreed with the doctor's diagnosis.

Speaker 1	☐	**Speaker 4**	☐
Speaker 2	☐	**Speaker 5**	☐
Speaker 3	☐		

Exam advice

- Don't answer each question until the speaker has finished speaking.
- You may need to get a general idea of what the speaker is saying, not just specific details.

Use of English Part 3

1 **Read this sentence from Reading Part 2 and choose the best answer to the question below:**

... the students at Appleton Central High School ... do not seem to misbehave.

1 What does *misbehave* mean?
 a behave badly or wrongly
 b behave differently

Now read these sentences and answer the questions below.

Please do not unfasten your seatbelt until the aircraft has come to a complete stop.

2 What does *unfasten* mean?
 a fasten something wrongly
 b release or open something which was fastened

You should disconnect the apparatus before trying to repair it, or you'll get an electric shock.

3 What does *disconnect* mean?
 a break the connection with the supply of electricity
 b connect something wrongly

4 Which prefix, *mis-*, *un-* or *dis-* has a different meaning from the other two?

2 **Complete these sentences using the negative form of the verb given in capitals. Remember to use the correct form of the verb.**

1 Could you help me ....*undo*........ the button on the back of my dress? DO
2 I know the news will .... you, but we are unable to offer you the job. APPOINT
3 If you .... the equipment it will probably break. USE
4 The knot was so tight that he couldn't .... it. TIE
5 Accommodation is a word which many students .... SPELL
6 I can't find my keys anywhere. They seem to have just .... ! APPEAR
7 This isn't a complete check-up, so you needn't .... – just take off your shirt. DRESS
8 I'm afraid you must have been .... ; there's no concert here tonight. INFORM

3 **Add a prefix *un-*, *dis-*, *in-*, *im-* or *mis-* to form opposites of these words (in some cases more than one answer is possible).**

expected *unexpected*		understood	satisfied	
respect	pronounce	pleased	obey	likely
interpret	healthy	happy	possible	capable
correct	aware	appoint	agree	complete
able	patient			

4 **For questions 1–10, read the text on page 111. Use the word given in capitals at the end of some of the lines to form a word that fits in the gap in the same line.**

Before you decide which word, decide what type of word you need (adjective, noun, etc.), whether you need a negative form, a plural form or the correct form of a verb.

Exam advice

- Check whether you need a singular or plural noun.
- Make sure you put verbs in the correct form.
- Be careful to spell your answers correctly. Remember:
  - there are many words which end in 'ght': *fight*, *night*, etc.
  - 'i' comes before 'e' except after 'c', e.g. *achieve*, *relief* but *receive*, *receipt*
  - be careful about double letters, e.g. *disapprove*, *disappointment*, *misspell*, etc. – check by looking at the spelling of the word given.

Is there a doctor on board?

You're on a plane in mid-air. You've just (0) ..*undone*.. your seatbelt and relaxed	DO
when you hear an (1) .... from one of the cabin crew: 'Is there a doctor on board?'	ANNOUNCE
As we all know, air travel can be an extremely (2) .... experience, especially after queuing in the airport and going through airport	STRESS
(3) .... checks. Studies of airline passengers reveal that we all	SECURE
(4) .... worry that we or another passenger may have an	OCCASION
(5) .... health problem far	EXPECT
from a hospital at a (6) .... of 10,000 metres. Well, now Lufthansa, the German airline, has calculated that	HIGH
on 80% of its (7) .... there is in fact a doctor amongst the passengers. Having previously obtained the doctor's	FLY
(8) ...., when there's a medical emergency on board one of the cabin staff will discreetly ask for his or her	AGREE
(9) .... It is hoped that in the future this system will avoid causing	ASSIST
(10) .... nervousness among the other passengers when these situations arise.	NECESSARY

Speaking Part 4

1 Work in pairs. Read the questions below and think of three things you can say to answer each of the questions.

a How important is a healthy diet?
b What advice would you give to young people to stay fit and healthy?
c Do schools in your country teach young people about keeping healthy? Do you think they should?
d Do you think people in general look after their health enough?
e Should people go to their doctors regularly for check-ups? Why (not)?
f If you could change one thing in your lifestyle to make it healthier, what would you change? Why?
g Do you agree that taking regular exercise helps people to do better work? Why (not)?

2 (10) Listen to four candidates answering questions in Speaking Part 4. Which question does each candidate answer? Write a letter a–g in each box. You will not need to use all the letters.

Candidate 1 ☐
Candidate 2 ☐
Candidate 3 ☐
Candidate 4 ☐

3 (10) Listen again and note down each candidate's ideas.

4 Change partners. Take turns to ask and answer the questions above with your own opinions and ideas.

Exam advice

- Think of a number of different things you can say to answer each question.
- Look confidently at the examiner while you are speaking.
- If your partner has been asked the same question, react to what he/she has said.

Writing Part 2 An essay

1 Work in small groups. Discuss your opinions about this question:

Do you think modern lifestyles are healthy or not?

During your discussion, you can talk about:

- the environment and health
- diet
- work activities
- information, e.g. about exercise, smoking
- free-time activities.

When you have finished, change groups and report what your group decided.

2 Read the writing task and the answer below (without paying attention to the gaps). Which of the ideas that arose in your discussion are mentioned in the answer?

You have had a class discussion on whether modern lifestyles are healthy or not. Now, your teacher has asked you to write an essay giving your opinions on the following statement:

Modern lifestyles can seriously endanger our health.

Write your **essay.**

3 Complete the essay by writing one word in each space.

4 Answer the following questions.

1 Which paragraph gives reasons why lifestyles often aren't very healthy?
2 Which paragraph gives reasons why lifestyles should be healthier now?
3 What is the purpose of the final paragraph?
4 Which two sentences in the essay give examples?
5 Can you find six relative clauses in the essay?

Modern lifestyles can seriously endanger our health

There's (1) .... of information available in the newspapers and on television about (2) .... is necessary for a healthy lifestyle. For instance, we know that smoking is dangerous, (3) .... is something our grandparents didn't realise. Moreover, people who live in rich countries are (4) .... to eat a healthy diet of good quality fresh food and they have access to sports facilities which allow them to take all the exercise (5) .... need.

However, in many ways (6) .... is more difficult to have a healthy lifestyle because the environment is becoming more and more polluted. What is (7) .... , we have a very sedentary way of life with less time for activities which keep us fit. For example, (8) .... work most people spend long hours sitting in front of computers, and in their free time they watch television or play computer games. In addition, people tend to eat a lot of fast food which is not very healthy.

So, although in terms of information it's easier to have a healthy lifestyle, in reality (9) .... are many things to prevent us from doing (10) ....

5 Work in small groups. Discuss whether you agree or disagree with this statement:

Young people generally don't pay enough attention to their health and fitness.

You can talk about:
- diet
- sport and exercise
- free-time activities
- smoking

6 Work in groups of three. You will hear five different people talking about their attitudes to health and fitness. Before you listen, discuss these questions.

- Which of the attitudes (A–F) do you think are most typical for young people in your country?
- Which attitudes would be unusual?

A I'd like to take more exercise than I do.
B I'll give up smoking sometime in the future.
C I'll worry about my health when I'm older.
D I'm keen to have a healthy lifestyle because of my parents.
E I'm not interested in doing sports.
F I've recently become a vegetarian.

7 (11) Now listen and choose from the list (A–F) what attitude each speaker expresses. Use the letters only once. There is one extra letter you do not need to use.

Marina ☐

Saleem ☐

Claire ☐

Paul ☐

Vicky ☐

8 Do the following writing task. Write between 120 and 180 words.

Before you write, make a plan.

When you write, you can use the essay on page 112 as a model.

You have had a class discussion on how interested young people are in health and fitness. Now, your teacher has asked you to write an essay giving your opinions on the following statement:

Young people generally don't pay enough attention to their health and fitness.

Write your **essay.**

Exam advice

A possible structure for an essay is
- Paragraph 1: Introduction saying why the subject is important
- Paragraph 2: Arguments in favour of the statement in the question
- Paragraph 3: Arguments against the statement
- Paragraph 4: Conclusion saying your opinion and the reason(s) for it.

Unit 11 *Vocabulary and grammar review*

Vocabulary

1 Complete this crossword with a word connected with money.

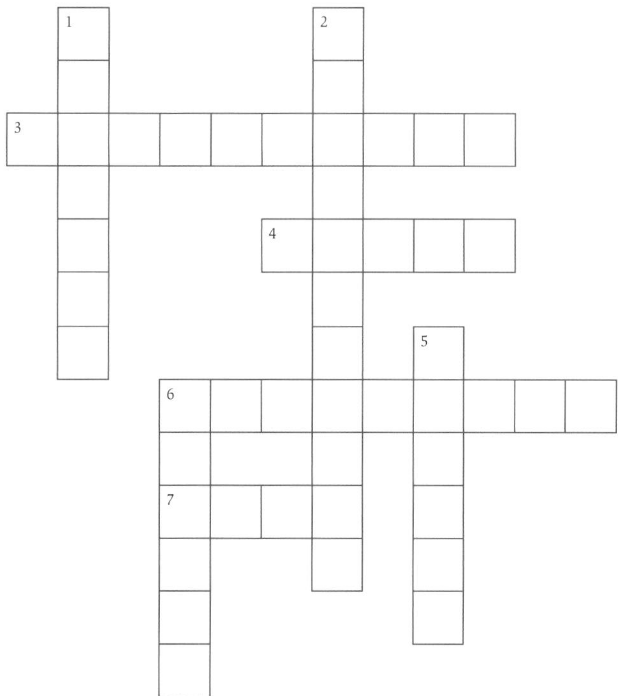

Across

3 If you haven't got the money in cash, you can always pay by .... (6, 4)

4 Life is very expensive, so it's hard to .... on such a low salary. (3, 2)

6 Piero gets an .... of 100 euros a month from his parents. (9)

7 We can take the bus if you've got the money for the .... (4)

Down

1 Prices in the market are really low, so it's quite easy to pick up a .... (7)

2 I have to do a part-time job because I don't get much .... from my parents. (6, 5)

5 I've been .... money all winter so I have enough for my summer holidays. (6)

6 I've spent all my money, so I can't .... to go to the cinema this weekend. (6)

Grammar

2 Use *can, can't, could, couldn't, be able to / not be able to* or *(not) manage to* in each of the following sentences. Sometimes more than one answer is possible.

1 I'm sorry I wasn't able to / couldn't / didn't manage to do any homework last weekend, but my mother was ill.

2 When we got to the top of the mountain we .... see for more than 50 kilometres.

3 I .... persuade my mum to get me the shoes, but only after she'd seen how cheap they were.

4 At the age of 7, Reggie .... already speak five languages fluently.

5 I'm going to classes because I would like to .... play the violin.

6 Dario must be very busy, because I have .... speak to him for several days.

7 Unfortunately for the police, the thief .... escape across the river by stealing a boat.

8 Silvie was quite an advanced child and she .... read before she even went to school.

3 Write *as* or *like* in each of the spaces below.

When my grandfather left school at the age of 14, he got his first job (1) as an office assistant in London. In those days he was extremely thin (2) .... he wasn't paid very much and couldn't afford to eat a lot. But he was in the same situation (3) .... a lot of boys at that time (4) .... most children left school at that age and had to look for a job. I have one or two photos of him from that time and he looks just (5) .... me, but thinner! When he grew older, he worked at all sorts of things, such (6) .... reporting for a local newspaper and working (7) .... a part-time mechanic. (8) .... many people of his generation, he worked hard all his life, but he always found time for the things he enjoyed, (9) .... walking in the country or spending time with his grandchildren. I hope I'll be (10) .... him when I'm an old man!

Unit 12 *Vocabulary and grammar review*

Vocabulary

1 Complete sentences 1–10 with a word from the box in the correct form.

check-up cure ~~diagnose~~ fit get over heal infection prescription put on treatment

1 After a brief examination, my doctor ...diagnosed... that I was suffering from a slight infection.
2 As long as you keep the cut clean, it should .... on its own quite soon.
3 Farouk has been having .... in hospital following an accident he had last month.
4 She's spent the last two or three days in bed because of a minor .... she picked up at school.
5 I have to be quite careful what I eat so that I don't .... too much weight.
6 It's a good idea to keep .... by taking regular exercise – at least 40 minutes a day.
7 Rana's doctor has given her a .... for antibiotics to treat her illness.
8 Take this medicine. It should .... you in a couple of days.
9 You may not be very ill, but it's still worth going to the doctor for a .... to make sure it's nothing serious.
10 It took her several weeks to .... her illness and she missed a lot of classes in that time.

Word formation

2 Complete each of the following sentences by using the word given in capitals at the end of the sentences to form a word that fits in the gap.

1 I'm sorry about the mistake. I'm afraid I ...misunderstood... your instructions. UNDERSTAND
2 If you .... me again I'll stop giving you pocket money for a week! OBEY
3 I felt very .... with the food at that restaurant and I'm thinking of complaining. SATISFY
4 I'm afraid that most of your answers were .... and you only got three right. CORRECT
5 I thought the film was rather .... after the good reviews it had in the newspapers. APPOINT
6 I think we could go for a walk this afternoon as it looks .... to rain. LIKELY
7 She was so shocked by the news that she was .... of speaking for some time. CAPABLE
8 When your children .... , do you punish them? BEHAVE
9 If it's too hot, you can .... one or two buttons on your shirt. DO
10 I looked in all the shops but I was .... to find a jersey I liked. ABLE

Grammar

3 Write a relative pronoun (*who, whose, which, that, what, why, when, where*) in each of the spaces below. If you think no relative pronoun is necessary, write – in the space. In some cases more than one answer is possible.

1 Is he the man ...who / that... was driving the car?
2 The girl ...who / that / –... you spoke to this morning has just phoned again.
3 I'm sorry but there never seems to be a time .... I'm not busy these days.
4 Look! That's the shop .... I bought the chocolates.
5 I'm afraid the hospital .... you went to doesn't have a very good reputation.
6 You remember Magda, don't you? She's that tall girl .... sister sits next to me in class.
7 I've already spent all the money .... you gave me this morning!
8 I really hate people .... interrupt me when I'm speaking!
9 In the street .... I live there are seven bus stops.
10 There's no reason .... you shouldn't get a very high mark.

4 Are the following sentences correct or incorrect? Correct any mistakes by adding, replacing or removing one word only. If you think a sentence is correct, write *correct* next to the sentence.

1 I think ~~that~~ you did was very clever. what
2 Mum! The man his car you scratched is at the front door!
3 The shirt that I want to wear tomorrow is dirty.
4 I haven't met anyone liked the film.
5 Mike Smith, that taught you last year, is going to be your teacher again this year.
6 I really like the car you're driving!
7 I'm sorry! I shouldn't have said that I said.
8 The girl her bike I borrowed is really angry with me.

Unit 13 Animal kingdom

Starting off

1 Work in pairs. Which of the animals in the photos are …?

- wild animals
- working animals
- pets

2 Which of the animals in the photos …?

- provide us with company
- entertain us
- provide us with food
- participate in a sport
- are used for transport
- help us in other ways

3 Imagine you are planning an article for your college magazine on the importance of animals in our lives. First discuss what role each animal in the photos plays in our lives and how these roles benefit people. Then decide which two photos would be best for the magazine article.

Listening Part 1

1 Work in pairs. Before you listen, answer the questions in the Exam round-up box.

Exam round-up

How much do you remember about Listening Part 1? Circle the correct alternative in *italics* in each of these sentences. In Listening Part 1:

1 you hear *six* / *eight* extracts
2 the extracts are on *the same subject* / *different subjects*
3 you hear each extract *once* / *twice*
4 you *read and hear* / *read but don't hear* the question before the extract.

2 (12) You will hear people talking in eight different situations. For questions 1–8, choose the best answer (A, B or C). As you hear the question, underline the main idea.

1 You overhear a woman talking about different animals. Which animal would she let her family have?
  A a cat
  B a dog
  C a horse
2 You hear part of a television programme about zebras. What does the presenter say about their appearance?
  A All members of a family of zebras have the same stripes.
  B Zebras can recognise each other by their stripes.
  C Male and female zebras have similar stripes.
3 You overhear a woman talking about the birds which come to her garden. How does she feel about them?
  A She enjoys watching them.
  B She finds them annoying.
  C She worries about them.
4 You overhear part of a conversation in which two men are talking about dogs. What do they say about them?
  A They are good company.
  B They are good at protecting property.
  C They shouldn't live in cities.
5 You hear a woman giving part of a lecture about animal rights. What does she say about zoos?
  A They are no longer necessary in modern times.
  B They should be closely supervised.
  C They should only be for endangered species.
6 You hear a young woman talking about some animals she worked with. How did she feel when she was with them?
  A frightened
  B relaxed
  C strange
7 You hear part of a radio programme in which a man talks about how he was attacked by a hippopotamus. What does he say about hippos?
  A They are one of the most dangerous animals in Africa.
  B They often attack people for no reason.
  C They're usually very timid animals.
8 You hear a woman talking to her husband. Why is she talking to him?
  A to make a suggestion
  B to make a complaint
  C to remind him of something

Vocabulary

Named and *called*

1 First Certificate candidates often confuse *named* and *called*. Which words were used in extract 8 in Listening Part 1? Choose the correct alternative.

Man: What's the circus *called* / *named* by the way?

Woman: Let's see … here it is. It's *called* / *named* Giffords Circus.

2 Read these extracts from the *Cambridge Advanced Learner's Dictionary* and answer the questions which follow.

> **call** *verb* [+ object + noun] to give someone or something a name, or to know or address someone by a particular name: *They've called the twins Katherine and Thomas. His real name is Jonathan, but they've always called him 'Johnny'. What's her new novel called?*
>
> **name** *verb* [T] to give someone or something a name: [+ two objects] *We named our dogs 'Shandy' and 'Belle'.*

1 Which verb(s) can you use to mean to give someone or something a name for the first time and only the first time: *call* or *name*, or both *call* and *name*?
2 Which verb(s) can you use when you mention someone or something for the first time, but you haven't given it a name for the first time: *call* or *name*, or both *call* and *name*?
3 Which verb(s) can you use to mean that it is someone's or something's name: *call* or *name*, or both *call* and *name*?

3 Correct the mistakes made in the following sentences by First Certificate candidates. Some sentences are correct. If you think a sentence is correct, write *correct*.

1 People who look after animals in zoos are ~~named~~ zoo keepers. *called*
2 We went to a bookshop in Oxford Street named Waterstones.
3 We named our children Kasper and Andrea.
4 You can get here by taking a bus with a company named ABC Coaches.

Grammar
Third conditional

1 Look at this sentence from Listening Part 1 (extract 7) and answer the questions below.

If I hadn't reacted quickly, the hippo would have killed me.

Are these statements true or false?

1 The speaker reacted quickly.
2 The hippo killed him.
3 The speaker is talking about the past.

2 Now look at these sentences (one is from extract 8) and answer the questions below.

a *I think if they'd had more acrobats, we'd have enjoyed the circus more.*
b *I think if they had more acrobats we'd enjoy the circus more.*

Which sentence (a or b) ...?

1 means: *They don't have enough acrobats, so we don't enjoy the circus very much.* ....
2 means: *They didn't have enough acrobats, so we didn't enjoy the circus very much.* ....
3 has this form: *if* + past simple, *would* + infinitive ....
4 has this form: *if* + past perfect, *would have* (*been/done/enjoyed*, etc.) ....
5 is second conditional (see Unit 5 page 46) ....
6 is third conditional ....
7 has the same form as *If I hadn't reacted quickly, the hippo would have killed me* in Exercise 1. ....

page 163 *Grammar reference: Third conditional*

3 Complete each of the following sentences by putting the verb in brackets into the correct tense.

1 If Martin had concentrated on his work, he .....*would have finished*..... (finish) it earlier.
2 If my mother had let me when I was a child, I .... (have) a pet dog.
3 If Don hadn't been wearing thick boots, the snake .... (bite) him.
4 If the shops .... (be) open, I could have bought you some bread.
5 We would have gone swimming if the weather .... (not be) so cold.
6 If John .... (pay) attention, he wouldn't have had the accident.
7 Sorry! I .... (not make) so much noise if I'd known you were asleep.
8 If the dog hadn't barked, we .... (not hear) the burglar downstairs.

4 Work in pairs. Answer these questions in any way you like.

- What would have happened if you'd got up an hour later this morning?
- Where was the last place you went on holiday? What would you have done if you hadn't gone on holiday there?
- What was the last exam you passed? What would have happened if you'd failed the exam?

Reading Part 3

1 Work in small groups.

- Name the animals in the photos. Which do you think is the most dangerous, and which the least?
- What should you do if one of these animals tries to attack you?
- Are there any dangerous wild animals in your country?

2 You are going to read a newspaper article about people who have been attacked by animals. Before you read the article, read the questions carefully and decide which questions refer to something which happened:

a before the attack
b at the same time as the attack
c after the attack.

Write **a**, **b** or **c** in the boxes provided. (For some questions more than one answer is possible.)

Which person

1 didn't immediately realise he'd been attacked? ☐
2 was photographed during the attack? ☐
3 made a noise to frighten the animal? ☐
4 thought he would be attacked again? ☐
5 was attacked while at work? ☐
6 was put in danger by someone he was with? ☐
7 was searching for something when he was attacked? ☐
8 was considered to have missed an opportunity? ☐
9 was sorry he wasn't injured? ☐
10 was warned by a companion? ☐
11 was happy at first to see the animal which later attacked him? ☐
12 was prevented from escaping by a piece of equipment? ☐
13 was returning when he was attacked? ☐
14 was seriously injured by the attack? ☐
15 didn't visit a doctor despite his injury? ☐

3 Now read the article and for questions 1–15, choose from the people (A–E). The people may be chosen more than once.

Surviving an animal attack

No matter how well prepared you are as a traveller, animals can still attack you. Our advice? Keep your distance!

A Colin Bristow

I was working as a safari guide in Botswana with four American clients. There was a sudden movement to my left and a charging elephant crashed through some small trees less than 20 feet away. I turned to face it and was immediately knocked over by one of the clients, who was screaming 'run, run' at the top of his voice. I landed on my back between the exposed roots of a large acacia tree. My backpack tangled with one of the roots so that I couldn't move. The elephant was kneeling over me and his thick trunk was smashing into the roots on either side of my body. I managed to free myself from my backpack. A very loud single enraged trumpet pierced the silence as I ran flat out to safety.

B Craig Bovim

I was attacked by a great white shark while snorkelling off Scarborough beach, south of Cape Town. I was about 80 metres out and had started swimming for shore when I saw it coming towards me at speed. Before I knew it, this huge mouth had taken both my arms with a crunching sound, and then its body hit me. It was the thought of dying without saying goodbye to my children that made me fight back.

I got my hands free and I knew that unless I got back to the beach quickly, I'd die. I was expecting the shark to come back for me at any moment, but somehow I made it. I'd lost a lot of blood by the time I got ashore.

C Chris Haslam

I was camping on a beach in Mexico. It was sunset and I was walking along the coast looking for firewood. Then I noticed a dead cactus which was perfect for the fire. I bent to lift it and felt the slightest prick against my middle finger, which I thought I'd brushed against a cactus spine. It was a scorpion. The pain was intense and sudden. By the time I arrived back at camp, my lips were numb and I was shaking. In the absence of qualified medical opinion, my companions carried on with their game of cards.

The next morning, I showed the sting to a local.

'Did you play cards with the other gringos last night?'

'Course not,' I replied. 'I was too ill.'

He raised his eyebrows. 'Too bad. Scorpion stings are very lucky, muchacho.'

D Baz Roberts

On our penultimate night on the ice, I was just falling asleep at about 11.30 pm when Paul's voice woke me: 'Guys, there's a bear in the camp. I'm serious!' I leant forward on my knees to unzip the tent door. Directly in front was a polar bear about ten metres away. It heard the sound of my tent zip and turned to face me, all 600 kilos or so of him.

I started screaming and waving my arms. When he got about one metre away, we grabbed pots and pans and threw them at him. I threw a large jar of coffee powder into the bear's face. If he hadn't turned and walked off at that moment, we wouldn't have survived.

E Zebedee Ellis (aged six)

I was at a zoo and dinosaur park with mummy and daddy two years ago. I had eaten about 400 tons of ice cream and now I wanted to see more animals. In a large open area next to a pond, daddy saw some big fat pelicans, all full of fish. 'There you are!' he said. 'Some animals for you to annoy.'

I was very pleased and danced up and down in front of them. The pelican was very big close up and looked at me for a long time. Then he tried to eat my T-shirt. It didn't really hurt and daddy got this great picture while mummy and another daddy had to rescue me. I wish it had made some kind of scratch on my skin to show my friends.

Adapted from *The Sunday Times*

4 **Work in small groups.**

Which incident do you think was ... ?

- the most dangerous
- the most frightening
- the least dangerous

Use of English Part 1

1 **Work in pairs. You will read a short article by someone who worked in a circus. Before you read, discuss these questions.**

- Do you enjoy circuses? Why (not)?
- What things do you enjoy most (or least) when you go to the circus?

2 **Before doing Use of English Part 1, answer the questions in the Exam round-up box.**

Exam round-up

How much do you remember about Use of English Part 1? Complete the following information with the words and phrases in *italics*.

12   after   all the questions   the text quickly
you have finished   15   the alternatives

1. There are .... questions in this part. You must choose A, B, C or D.
2. You should spend about .... minutes doing it.
3. Read .... before attempting the questions.
4. Read the words before and .... the spaces carefully.
5. Try all .... in the gaps before deciding.
6. Read the text again carefully when ....
7. Answer ....

3 **Read the article quickly without paying attention to the spaces. What animals do Nell and Toti have in their circus?**

My sister's circus

My sister and brother-in-law, Nell and Toti, **(0)** ..*C*... a circus. It is **(1)** .... Giffords Circus, and it tours some of the loveliest parts of south-west England. Circuses have always been a part of Nell's life, even when we were children. When she **(2)** .... Toti, she had already worked in **(3)** .... circuses in Britain and Europe. She had ridden elephants and worked as a ring mistress, but what she really **(4)** .... for was a circus of her **(5)** ....

If the word 'circus' **(6)** .... you of images of clowns and lions, think again. The show is **(7)** .... on traditional travelling circuses and aimed at a rural **(8)** .... There are no wild animals, but horses play a **(9)** .... role in performances, which are a mixture of theatre, dance, traditional circus acts and clowns, all **(10)** .... by a circus band.

The circus **(11)** .... to people because it feels intimate, almost home-made. The tent seats only a few hundred people, the performers moving in a ring small enough for you to reach out and touch them.

I had visited Nell at the circus a lot, but this time I was going to **(12)** .... the summer there.

Adapted from *The Daily Telegraph*

4 **For questions 1–12, read the text again and decide which answer (A, B, C or D) best fits each gap.**

0	A belong	B keep	C own	D possess
1	A called	B known	C named	D titled
2	A found	B knew	C met	D saw
3	A few	B number	C plenty	D several
4	A desired	B longed	C wanted	D wished
5	A belonging	B own	C possession	D property
6	A recalls	B recollects	C remembers	D reminds
7	A based	B built	C put	D set
8	A spectator	B public	C crowd	D audience
9	A winning	B ruling	C leading	D main
10	A combined	B accompanied	C joined	D linked
11	A appeals	B interests	C attracts	D suggests
12	A be	B pass	C spend	D stay

5 **Work in pairs.**

- Many people think it's cruel to use animals in circuses. Do you agree?
- Do you think it's cruel to keep animals in zoos as well? Why (not)?

Grammar

Wish, if only and *hope*

1 **Read sentences a–f below and answer questions 1–8 which follow.**

a My aunt has a white cat and I wish I had one too.
b I wish the dog next door wouldn't bark, especially at night.
c I wish it had made some kind of scratch on my skin to show my friends.
d If only I was back in Italy!
e We get quite a variety of birds at this time of year. I always hope the cats don't get them.
f I hope you enjoy your holiday and have good weather!

1 In which sentences is the speaker talking about something in the present?
2 In which two sentences is the speaker saying he/she would like the present situation to be different?
3 In which sentence is the speaker complaining about an activity which is annoying?
4 What tenses are possible after *wish* and *if only* when referring to present time?
5 In which sentence is the speaker talking about something which happened in the past?
6 What tense is used after *wish* and *if only* when referring to past time?
7 In which sentences is the speaker talking about something in the future?
8 What tense is used with the verb after *hope* when we talk about the future?

page 164 *Grammar reference:* Wish, if only *and* hope

2 **First Certificate candidates often use *wish* when they should use *hope*. Read the following sentences and decide when *wish* is used correctly and when you should use *hope*. If you think a sentence is correct, write *correct*.**

1 It was lovely seeing you and I ~~wish~~ to see you again very soon in my house. *hope*
2 Going to the theme park together was great and I wish you enjoyed the experience.
3 I wish I'd visited you last summer when I had the chance.
4 I'm looking forward to having news from you soon and I wish you have a good time in New York.
5 My neighbour's children are always shouting; I wish they wouldn't be so noisy.
6 The performance was really good but I wish more people will come next time.
7 I don't get many letters from you and I wish you'd write to me more often.
8 We wish you enjoy your stay at our hotel while you're here in Tokyo.

3 **For questions 1–5, complete the second sentence so that it has a similar meaning to the first sentence, using the word given. Do not change the word given. You must use between two and five words, including the word given.**

1 It's a pity I can't cook well.
BETTER
I wish I ....was a better.......... cook.

2 I regret not studying harder when I was at school.
STUDIED
If only .... when I was at school.

3 I want the neighbours to stop making so much noise.
MAKE
I wish the neighbours ....
.... noise.

4 What a pity that they cancelled the match!
NOT
If only they .... the match.

5 I'm sorry you didn't meet my brother.
WISH
I .... my brother.

Speaking Part 1

1 **Before doing Speaking Part 1, answer the questions in the Exam round-up box.**

Exam round-up

How much do you remember about Speaking Part 1? Circle the correct alternative in *italics* in each of these sentences. In Speaking Part 1:

1 you are asked questions about *yourself, your life and your interests / your opinions*
2 you should *answer very briefly / answer giving reasons and examples if possible*
3 this part takes *about three minutes / just one minute.*

2 **Work in pairs. Here are some questions like the ones you may be asked in Speaking Part 1. Discuss your answers to each of them.**

- Do you have any pets or animals at home?
- Do you enjoy visiting zoos? Why (not)?
- Do you enjoy watching programmes about animals on television?

3 (13) **Listen to three students answering these questions and write a, b or c in the boxes.**

Who …
a gives a reason for his/her answer?
b adds extra information?
c offers an opinion?

Student 1	☐	☐
Student 2	☐	☐
Student 3	☐	☐

4 **Change partners and take turns to ask each other these questions.**

- Do you live in the city or the country?
- What do you like about the area where you live?
- What things are there for people to do in their free time in your area?
- Do you enjoy doing things outside in the open air?

Writing Part 2 A letter

1 **Before doing Writing Part 2, answer the questions in the Exam round-up box.**

Exam round-up

How much do you remember about Writing Part 2? Circle the correct alternative in *italics* in each of these sentences.

1 You must choose to do ONE writing task from a choice of *two / four.*
2 You must write between *100–150 words / 120–180 words.*
3 Possible tasks are *a letter, a review, a report, a story / a letter, a review, a report, a story, an essay or an article.*
4 You have *about 40 minutes for this part / about one hour for this part.*

2 **Work in pairs. Read the following exam task and discuss the questions which follow.**

A British friend, Valerie, has written to you for some advice. This is part of the letter you have received.

> I'm thinking of visiting your country this summer. I'd be interested in seeing some of the most beautiful countryside and scenery. Also, if possible, I'd like to see some of the wildlife. Can you advise me on where to go, what to see and the best way of getting around to see these things?
>
> Best wishes,
>
> Valerie

Write your **letter**. Do not write any postal addresses.

1 What three things must you deal with in your letter?
2 What advice would you give Valerie about your country?
3 What style would you use: formal or informal? Why?

3 **Read Manolo's reply to Valerie's letter and answer these questions.**

1 How does he make a reference to Valerie's letter?
2 Has he answered all three things from the question? What advice did he give about each?
3 Does Manolo give reasons for his advice?
4 What style does he use: formal or informal?

4 **Find and underline these ways of giving advice in Manolo's letter.**

1 *I'd advise you* + infinitive
2 *You should* + infinitive (without *to*)
3 *If I were you, I'd / I would* …
4 *The best idea would be* + infinitive
5 *Make sure that* …

5 **Write five similar sentences using each of the five phrases above once to give advice to Valerie for visiting your country.**

6 **Write your own answer to the question. Use Manolo's letter as a model. Write between 120 and 180 words.**

Dear Valerie,

I'm very glad to hear that you're thinking of visiting my country this summer. You can see beautiful countryside and scenery in many parts of the country, although it varies a lot, depending on the region.

If you want somewhere that's not usually too hot in summer, I'd advise you to go to Asturias, in the north of Spain. It's a region which has some fantastic mountains as well as green countryside and beautiful rivers. You should visit the 'Picos de Europa', which are really spectacular mountains and canyons. All the paths are clearly marked, which makes walking quite safe, and you're sure to see a lot of wildlife while you're there. You may even see bears and wolves if you're lucky!

If I were you, I'd hire a car to get around. The best idea would be to hire it online before you leave home. Make sure that you take warm clothes and a raincoat as we can have heavy rain, even in summer.

I hope you enjoy your holiday and have good weather!

Best wishes,

Manolo

Unit 14 House space

Starting off

1 Work in pairs. Match each of these types of place to live with thc photos.

- a a castle
- b a country cottage
- c a block of flats with several storeys
- d a townhouse
- e a housing estate
- f a houseboat

2 Discuss which of these things you think are important when choosing where to live and which are not so important.

- a quiet neighbourhood
- a good view
- shops within walking distance
- a garden
- space for parking
- public parks or gardens
- good public transport
- a good local school

3 What other things would you consider when choosing somewhere to live?

4 The photos show different places to live. Why might people choose to live in each of these places?

5 Work in small groups. Imagine you are going to live together for a year. Decide which type of place shown in the photos would be best for all of you.

Reading Part 1

1 Work in pairs. You are going to read an extract from a historical novel about a house in Venice. Before you read, look at the painting. Do you think you would have enjoyed life in 18th-century Venice? Why (not)?

2 Before doing Reading Part 1, answer the questions in the Exam round-up box.

Exam round-up

How much do you remember about Reading Part 1? Circle the correct alternative in each of these sentences. In Reading Part 1:

1. There are *six / eight* questions; you must choose the best alternative A, B, C or D.
2. You have about *20 / 30* minutes for this part.
3. You should read *the text quickly before reading the questions / the questions quickly before reading the text.*
4. You should read the alternatives *before / after* reading the section of text where a question is answered.
5. There *must / needn't* be words in the text which support the alternative you've chosen.

3 Read the text quite quickly to find out why the writer thinks the house is in a good location.

My new home in Venice, 1733

Uncle Leo gives me a suspicious look when I call this place the 'Scacchi Palace'. It is really a house, called Ca' Scacchi in Venetian. Anywhere else in the world this would surely be regarded as a palace, although it is one in need of a little care and attention.

Our house is by the side of the little San Cassian canal and a small square of the same name. We have a door which leads onto the street and two entrances from the water. One runs under a grand, rounded arch into the ground floor of the house, which, as is customary in the city, is used instead of a cellar for storing things. The second is used for our commercial activities and it is situated in another building which is three storeys high, attached to the north side, towards the Grand Canal.

Finally, there is yet another exit: a wooden bridge, with handrails, runs from the first floor of the house between the two river entrances straight over the canal and into the square itself. Consequently I can wander over it in the morning and find fresh water from the well in the centre of the square while still rubbing the sleep from my eyes. Or I may call a gondola from my bedroom window, find it waiting for me by the time I get downstairs and, just one minute later, be in the middle of the greatest waterway on earth: the Grand Canal of Venice.

The house is almost 200 years old, I am told, and built of bricks of a rich dark brown colour. It has elegant arched windows and green-painted shutters to keep out the cruel summer heat. I live on the third floor in the third room on the right with a view over the canal and the square. When I lie in bed at night I can hear the chatter and songs of the passing gondoliers and the conversations in the square nearby. I understand why Uncle runs his business here. The prices are not too steep. The location of the house is near the city centre and easy for our clients to find. Furthermore, the printing trade has many roots in this area of Venice, even if some of the old publishers from the area no longer exist.

Oh sister! I long for the day when I can show you these things instead of struggling to describe them in a letter which may take a long time to reach you in Spain! Venice is like a vast imitation of our old library at home, full of dark corners and unexpected surprises, some very close to me. Last night, while searching in the jumbled corners of the warehouse cellar, I found a single copy of Aristotle's *Poetics*, published in the city in 1502. I raced to Uncle Leo with my discovery and – now here's a victory – a smile almost appeared on his face. 'A find, boy! This'll fetch good money when I sell it down in the market.'

'May I read a little first, sir?' I asked, and felt some anxiety when I made the request. Leo has a frightening manner at times.

'Books are for selling, not reading,' he replied immediately. But at least I had it for the night, since the dealers were by that time closed.

Adapted from *Lucifer's Shadow* by David Hewson

4 Now, for questions 1–8, choose the answer (A, B, C or D) which you think fits best according to the text.

1 What do we learn about the house in the first paragraph?
- **A** It has an unsuitable name.
- **B** It's an impressive building.
- **C** It's being repaired.
- **D** It used to be a palace.

2 In what way is the house typical of Venice according to the writer?
- **A** There are several ways of entering it.
- **B** People live and work in the same building.
- **C** The storage area is not below ground.
- **D** It consists of two separate buildings.

3 What does 'it' refer to in line 10?
- **A** the family business
- **B** an entrance
- **C** a floor
- **D** a building

4 What do we understand about the house from the third paragraph?
- **A** There is no supply of fresh water in the house.
- **B** The writer's bedroom is on the ground floor.
- **C** The bridge is the only way out of the house.
- **D** The house has its own gondola.

5 What does the writer say about his uncle's printing business in the fourth paragraph?
- **A** His printing business is less expensive than others.
- **B** The business has plenty of customers.
- **C** There are other similar businesses in the district.
- **D** It's the only printing business left in the district.

6 What do we understand about the writer and his sister in the fifth paragraph?
- **A** They both enjoy reading.
- **B** They both used to live in Venice.
- **C** They write to each other often.
- **D** They don't expect to see each other soon.

7 What does the incident with the book show about Uncle Leo?
- **A** He dislikes having the writer in his house.
- **B** He has a good sense of humour.
- **C** He has problems with money.
- **D** His main interest is making money.

8 Which sentence best summarises the writer's attitude to Venice throughout the text?
- **A** It's a strange and special place to live.
- **B** It's a depressing place to live.
- **C** It's a place where it's easy to get lost.
- **D** It's a place where money is the most important thing.

5 **Work in pairs. You should each speak for about one minute and take turns to describe a house which you have really enjoyed living in or visiting.**

- Before you speak, spend a few minutes planning what you are going to say.
- When your partner speaks, listen and think of one or two questions to ask at the end.

Vocabulary

Space, place, room, area, location and *square*

1 **First Certificate candidates often confuse the following words: *space, place, room, area, location* and *square*. Circle the correct alternative in *italics* in these sentences from Reading Part 1.**

1 Uncle Leo gives me a suspicious look when I call this (*place*)/ *area* the 'Scacchi Palace'.
2 When I lie in bed at night I can hear the chatter and songs of the passing gondoliers and the conversations in the *square* / *place* nearby.
3 The *place* / *location* of the house is near the city centre and easy for our clients to find.
4 Furthermore, the printing trade has many roots in this *area* / *place* of Venice.

2 **Look at these extracts from the *Cambridge Advanced Learner's Dictionary*. Then do the exercise below.**

space EMPTY PLACE *noun* [C or U] an empty area which is available to be used: *Is there any space for my clothes in that cupboard?*

place AREA *noun* [C] an area, town, building, etc.: *Her garden was a cool pleasant place to sit.* [U] a suitable area, building, situation or occasion: *University is a great place for making new friends.*

room SPACE *noun* [C or U] the amount of space that someone or something needs: *That sofa would take up too much room in the flat.*

area PLACE *noun* [C or U] a particular part of a place, piece of land or country: *All areas of the country will have some rain tonight.*

location POSITION *noun* [C or U] *SLIGHTLY FORMAL* a place or position: The hotel is in a lovely location overlooking the lake. A map showing the location of the property will be sent to you.

square SHAPE *noun* [C] an area of approximately square-shaped land in a city or a town, often including the buildings that surround it: *A band were playing in the town square.*

Circle the correct alternative in *italics* in each of the following sentences.

1 We don't have enough *area* /(*space*) in our garden to hold the party.
2 I hope I will have enough *place* / *room* for all the things I am bringing.
3 I was late because I was unable to find a parking *place* / *space* nearby.
4 I'm enclosing a map which shows the *location* / *place* of my house.
5 It's dangerous to go walking in a mountainous *area* / *place* without the correct equipment.
6 The animals in this zoo have a lot of *area* / *space* to move around.
7 The concert will take place in the main *square* / *place* in front of the cathedral.
8 The *area* / *space* of forest where they're going to build a new shopping centre is over 500 years old.
9 There isn't enough *place* / *space* to build more houses in this neighbourhood.
10 You'd be welcome to stay in my house as I have enough *room* / *place* for you.

Listening Part 2

1 **You will hear part of an interview with a writer called Jeff Bowen, who believes his house is haunted. Before you listen, work in pairs: do you think it's possible for houses to be haunted? Why (not)?**

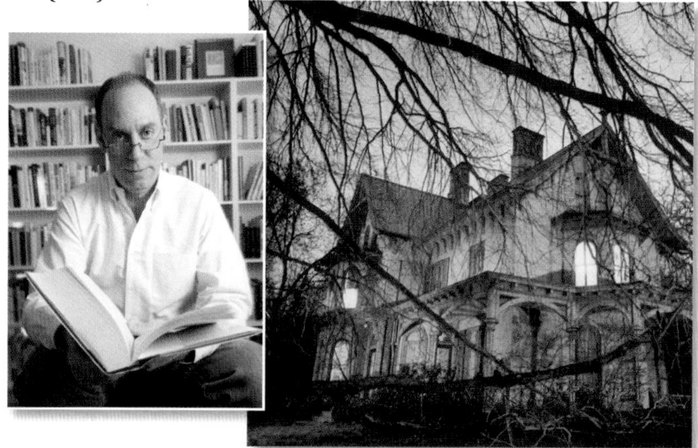

2 **Answer the questions in the Exam round-up box.**

Exam round-up

How much do you remember about Listening Part 2? Say whether the following statements are true (T) or false (F). If a statement is false, write what is correct.

1 Listening Part 2 has eight questions.
2 You will need just one or two words for each space.
3 You hear the actual words you need to write.
4 You must spell your answers correctly.
5 Before you listen, read the questions as quickly as possible.
6 When you finish, make sure your answers form grammatical sentences.

3 **Now read the sentences on page 127 and predict what type of information or what type of words you need for each space, e.g. question 1 is *probably a length of time*.**

Jeff has lived in the house for (1) ....

He thinks his house is haunted because of the (2) .... which people have had there.

His (3) .... saw medieval soldiers.

Another visitor saw furniture moving in (4) ....

When working in his study, Jeff has felt there was a person (5) .... him.

He decided to convert a (6) .... into a study.

An expert told him the house was built on the site of a (7) ....

He recently had a (8) .... installed in his garden.

One of the workers saw a man with (9) .... on his shirt.

Jeff only lives in the house (10) ....

4 (14) **For questions 1–10, listen and complete the sentences.**

5 Work in small groups.

Would you be happy to live in a house with a reputation for being haunted? Do you know of any haunted houses?

Grammar

Causative *have*

1 In Listening Part 2, Jeff describes two changes to the house. What were they? Listen again if necessary.

2 Look at the sentences below and answer the questions which follow.

a *I turned a bedroom into a study.*
b *I had a bedroom turned into a study.*

a *I was building the tennis court.*
b *I was having the tennis court built.*

1 Which sentences (a or b) did you hear in the interview?
2 Which sentences (a or b) mean …?
- I did it myself?
- I asked someone else to do it for me?

3 In the b sentences, who do you think did these things?

page 164 *Grammar reference: Causative* have

4 Complete the sentences below by writing the correct form of *have* and one of the verbs in the box in each space.

cut down	delivered	pulled out	extended
painted	~~renewed~~		

1 You'll need ......to have...... your passport ......renewed...... before you go to America next autumn.
2 She went to the dentist yesterday and .... a tooth .... , so she's not feeling too well today.
3 We're thinking of .... the house .... blue. What do you think?
4 There's a tree hanging dangerously over the house and I think we ought to .... it ....
5 Our house is too small. If we could afford it, we'd .... it ....
6 He hates cooking and .... all his meals .... from the restaurant opposite.

5 Work in small groups.

You have just bought this house to use as a holiday home. You have £3,000 for repairs and redecoration. Decide together:

- what you will do yourselves, e.g. *We can paint the house ourselves.*
- what you will pay someone else to do, e.g. *We'll have the roof repaired.*

When you have finished, compare your decisions on how you spent your money with another group.

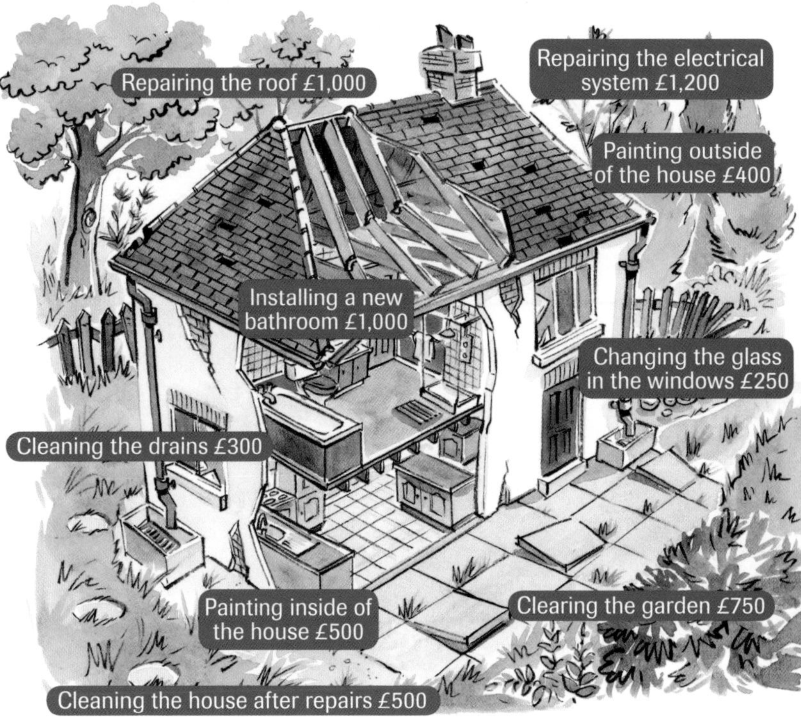

Use of English Part 2

1 Work in pairs. Look at the photo.

Would you like to live here? Why (not)?

2 Before doing Use of English Part 2, answer the questions in the Exam round-up box.

Exam round-up

How much do you remember about Use of English Part 2? Complete the following sentences with the words and phrases in *italics*.

12 before and after every question general idea grammar the completed text

1 There are .... questions in this part.
2 The words you need are .... words: articles, pronouns, auxiliary verbs, etc. and parts of expressions, e.g. *take part in*, or phrasal verbs, e.g. *make up*.
3 First read the text quickly to get a .... of what it's about.
4 Read the words .... the gaps to decide what type of word you need.
5 Answer .... with one word ONLY, making sure you have spelled it correctly.
6 Read .... when you have finished to check.

3 Read the article below quickly without paying attention to the gaps. Do you think you'd enjoy living on a houseboat?

Living on a houseboat

When the Skeens family first moved onto their houseboat on the River Crouch, there (0) ....*was*.......... a big storm. The lights swung backwards and forwards (1) .... though they were at sea, but in (2) .... of the bad weather, not a single cup or saucer fell off the shelves. In fact, in the four years (3) .... they moved from their small house in the local town, hardly anything has been broken.

The boat is huge: 20 metres long and four metres wide. There are five bedrooms. 'It's about four times bigger (4) .... our old house,' says Nick, (5) .... works as a media consultant. The kitchen (6) .... up about half of the main living space and is not separated from the rest of it so that whoever is cooking doesn't feel left (7) .... 'I've always thought that the kitchen (8) .... be the centre of the home, otherwise you just don't want to be there,' says Nick's wife, Leda. Their children's friends tend (9) .... come round to hang out on the boat after they've (10) .... to school. In the living area (11) .... is even room for a ping-pong table, and the rest of the area is occupied by a sofa and an enormous table which is big (12) .... to seat 16 hungry people. Friends enjoy the novelty of visiting a houseboat.

Adapted from *The Observer*

4 Now think of the word which best fits each gap. Use only one word in each space.

5 Work in pairs.

Which do you prefer: when friends visit you, when you visit them, or when you go out together?

Speaking Part 2

1 Work in pairs. Before doing Speaking Part 2, answer the questions in the Exam round-up box.

Exam round-up

How much do you remember about Speaking Part 2? Say whether the following statements are true (T) or false (F). If a statement is false, write what is correct.

1 Each candidate must speak alone for about one minute.
2 You have to compare four photos and answer a more general question about them.
3 You should describe the general ideas behind the photos.
4 After your partner has spoken, you will be asked a question about the same photos.

2 Take turns to talk about the photographs for a minute.

Student A: The photographs show two different places to live. Compare these photographs and say what you think it would be like to live in these places.

What would it be like to live in each of these places?

Student B: The photographs show two different places to spend a holiday. Compare these photographs and say what you think it would be like to spend a short holiday in these places.

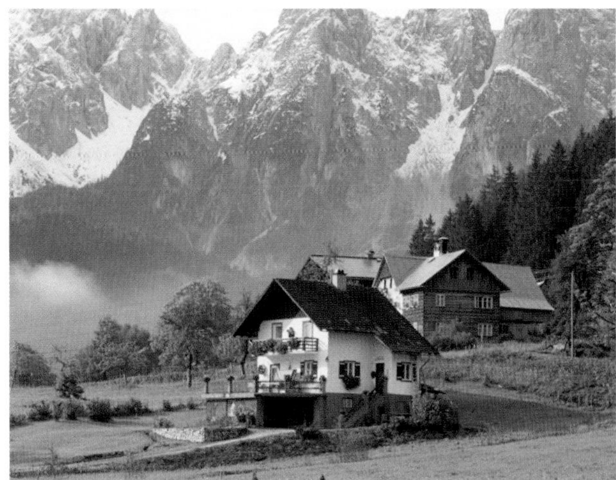

What would it be like to spend a short holiday in each of these places?

Grammar

Expressing obligation and permission

1 You will hear five students who are staying with host families while studying in Britain.

- Work in pairs. Before you listen, make a list of things students who stay with a host family in your country should and shouldn't do. Examples: *You should help with the housework. You shouldn't come home too late.*
- What are the advantages and disadvantages of living with a host family for students learning English?

2 Look at the sentences below and then answer the questions which follow.

A *I can* invite my friends to dinner sometimes.
B *I have to* help with the housework.
C *I can't* take food from the fridge.
D I'm supposed to be back home early.
E *They let me* borrow their car.
F *They won't let me* do any cooking.

1 Which phrases in *italics* mean ...?
   a I must ...I have to...
   b I'm not allowed to ......
   c I'm allowed to ......
2 What does *I'm supposed to be* mean?
   a I must be
   b I should be, but sometimes I'm not

3 (15) Listen and for questions 1–5, choose which sentence A–F best summarises what each student says. There is one extra letter which you do not need to use.

1 Marcos ☐
2 Lidia ☐
3 Ana ☐
4 Erich ☐
5 Claudia ☐

4 Which speaker said each of the following sentences? If necessary, listen again to check.

1 *I don't have to* do anything around the house.
2 *I had to* buy the food and cook it.
3 *They don't allow me to* have a real party.
4 Apparently *I was supposed to* phone to say I wasn't coming.
5 *They didn't let me* invite a couple of friends to dinner the other day.
6 *I needn't* clean the bathroom or do any shopping.

5 Work in pairs. Copy the table below into your notebook. Complete it using the phrases from Exercises 2 and 4 above.

	obligation	prohibition	permission	no obligation
present	I must	I can't	I can	
past				

page 164 *Grammar reference: Expressing obligation and permission*

6 For questions 1–5, complete the second sentence so that it has a similar meaning to the first sentence, using the word given. Do not change the word given. You must use between two and five words.

1 'You can't go to the discotheque,' Steve's father told him.
ALLOW
Steve's father did ......not allow him...... to go to the discotheque.

2 When you do the exam, it's not necessary to copy out the question.
HAVE
You ...... copy out the question when you do the exam.

3 I shouldn't wear shoes inside the house.
SUPPOSED
I ...... off my shoes before I enter the house.

4 You can't enter the room marked 'Private'.
ALLOWED
You ...... into the room marked 'Private'.

5 Diane wouldn't lend Celia her car.
LET
Diane refused ...... her car.

Writing Part 2 An article

1 Work in pairs. Before working on Writing Part 2, answer the questions in the Exam round-up box.

Exam round-up

How much do you remember about how to approach Writing Part 2? Put the following tasks in the correct order by writing a number 1–7 by each.

a Check what you have written looking for specific mistakes you know you make. ☐
b Organise your notes into a plan. ☐
c Read all the questions and choose the one you think is easiest. ☐
d Think and make notes. ☐
e Underline the things you must deal with in your answer. ☐
f Write your answer (120–180 words) following your plan. ☐
g Take about 40 minutes to do the whole task. ☐

❷ **Work in groups of three. Read the writing task below and discuss the questions which follow.**

> You have seen this announcement in your college magazine.
>
> **My ideal home**
>
> If you could choose the type of house you would like to live in and its location, where would you live, what sort of house would it be and what features would it have?
>
> The best articles will be published in the next issue of our magazine.
>
> Write your **article**.

- What would be the ideal location for your house?
- What sort of house would you choose?
- What features would your ideal house have?

❸ **Work in pairs with someone from another group.**

- Take turns to give a short talk describing your ideal house.
- When your partner finishes speaking, ask a few questions to find out more details.

❹ **Look at the writing task again and discuss these questions.**

1 Who will read your article?
2 What style would be suitable for this article?
3 Which of these tenses should your article particularly use: present simple, future simple, conditional? Why?
4 What information must it contain?
5 How can you make the article interesting for your readers?

❺ **Read the following sample answer to the writing task without paying attention to the gaps.**

1 How does this ideal home compare with your own?
2 Has the writer answered the question completely?

My dream home

I dream of living in a small, stylish modern flat in a historic old building near the centre of a large city (1) ....such........ as Paris or Vienna. This would be quite different (2) .... the small suburban house (3) .... I live at present. It would be conveniently close to theatres, art galleries and the best shops and I hope I'd have many good friends living nearby (4) .... would come to visit, or go out with me.

I don't need a large flat because I'd live on my (5) .... This would give me the freedom to do (6) .... I wanted when I wanted. It would consist (7) .... a cosy bedroom, a light, comfortable sitting room, and well-equipped kitchen. Ideally it would (8) .... a small balcony with a few plants where I could sit on sunny days. It would be in a quiet street lined with trees which flower in spring.

I wouldn't need (9) .... space. I'd just want enough room to keep my books and my music. (10) .... I had all these things, I'd be happy for years.

❻ **Complete the sample article by writing one word in each space.**

❼ **Work in pairs. Discuss whether the following statements are true (T) or false (F).**

		T/F
1	The article uses plenty of adjectives.	T
2	It uses conditional tenses.	
3	The writer mentions the furniture he/she would need.	
4	You can tell something about the writer's personality and tastes from the article.	
5	There are plenty of relative clauses.	
6	The writer doesn't say where he/she lives now.	

❽ **Write your own article.**

- Before you write, decide what features of the sample article above you could also use. Then think and write a plan.
- When you write, follow your plan.
- Write 120–180 words.

Unit 13 *Vocabulary and grammar review*

Vocabulary

1 Write either *named* or *called* in each space below. In one sentence, both words may be possible.

1 We saw some extraordinary animals in the zoo including one ......called...... an elephant shrew.
2 Is there anyone here .... Marsden? I've got a letter for him.
3 We've .... our new dog Goofy, after the cartoon character.
4 Brenda has just had a baby daughter, but she hasn't .... her yet.
5 What's that bird .... – the one that sings all night?

Grammar

2 Match the beginnings and endings of these sentences about the reading text on page 119, putting the verb in brackets into the correct form.

1 If one of the clients ......hadn't...... ......knocked...... (not knock) Colin over,
2 If Chris .... (not pick up) the cactus,
3 If Zebedee .... (not provoke) the pelican,
4 If Craig .... (not reach) the shore,
5 If no one .... (hear) the polar bear,

a he .... (die).
b he ......would have...... ......escaped...... (escape) from the elephant more easily.
c the scorpion .... (not sting) him.
d it .... (not attack) him.
e it might .... (attack) them without warning.

3 Complete these sentences with the correct form of the verb in brackets. In some sentences more than one answer is possible.

1 The lions wouldn't have attacked us if they ......hadn't been...... (not be) so hungry.
2 I wish it .... (be) summer – then we could go to the beach!
3 If the weather had been warmer, we .... (have) lunch on the terrace.
4 If only you .... (not make) so much noise! I can't concentrate on my studies and it's really annoying me!
5 I wish I .... (live) near the city centre. It's such a long bus ride from here.
6 Nick hasn't rung. You .... (hear) the telephone if he had.
7 Where's Candice? I hope she .... (not miss) the train.
8 I wish you .... (speak) more clearly so I could understand you better.
9 I think this soup .... (be) nicer if I'd used a bit less salt, don't you?
10 If only Amanda .... (not be) so moody! I find her very difficult to get on with sometimes.
11 I hope you .... (change) your shirt before we go out to the restaurant.
12 I know my mother wishes she .... (study) harder when she was my age.

4 Imagine a friend of yours is thinking of buying a dog but she lives in the centre of a busy town. Write some advice for her using these ideas and beginning with the phrases below.

take it for walks twice a day
take it to the vet for vaccinations
train it to behave properly
give it baths from time to time
don't let it bark at night

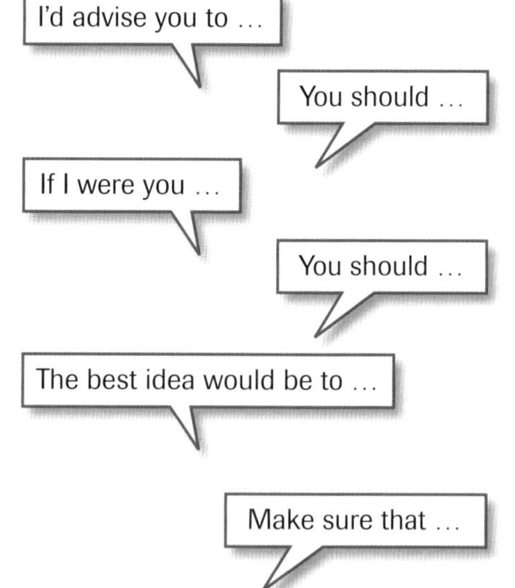

I'd advise you to …
You should …
If I were you …
You should …
The best idea would be to …
Make sure that …

Unit 14 *Vocabulary and grammar review*

Vocabulary

1 Circle the correct alternative in *italics* in sentences 1–8 below.

1 You can leave your car in the parking *space* / *place* just outside my house.
2 Bring your family to stay with us – we've got plenty of *room* / *place* for all of you.
3 He loves travelling and the first thing he does when he arrives in a new *location* / *place* is take a photo.
4 The university campus is in an excellent *location* / *space* surrounded by countryside, but within easy reach of the city centre.
5 The schools are excellent in this *area* / *location*, so it might be a good place to buy a house.
6 There's an empty *place* / *room* at that table if you want to sit there.
7 We may have to take two taxis because I don't think there's *space* / *place* in one for all of us.
8 You can buy international newspapers at the newsagent's in the main *square* / *place*, just behind the station.

Grammar

2 Complete each of the sentences below using one of the words in the box.

~~allowed~~	can	can't	couldn't	had
have	let	must	needn't	supposed

1 Please ask any questions now as you won't be ...allowed... to speak during the exam.
2 Veronique got into trouble because she went shopping when she was .... to be at school.
3 The family I'm staying with are very annoying. They won't .... me use the phone to call my mum!
4 You .... go in there – it's the headmaster's study and it's locked.
5 Meryl was in a great hurry because she .... to buy something for supper before the supermarket closed.
6 You .... shout! I can hear you perfectly clearly if you just speak normally.
7 James has a lovely life. His mother does all the housework and he doesn't even .... to make his own bed!
8 I wonder what time the film starts. .... I look at your newspaper to check?
9 I .... remember to buy some new sunglasses before I go on holiday.
10 When I was a teenager, my parents let me stay out late at weekends, but I .... stay out late on weekdays.

3 For questions 1–8, complete the second sentence so that it has a similar meaning to the first sentence, using the word given. Do not change the word given. You must use between two and five words.

1 Someone is going to paint the kitchen for us next week.
HAVE
We're going ...to have the kitchen painted... next week.

2 You're looking smart. Has someone cut your hair?
YOU
You're looking smart. Have .... cut?

3 We're hoping to employ someone to build a tennis court for us in the garden.
HAVE
We're hoping to .... for us in the garden.

4 Make sure that someone checks the car before you buy it.
HAVE
Make sure that .... before you buy it.

5 If someone cut the tree down for you, the view would be better.
HAD
If you .... down, the view would be better.

6 They make us do three hours of homework a day in this school.
HAVE
We .... three hours of homework a day in this school.

7 In this restaurant you should pay for your food when you order it.
SUPPOSED
In this restaurant you .... for your food when you order it.

8 They won't let you speak during the exam.
ALLOWED
You .... during the exam.

Unit 15 Fiesta!

Starting off

1 **Work in pairs. Write one of the verbs from the box in each of the spaces below to complete the descriptions of festivals and celebrations. Use each verb once only.**

~~celebrate~~	commemorate	dress up
gather round	hold	let off	march
perform	play	wearing

We hold a festival every March to (1) ...*celebrate*... the arrival of spring.

People in our region (2) .... in **traditional costumes** and then they (3) .... one of our **traditional dances**.

People (4) .... through the town in a spectacular **parade** to (5) .... a famous battle.

In many parts of the town residents (6) .... **street parties**.

Bands (7) .... dance music all night long.

Crowds (8) .... **street performers** who perform **street theatre**.

During the festival we (9) .... **fireworks**.

People from the town go out in the streets (10) .... **disguises**.

2 **Find the words and phrases in bold above illustrated in the photos.**

3 **Look at the photos again. They show different events which take place during festivals. Discuss these questions.**

1. Why do people do these different things at festivals?
2. Which type of activity is most enjoyable for people to watch?
3. Which country do you think each of the photos was taken in?

4 **Take turns to talk about a festival in your town or country.**

- What happens during the festival?
- What does the festival celebrate?
- Do you participate? Why (not)?

Listening Part 4

1 Work in pairs. You are going to hear an interview with a man who performs street theatre during festivals including one called the *Hat Fair*. Before you listen discuss these questions.

- What sort of things do street performers do?
- Do you enjoy watching street theatre? Why (not)?

2 Answer the questions in the Exam round-up box.

Exam round-up

How much do you remember about Listening Part 4? Complete the following sentences with the words and phrases in *italics*.

seven general ideas interview underline different words

1 Listening Part 4 is normally an ....
2 There are .... questions; you must choose A, B or C.
3 Read the questions carefully and .... the main ideas. These will be expressed using .... from the question.
4 Listen for .... as well as specific information.

3 (16) Now listen, and for questions 1–7, choose the best answer (A, B or C).

1 Why is the festival called the *Hat Fair*?
A It was started by local hat-makers.
B Many participants wear hats.
C Street performers collect money in hats.

2 What does Max most enjoy about the Hat Fair?
A the type of audiences he gets
B the other street performers he meets
C the shows he can do

3 How did Max start in street theatre?
A He lost his job in a circus.
B He did it while he was at university.
C He learnt it from his father.

4 What do audiences enjoy most about Max's act?
A the jokes
B the acrobatics
C the danger

5 What does he say is the main advantage of street theatre?
A Performers earn more than in conventional theatre.
B Performers are only paid if their performance is good.
C Performers can work independently.

6 What does he say is usually the main problem with street theatre?
A the weather
B the location
C the police

7 According to Max, how does the Hat Fair help the city?
A It attracts visitors to the town.
B It encourages local people to work together.
C It helps local people to relax together.

4 Work in pairs. Sometimes towns and cities discourage street theatre. Why do you think this is?

Grammar

The passive

1 Read the following extracts from the recording script and underline the verbs in the passive.

a I've been told the fair was only started in 1976, as a way of encouraging street performers like myself.
b A hat is passed around so that people like me can earn a living.
c They really seem to love it when they're being laughed at by other members of the audience.
d I actually went to quite a famous circus school in Canada when I was a teenager and I was taught juggling and acrobatics there.
e Here we're given the main shopping street, which is fine. In other places, if you haven't got permission, you'll get moved on by the police.

2 Work in pairs. In which extracts (a–e) does the speaker do the following? (You can use the extracts for more than one answer.)

1 He tells us who or what does/did the action.
In extract c and part of extract e
2 He uses the passive because he doesn't know who or what does/did something.

3 He uses the passive because he doesn't need to say who or what does/did something because it's obvious from the situation or context.
4 He uses the passive because what happens is more important than who does it.

page 165 *Grammar reference: The passive*

3 Rewrite these sentences in the passive, starting with the words given.

1 They discovered America in 1492.
America ......was discovered in 1492.......
2 Someone has stolen my wallet!
My wallet ....
3 You won't be able to ring me while they are repairing my mobile.
You won't be able to ring me while my mobile
....
4 Have you heard? They've given me a place on the course!
Have you heard? I ....
5 If you'd interrupted the meeting, the police would have arrested you.
If you'd interrupted the meeting, you
....

4 Read the following text quickly to find out what happens at the Egyptian festival of Sham el Nessim.

5 For questions 1–10, read the text again and think of the word which best fits each space. Use only one word in each space.

6 Look at this sentence from the text about Sham el Nessim and answer the questions which follow.

It is thought to have been the first festival to celebrate the beginning of spring.

1 What does the sentence mean?
 a People think that this was the first festival that celebrated the beginning of spring.
 b It used to be the first festival to celebrate spring.
2 It follows this pattern: subject + passive verb + infinitive. Here are some other verbs which can be used in this way: *believe, report, say, consider, expect*. Which other two sentences in the text follow the same pattern?

The sentence could also be expressed as follows:
It is thought that this was the first festival to celebrate the beginning of spring.

page 166 *Grammar reference: The passive with reporting verbs*

Sham el Nessim

A large number of contemporary Egyptian traditions (1) ......are...... said to have their origins in very ancient times. These include the holiday which is known (2) .... Sham el Nessim. This holiday may have (3) .... celebrated as early as 4,500 years ago. It is thought (4) .... have been the first festival to celebrate the beginning of the spring.

Nowadays, in the early morning of Sham el Nessim millions of Egyptians come out to crowd public parks and other open areas. Young men swim in the Nile and families generally enjoy the cool breeze of spring.

Sham el Nessim (5) .... also celebrated by eating traditional foods and these include salted fish, coloured eggs, sunflower seeds and raw onions. The reason for each of these foods (6) .... eaten is supported (7) .... a different myth. For example, offerings of fish are believed to (8) .... been made to the ancient gods and by (9) .... this a good harvest was ensured. Salted fish symbolised welfare to the ancient Egyptians and in ancient times fish (10) .... easily caught by being trapped in natural pools created by the movement of the Nile.

7 Rewrite the following sentences beginning with the words given.

1 Offerings of fish are believed to have been made to the ancient gods.
It is believed that offerings of fish were made to the ancient gods.

2 A large number of contemporary Egyptian traditions are said to have their origins in very ancient times.
It is said that ....

3 It is reported that five thousand people joined in the festivities.
Five thousand people are reported ....

4 It is said that our festival has the best fireworks in the world.
Our festival is said ....

8 For questions 1–5, complete the second sentence so that it has a similar meaning to the first sentence, using the word given. Do not change the word given. You must use between two and five words, including the word given.

1 People believe that the festival originated in the eighteenth century.
HAVE
The festival is believed to have originated in the eighteenth century.

2 People expect that she will be chosen as carnival queen.
BE
She is .... as carnival queen.

3 The festival is said to be more popular than ever.
THAT
It is .... more popular than ever.

4 They think Channel 4 is the only channel which will broadcast the opening ceremony.
THOUGHT
Channel 4 .... the only channel which will broadcast the ceremony.

5 People think that Carnival is the best festival of the year.
CONSIDERED
Carnival .... the best festival of the year.

Reading Part 2

1 Work in small groups. You are going to read an article about a Spanish fiesta. Before you read, look at the fiesta in the photo.

What do you think is happening? Would you enjoy a fiesta like this? Why (not)?

2 Answer the questions in the Exam round-up box.

Exam round-up

How much do you remember about Reading Part 2? Say whether the following statements are true (T) or false (F). If you think a statement is false, write what you think is correct.

1 In the exam this part will contain eight questions including the example.
2 You should first read the whole text carefully to form an idea of how it develops.
3 Underline clues in the text while you read, e.g. pronouns: *this*, *he*, etc., adverbs which suggest something mentioned before, e.g. *the second point*, *however*, etc., relationships of meaning, e.g. *it was expected to be huge … in fact it was tiny …*, etc.
4 Read each sentence carefully, thinking about where it could fit and looking for clues.
5 When you have decided on a sentence for a gap, don't change your mind.
6 When you've finished, don't read the complete text again.

3 Seven sentences have been removed from the article.

- Read the article (but not the missing sentences) quite carefully.
- Underline words and phrases which may refer to the missing sentences (two are done for you as examples).

The tomato fight fiesta

Every year on the last Wednesday of August thousands of people gather in the small town of Buñol for a spectacular tomato fight. ***Michelle O'Connor*** *joined in.*

Along with my two friends, I had done nothing to prepare for La Tomatina, the biggest and most well-known food fight in the world. Yet no amount of planning could have really prepared us for the battle that lay ahead. As our taxi pulled into the usually sleepy town of Buñol, we realised this fight was going to be a whole new experience for us.

The nearest Spanish city to Buñol is Valencia. Despite missing the last train, we were keen not to miss the penultimate evening of Buñol's seven day fiesta, so we had found a taxi to take us the thirty kilometres. **1** ___ However Buñol holds a week-long party in preparation for the tomato-throwing frenzy and, if every night of that week is like the Tuesday night we were there, this is one party it's not cool to arrive for late.

There are a number of explanations of how the festival began. **2** ___ The owner of a nearby vegetable stall provided the perfect weapons, people got caught in the crossfire and soon joined in. Because people had enjoyed themselves so much, the fight was remembered and repeated the following year. With time a tradition formed and eventually the fiesta was organised by the town hall. Nowadays people flock from all over the world to attend La Tomatina.

The evening we arrived, the streets were lined with bright lights and lively cafés full of people laughing and enjoying huge sizzling pans of paella. **3** ___ In the main square a huge party was taking place with bands playing upbeat jazzy Salsa. People pushed against each other shouting and dancing.

Feeling hungry, we scoured the streets looking for somewhere to eat. Finally we found a restaurant that had a free table. The atmosphere inside was lively and the food was tasty and inexpensive. **4** ___ When we awoke on a patch of grass on the roadside the next day, all we could see were thousands of people all wearing goggles to protect their eyes.

By this time, the atmosphere was manic as people poured into the town for the fight. **5** ___ From there they went and immersed themselves in the party spirit. We crammed into the narrow main street while firemen poured water over the crowd from the rooftops above.

At 12.00 a firework signalled the beginning of the fight. Six huge lorries trundled through the town carrying loads of stale, sour tomatoes that were then hurled into the crowd by teams of men. **6** ___ Water poured from the rooftops and we found ourselves swimming in a sea of red tomato juice. It was fantastic. The trucks then emptied their contents onto the ground before continuing down the street. It was manic, chaotic, crazy, brilliant fun!

At 13.00 another firework signalled the end, the crowd of some thirty thousand people walked down to the river and washed themselves in it turning it red. **7** ___ Nor could I look at or eat another tomato. But it was without a doubt worth it.

Adapted from **La Tomatina Festival** by Michelle O'Connor on *www.attitudetravel.com*

4 Now choose from the sentences A–H the one which fits each gap (1–7) in the text. There is one extra sentence which you do not need to use.

A As they arrived, they stored their belongings in shops that offered temporary cloakrooms.

B At this point the crowds went crazy chucking tomatoes at each other and squashing them on the heads of their closest opponents.

C The most likely is that sometime in the 1940s a fight broke out in the town square.

D For days afterwards I was unable to remove the smell of tomato from my skin and hair.

E Fortunately, people were friendly and we were soon invited to join them.

F Spanish guitar music drifted through the little town and locals and visitors danced in the streets as night fell.

G While we were there we got talking to a friendly group of Australian tourists and spent the rest of the night enjoying this astonishing party with them.

H Unlike us, most people come to Buñol just for the tomato fight on the final morning and then go home straight after.

5 Work in small groups. Imagine that your town is thinking of starting a new festival to attract tourists to the town.

- Decide what events should happen during the festival and what other features the festival should have.
- When you have finished, change groups and explain to another group what you have decided.

Use of English Part 3

1 Look at these three extracts from Reading Part 2 and use the word given in capitals at the end to form a word that fits in the gap. Then check your answer by looking at the text again.

1 The .... of a nearby vegetable stall provided the perfect weapons. **OWN**
2 We got talking to a friendly group of Australian .... and spent the rest of the night enjoying this astonishing party with them. **TOUR**
3 We crammed into the narrow main street while .... poured water over the crowd. **FIRE**

2 You can form personal nouns (nouns which describe people who do particular activities) by adding:

- *-er, -or, -ant* to a verb, e.g. *teach – teacher, sail – sailor, account – accountant*
- *-ist, -ian, -man/-woman* to a noun, e.g. *motor – motorist, mathematics – mathematician, police – policeman/policewoman.*

Form personal nouns from the noun or verb given.

noun / verb	person
1 design	designer
2 art	
3 perform	
4 collect	
5 create	
6 participate	
7 music	
8 politics	
9 fish	
10 cycle	

3 Work in pairs. Think of two other examples for each of these suffixes *-er, -ist, -or, -man.*

4 Answer the questions in the Exam round-up box.

Exam round-up

How much do you remember about Use of English Part 3? Circle the correct alternative in *italics* in the following sentences.

1 This part contains *10 / 12* questions.
2 *Write an answer as soon as you see a gap / Read the whole text quickly before answering the questions.*
3 When you look at a gap, think *what word would fit / what type of word (adjective, noun, verb, etc.) you need.*
4 *Make sure you have spelled the word correctly (look at the base word you have been given) / Correct spelling is not important in this part.*
5 When you have finished, *go to Part 4 / read the completed text again.*

5 For questions 1–10, read the text below. Use the word given in capitals at the end of some of the lines to form a word that fits in the gap in the same line. There is an example at the beginning (0).

My local festival

The (0) ....preparations........ for the festival in my town are an extremely (1) .... time. Months before, the organisers on the committee start making all the necessary (2) .... and finalising the details of the processions and other (3) .... that are going to take place. They also keep the main (4) .... up to date with what is going on.
When the day finally arrives, it becomes (5) .... to drive in the city since the streets are really crowded with local people, (6) .... from other nearby towns and even some tourists. The whole town appears (7) .... and chaotic. People dress up in (8) .... costumes, young people stay out all night with their friends and it is quite normal to see people who are (9) .... quiet and respectable dancing in the streets. For me, however, the firework displays are the most (10) .... part.

PREPARE
EXCITE
ARRANGE
ACT
PARTICIPATE
POSSIBLE
VISIT
ORGANISE
TRADITION
USUAL
IMPRESS

Speaking Part 3

1 Work in pairs. Decide which of the occasions below is shown in each picture (two of the occasions are not shown).

a sporting triumph	an engagement	a new job
a new house	getting promotion	graduating
a new baby	the first car	good exam results

What would be the best way of celebrating each of these occasions?

Which of these occasions would you be happiest to celebrate?

2 (17) Listen to two students, Nikolai and Antonia, practising Speaking Part 3. What ways of celebrating do they mention?

3 Work in pairs. Can you think of any other ways of celebrating?

4 (17) Listen again. Decide whether the following statements are true (T) or false (F).

1 The candidates ask each other's opinions. *T*
2 When they don't know a word in English, they keep quiet.
3 They make alternative suggestions.
4 They give reasons for their ideas.
5 They discuss everything very seriously.
6 They sometimes interrupt each other.
7 They discuss both questions.

5 (17) Complete these phrases used by the students by writing one word from the box in each space. Then check your answers by listening again.

~~called~~	case	could	depends	idea
move	suggest			

1 I think that the event – **I'm not sure what it's** ......*called*...... **in English** – the event when you graduate …
2 You .... be right.
3 Or **perhaps I'd** .... a holiday somewhere really nice.
4 **I think that's a really good** .... **How do you think people should** celebrate buying a new house?
5 **Maybe in this** .... I'd celebrate by going out and buying a nice piece of furniture to put in the house.
6 **I think it** .... **on** how I'm feeling. **I think I might** just go out to a restaurant with a friend to celebrate that one.
7 **Shall we** .... **on to** the second question?

6 Which of the phrase(s) in bold above can you use when you want to say these things?

1 You don't know how to express an idea.
I'm not sure what it's called in English …
2 You want to talk about something new or different.
3 You want to make a suggestion.
4 You want to say you agree.
5 You're not sure how to answer.

7 Before doing Speaking Part 3, answer the questions in the Exam round-up box.

Exam round-up

How much do you remember about Speaking Part 3? Say whether the following statements are true (T) or false (F). If you think a statement is false, write what you think is correct.

1 You do Speaking Part 3 alone.
2 You have about five minutes for this part.
3 You must discuss two different questions.
4 You should try to reach a decision together.
5 You should try to have a natural conversation.
6 You should only discuss the pictures and prompts which interest you.
7 You should ask for your partner's ideas.

8 Work in pairs. The pictures show important moments in people's lives.

- Discuss together what would be the best way of celebrating each of these occasions.
- Decide which two of these occasions you would be happiest to celebrate.

Writing Part 1

1 Before doing Writing Part 1, answer the questions in the Exam round-up box.

Exam round-up

How much do you remember about Writing Part 1? Choose the best alternative in *italics* in the sentences below. In Writing Part 1:

1 *there is one question you must do / you can choose from two questions*
2 you must write between *100–120 words / 120–150 words*
3 the task is *a letter / a letter or an email*
4 *you can write whatever you want / you must deal with four specific points in the task*
5 you have about *40 minutes / 60 minutes* to do this

2 Work in pairs. Look at the following exam task and discuss the questions which follow.

You have received an email from your English-speaking friend, Sam, asking you about a festival in your country. Read Sam's email and the notes you have made. Then write an email to Sam, using **all** your notes.

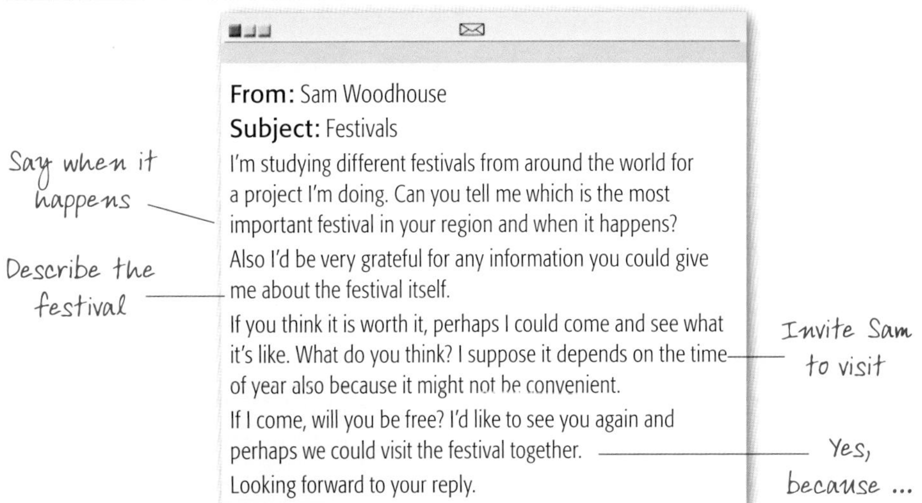
From: Sam Woodhouse
Subject: Festivals

I'm studying different festivals from around the world for a project I'm doing. Can you tell me which is the most important festival in your region and when it happens?

Also I'd be very grateful for any information you could give me about the festival itself.

If you think it is worth it, perhaps I could come and see what it's like. What do you think? I suppose it depends on the time of year also because it might not be convenient.

If I come, will you be free? I'd like to see you again and perhaps we could visit the festival together.

Looking forward to your reply.

Write your **email**. You must use grammatically correct sentences with accurate spelling and punctuation in a style appropriate for the situation.

1 Who is the target reader?
2 What style would be suitable?
3 What four things must you deal with, and in what order would you deal with them?
4 Which festival would you tell Sam about, and what would you say about it?

3 The email below contains 15 spelling mistakes commonly made by First Certificate candidates. Find the mistakes and write the correct spelling (e.g. ~~bout~~ – *about*).

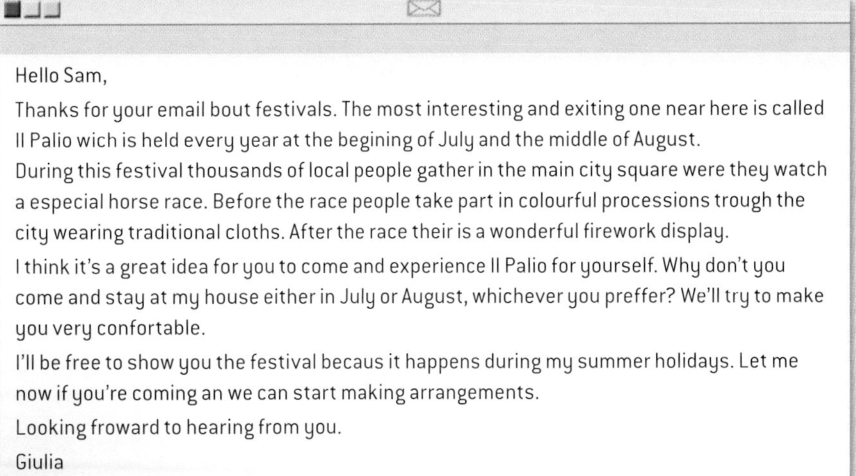
Hello Sam,

Thanks for your email bout festivals. The most interesting and exiting one near here is called Il Palio wich is held every year at the begining of July and the middle of August.

During this festival thousands of local people gather in the main city square were they watch a especial horse race. Before the race people take part in colourful processions trough the city wearing traditional cloths. After the race their is a wonderful firework display.

I think it's a great idea for you to come and experience Il Palio for yourself. Why don't you come and stay at my house either in July or August, whichever you preffer? We'll try to make you very confortable.

I'll be free to show you the festival becaus it happens during my summer holidays. Let me now if you're coming an we can start making arrangements.

Looking froward to hearing from you.

Giulia

4 Write your own email to Sam. Write between 120 and 150 words. Make sure you include all four points from the notes.

Unit 16 Machine age

Starting off

1 **Work in pairs. Choose from the words in the box and write the name of each of these items by each photo.**

digital camera	digital TV	DVD player	~~laptop~~
mobile phone	MP3 player	SatNav	webcam

2 **Complete reasons for using these items by writing a word from the box below in each space. Use each word only once.**

give	date	do	find	~~keep~~
save	store	take	wherever	

1 To ....Keep.......... in touch with friends.
2 To .... my way.
3 To keep up to .... with what's going on.
4 To .... me more choice of what I watch.
5 To help me .... my homework.
6 To .... time and effort.
7 To listen to music .... I want.
8 To .... good photos easily and .... them on my computer.

3 **Say which item you would use for each of the reasons above, e.g.**
I would use a laptop and a webcam to keep in touch with friends.

4 **Which two items do you think are the most useful? Why?**

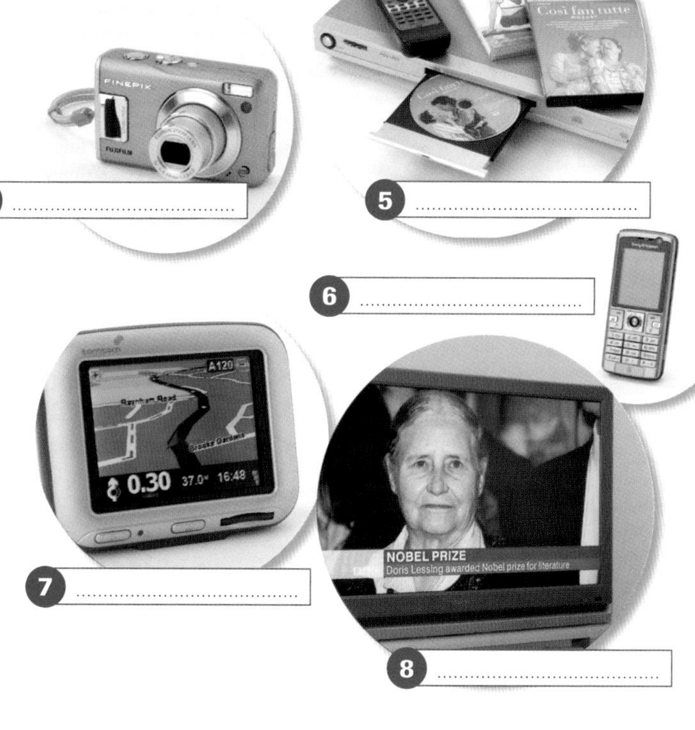

Reading Part 3

1 **Work in small groups. You are going to read a newspaper article about five innovative new products. Before you read, look at the photos on page 143.**

What do you think the purpose of each of these devices is?

2 **Before doing Reading Part 3, do the exercise in the Exam round-up box.**

Exam round-up

How much do you remember about Reading Part 3? Say whether the following statements are true (T) or false (F). If you think a statement is false, write what you think is correct.

1 In Reading Part 3 there are 12 questions.
2 You have to match the questions with different texts or different parts of a text.
3 You should read the text(s) carefully before reading the questions.
4 You should underline the main ideas in the questions.
5 You have 10 minutes to do this part of the Reading Paper.
6 If you can't find an answer, leave the space blank.

❸ **For questions 1–15, choose from the devices (A–E). The devices may be chosen more than once.**

Which device(s)		
allows the owner to change the way it looks?		1
can save time for the owner?		2
can make signals to attract its owner's attention?		3
is a machine which usually has a different appearance?		4
is intended to protect its owner from danger?		5
is the writer uncertain about how many will be sold?		6
may not work in all countries?		7
allows you to decide your objectives and measure your progress?		8
can be used when other similar devices are not allowed?		9
may save money?		10
allows the owner to do something in private instead of in public?		11
can be used to deceive other people?	12	13
are superior to most other products of the same type?	14	15

New Products Review

A The Nabaztag

Nabaztag is a wi-fi connected rabbit. It'll wake you up in the morning with the latest weather report, give an electronic signal to tell you when an email or text message has arrived and even play your favourite tunes. All you do is plug the rabbit in and let it find your internet connection. As well as communicating using its little loudspeaker, Nabaztag also has lights built into its body and it can move its ears. You can even link or marry your rabbit to another one anywhere else on the internet. Nabaztag is just the first of many wi-fi connected devices that don't resemble computers, even though that's what they are. I hope this one will disappear, but it could equally become a global fashion.

B The X-Bike

We all know cycling's supposed to be a pretty good form of exercise. It gives your whole body a good workout and develops your natural coordination. Sadly, there are rather a lot of downsides in the form of weather, bad roads, drivers and clothes. Cycling clothes make most cyclists look ridiculous. The X-Bike is a sensible alternative, giving all the fitness benefits of riding a mountain bike without the embarrassment because you're indoors.

With the X-Bike you can set targets and check how your fitness is improving. You can also choose the programme that suits those exercise goals, which is something that a wheeled bicycle simply cannot do.

C The Tulip Ego

The Tulip Ego is the first laptop computer I've seen that's aimed at people who want to look fashionable. It even has special software for turning the screen into a mirror in case you want to check your make-up using a built-in camera. At the same time most current laptops are very similar inside, with far more power than any normal user could ever require. And the Ego is at the top end of specifications, as you'd expect from its substantial price tag. You could spend the same on four or five normal laptops. But most buyers won't be as interested in the power of the processor as in the fashion extras. These come mostly in the form of 'skins' that alter the appearance of the laptop. They vary from antique wood or dark leather to bright pink or zebra skin.

D The Pretender

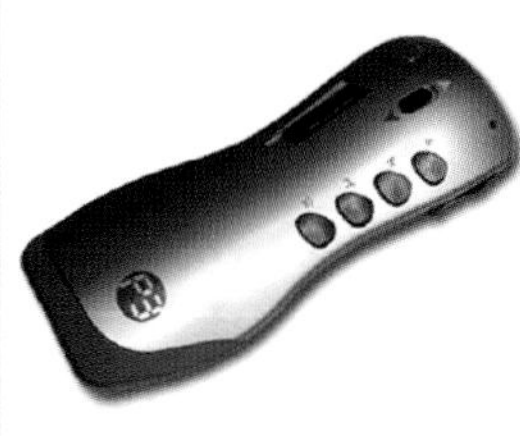

There are times when I would like to be able to control my electronic communication a little more, particularly when it comes to unwanted, unnecessary or overlong phone calls. What the Pretender does is act as a voice changer. The idea is that when you're trying to get somebody off the line, you press a button and they hear the sound of a baby crying or something else that demands immediate attention. Suddenly, saying goodbye is easy. The Pretender is only currently available as an import from the United States, so it's uncertain whether or not it is compatible with other phone systems. However, it seems to work better than many other voice changers because it's attached to the phone line. You can even persuade a caller that they're speaking to somebody of the opposite sex.

E The Sazo

The Sazo is a device about the size of a small box of matches that can pinpoint the location of its owner, sometimes to within a metre, using the internet. It's clearly aimed at parents who can use it to check where their children are even though it doesn't allow them to supervise what they are doing. Although parents could use a mobile phone, the company reminds them of the possible health risks from mobiles. There are other problems with phones: parents can't control the costs of their children's phones and schools are not keen on pupils having them switched on in class.

The Sazo does have some mobile features, such as the ability to receive calls, dial three pre-programmed numbers, and a panic button which automatically sends a text message to those numbers. It sounds well thought out. On the other hand, if I had had one in my teens, I would have 'accidentally' left the tracker at the place I was supposed to be, while I was up to no good elsewhere.

Adapted from articles by Nick Clayton in *The Scotsman*

4 Work in pairs.

- Which of these products do you think is the most useful? And the most useless?
- Describe a product you would like to see invented.

Vocabulary

Check, supervise and *control*

1 First Certificate candidates often confuse these words: *check, supervise* and *control*. Write the correct word in each of these sentences from Reading Part 3. Then check your answers by looking at the text again.

- With the X-Bike you can set targets and (1) ......check...... how your fitness is improving.
- There are times when I would like to be able to (2) .... my electronic communication a little more ...
- It's clearly aimed at parents who can use it to (3) .... where their children are even though it doesn't allow them to (4) .... what they are doing.
- ... parents can't (5) .... the costs of their children's phones ...

2 Now match the words with their definitions.

1 control — **a** to be responsible for watching over the activity of another person or over a process to make certain that it is always done correctly or safely

2 check — **b** to order, limit, instruct or rule something or someone's actions or behaviour (NOT to test something to see that it is correct)

3 supervise — **c** to quickly examine something (or someone) to make certain that it is correct, working properly, suitable or safe to use

3 Complete the sentences below by writing the correct word, *check, supervise* or *control* in the spaces.

1 He has very little authority over his children and can't ......control...... them at all.
2 In my job I .... ten other workers.
3 Make sure you .... your answer for mistakes before you hand it in.
4 The children play while two teachers .... them.
5 We should always respect the forces of nature because we will never be able to .... them.
6 You should always .... the tyres on your car before a long journey.

4 Work in pairs.

- Do you think having so many machines and gadgets helps us to control our lives more or less? Why?
- What things do you have to check before going on holiday?
- When do you think teachers should supervise students?

Grammar

Linking words: *when, if, in case, even if, even though* and *whether*

1 First Certificate candidates often confuse *when* and *if*. Look at this extract from the *Cambridge Advanced Learner's Dictionary* and then do the exercise which follows.

> Common Learner Error
>
> **when** or **if**?
>
> In conditional sentences **when** is used to describe a situation which is always true or a situation which you are sure will happen in the future.
>
> *I always get migraines when it's this hot.*
>
> *When I finish school, I'm going to go to college.*
>
> **If** is used to describe a possible situation.
>
> *It would be better for the environment if everyone went by bicycle.*
>
> ~~*It would be better for the environment when everyone went by bicycle.*~~

Some of the sentences below contain errors made by First Certificate candidates and some sentences are correct. Where you think there is an error, correct it. If you think a sentence is correct, write *correct*.

1 I'd be very happy ~~when~~ my parents gave me a new computer. if
2 I'll have dinner waiting for me if I get home tonight.
3 It would be wonderful if the number of tourists increased.
4 It would be a great opportunity for me when I could go to study in Copenhagen.
5 We would like to go to the show if you think it's possible.
6 Marta will be able to study medicine when she gets high marks in her exams next month.

2 **First Certificate candidates often confuse *even if* and *even though*. Read these two extracts from the *Cambridge Advanced Learner's Dictionary*. Then correct the mistakes in the sentences below. One sentence is correct.**

> **even if** whether or not: *Even if you take a taxi, you'll still miss your train.*
>
> **even though** although: *Even though he left school at 16, he still managed to become prime minister.*

1 I agreed to go dancing with her ~~even~~ I had planned something else to do. even though
2 We gave Amina a very responsible job even if she was only 18 years old.
3 Sasha didn't get a high mark even if his answer to the last question was excellent.
4 I decided to buy a ticket to the music festival even though I had to cancel my trip to Berlin.
5 Even if we had to walk for just ten minutes we felt very tired when we reached the river.
6 Nico won't come to the party even though we move it to Saturday.

3 **First Certificate candidates often confuse *if* and *in case*. Read the explanation below and then write *if* or *in case* in the sentences which follow.**

We use *in case* or *just in case* to explain why someone does/did something: *Karen took her swimsuit in case she had a chance to swim. I always take my mobile phone with me just in case my car breaks down.*

Compare:
Instead of going camping, we'll stay in a hotel in case the weather is bad (perhaps the weather will be bad – we have already decided to stay in a hotel for that reason).
Instead of going camping, we'll stay in a hotel if the weather is bad (perhaps the weather will be bad – if that happens, we'll stay in a hotel, otherwise we'll go camping).

1 You ought to take a raincoat ......in case...... there's a thunderstorm while you're out.
2 Could you call me .... your plane is delayed?
3 I think you should always take out insurance before you go on holiday .... you have an accident.
4 I've brought an extra pair of shoes with me .... these ones get wet.
5 He brought a book with him to study in class .... his teacher was ill and didn't come.
6 She'd have to buy a new MP3 player .... she lost that one.

page 166 *Grammar reference: Linking words and phrases*

4 **Complete the following text using *when, if, in case, even if* and *even though* in the spaces. In some cases more than one answer is possible.**

I'm one of those people who couldn't live without a computer (1) ......even if...... I lived on a desert island. It does everything for me. It always plays me music (2) .... I want to listen to music, and it allows me to email my friends (3) .... their phone is engaged. It also gives me things to read and games to play. I even save all my work on my computer (4) .... I lose my notebooks. Actually, I bought a top-of-the-range new computer only last month (5) .... the one I had was working perfectly, but then I'm a computer addict and I think it's a good idea to have two computers (6) .... one of them breaks down. The only reason I can think of for giving up my computers would be (7) .... someone managed to invent a robot to replace them!

Listening Part 3

1 **Work in small groups. You are going to hear five young people talking about their parents and computers. Before you listen, discuss these questions.**

- Who in your family understands technology best?
- Does your family ever argue about using the television, computers and other devices?

2 **Before doing Listening Part 3, do the exercise in the Exam round-up box on page 146.**

Exam round-up

How much do you remember about Listening Part 3? Choose the best alternative in each sentence below.

1 You listen to *four speakers / five speakers* and you must choose the statement which best summarises what they say from *six alternatives/ seven alternatives*.

2 Before listening, you should *read and* underline *the main idea in each alternative / read through the alternatives, then wait patiently for the listening to begin*.

3 When listening, you should listen for *small details / the main idea of what each speaker is saying*.

3 (18) **You will hear five young people talking about their parents and computers. For questions 1–5, choose from the list (A–F) the sentence which best summarises what each person says. Use the letters only once. There is one extra letter which you do not need to use.**

Speaker 1 ☐

Speaker 2 ☐

Speaker 3 ☐

Speaker 4 ☐

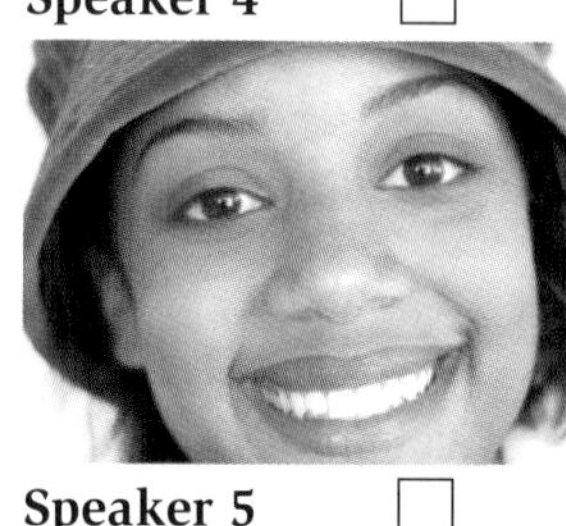

Speaker 5 ☐

A They offered to help me to use the computer.
B They complained about not having access to the computer.
C They suggested buying a new computer.
D They said they were proud of my computer skills.
E They advised me to go on a computer course.
F They told me to send fewer messages to my classmates.

4 **Work in pairs.**

1 How can computers help students with their studies?
2 What useful skills can young people learn by using computers?

Grammar

Reported speech 2: reporting verbs

1 **Look at sentences A–F from Listening Part 3 above. Which reporting verb (*offer, complain, suggest, say, advise, tell*) follows each of these patterns? Make a chart in your notebook like the one below and write the verbs in the columns.**

reporting verb + infinitive	reporting verb + object + infinitive	reporting verb + preposition + noun or verb + *-ing*	reporting verb + verb + *-ing*	reporting verb + *(that)* + sentence
offered to help				

page 167 *Grammar reference: Reported speech 2: reporting verbs*

2 **Circle the correct alternative in *italics* in each of the sentences.**

1. She admitted *steal* / *stealing* the watch.
2. Susan accused Brian *that he had lied* / *of lying*.
3. Mark's mother agreed *to buy* / *buying* him a new car.
4. The children apologised *that they had broken* / *for breaking* the window.
5. Martha asked me *to go* / *going* for coffee with her.
6. Peter has invited me *to visit* / *that I visit* him in Switzerland this summer.
7. Vicky offered *to help* / *helping* Tanya with her homework.
8. Ewan persuaded his mother *to buy* / *buying* him a new bike.
9. Karen has promised *to visit* / *visiting* me after the summer.
10. I would recommend *to install* / *installing* new computers in the office.
11. Can I remind you *to buy* / *buying* some fruit?
12. Martin warned me not *to use* / *using* that machine.

3 **Write the verbs from Exercise 2 in the correct column of the table in Exercise 1.**

Example: 1 *admitted stealing* – reporting verb + verb + *-ing*

4 **For questions 1–6, complete the second sentence so that it has a similar meaning to the first sentence, using the word given. Do not change the word given. You must use between two and five words, including the word given.**

1. 'You should buy a more powerful computer, Pablo,' his friend said.
   ADVISED
   Pablo's friend ...advised him to buy... a more powerful computer.
2. 'Why don't we go swimming this afternoon?' said Marie.
   SUGGESTED
   Marie .... afternoon.
3. 'Turn off the computer when you finish,' my father said to me.
   TOLD
   My father .... the computer when I finished.
4. 'Don't forget to post the letter,' Silvia told Natasha.
   REMINDED
   Silvia .... the letter.
5. 'You haven't been paying attention to me,' our teacher told us.
   ANY
   Our teacher accused us .... notice of him.
6. 'I'll try as hard as I can to pass the exam,' said Paola.
   BEST
   Paola promised .... to pass the exam.

Speaking Part 4

1 **Work in pairs. Answer the questions in the Exam round-up box.**

Exam round-up

How much do you remember about Speaking Part 4? Choose the correct alternative in *italics* in the following sentences.

1. This part of the Speaking paper lasts about *4 minutes* / *5 minutes*.
2. You are asked your opinions connected with *the same theme as Speaking Part 3* / *a completely new theme*.
3. You and your partner *will both be asked the same questions* / *may be asked the same questions or different questions*.
4. Give *your opinion plus an explanation, reason or example* / *just your opinion*.
5. When your partner is speaking you should *listen carefully* / *relax* because you *may have to* / *won't have to* comment on what they say.

2 (19) **Read the questions in the two boxes below. Then listen to two candidates, Irene and Miguel, answering one of the questions. Which question are they answering?**

Student A	Student B
• Is it important for everyone to be able to use computers? Why (not)? • Tell me about a machine or gadget you couldn't live without. Why (not)? • What invention would you like to see in the future? • Some people say that we depend too much on machines. Do you agree?	• Do you think young people are more comfortable using modern technology than old people? Why (not)? • How have mobile phones changed the way we live? • How do you think technology will change our lives in the future? • Would you like to have a robot? What could it do for you?

3 (19) **Now listen again and note down how they answer the question and what explanation they give.**

4 Complete this table.

Which candidate ...	Irene	Miguel	both candidates
1 gives one answer?			
2 mentions several possibilities?			
3 gives reasons for their answer?			
4 do you think gives the best answer?			

5 The candidates didn't answer the question immediately. Which of the following phrases did they use to show they understood the question but they were thinking about their answer?

1 That's quite a hard question to answer because …
2 I'm not too sure because …
3 I don't know because …
4 I'd have to think about that because …

6 Work in pairs. Look at Exercise 2 again and take the part of Student A or Student B. Take turns to ask each other the questions in your box.

Use of English Part 4

1 Do the exercise in the Exam round-up box below.

Exam round-up

How much do you remember about Use of English Part 4? Complete the following sentences by writing one word from the list below in each space.

word contractions change vocabulary
same number given five eight

- Use of English Part 4 has (1) .... questions.
- You must write between two and (2) .... words in each space, using the (3) .... given.
- (4) .... count as two words.
- You must not (5) .... the word given.
- This part tests your knowledge of grammar and (6) .... , including expressions and phrasal verbs.

Read the question and decide what grammar and vocabulary you need. When you have finished read your answer and check:

- if it means the (7) .... as the original sentence
- if you have used the correct (8) .... of words
- you haven't changed the word (9) ....

2 For questions 1–8, complete the second sentence so that it has a similar meaning to the first sentence, using the word given. Do not change the word given. You must use between two and five words, including the word given.

1 No one helped Tracey with any of her homework yesterday.
OWN
Tracey did all .... yesterday.

2 Candice dialled your number by accident.
MEAN
Candice .... your number.

3 It is predicted that sea levels will rise by about 10 centimetres in the next century.
EXPECTED
Sea levels .... by about 10 centimetres in the next century.

4 It looks as if Tony has lost his way while coming here.
GOT
Tony seems .... on his way here.

5 One of our friends installed the system for us.
HAD
We .... a friend of ours.

6 The fight started in the market because the customer refused to pay.
BROKEN
If the customer had paid, the fight .... in the market.

7 I'm sure Sheila didn't borrow your bike because she's still in her room.
HAVE
Sheila is still in her room so she .... your bike.

8 It's a pity Don won't stop working so hard.
CUT
If only .... on the amount he works.

Writing Part 2 A review

1 Work in pairs. Look at the following writing task and discuss the questions which follow.

You have seen this announcement on a website called www.gadgets.com.

Have you bought a new gadget recently? If so, could you write us a review of it? We'd like to know why you bought it, if it meets your requirements and if you'd recommend it to other people.

The best reviews will appear on our website.

Write your **review**.

1 Which gadget would you write about?
2 What things must you mention in your review?
3 What would you say about each of these things?

2 Read the sample answer below. Has the writer answered all the points in the writing task?

I've recently bought a new mobile phone made by Alcitel because I'd lost my previous one. I didn't want to spend a lot of money because I lose things quite often. I bought it for three reasons. Firstly it has reasonably large keys which means it's easy to send messages and dial numbers. Secondly, it has quite a large colour screen which makes it easy to read. Finally it flips open, so that when you carry it in your pocket, you can't dial a number by accident.

I've found that this phone is easy to use with clear instructions on the screen. Also, I can hear callers very clearly even in a noisy environment. However, I have one small complaint. Its ring tones are all musical tunes whereas I'd prefer something which sounds more like a traditional telephone.

This phone is not very sophisticated or complicated because, for example, it doesn't have a camera. However, it meets my needs and, at 35 euros, I think its price is very reasonable.

3 Write your own answer to the writing task.

After you have done Vocabulary and grammar review Units 15 and 16, remember to look at the Grammar reference section. Then there are reference sections on Writing and Speaking and a complete practice paper from Cambridge ESOL – all to help you get more practice. Good luck with the exam!

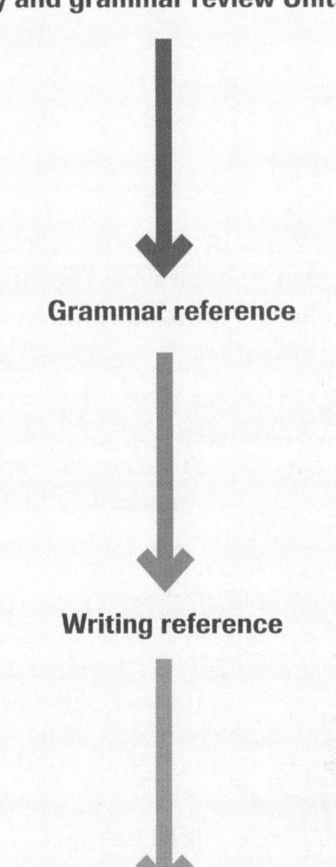

Unit 15 *Vocabulary and grammar review*

Word formation

1 Write personal nouns for each of these words.

1 visit ....visitor.........
2 science ....
3 sing ....
4 chemistry ....
5 magic ....
6 geology ....
7 manage ....
8 electric ....
9 assist ....
10 post ....

2 Complete each of the following sentences by using the word given in capitals at the end of each question to form a word that fits in the gap.

1 There were tremendous ....celebrations.... in the main square last night after Bayern Munich won the cup. CELEBRATE
2 In this airline we make sure that we follow all the .... procedures in order to avoid accidents. SAFE
3 My teacher just looked at me in .... when I answered all the questions perfectly. AMAZE
4 The article was badly written and contained a lot of .... of the same ideas. REPEAT
5 Visitors are often confused to find the .... of two streets with similar names in the town. EXIST
6 If only Maria would tell us the .... instead of trying to deceive us with obvious lies! TRUE
7 Pierre parachuted from a .... of 4,000 metres. HIGH
8 The .... of a swimming pool has made the hotel much more popular. ADD
9 Can you tell the .... between this fake Rolex and the original one made in Switzerland? DIFFER
10 Edison was responsible for many other ...., not just the light bulb. INVENT

Grammar

3 For questions 1–6, complete the second sentence so that it has a similar meaning to the first sentence, using the word given. Do not change the word given. You must use between two and five words, including the word given.

1 We think the flight will arrive on time.
EXPECTED
The flight ....is expected to arrive.......... on time.

2 Thieves entered my house last night.
BROKEN
My house .... thieves last night.

3 According to reports, seven firemen were injured in the fire.
REPORTED
Seven firemen .... been injured in the fire.

4 It's five months since my car was serviced.
BEEN
My car .... five months.

5 According to many people, she's living in Mexico.
SAID
She .... in Mexico.

6 Most of the cakes were still left uneaten at the end of yesterday's party.
EATEN
Almost none of .... at the end of yesterday's party.

Unit 16 *Vocabulary and grammar review*

Vocabulary

1 Write either *check*, *supervise* or *control* in the correct form in each space below.

1 Fred's car became difficult to ....control.... on the icy road.
2 Nancy is not very good at .... her emotions when she disagrees with people.
3 Cooking is a good way for young children to learn, but they must be .... by an adult as kitchens can be dangerous.
4 The police were .... passengers to make sure none of them was carrying a weapon.
5 Two teachers stood at the front of the room .... the exam to make sure no one was cheating.
6 You should .... that you have enough money in your bank account before you buy that computer.

Grammar

2 Write either *when*, *if*, *in case*, *even if*, *even though* or *whether* in each space below. In some cases more than one answer is correct.

1 You shouldn't go paragliding with him ....even if.... he tells you it's perfectly safe.
2 Could you tell me .... you'll be coming to the party, or not?
3 Don't worry .... you've lost your key because I have a spare one.
4 She carried on working .... the noise from the street made it difficult to concentrate.
5 He took his driving licence with him .... he had to identify himself.
6 I'll always remember you .... I never see you again.
7 It's much better to go fishing .... it's raining because the fish can't see you.
8 Sally feels so angry that she says she won't speak to him .... he apologises.
9 Take a book with you .... you have to wait a long time to see the doctor.
10 We bought the car .... it cost twice as much as we wanted to pay.

3 Put each of the following sentences into reported speech starting with the words given.

1 'If I were you, I'd wear a tie to the party,' said Terry.
Terry advised ....me to wear a tie to the party....
2 'Mark, you were the one who caused the accident,' said Patrick.
Patrick accused ....
3 'I'm sorry I didn't ring you!' said Mandy to Maria.
Mandy apologised ....
4 'Would you like to come skiing with me?' Alicia said to me.
Alicia invited ....
5 'I'll do the photocopies for you,' Frankie said to Trish.
Frankie offered ....
6 'I'll give you all the money back at the end of the month,' Gloria told me.
Gloria promised ....
7 'You ought to visit the Musée d'Orsay while you're in Paris,' I said to them.
I recommended ....
8 'Don't forget to buy some eggs while you're out,' Andy said to me.
Andy reminded ....
9 'Walk very carefully because the path is slippery,' Carl told her.
Carl warned ....
10 'Drop your guns and put your hands on your heads,' the police shouted at the thieves.
The police ordered ....

Grammar reference

Contents

Unit 1

Present simple and present continuous

The present simple is used to describe:

- a permanent state or situation: *I live in the town where I was born.*
- a fact or something which is always true: *The earth revolves around the sun.*
- an activity which happens regularly or occasionally: *He gets up at six o'clock every day.*

The present continuous is used to describe:

- a temporary situation: *I'm living with my uncle while the builders finish decorating my house.*
- an activity happening at the present moment: *I'm sorry you can't talk to her at the moment. She's having a shower.*
- an activity in progress but not exactly at the present moment: *I'm studying three foreign languages, so I'm quite busy nowadays.*
- a situation which is changing or developing: *Lots of people are coming to live here, so the town is growing quickly.*
- things the speaker finds strange or irritating, with *always*. This is a way of complaining: *You're always using the telephone. Our phone bill will be enormous!*
- something which happens frequently, with *always*: *My girlfriend is always cooking me special meals!*

State verbs

Verbs which describe states, not actions, are not usually used in the continuous. These verbs describe:

thoughts: *believe, know, remember, think* (meaning *believe*), *feel* (meaning *believe*), *suppose*, etc.

feelings: *love, like, hate, want, prefer*, etc.

senses: *smell, hear, taste, see*

possession: *have, belong, own*, etc.

the verb *to be*.

Present perfect simple and present perfect continuous

Both the present perfect simple and present perfect continuous talk about something which started in the past and:

- either has a result in the present: *He's lost his job* (i.e. he's unemployed now). *I've been partying all weekend, so I'm feeling pretty tired now.*
- or is still happening now: *We've been building an extension to our house* (and we haven't finished yet).

Often they are interchangeable. However:

The present perfect simple	The present perfect continuous
• emphasises the result: *I've phoned all my friends and they're coming to the party.*	• emphasises the activity: *I've been phoning my friends* (that's why I haven't done my homework).
• says how much you have done: *I've cooked three pizzas.*	• says how long you've been doing something: *I've been cooking all afternoon.*
• may give the idea that something is more permanent (and may be accompanied by a time expression which shows this): *He's worked in this shop all his life. I've always lived here.*	• may give the idea that something is temporary (and may be accompanied by a time expression which shows this): *I've been working here for the last two months until I go to university. We've been eating dinner in the garden while the weather has been so warm.*
• is used when we want to say how many times something has been repeated: *I've invited her two or three times but she always says she's busy.*	• when we want to emphasise the process of change over a period of time and that these changes are not finished: *Your English has been improving tremendously since you started doing your homework!*

Remember: state verbs are not normally used in the continuous (see left).

Unit 2

Adjectives with *-ed* and *-ing*

There are many adjectives which can be formed with *-ed* or *-ing*.

- Adjectives with *-ed* express how the person feels about something: *She was terrified as Dracula approached her.*
- Adjectives with *-ing* are used to describe the person or thing which produces the feeling: *There's a surprising article in today's newspaper* (I felt surprised when I read it).
- Not all of these types of adjective have both forms, e.g. *elated* but not ~~*elating*~~.

Comparative and superlative forms of adjectives and adverbs

Comparative forms		
adjective/adverb + *-er* *more* + adjective/ adverb	+ *than*	*Tennis is cheaper than golf.* *Golf is more expensive than tennis.*
Superlative forms		
the + adjective/ adverb + *-est* *the most* + adjective/ adverb		*Chess is one of the cheapest hobbies.* *Playing team sports is the most sociable free-time activity.*

Comparison of adjectives

Add *-er* and *-est* with:	**Use *more* and *most* with:**
• one-syllable adjectives: *Fiona is fitter than last year.* • two-syllable adjectives ending in '-y' and '-ly', e.g. happy, friendly: *My brother's the friendliest person in my family.*	• adjectives of two syllables or more (except two-syllable adjectives ending in '-y' or '-ly'): *Biking is the most dangerous activity.*

These adjectives form irregular comparisons:

good – better – best	bad – worse – worst
much – more – most	many – more – most
little – less – least	far – farther/further – farthest/furthest
old – elder – eldest (for brothers and sisters)	

Spelling

When there is just one vowel before one final consonant, the final consonant is doubled: *hot – hotter, fat – fatter* (BUT *clean – cleaner, safe – safer.*)
Final '-y' becomes 'i': *easy – easier, healthy – healthier.*

To say two things are the same, use *as* + adjective + *as*: *She finds doing aerobics as interesting as playing team sports* (this means: she finds doing aerobics and playing team sports equally interesting).

To say that one thing is less than another, use:

- *not so/as* + adjective + *as*: *Window shopping is not so/as enjoyable as clubbing.*
- *less/least* + adjective: *Playing chess is less healthy than playing team sports. Clubbing is the least healthy.*

Comparison of adverbs

Add *-er* and *-est* with:	**Use *more* and *most* with:**
• one-syllable adverbs, e.g. hard, fast, straight: *My mum works harder than my dad.*	• two-syllable adverbs including adverbs ending in '-ly': *Maria read the text more quickly than Susanna. She visits me more often than in the past.*

These adverbs form irregular comparisons:

well – better – best   badly – worse – worst

To say two things are the same, use *as* + adverb + *as*: *Julia finished the exercise as quickly as Mark* (Julia and Mark finished the exercise equally quickly).

To say that we do one thing differently from another, use:

- *not so/as* + adverb + *as*: *Sophie doesn't speak Spanish so/as well as Gordon.*

Unit 3

Past simple, past continuous and *used to*

The past simple is used for:

- actions or events in the past: *I visited Egypt last year.*
- actions or events which happened one after another: *I saw the Pyramids, then I went round the Cairo Museum and later I went to a traditional restaurant.*
- things which happened for a long time in the past: *She lived in Zurich for ten years from 1992 to 2002.*

The past continuous is used for:

- an activity which started before and continued until an event in the past: *He was driving to work when his car broke down* (the activity of driving was interrupted by the problem with the car).

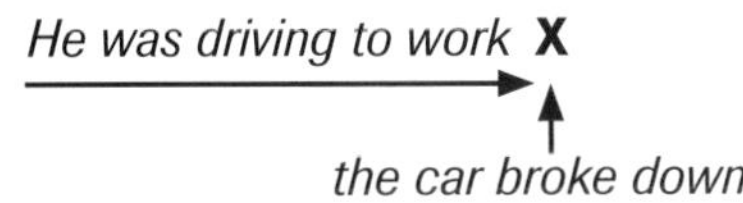

He was driving to work X
the car broke down

- an activity which started before and continued after an event in the past: *I was watching television when the news was announced* (and I continued to watch television afterwards).

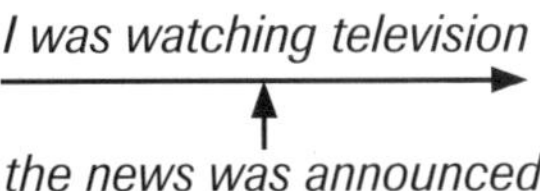

I was watching television
the news was announced

Remember: state verbs are not normally used in the continuous (see *Present simple and present continuous* on page 153).

***Used to* is used for:**

- situations or states in the past which are not true now: *He used to be in the army but now he's a teacher.*
- repeated activities or habits in the past which do not happen now: *She used to run in the London Marathon every year until she injured her leg.*

Note:

- *Used to* is a verb which is only used in the past: *She used to run in the Marathon. Did you use to run in the Marathon? I didn't use to run in the Marathon.*
- To talk about habits in the present, use the present simple with an adverb like *usually, every day*, etc.: *I usually drink tea with my lunch. He catches the same train every day.*

Past perfect tenses

The past perfect simple is used:

- to indicate that we are talking about something which happened **before** something which is described in the past simple: *When he got to the station, his train had already left.* Compare this with: *When he got to the station, his train left.* This indicates that the train left at the time he arrived.
- typically with time expressions like: *when, as soon as, after, before*, etc.: *She started driving before he'd fastened his seatbelt.*
- often with these adverbs: *already, just, never*: *He'd never eaten steak and kidney pie until he came to England.*

The past perfect continuous is also used

- to indicate that we are talking about something which happened before something which is described in the past simple, but it:
- focuses on the length of time: *Mandy needed a walk because she'd been sitting down all day.*
- says how long something happened up to a point in the past: *It was two months before any of the teachers noticed that Paula hadn't been coming to school. He'd been playing for Arsenal for only two games when he scored his first goal.*

Unit 4

So and *such*

***So* and *such* (*a/an*) mean very, extremely:** *That was so kind of you! You have such a beautiful house.*

***So* and *such* (*a/an*) are used to talk about cause and effect:** *He was so late that he missed the beginning of the exam. She gave such a good performance that she won an Oscar.*

so	*such*
so + adjective or adverb (+ *that*): • *He was so nervous before the exam that he couldn't sleep at all.* • *That remark was just so silly!* • *He cooks so well that I think he'll win the competition.*	***such*** + adjective + uncountable noun / plural noun (+ *that*): • *She has such nice children!* • *Switzerland has such spectacular scenery that we always choose it for our holidays.*

so	such
so + *much/many/few/ little* + noun (+ *that*): • *We had so little money left at the end of our holiday that we had to sleep at the station.* • *Marta makes so many mistakes when she's speaking!*	***such a/an*** + adjective + singular countable noun (+ *that*): • *Why did you come in such an old pair of jeans?* • *It was such a beautiful day that we decided to go for a picnic.* ***such a lot of …*** • *Elena's got such a lot of friends that the telephone never stops ringing.*

Too and *enough*

***Too* means more than is needed or wanted:** *She's too old to join the police.*

***Enough* means as much as is necessary or needed:** *Have we got enough eggs to make a cake?*

too	enough
too + adjective (+ noun) + (for somebody) (+ infinitive): • *He's too young to drive.* • *That suitcase is too heavy for me to lift.* ***too*** + adverb + (for somebody) (+ infinitive): • *You're driving too dangerously. Please slow down.* ***too much/too many*** + noun + (for somebody) (+ infinitive): • *They brought too much food for us to eat.* • *I've received too many emails to answer.*	adjective/adverb + ***enough*** + (for somebody) (+ infinitive): • *This coffee is not warm enough! Please heat it up again.* • *Franz didn't answer the questions convincingly enough to get the job.* • *That hotel is not smart enough for her.* ***enough*** + noun + (for somebody) (+ infinitive): • *Have you got enough money to get to London?* • *There isn't enough cake in the cupboard for me to give some to everyone.*

Unit 5

Zero, first and second conditionals

Conditional sentences express a condition (*If* …) and the consequence of the condition.

The consequence can be expressed before or after the condition: *If you come to Canada, we can visit Vancouver. We can visit Vancouver if you come to Canada.*

Note: If the condition comes first, a comma is used. If the consequence comes first, no comma is used.

Zero conditional

***If* + present tense, – present tense:** *If the teacher is late, it sets a bad example to the class.*

Zero conditional is used to express:

- things which are always or generally true: *People get annoyed if you shout at them.*
- scientific facts: *If water boils, it evaporates.*

First conditional

***If/Unless* + present tense, – future tense / modal verb (*may, can, should*, etc.) / imperative:** *If you wash the car, it will look much smarter. You can have an ice cream if you behave well. If he phones, tell him I'm in a meeting. I won't phone you unless it's urgent. You shouldn't go swimming unless you think it's safe.*

The first conditional is used to express a future condition the speaker thinks is possible or likely: *If I get the job, I'll buy myself a new car.*

Second conditional

***If/Unless* + past tense, – *would/could/might* + infinitive:** *If she wasn't so busy, she could come to the party. I would go for a walk, if it wasn't so cold.*

The second conditional is used to express a present or future condition which is imaginary, contrary to the facts, impossible or improbable:

If I was as rich as Bill Gates, I wouldn't work (this is imaginary).

I wouldn't fly in a helicopter unless I was sure it was completely safe (this is imaginary).

Her English would be better if she came to class more often (contrary to the facts – she doesn't come to class often enough).

Indirect questions

Indirect questions are questions which you introduce with a short phrase, e.g. *Do you know …, Could you tell me …, I wonder …, I'd like to know …*

This type of question is used when:

- you are talking to someone you don't know, or
- you are writing a letter or email.

When you ask an indirect question:

- the order of the words in the question is the same as a normal sentence, e.g.

  direct question: *How long* ***have you been*** *studying English?*

  indirect question: *Can you tell me how long* ***you have been*** *studying English?*

  direct question: *When* ***can I phone*** *you?*

  indirect question: *I wonder* ***when I can*** *phone you.*

- the auxiliary verbs *do*, *does* and *did* are not used to form questions; the question has the same form as a normal sentence, e.g.

  direct question: ***Does the train to Paris*** *leave from this platform?*

  indirect question: *Could you tell me if* ***the train to Paris leaves*** *from this platform?*

  direct question: ***Did she speak*** *to the headmaster?*

  indirect question: *Do you know* ***if she spoke*** *to the headmaster?*

- use a question mark (?) when the introductory phrase is a question, e.g.

  Could you tell me *why you haven't done your homework yet?*

- do not use a question mark (?) when the introductory phrase is not a question, e.g.

  I'd like to know *how much the course costs*

- use *if* or *whether* to introduce questions where you expect the answer yes or no, e.g.

  direct question: *Is the university near the city centre?*

  indirect question: *Can you tell me* ***if/whether*** *the university is near the city centre?*

Unit 6

Ways of expressing the future

There are many ways of talking about the future in English. Here is a list of the most important ones.

tense	use	examples
future simple	1 with things which are not certain, especially with *I think, I hope, I expect, probably* and *maybe*	*She'll probably phone later.* *I think it'll be warmer next week.*
	2 predictions for the future	*Sea levels will rise by several centimetres.* *The climate will change.*
	3 *will* can also be used to: • make requests • make promises • make offers • express a decision made at the moment of speaking	 *Will you help me with my homework?* *I won't forget.* *I'll buy you a sandwich if you're hungry.* *That's the phone ringing – I'll get it!*
future continuous	for something happening / in progress at a specific time in the future, or over a period of time in the future	*Don't phone me at 9 o'clock because I'll be having dinner.* *In 2050, sea levels will still be rising.*
future perfect	for things completed *before* a time mentioned in the future	*You can phone me at 10 because I'll have finished dinner by then.* *He'll have made $1 million by the time he's 25.*
'going to' future	1 predictions about the future based on present evidence	*Your work is so good that I reckon you're going to get a Grade A.* *Look at the clouds! I think it's going to snow.*
	2 future plans and intentions	*I'm going to study biology at university.* *He says he's going to phone you tomorrow.*
present continuous	things arranged between people for the future	*I'm seeing the dentist tomorrow – I made the appointment last week.*
present simple	events fixed on a timetable	*The flight to Paris takes off at six.*

Unit 7

Countable and uncountable nouns

Nouns can be either countable [C] or uncountable [U].

Some nouns can be both countable [C] and uncountable [U], but with a difference in meaning: *They say it's healthy to drink tea [U]* (tea in general). *Would you like a tea [C]* (a cup of tea)? *Living in a large house is a lot of work [U]. That picture is a work [C] of art.*

The grammar for countable nouns is different from the grammar for uncountable nouns.

Countable nouns:	**Uncountable nouns:**
• use *a* or *an* in the singular, e.g. *a job, an animal* • can be made plural, e.g. *cars, books* • use *some* and *any* in the plural, e.g. *some friends, any answers* • use *few* and *many* in the plural, e.g. *few students, many years*	• do not use *a* or *an* • cannot be made plural, e.g. *work, music* • use verbs in the singular, e.g. *the news is good, music helps me relax* • use *some* and *any* in the singular, e.g. *some food, any advice* • use *little* and *much*, e.g. *little information, much homework* • use other words to refer to a quantity, e.g. *a piece of advice, an amount of money*

Some common uncountable nouns in English

accommodation	advice	behaviour	countryside	damage	equipment
experience	food	furniture	homework	housework	information
knowledge	luggage	media	music	news	paper
pollution	research	scenery	smoke	software	stuff
transport	work				

Articles

The indefinite article

***A* or *an* are used:**

- with singular, countable nouns mentioned for the first time: *A blue car came round the corner. A strange man with a black beard walked through the door.*
- to express rates: *He drove at 50 kilometres an hour. She earns €50,000 a year.*

***A* or *an* are not used with uncountable nouns or plural countable nouns:** *More women go to university in Spain than men. Knowledge makes people powerful.*

- Use *an* before vowels: *an email* (but not when 'u' or 'e' produces a 'y' sound: *a useful tool, a European student, a university*).
- When 'h' is silent, use *an*: *an hour, an honest man.*

The definite article

***The* is used:**

- with things we have mentioned before or it's clear who or what we are referring to from the context: *I've got a new teacher. The teacher is from California. Could you go to the bank for me, please?* (i.e. the bank we always use)
- with things which are unique: *the internet, the moon*
- with adjectives to express groups: *In this country, the rich are growing richer and the poor are growing poorer.*
- with nationalities: *the French, the Spanish, the Italians* (**Note:** Nationality adjectives ending in *-sh, -ch, -ese,* and *-ss* have a singular form but are plural in meaning: *the English, the Dutch, the Chinese, the Swiss; the English drink a lot of tea, the Chinese are very hard-working.* Other nationality adjectives have a plural form and a plural meaning: *the Americans, the Poles; I think the Brazilians are going to win the World Cup again.*
- with superlatives: *the best, the longest*, etc.
- with *the first, the second, the third* used as adjectives: *Manolo won the first prize and Igor won the second.*
- with names of countries which include these words *Republic, Kingdom, States,* or *Emirates*: *The United States, The Czech Republic, The United Kingdom*, etc.
- with names of rivers, mountain ranges, seas and oceans: *the Nile, the Alps, the Mediterranean, the Pacific.*

Do not use *the*:

- when talking in general and in the plural: *Teachers are not paid enough. I can't imagine offices without computers. Life is hard. Everyone needs love.*
- with many common expressions:
  in/to bed   *to church*   *at home*
  in/to hospital   *in/to prison*   *at/to school*
  at/to university   *at/to work*
  He's in bed. I'm at university. What time do you go to work? She's been taken to hospital.

Unit 8

Infinitives and verb + *-ing* forms

Infinitive

The infinitive is used:

- to say why you do something: *I've just gone running to get some exercise. He's taken up tennis to make friends.*
- to say why something exists: *There's an example to help you.*
- after *too* and *enough*: *It's too cold to go swimming today. He isn't good enough to make the national team.*

The infinitive is used after these verb patterns:

- **verb + *to* infinitive:** *She agreed to meet him after work.*

  agree appear begin bother decide demand fail hope learn manage offer plan refuse seem be supposed threaten

- **verb + (somebody/something) + *to* infinitive:** *She expected to win the race. I expect you to play in the match.*

  ask choose expect help intend promise want

- **verb + somebody/something + *to* infinitive:** *The money enabled him to go to university.*

  advise allow enable encourage forbid force invite order permit persuade recommend remind teach tell warn

The following verbs from the lists above can be used to report speech:

advise agree allow ask decide encourage forbid invite offer order permit persuade promise recommend refuse remind tell threaten warn

Note: For more information on how to use these verbs, see *Reported speech 2: reporting verbs* on page 167.

Verb + *-ing*

The verb + *-ing* is used:

- after prepositions: *He's made a lot of friends by joining the tennis club. We watched a film about climbing in the mountains.*
- as subjects or objects of a sentence: *Climbing is safer than it looks. He decided to take up adventure racing.*

The verb + *-ing* is used after these verbs:

admit appreciate avoid celebrate consider delay deny dislike enjoy finish imagine involve keep mind miss postpone practise regret risk stop suggest

I really enjoyed winning that match. She suggested playing a game of squash after school.

The following verbs from the list can be used in reported speech:

admit deny regret suggest

Note: For more information on how to use these verbs, see *Reported speech 2: reporting verbs* on page 167.

The verb + *-ing* is used after these expressions:

it's no good it's not worth it's no use it's a waste of time can't stand can't bear can't help

It's not worth joining that sports club. It's a waste of time entering the competition unless you're really fit. I can't bear watching my team when they play badly.

Verbs followed by either an infinitive or a verb + *-ing* with the same meaning:

love begin continue hate* prefer* like* start*

I love playing tennis. I love to play tennis.
It continued raining all day. It continued to rain all day.

* When these verbs are used with *would*, they are always followed by the infinitive: *I wouldn't like to do an adventure race. I'd prefer to watch it on television.*

Verbs followed by either an infinitive or a verb + *-ing* with a difference in meaning

	verb + infinitive	verb + *-ing*
remember	*Did you remember to bring your running shoes?* (an action you have to do)	*I remember feeling very tired at the end of the race* (a memory of something in the past).
forget	*Don't forget to bring your tennis racket* (an action you have to do).	*I'll never forget winning my first tennis championship* (a memory of something in the past).*
regret	*I regret to tell you the race has been cancelled* (*regret + to say / to tell / to inform* means: I'm sorry to give you this information).	*I regret not training harder before the race* (I'm sorry I didn't do this).
try	*I'm running every day because I'm trying to get fit* (my objective is to get fit).	*If you want to get fit, why don't you try swimming?* (swimming is a method to reach your objective)
mean	*Nadal means to win the championship* (this is his intention).	*I wanted to be a swimming champion, but it meant going to the pool every day at 5.30* (it involved).
stop	*Halfway through the marathon, he stopped to drink some water* (in order to drink some water).	*When he realised he couldn't win, he stopped running* (he didn't continue).

* This form is unusual. It is more normal to use *(not) remember*:
I don't remember riding a bike the first time.
~~*I forget riding a bike the first time.*~~

Unit 9

Reported speech 1

Tense changes in reported speech

If the reporting verb (*said, told, admitted, warned,* etc.) is in the past, make the following tense changes:

- present simple → past simple: *'I live in Berlin.'* → *She said she lived in Berlin.*
- present continuous → past continuous: *'I'm watching TV.'* → *He said he was watching TV.*
- present perfect → past perfect: *'I've seen the film already.'* → *She said she had seen the film already.*
- past simple → past perfect: *'I missed the concert.'* → *He told me he had missed the concert.*
- *will* → *would*: *'I'll phone you soon.'* → *She promised she would phone me soon.*

These modal verbs also change:

- *can* → *could: 'I can understand German, but I can't speak it.'* → *She said she could understand German but she couldn't speak it.*
- *may* → *might: 'I may give the book to John.'* → *The teacher suggested he might give the book to John.*
- *must* → *had to: 'I must cook supper.'* → *Tanya said she had to cook supper.*

The following modal verbs do not change in reported speech: *could, would, should, might, ought to* and *used to.*

***Would* doesn't change:** *'I would prefer to study in London.'* → *She said that she would prefer to study in London.*

***Must* usually changes to *had to*:** *'You must read this text for the next lesson.'* → *My teacher told me I had to read the text for the following lesson.*

***Must* doesn't change:**

- when it's negative: '*You mustn't tell Katya our secret.*' → *Ana told Stefan he mustn't tell Katya their secret.*
- when it expresses a deduction: *'Arturo must still be asleep.'* → *She said that Arturo must still be asleep.*

Note: If the reporting verb is in a present tense, no tense changes are necessary: *'I'll help you with your homework.'* → *She says she'll help me with my homework.*

Questions in reported speech

To report a question, make the following changes.

- Change the word order in the question to the same as a normal sentence (see *Indirect questions* on page 156).
- Make the same tense changes as above.
- Use the same question words (*when, where, how,* etc.).
- Use a full stop (.), not a question mark (?): *'How long **have you been** living in London?'* → *She asked me how long **I had been** living in London. 'When **can I phone** you?'* → *Abdullah asked Magdi **when he could** phone him.*
- The auxiliary verbs *do, does* and *did* are not used; the question has the same form as a normal sentence: *'What time **does the lesson start**?'* → *Ludmila asked what time **the lesson started**.*
- 'Yes/No questions' use *if* or *whether*: '*Can I come to your party?'* → *Aniela wanted to know **whether** she could come to our party.*

Verbs and phrases used to introduce reported questions: *ask, wonder, want to know, enquire.*

Pronoun, adjective and adverb changes in reported speech

We usually make the following changes:

- *you* → *he / she / they: 'I spoke to you earlier.'* → *He said he had spoken to her earlier.*
- *your* → *his / her / their; our* → *their: 'I'll come to your house later.'* → *He promised that he would come to her house later.*
- *this / that* (pronouns) → *it: 'You should give this to Joan.'* → *She told him he should give it to Joan.*
- *this / that work* (etc.) → *the work; these / those cars* (etc.) → *the cars: 'This work is very good.'* → *She told him the work was very good.*
- *today / this week / this month / this year* → *that day / that week / that month / that year*
- *tomorrow / next month / next year* → <u>*the*</u> *next /* <u>*the*</u> *following day / month / year*
- *yesterday / last week / month / year* → *the day before / the previous day / the previous week / month / year; the week / month / year before*
- *here* → *there*

Note: For more on reported speech, see these Grammar reference sections:

page 159: Infinitives and verb + *-ing* forms

page 166: The passive with reporting verbs

page 167: Reported speech 2: reporting verbs

Linking words for contrast

Although, even though, while and *whereas*

- *Although, even though, while* and *whereas* are used to put two contrasting ideas in one sentence: *I didn't buy the car although I thought it was beautiful.*
- They can be placed at the beginning of the sentence or in the middle, between the two contrasting ideas: *It was late. She decided to phone him.* → *Although it was late, she decided to phone him.* OR *She decided to phone him although it was late.*
- When the sentence begins with *although, even though, while* or *whereas*, we separate the two parts with a comma. When these words are placed in the middle, no comma is used: *Berlin is a noisy city. My home village is*

quite peaceful. → *While Berlin is a noisy city, my home village is quite peaceful.* OR *Berlin is a noisy city whereas my home village is quite peaceful.*

- *Even though* is stronger than *although*: *I didn't buy the car even though I had the money ready in my pocket.*

However

- *However* normally starts a new sentence and refers to the sentence before.
- It is usually followed by a comma: *He decided to go out to the cinema. However, he didn't tell his family where he was going.*

Despite and *in spite of*

- *Despite* and *in spite of* mean without taking any notice of or being influenced by; not prevented by: *He got into the army despite being quite short. She went swimming in spite of the cold weather.*
- They can be placed at the beginning of the sentence or in the middle. They are followed by a noun or a verb + *-ing*.
- When used at the beginning of a sentence, a comma is also used to separate the two parts of the sentence: *Despite working all day, Teresa didn't feel at all tired. We got to school on time in spite of the heavy traffic.*

But

- *But* can be used to join two sentences. In this case it is used in the middle of the sentence and it usually follows a comma: *We warned her, but she didn't pay any attention.*
- It can sometimes be used at the beginning of a new sentence: *He likes romantic films. But don't tell anybody!*

Unit 10

Modal verbs to express certainty and possibility

To express certainty about the present	• Use ***must***: *She's been in over 15 films, so she must be very well known.* **Note**: we usually have a good reason for expressing this certainty, e.g. *She's been in over 15 films.* • Use ***can't*** or ***couldn't*** for the negative (**not** ~~*mustn't*~~). *You can't be tired. You've just got out of bed! Mark couldn't be coming to the party – he's on holiday in America at the moment.*
To express certainty about the past	• Use ***must have*** + past participle: *You have a very big part in the play. It must have taken you ages to learn all the lines.* • Use ***can't have*** and ***couldn't have*** + past participle for the negative: *She can't have left her glasses at home – I saw her wearing them on the bus. She couldn't have stolen the money because she's far too honest!*
To express possibility about the present or future	• Use ***may***, ***might*** or ***could***: *I may come and visit you next summer. We might go to the cinema this evening if we finish all our work in time. We'd better go out for a walk now because it could rain later.* • Use ***may not*** and ***might not*** (**not** ~~*mayn't*~~ or ~~*mightn't*~~) for the negative (**not** ~~*can't*~~ or ~~*couldn't*~~ which express certainty): *Frankie is looking very pale. He may not be very well. Don't cook any dinner for me because I might not be back in time.*
To express possibility about the past	• Use ***may have, might have, could have, may not have, might not have*** + past participle: *It's unlike Sally to be late. She may have overslept, or she might not have remembered the appointment.*

Unit 11

Expressing ability

To say someone has an ability, use *can, can't, could, couldn't, be able to*, and *manage*.

- **In the present, use:**
  - ***can*** or ***am / is / are able to*** for things which are possible: *Francesca can speak five languages, but she can't speak Russian. She's able to play the piano but she isn't able to play the violin.*
  - ***can't*** or ***am not / isn't / aren't able to*** for things which are not possible (see examples above).

  Note: We usually use *can* and *can't* when speaking because they are shorter.
- **In the past, use:**
  - ***could*** only when you are speaking in general: *When I was a child, I could read without glasses.* (**not** ~~*I was able to read without glasses.*~~)
  - ***was / were able to*** when you are speaking about one particular occasion: *Dad didn't have any money on him, but fortunately he was able to use his credit card to pay the bill.* (**not** ~~*he could use his credit card to pay the bill.*~~)
  - ***couldn't*** and ***wasn't / weren't able to*** when you are speaking in general and also when you are speaking about one particular occasion: *Pascual wasn't able to / couldn't do all the questions in the maths exam. Olga couldn't / wasn't able to ride a bike till she was 18.*
- **Use *can* only in the present and *could* only in the past. For perfect and future tenses, use *able to*:** *I've been very busy so I haven't been able to finish reading the novel* (present perfect). *When you finish the course, you'll be able to speak English really well* (future simple). Remember the verb *to be* is not used in the continuous.
- **Use *be able to* after an infinitive:** *She hopes to be able to study medicine when she goes to university.*
- **Use *be able to* after modal verbs (*might, should, may*, etc.):** *If I'm free this weekend, I might be able to help you paint your house. When you've finished this course, you should be able to speak English very well.*
- **Use *can* and *could* with *see, hear, smell, feel* and *taste*:** *From the top of the mountain we could see for more than 50 km. I can hear a strange noise coming from upstairs.*
- **Use *manage* when you succeed in doing something quite difficult to do:** *I know you've been busy, but did you manage to phone my mum? He managed to pass the exam although he was feeling ill when he did it.* Remember *could* is only possible when speaking in general: ~~*He could pass the exam although he was feeling ill when he did it.*~~

As and *like*

As

Use *as*:

- to say someone or something is that thing, or has that function: *He works as a nurse. She uses email as a way of keeping in touch with her friends. Can I give you some advice as a friend?*
- before a subject + verb: *Things happened exactly as I had predicted* (in the way I predicted).
- to mean because: *As Mum is away, I'm going to cook lunch today.*
- after certain verbs including *describe as, consider as, regard as*: *The teachers regard you as the best group of students in the school. The police are describing him as extremely dangerous.*
- with adjectives and adverbs to make comparisons: *Mike is not as clever as his sister.*
- to mean for example in the phrase *such as*: *I spent the summer travelling round Europe and visiting lots of places such as Venice, Florence and Barcelona.*
- with *same … as*: *You're wearing the same colour shirt as me!*
- in these phrases:
  - *as far as I know* (I think it's true but I don't know all the facts): *As far as I know, Woody Allen has never won an Oscar.*
  - *as far as I'm concerned* (this is my personal opinion): *I don't mind how much money you spend on clothes – you can spend all your money on clothes as far as I'm concerned.*
  - *as far as I can see/tell* (this is what I've noticed or understood): *Arsenal aren't going to win the cup this year as far as I can see.*

Like

Use *like*:

- to mean similar to (especially with *look, sound, smell, seem, taste*, etc.): *My boyfriend looks just like Brad Pitt! This swimming pool is fantastic – the artificial waves mean it's like swimming in the sea.*
- to mean for example: *He enjoys all sorts of adventure sports like paragliding, windsurfing and canoeing.*

Look, seem and *appear*

You can use these verbs to express your impressions of something or someone: *I haven't talked to him very much, but he seems very intelligent. You still look tired even if you have slept all night.*

These verbs can be used with the following patterns:

- *look / seem / appear* + adjective: *She looks very old. He seems hungry. Marga appeared tired.*
- subject + *look* + *as if* + sentence: *The car looks as if it needs washing. You look as if you've had a bad day.*
- *it looks / seems* + *as if* + sentence: *It looks as if the car needs washing. It seems as if you've had a bad day.*
- *seem / appear* + infinitive: *The weather seems to have changed. She appeared to be crying.*
- *look / seem* + *like* + noun: *He looks like my uncle. It may seem like an impossible task, but it isn't really.*

Unit 12

Relative pronouns and relative clauses

relative clause

The man [*who phoned you*] *is my doctor.*

A clause is part of a sentence. Relative clauses start with these relative pronouns: *who, which, that, whose, where, when* and *why*.

Defining relative clauses

Relative clauses which tell you which person or thing the speaker is talking about are called ***defining relative clauses***. They give essential information, e.g. *The doctor who treated me is my cousin.* The relative clause (underlined) tells us which doctor we are talking about.

Non-defining relative clauses

Relative clauses which give you extra information are called ***non-defining relative clauses***: *My doctor, who belongs to the same tennis club as you, vaccinated me yesterday.* We already know which doctor (it's my doctor); *who belongs to the same tennis club as you* does not tell us which doctor we are talking about; it just adds extra information.

There are differences in grammar.

Defining relative clauses	Non-defining relative clauses
• Don't have commas. • Use the following relative pronouns: *who, which, whose, where, when, why.* • *That* can be used instead of *who* or *which.* • *Who, which* or *that* can be omitted when they are the object of the clause: *The medicine (which/that) the doctor gave me should be taken twice a day* (*the doctor* is the subject and *which/that* the object of the clause).	• Use commas (or pauses in spoken English). • Use the following relative pronouns: *who, which, whose, where, when, why.* • Don't use *that.* • The relative pronoun cannot be omitted.

Unit 13

Third conditional

The third conditional is used to talk about:

- something which did not happen in the past and
- its results, which are imaginary.

If I had lived in the 19th century, I would have gone to school by horse. (*If I had lived in the 19th century* (something which did not happen – I am alive now), *I would have gone to school by horse* (an imaginary consequence because I didn't live in the 19th century).

If I hadn't reacted quickly, the hippo would have killed me (I reacted quickly, so the hippo didn't kill me).

The third conditional has the following form:

If + past perfect tense, – *would have* + (*done / been / eaten,* etc.):

If you had phoned me this morning, I would not have been late for school.

If you had gone to the concert, you would have enjoyed it a lot.

Note: You can contract the third conditional as follows:

If I'd lived in the 19th century, I'd have gone to school by horse.

If he hadn't been in such a hurry, he wouldn't have had an accident.

You can use *could* and *might* instead of *would*:

- *If our team had played harder, they could have won the match* (they had the ability to win the match, but they didn't, because they didn't play hard enough).
- Compare this with: *If our team had played harder, they would have won the match* (they were sure to win, but they didn't because they didn't play hard enough).
- *If the weather had been better, we might have gone swimming* (swimming was a possibility).
- Compare this with: *If the weather had been better, we would have gone swimming* (swimming was a certainty).

Wish, if only and *hope*

Use *wish / if only* + past simple to say we would like a present situation to be different: *I wish I had a bigger car* (because my car is too small). *If only it was the summer holidays* (but it isn't – I'm still at school).

Use *wish / if only* + *would* to say:

- we want something to happen: *I wish my car would start* (I can't make it start and I want it to start). *If only the lesson would end* (I want it to end).
- we want someone to start doing something they do not do: *If only you'd listen to me!* or we want someone to stop doing something which annoys us: *I wish you wouldn't borrow my clothes! If only my mum wouldn't phone me every five minutes!*

Use *wish / if only* + past perfect to talk about things which we are unhappy about which happened in the past: *He wishes he had studied harder when he was at school* (he didn't study hard enough – perhaps if he had studied harder he would have gone to university). *If only they hadn't scored that goal!* (they scored a goal and as a result we probably won't win the match).

***If only* means *I wish*. When talking about other people we use *he wishes*, *they wish*, etc. We use *if only* when we feel something very strongly. Otherwise we use *I wish*.**

Use *hope* when we want something to happen or to be true, and usually have a good reason to think that it might: *I hope you have a good holiday. She hopes she'll get a high grade in her exams. He hopes to go into politics in the future.*

We can use *hope* when we want something to be true about the past, but we don't know if it is true: *I hope you had a good flight* (but I don't know if you had a good flight). *I hope you had good weather for your party* (but I don't know if the weather was good).

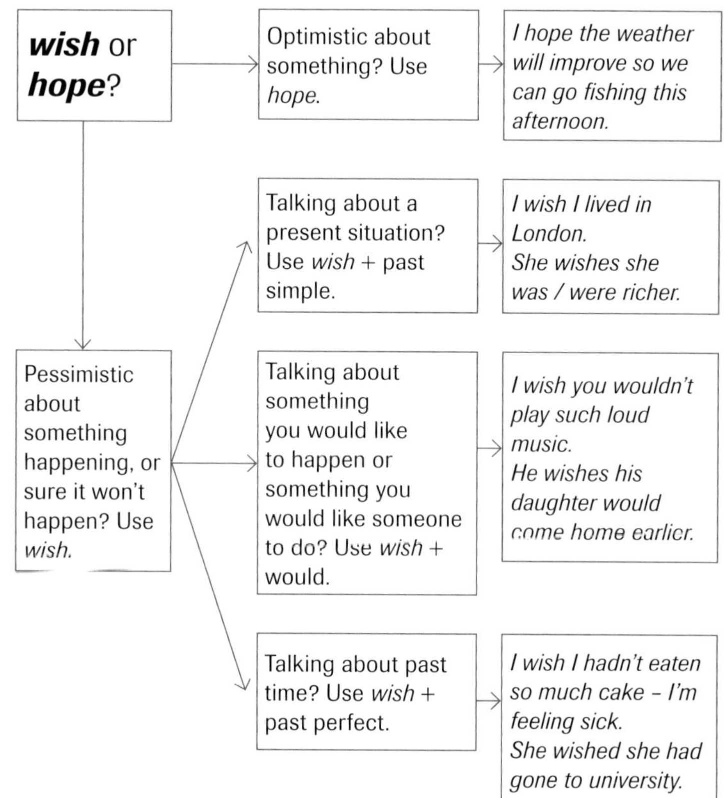

Unit 14

Causative *have*

- We use this structure *have + something + done / made / cleaned* when we ask someone else to do something for us: *We're having the house painted* (i.e. the decorators are painting our house for us). *I've just had my watch repaired* (i.e. a watchmaker has just repaired my watch).
- Usually it's not necessary to say who did it for us, but it is possible: *I've just had my hair cut by my brother-in-law* (i.e. my brother-in-law has just cut my hair for me).
- *Have something done* can be used in any tense or form: *I'm thinking of having my hair dyed green. Maggie's going to have her shoulder tattooed.*

Expressing obligation and permission

Obligation – *must* and *have to*

- Only use ***must*** in the present tense. For other tenses use ***have to***: *I'd like to go camping with you, but I'll have to ask my parents first. In order to escape from the guards they had to swim across a river.*
- Use ***must*** when the obligation is something you agree with. Teacher to students: *You must hand in your homework on Monday.*
- Use ***have to*** when the obligation comes from someone else: *My teacher has given me a lot of homework which I have to do for Monday.*

- Use ***must*** for strong advice: *You must be careful if you stay out late at night.*
- Use ***be supposed to*** to talk about an obligation which may be different from what really happens: *We're supposed to do five writing tasks each term* (but most people only do two or three). *Aren't you supposed to be in class* (not out here playing football)?
- Use ***should*** to talk about the right thing to do, but which is different from what really happens: *I should do the housework instead of watching television in the middle of the afternoon. He should write his own answers instead of copying them from the internet.*
- The past of ***should*** is ***should have***: *You shouldn't have shouted at your father like that!*

Prohibition

- Use these modal verbs and phrases to express prohibition: ***can't, mustn't, not let, am not allowed to, don't allow (me) to.***

  You can't go in there – it says 'No entry!'

  You mustn't speak during the exam – it's forbidden.

  My sister won't let me listen to her CDs.

  I'm not allowed to use the kitchen in my host family's house.

  My parents didn't allow me to play computer games when I was small.
- Do not use ***don't have to*** to express prohibition: *You mustn't use your mobile phone in class* (it's not allowed). Compare this with: *You don't have to use your mobile phone to speak to Fayed. Look! He's over there* (i.e. it's not necessary).
- To talk about the past use: ***couldn't, didn't let, wasn't allowed to, didn't allow (me) to***. *I couldn't leave the room until the end of the meeting. She wasn't allowed to invite her boyfriend to the party.*
- Do not use ***mustn't*** to talk about the past. *We ~~mustn't~~ couldn't use our dictionary in the exam last week.*

Permission

- To express permission use: ***can*** (past ***could***), ***let, am allowed to*** and ***may*** (past ***was/were allowed to***). *You can only smoke in open spaces, not inside buildings. Are we allowed to use the phone in the office for private calls? She let him borrow her bicycle to get to the station.*
- Only use ***may*** in formal situations: *It's not necessary to stay until the end of the examination. When you have answered all the questions, you may leave the room.*

No obligation

- To say that there is no obligation, or it's not necessary use: ***don't have to, don't need to*** and ***needn't***: *This is a really good exercise on phrasal verbs for anyone who's interested, but it's not for homework, so you don't have to do it if you don't want to. You needn't learn all the vocabulary on this page – only the words you think are useful.*
- ***I didn't need to*** means it wasn't necessary and I didn't do it; ***I needn't have*** means it wasn't necessary but I did it: *I didn't need to buy a newspaper to find out the story because I'd already heard it on the radio. What lovely roses! You needn't have bought me so many, but it was very generous of you.*

Unit 15

The passive

Form

The passive is formed by the verb *to be* + *done* / *eaten* / *cleaned*, etc.

Active	Passive
They ate all the food very quickly.	*All the food was eaten very quickly.*
We've sold the car.	*The car has been sold.*
It's nice when people invite me to dinner.	*It's nice when I'm invited to dinner.*
On a clear day you can see Ibiza from the mainland.	*On a clear day Ibiza can be seen from the mainland.*

Uses

The passive is used when:

- the speaker doesn't know who or what does/did something: *My car has been stolen!*
- the speaker doesn't need to say who or what does/did something because it's obvious from the situation or context: *The law was passed earlier this year* (obviously by parliament).
- what happens is more important than who does it: *The car has been repaired so we can go away this weekend.*
- when writing in a formal style: *Your ticket has been booked and can be collected from our office.*

The passive with *get*

- You can use *get* instead of *be* to form the passive, especially when you want to say that something happened to someone or something: *He got hurt playing football yesterday* (He was hurt). *I'm afraid we were playing football and one of your windows got broken* (one of your windows was broken).
- Only use *get* when something happens or changes: *He got arrested by the* police. It is not possible with state verbs (see page 153): ~~*The car got owned by a film star.*~~ *The car was owned by a film star.*
- *Get* is used mainly in informal spoken English.

The passive with reporting verbs

The passive is often used to report what people say, think, etc. especially when we don't know who said it or thought it, or it's not important: *The Queen is thought to be suffering from a heavy cold. Fernando Alonso is considered to be the best Spanish Formula One driver of all time.*

This use of the passive is common in news reports.

We use three possible forms.

- *He/She is said, thought, considered*, etc. + infinitive: *Lions are known to hunt in this area. Elena is thought to be highly intelligent.*

  Verbs that can be used with this pattern are: *consider, discover, expect, feel, know, say, suppose, think, understand.*

  To talk about the past we can use: *She is said to have played / eaten / been*, etc.: *The Prime Minister is understood to have spoken to the rebels on the phone.*
- *It is said, thought, considered*, etc. + *that* + a sentence: *It is thought that Elena is highly intelligent. It is known that lions hunt in this area.*

  Verbs that can be used with this pattern are: *agree, announce, consider, decide, discover, expect, feel, find, know, mention, propose, recommend, say, suggest, suppose, think, understand.*
- *It is agreed, planned*, etc. + infinitive: *It has been agreed to change the dates of the meeting.*

  Verbs that can be used with this pattern are: *agree, decide, forbid, hope, plan, propose.*

Unit 16

Linking words and phrases: *when, if, in case, even if* and *even though*

Use *when* to talk about:

- a situation: *I feel very uncomfortable when the weather is so hot.*
- something you know will happen at some point in time: *I'm writing an essay at the moment. When I finish, I'll phone you back.*

Use *if* to describe:

- something you are not sure will happen: *We'll miss the beginning of the film if the bus is late.*

Compare:

- *If I get a place at university, my parents will buy me a new car* (I'm not sure if I'll get a place at university).
- *When I get a place at university, my parents will buy me a new car* (I'm confident I'll get a place at university).

Use *in case*:

- with the present tense to talk about something which might happen in the future: *I'll take a book to read in case I have to wait a long time for the train. Take a bottle of water with you in case you get thirsty.*
- with the past simple to explain why someone did something: *Clara turned off her mobile phone in case it rang during the exam* (she thought it might ring during the exam, so she turned it off).

***In case* and *if* are different. Compare:**

- *I'll take my swimming costume in case we go to the beach* (I'll take it now because we might go to the beach later).
- *I'll take my swimming costume if we go to the beach* (I won't take my swimming costume now, because I don't know if we will go to the beach – we might not go to the beach).

Use *even though* as a stronger way of saying *although* when we are certain about something:

- *He bought a new computer even though his old one was working perfectly* (the speaker is certain the old one was working perfectly).
- *I'm really looking forward to my holiday even though the weather forecast is for rain* (the speaker knows the weather forecast is for rain).

Use *even if* as a stronger way of saying *if*, when you are not certain about something:

- *I'm going to have a holiday in the USA this summer even if I fail all my exams* (I'm not sure if I'm going to fail my exams – but I'm going to have the holiday anyway).
- *I'll come to your party even if I have to walk there* (I don't know if I'll have to walk there, but I'll make sure I come to your party).

Reported speech 2: reporting verbs

There are many verbs which can be used to introduce reported speech, each followed by different grammatical patterns. You will see that most verbs can be followed by more than one grammatical pattern.

Verb + infinitive

agree: *Magda agreed to look after the children.*

offer: *She offered to take the children to the zoo.*

promise: *She's promised to phone me later.*

Verb + object + infinitive

advise: *The doctor advised Mrs Carter to take a long holiday.*

ask: *The neighbours asked us to turn our music down.*

invite: *Patsy has invited me to go to the party with her.*

order: *The police ordered everyone to leave the building.*

persuade: *I persuaded my mother to take a holiday.*

remind: *Can I remind you to phone Stephen?*

tell: *Carl told Jane to close all the windows.*

warn: *They warned us not to walk on the ice.*

Verb + preposition + noun or verb + *-ing*

accuse of: *Biggs was accused of robbery. Sophie was accused of stealing books.*

admit to: *Bill admitted to the mistake. Sally admitted to taking the money.*

apologise for: *Tommy apologised for the accident. Mandy apologised for being late.*

complain about: *The neighbours have been complaining about the noise. We complained about being given too much homework to do.*

Verb + noun or verb + *-ing*

admit: *Danny admitted the theft. Sue admitted stealing the money.*

deny: *Silvia denied the theft. Sean denied causing the accident.*

recommend: *I can really recommend this book.*
I recommend cycling as a way of getting fit.

suggest*: *Jasmine suggested the solution to the problem. Mike suggested going climbing at the weekend.*

Verb + (*that*) + sentence

admit: *Sally admitted (that) she had taken the money.*

agree: *The headteacher agreed (that) the exam had been too difficult.*

complain: *We complained that we had been given too much homework to do.*

deny: *Pablo denied that he had caused the accident.*

explain: *She explained that she wasn't feeling very well.*

promise: *Mandy promised (that) she would phone later.*

recommend: *The doctor recommended (that) I take more exercise.*

say: *Robin said (that) he was going swimming later.*

suggest*: *Liz suggested (that) I should try the shopping centre on the edge of town.*

Verb + object + (*that*) + sentence

persuade: *I persuaded my mother that she should take a holiday.*

promise: *Mandy promised Charlie (that) she would phone him later.*

remind: *Can I remind you (that) you've got to phone Stephen?*

tell: *The school told the students (that) they had the rest of the day free.*

warn: *Nobody warned me (that) my grandmother was visiting us today.*

Others

ask + *if / what*, etc. + sentence: *She asked me what I was doing. He asked me if I was free.*

invite + object + *to* + noun: *Patsy has invited me to the party.*

*** Note: *Suggest* is never followed by the infinitive. The following patterns are possible:**

suggest + verb + *-ing: Maria suggested buying a new computer.*

suggest + noun: *Phil suggested the idea.*

suggest + *(that)* + sentence with a verb in a tense: *Tony suggested that they played football that afternoon.*

suggest + *(that)* + should: *Chantal suggested I should write a letter.*

Irregular verbs

verb	past simple	past participle
arise	arose	arisen
be	was/were	been
beat	beat	beaten
become	became	become
begin	began	begun
bend	bent	bent
bite	bit	bitten
bleed	bled	bled
blow	blew	blown
break	broke	broken
bring	brought	brought
broadcast	broadcast	broadcast
build	built	built
burn	burnt/burned	burnt/burned
burst	burst	burst
buy	bought	bought
catch	caught	caught
choose	chose	chosen
come	came	come
cost	cost	cost
creep	crept	crept
cut	cut	cut
deal	dealt	dealt
dig	dug	dug
do	did	done
draw	drew	drawn
dream	dreamt/dreamed	dreamt/dreamed
drink	drank	drunk
drive	drove	driven
eat	ate	eaten
fall	fell	fallen
feed	fed	fed
feel	felt	felt
fight	fought	fought
find	found	found
fly	flew	flown
forbid	forbade	forbidden
forget	forgot	forgotten
forgive	forgave	forgiven
freeze	froze	frozen
get	got	got
give	gave	given
go	went	gone
grow	grew	grown
hang	hung	hung
have	had	had
hear	heard	heard
hide	hid	hidden
hit	hit	hit
hold	held	held
hurt	hurt	hurt
keep	kept	kept
kneel	knelt	knelt
know	knew	known
lay	laid	laid
lead	led	led
lean	leant/leaned	leant/leaned
learn	learnt/learned	learnt/learned
leave	left	left
lend	lent	lent
let	let	let
lie	lay	lain
light	lit	lit
lose	lost	lost
make	made	made
mean	meant	meant
meet	met	met
pay	paid	paid
put	put	put
read	read	read
ride	rode	ridden
ring	rang	rung
rise	rose	risen
run	ran	run
say	said	said
see	saw	seen
sell	sold	sold
send	sent	sent
set	set	set
sew	sewed	sewn
shake	shook	shaken
shine	shone	shone
shoot	shot	shot
show	showed	shown
shrink	shrank	shrunk
shut	shut	shut
sing	sang	sung
sink	sank	sunk
sit	sat	sat
sleep	slept	slept
slide	slid	slid
smell	smelt/smelled	smelt/smelled
sow	sowed	sown
speak	spoke	spoken
spell	spelt/spelled	spelt/spelled
spend	spent	spent
spill	spilt/spilled	spilt/spilled
spit	spat	spat
split	split	split
spoil	spoilt/spoiled	spoilt/spoiled
spread	spread	spread
spring	sprang	sprung
stand	stood	stood
steal	stole	stolen
stick	stuck	stuck
sting	stung	stung
strike	struck	struck
swear	swore	sworn
sweep	swept	swept
swell	swelled	swollen
swim	swam	swum
swing	swung	swung
take	took	taken
teach	taught	taught
tear	tore	torn
tell	told	told
think	thought	thought
throw	threw	thrown
understand	understood	understood
wake	woke	woken
wear	wore	worn
weep	wept	wept
win	won	won
write	wrote	written

Writing reference

What to expect in the exam

The Writing paper is Paper 2. It lasts 1 hour and 20 minutes.

You do two tasks.

- In Part 1, there is one task which you **must** do.
- In Part 2, you choose **one** of four tasks.

Part 1

You are given a letter, email or another short text with four points on it.

- You must write a letter or email to include the four points.
- Your letter or email must be between 120–150 words.

You are expected to:

- include the four points
- organise your answer in a logical way
- make requests, give information, suggest, write, complain, apologise, explain, etc.
- use a formal or informal style, depending who your readers are
- write grammatically correct sentences
- use accurate spelling and punctuation.

You have approximately 40 minutes to do this part (the Writing Paper lasts 1 hour 20 minutes, so if you spend more time on this part, you will have less time for the other part).

You studied and practised writing Part 1 in Units 1, 5, 7 and 15.

How to do Part 1

1 Read the instructions, the text (e.g. letter) and notes carefully.

2 Find and underline the four points you must deal with. You'll lose marks if you don't deal with them all.

3 Read the instructions to find out who will read the letter or email. Then decide whether you should write in a formal or informal style.

4 Make notes and organise your notes into a plan. When writing your plan, decide how many paragraphs you need and what you'll say in each paragraph.

5 Before writing your final letter, check that your plan covers the four points.

6 Write your letter or email following your plan.

7 When you have finished, read your answer carefully. Check you have written at least 120 words and correct any mistakes you find.

Exercise 1

Look at the following Part 1 task.

1 What are the four points you must deal with?

2 Should you use a formal or an informal style? Why?

3 Some of the notes tell you what to say. For others you have to think of information yourself. What information do you have to think of?

You **must** answer this question. Write your answer in 120–150 words in an appropriate style.

You help to organise meetings at your college and recently you have invited people with interesting jobs to speak to students about their work. You have received this email from a policewoman, Barbara Winslow, who you invited to speak on 2nd November. Read Barbara Winslow's email and the notes you have made. Then write an email to her using **all** your notes.

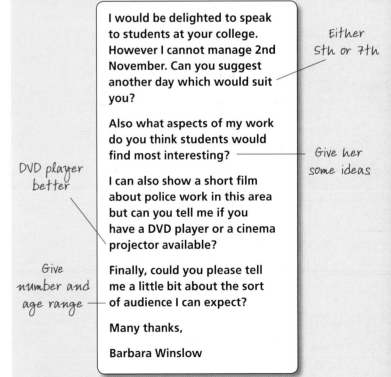

I would be delighted to speak to students at your college. However I cannot manage 2nd November. Can you suggest another day which would suit you? — *Either 5th or 7th*

Also what aspects of my work do you think students would find most interesting? — *Give her some ideas*

I can also show a short film about police work in this area but can you tell me if you have a DVD player or a cinema projector available? — *DVD player better*

Finally, could you please tell me a little bit about the sort of audience I can expect? — *Give number and age range*

Many thanks,

Barbara Winslow

Write your **email**. You must use grammatically correct sentences with accurate spelling and punctuation in a style appropriate for the situation.

Exercise 2

Read this answer to the task in Exercise 1.

1 What information has the writer invented for his/her answer?

2 Is the style formal or informal? (For differences between formal and informal styles, see page 76.)

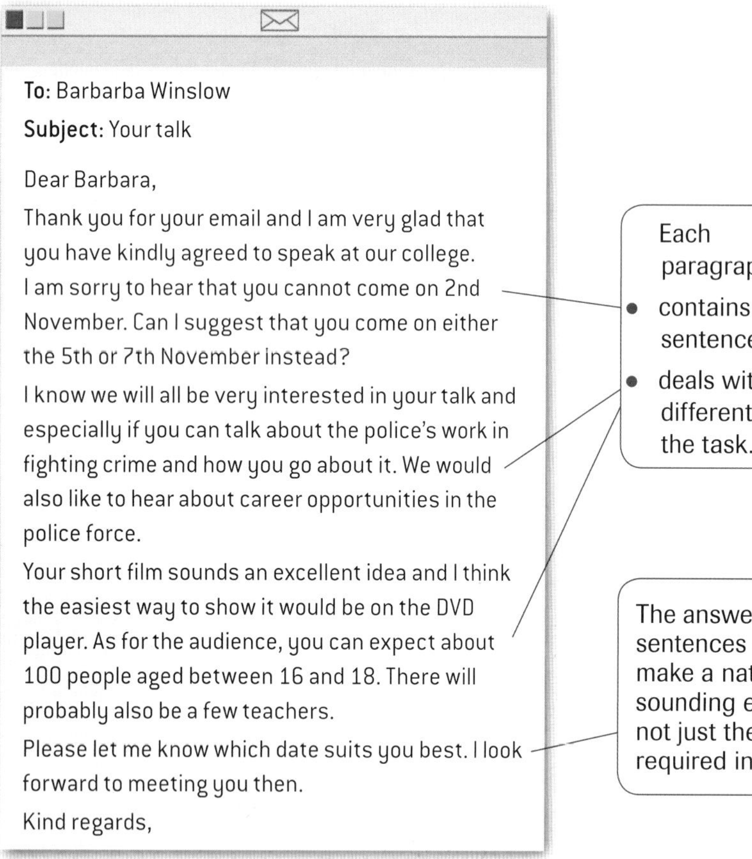

To: Barbarba Winslow

Subject: Your talk

Dear Barbara,

Thank you for your email and I am very glad that you have kindly agreed to speak at our college. I am sorry to hear that you cannot come on 2nd November. Can I suggest that you come on either the 5th or 7th November instead?

I know we will all be very interested in your talk and especially if you can talk about the police's work in fighting crime and how you go about it. We would also like to hear about career opportunities in the police force.

Your short film sounds an excellent idea and I think the easiest way to show it would be on the DVD player. As for the audience, you can expect about 100 people aged between 16 and 18. There will probably also be a few teachers.

Please let me know which date suits you best. I look forward to meeting you then.

Kind regards,

Each paragraph:
• contains several sentences
• deals with a different aspect of the task.
The answer contains sentences which make a natural-sounding email, not just the points required in the task.

Ways of starting and finishing emails

To someone you don't know well:

- start with: *Dear* + first name: *Dear Barbara* (if you would use their first name when you speak to them), or *Dear* + surname: *Dear Mr Hatton* (if you don't feel comfortable using their first name)
- finish with: *Best wishes* or *Kind regards.*

To someone you know well:

- start with: *Dear / Hello / Hi* + name: *Hi Magda, Hello Francesco*
- finish with: *Best wishes* or *All the best.*

Ways of starting and finishing letters

If you know the person's name:

- start with: *Dear Barbara, Dear Mr Hatton*
- finish with:
- *Best wishes* (if you're writing to a friend)
- *Love* or *With love* (if you're writing to a very close friend or a member of your family)
- *Yours sincerely* or *Yours* (if you're writing to someone you don't know too well).

If you don't know the person's name:

- start with: *Dear Sir or Madam*
- finish with: *Yours faithfully.*

Ways of starting the first paragraph of a letter or email

Thanks for your email … (informal)

Thank you for your letter about … (formal)

I am writing to request information about / complain about / apologise for / explain, etc. (formal)

Other useful phrases at the end of the letter or email

(I'm) looking forward to seeing you / hearing from you. (informal)

I look forward to seeing you / hearing from you / meeting you. (formal)

Ways of referring to something in a letter or email which you're replying to

Your short film sounds an excellent idea and … (formal and informal)

As for the audience … (formal and informal)

With reference to the audience … (formal)

You mentioned / asked about the audience in your letter and … (formal)

Ways of making suggestions

How about + verb + *-ing* (informal): *How about holding the meeting on the 5th?*

What about + verb + *-ing* (informal): *What about having a meal in a restaurant afterwards?*

It might also be a good idea to … (formal): *It might also be a good idea to visit the museum on the ground floor.*

Can I suggest that …? (formal): *Can I suggest that you give your talk on the 5th November?*

I suggest + verb + *-ing* (formal): *I suggest holding the meeting on the 5th November.*

Ways of asking for information

Could you tell me … (formal and informal)

I would / I'd like to know if … (formal and informal)

I would / I'd like information on … (formal and informal)

Do you know if / whether / when / what, etc. (formal and informal)

page 156 *Grammar reference: Indirect questions*

Ways of complaining

I'm not very happy about + noun / verb + *-ing* (informal): *I'm not very happy about the price. I'm not very happy about paying so much.*

I would like to complain about + noun / verb + *-ing* (formal): *I would like to complain about traffic noise in our district. I would like to complain about children playing football in our street.*

I am writing to complain about + noun / verb + *-ing* (formal): *I am writing to complain about the service I received at your hotel recently.*

Ways of apologising

Sorry about + noun / verb + *-ing* (informal): *Sorry about being late for the concert last Saturday.*

I would like to apologise for + noun / verb + *-ing* (formal): *I would like to apologise for arriving late for the concert on Saturday.*

Ways of inviting

How about …? (informal): *How about coming windsurfing with me next weekend?*

Would you like to …? (formal and informal): *Would you like to travel together?*

I would like to invite you to … + noun / infinitive (formal): *I would like to invite you to visit our town next summer. I would like to invite you to my house next weekend.*

Ways of giving advice

You should … (formal and informal)

If I were you, I would / I'd … (formal and informal)

It would be a good idea to … + infinitive (formal)

Part 2

In Part 2 you must choose from **one** of four writing tasks.

Note: The last task is a choice of questions on the set texts. If you wish to read a set text, you can visit the Cambridge ESOL website at www.cambridgeesol.org to find which are the set texts for this year. This book doesn't deal with set texts because they change every year. If you haven't read a set text, you choose from three tasks.

- The tasks you choose from will be four of the following: a letter, a report, a short story, an essay, a review or an article.
- For each of these tasks, the instructions are much shorter than in Part 1. You must answer the task with your own ideas. In most tasks there are **two** things you must deal with.
- You must write 120–180 words.

This part tests your ability to:

- deal with the type of task you have chosen
- use an appropriate style for the task you have chosen
- organise and structure your writing
- express opinions, describe, explain, make recommendations, etc.
- use an appropriate range of vocabulary and grammatical structures.

How to do Part 2

1 Read the questions and choose the task you think you can do best.

2 Read the task you choose carefully and underline:

- who will read what you write
- the points you **must** deal with
- anything else you think is important. For example:

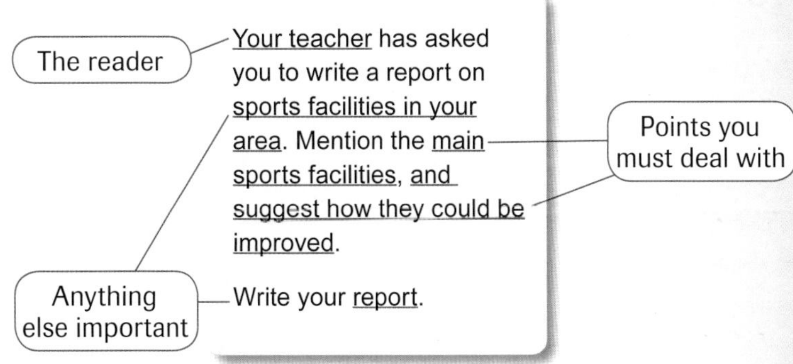

3 Decide if you need a formal or informal style.

4 Think of ideas you can use to deal with the question and note them down while you're thinking.

5 Decide which ideas are the most useful and write a plan. When writing your plan, decide how many paragraphs you need and what to say in each paragraph.

6 Think of useful vocabulary you can include in your answer and note it down in your plan.

7 Write your answer following your plan.

8 When you have finished, read your answer carefully. Check you have written at least 120 words and correct any mistakes you find.

Letters

You studied and practised writing a letter for Part 2 in Unit 13.

Exercise 1

Read the following writing task and underline:

1 who the reader(s) will be
2 what points you must deal with
3 anything else you think is important.

> An English friend, Pat, has written to you for some information. This is part of the letter you have received.
>
> > I'm doing a project on family life in different countries and I wonder if you could tell me a bit about family life in your country. I'd like to know what a typical family in your country is like and how family life is changing.
>
> Write your **letter**.

Exercise 2

Read Teresa's answer below.

1 What details does she give of a typical family in Spain?
2 How is family life changing?

Dear Pat,

Thanks for your letter asking for information about family life in Spain. Families in Spain are still very close and family members take a lot of trouble to spend time together and help each other. Families often get together at weekends and young people normally live with their parents until they are 25 or 30. People tend to get married in their 30s, which means that they start to have children quite late. As a result, families usually have just one or two children.

However, family life is changing. One of the main reasons is that most women now work. As a consequence, men have to take more responsibility in the home.

Another change is that, because both partners work, people are richer, so more and more families are now moving out of the cities to larger houses in the suburbs.

I hope that answers your questions. Please write to me if you need any more information. I'd love to see your finished project and read what you say about family life in other countries too.

Love,

Teresa

Write a natural introduction and conclusion

Use linking words and phrases, e.g. *However, As a result, One of the main reasons is that …*

Ways of expressing causes and results

*People tend to get married in their 30s, **which means that** they start to have children quite late.*

***As a result**, families usually have just one or two children.*

***One of the main reasons is that** most women now work.*

***As a consequence**, men have to take more responsibility in the home.*

*… **because** both partners work, people are richer, so more and more families are now moving out of the cities …*

Ways of expressing contrasts

***However**, family life is changing.*

***On the one hand** young people have more freedom than in the past. **On the other hand**, they have to study harder than ever before to pass exams.*

page 160 *Grammar reference: Linking words for contrast*

Reports

You studied and practised writing reports in Units 8 and 11.

Exercise 1

Read the following writing task and answer the questions below:

> Your teacher has asked you to write a report on things for young people to do in their free time in the area where you live. In your report, you should mention what free-time facilities there are and recommend improvements.
>
> Write your **report**.

1 Do you think you should use a formal or informal style for this report?

2 Read Christine's report below.
- Is the style formal or informal?
- Does it answer the question completely?

Notice the layout. The report:
- has a title
- is divided into sections
- each section has a heading.

Report on free-time facilities in my area

Introduction

The aim of this report is to outline what young people do in my area in their free time, what facilities exist for them and how these could be made better.

Normally, we state the aim or purpose of the report at the beginning.

Avoid repeating exactly the words of the question, e.g. the question says *recommend improvements*. The report says *how these could be made better*.

Free-time activities

My town, Beauvoir, is quite small, so it does not have a cinema or theatre and there is only one club for young people. As a result, young people have to take the train or bus to Nantes, which is about 30 kilometres away if they want these things. On the other hand, it is situated by the sea, so many young people spend their free time on the beach or doing water sports.

Other facilities

Beauvoir has a sports centre with tennis courts, a football pitch and a swimming pool. There are also a number of cafés where young people normally go to meet each other and spend their free time.

Recommendations

I recommend that the town council should set up a youth club where young people could meet, do other activities and also see films. This would encourage young people to stay in the town at weekends and improve their social life.

Give reasons for your recommendations.

Ways of starting a report

The aim of this report is + infinitive: *The aim of this report is to outline …*

The purpose of this report is + infinitive: *The purpose of this report is to describe …*

Ways of making recommendations and suggestions

I recommend that: *I recommend that the town council should set up a youth club …*

I (would) recommend + verb + *-ing*: *I would recommend setting up a youth club …*

I suggest + verb + *-ing*: *I suggest buying more equipment for the sports centre.*

I suggest that: *I suggest that the council should provide cheap transport for young people and students.*

It would be a good idea (for somebody) + infinitive: *It would be a good idea for the council to provide cheap transport for young people and students.*

Stories

You studied and practised writing stories in Units 3 and 10.

Exercise 1

Read the following writing task.

1 Underline the words you must use.
2 Underline anything else you think is important.
3 Who will read your story?

> You have read the following announcement in your school's English-language magazine.
>
> **Short stories wanted!**
>
> Students are invited to send short stories for next month's magazine starting with the words: *When I got up that morning, I thought it would be just another ordinary day …*
>
> Write your **story**.

Exercise 2

Which of these things should you try to do when you do this writing task? Write *yes*, *no* or *maybe* by each.

You should …

1 start with exactly the same words as the ones which are given in the question. Yes
2 use only the past simple when you write the story.
3 try to use a range of vocabulary.
4 say what was happening when the story began.
5 say what had happened before the story began.
6 say how you feel at different stages in the story.
7 give the story a title.

Exercise 3

Read the answer to the writing task below. Which of the things in Exercise 2 did the writer do?

Under arrest

When I got up that morning, I thought it would be just another ordinary day at school. I had gone downstairs and I was having breakfast when there was a ring on the doorbell. 'That's the postman,' I thought to myself as I went to the door.

Notice the range of tenses that are used.

Just as I was about to open the door, the doorbell rang again. As I opened it, I saw there were three policemen standing there. 'Helga Schmidt?' one of them asked.

Notice the different time conjunctions.

'Yes,' I answered, feeling a little surprised.

'Helga Schmidt, you're under arrest for robbery,' he said. The three policemen grabbed me and took me out to their waiting car. I was so shocked that I could not say anything until they were all in the car.

Using direct speech makes the story more immediate.

'But what have I stolen?' I asked in a frightened voice while they were driving me to the police station.

'You were identified on a hidden camera as the thief who was stealing clothes from Prada in the city centre,' said the policeman. 'And you're wearing them now!' I knew it was all a horrible mistake, but how was I going to prove my innocence and get to school on time?

Try to have a little surprise at the end!

Reviews

You studied and practised writing reviews in Units 4 and 16.

Exercise 1

Read the following writing task.

1 Underline the points you must deal with.
2 Underline anything else you think is important.
3 Who will the reader(s) be and where will your answer appear?

> You have seen this announcement in your school's English-language magazine.
>
> Have you seen a film or read a book recently that you think everyone would enjoy? We want to know about it! Write a review of the film or book saying what it's about and why we would all enjoy it.
>
> Write your **review**.

Exercise 2

Read Franz's review below. Which paragraphs say ...?

1 what the book is about
2 why we would all enjoy it

The Time Traveler's Wife by Audrey Niffenegger

This is an original and moving love story told from the point of view of the two main characters, Henry and Clare. Henry is a librarian who has a genetic problem which causes him to move backwards and forwards in time. Without warning, he disappears leaving everything behind and arrives at another time in his life. He can't control when or where he's going.

When he travels, he often meets the same girl, Clare, at different times in her life. Eventually they fall in love even though sometimes when they meet he is much older than her and at other times they are the same age.

I think everyone will enjoy this unusual story because it combines a little science fiction with a wonderful romantic story. Henry's problem causes situations which are funny, sometimes frightening, usually awkward and often very strange. The novel is fascinating because it makes you think about the nature of time. At the same time, you see how the characters and their relationships change during their lives but how their love grows stronger.

Give your review a title.

Mention:
- the type of book/film
- the characters
- some of the story
- what makes the book/film different.

Use plenty of adjectives to describe:
- the book/film
- how you feel about it.

Ways of praising

I think everyone will enjoy this ... [book / film / restaurant, etc.] *because* ...

The ... [book / film / restaurant, etc.] *is fascinating / wonderful / marvellous because* ...

This ... [book / film / restaurant, etc.] *is really worth* [*reading / seeing / visiting*, etc.] *because* ...

Articles

You studied and practised writing articles in Units 2 and 9.

Exercise 1

Read the following writing task.

> You have seen the following announcement on your college noticeboard.
>
> **My Best Friend**
> Tell us about your best friend for the college newspaper. We want to know:
> - how you met this person
> - why he or she is so special to you.
>
> We will publish the most interesting articles next week.
>
> Write your **article**.

Match the beginnings and endings of these sentences to make advice about how to write articles.

1 Before writing, identify
2 You can identify the readers by
3 Decide what style
4 Write things you think your readers
5 Before writing the article,
6 In your plan, decide what you will put
7 Make sure that the plan
8 Write the article following
9 While you are writing, think about

a answers the question.
b in each paragraph.
c make a plan.
d looking at the type of newspaper or magazine you are writing for.
e is suitable for your readers.
f the effect on your readers.
g who will read the article.
h will find interesting.
i your plan.

Exercise 2

Read Luis's article below and match the notes for his plan a–d with the paragraph numbers.

Para 1	a	How we became friends – same table at school, playground, visit each other's houses
Para 2	b	My first impressions of Thea – contrast with other kids
Para 3	c	When I met Thea – on school bus
Para 4	d	Why so special – share secrets, help each other, spend time together, sit together

An article should have a title.

An Inseparable Friend

Thea has been my best friend from that day when, aged seven, I climbed onto the school bus to go to my new primary school.

I wandered nervously down the bus, which was full of noisy kids shouting and laughing excitedly, and found a place beside a quiet girl with fair hair and friendly green eyes.

Notice the adverbs. You will get higher marks if you use a range of vocabulary.

Instead of using the same word again, use different words with similar meanings e.g. *shy – timidly*.

We were both very shy, so we didn't talk much to each other on the way to school, although we smiled at each other timidly. And when we went into class we naturally sat down together at the same table. Gradually we got to know each other, we played together in the playground, we visited each other's houses and our parents soon became firm friends as well.

We still share each other's secrets and we have complete confidence in each other. When either of us has a problem, the other is always ready to help. We have so much in common that we spend most of our free time together. We've even been on holiday together sometimes. And we still share the same table at school ten years later!

Good to have a small joke at the end!

Essays

You studied and practised writing essays in Units 6 and 12.

Exercise 1

Read the following writing task and underline:

1 who the reader(s) will be

2 the points you must deal with.

> You recently had a class discussion about how long young people should stay in education. Your teacher has now asked you to write an essay giving your opinions on the following statement:
>
> *All young people should continue at school or college until at least the age of 18.*
>
> Write your **essay**.

Exercise 2

Read the essay below and complete the plan for this essay.

> Para 1: Introduction: the situation now
>
> Para 2: Points in favour:
>
> 1 .... + reason ....
>
> 2 .... + reason ....
>
> Para 3: Points against:
>
> 1 .... + reason ....
>
> 2 .... + reason ....
>
> Para 4: My opinion(s) ....
>
> + reason(s) ....

Write a short introduction to the essay.

In my country, education is compulsory until the age of 16. After that young people can leave and look for a job if they wish.

Use words like *firstly, secondly, finally, also, what is more*, etc. to list your points.

However, there are two good reasons for making young people stay at school. Firstly, it is very difficult for 16-year-olds leaving school to find work. This is because jobs are becoming more and more specialised and technical. Secondly, if young people stay at school and receive education and training they will have more opportunities in the future.

Support your arguments with reasons.

On the other hand, many students would like to leave school at 16. This is because they find school difficult or they do not enjoy studying. They would prefer to be working and earning money. Also, because they are not motivated, they cause problems for students who do want to study.

Make sure you have expressed your opinion clearly in the essay.

I believe that in these cases, they should stay at school and choose technical or practical subjects which interest them. In my opinion, it is a mistake for people to leave school too soon, because they will miss opportunities which may arise in the future.

Show your range of grammar by using conditional sentences, relative clauses, etc.

Expressing opinions

In my opinion ...

I think ...

I feel ...

I believe ...

Putting your ideas in order

There are two good reasons for *making young people stay at school.*

On the other hand there are a number of reasons against *young people staying at school when they do not want to.*

Firstly ...

Secondly ...

Finally ...

Also ...

Furthermore ...

What is more ...

Speaking reference

What to expect in the exam

The Speaking paper is Paper 5.

- It lasts approximately 14 minutes.
- You do the Speaking paper in pairs.
- There are two examiners in the room; one gives you instructions and asks you questions, the other just listens.
- You may do the Speaking paper on a different day from the written exam.
- The Speaking paper has four parts.

Part 1

Part 1 is a conversation between the examiner and each candidate. You will be asked questions about yourself, your family, your hobbies and interests, your studies or your work, your likes and dislikes. Questions may also be about your past experiences and your future plans.

You studied and practised Part 1 in Units 1, 5, 9 and 13.

How to do Part 1

1 **Don't** prepare detailed answers before you go to the exam, but **do** make sure that you know the vocabulary you will need to talk about your studies, your job, your family, your town and your free-time activities.

2 Listen to the examiner's questions carefully.

3 Look confidently at the examiner and perhaps smile a little when you answer the questions.

4 Answer the questions openly and, when suitable, answer with a few extra details, or a reason; try to speak fluently and confidently.

Exercise 1

Read the advice and the example questions. Then match the answers with the questions.

Advice and example questions

1 Don't just answer the question – give some extra details if you can. Question: *Where are you from?* [b]

2 You can offer several ideas or answers to the same question. Question: *What do young people do in their free time in your town?* ☐

3 Avoid giving simple Yes/No answers which end the conversation. Question: *Do you like doing sports?* ☐

4 A question which starts, '*Tell us a little about …*' gives you an opportunity to say quite a lot. Question: *Tell us a little about your family.* ☐

5 When you speak about things you like or enjoy, sound enthusiastic. Be ready to use past tenses and time adverbs. Question: *Tell us about something you really enjoyed doing recently.* ☐

6 Be ready to talk about the future and use different tenses to do so. Question: *What do you hope to do next summer?* ☐

7 If you don't understand or don't hear the question, ask the examiner to repeat it. Question: *Which do you prefer: reading books or watching TV?* ☐

8 Use a range of grammar and vocabulary which is appropriate. The examiners want to hear how well you can speak English. Question: *Do you enjoy travelling?* ☐

9 When appropriate, give reasons for your answers. Question: *Tell me about a place you'd like to visit.* ☐

10 When the question gives you the opportunity, use a range of tenses in your answer. Question: *What job would you like to do in the future?* ☐

Good answers

a I'd really like to visit Venice. I've seen photos of it and I've read about it, but it must be an amazing place to actually be in and explore.

b I'm from Ostrava. It's a large industrial town in the east of the Czech Republic.

c I'm going to London in July. I hope to get a job there and at the same time I'll try to improve my English.

d Yes, I do, especially competitive sports like football or tennis, because I like to win.

e Sorry, could you say that again, please?

f They go to the cinema, they go out with friends, they go clubbing. You know, basically, they do the normal things which I think young people do everywhere.

g Two weeks ago I went skiing with two of my friends in the mountains. It was beautiful. We had a really good time.

h Well, I'm hoping to study architecture at university and become an architect. I've always liked beautiful buildings and I'd like to design them too.

i Well, there's just my mother, my father and myself. I'm an only child. My mother's a lawyer and my father manages a restaurant.

j Yes, I love it. I love seeing new places, meeting new people and getting away from my daily routine. I wish I could do it more.

Part 2

In Part 2, you work alone.

- The examiner gives you two photos on the same topic to speak about.
- He/She asks you to speak for one minute, compare the photos and answer a question about the topic of the two photos.
- The question is also printed above the photos.
- When your partner speaks about his/her photos, you should listen. After your partner has finished, the examiner asks you a brief question about your partner's topic.

You studied and practised Part 2 in Units 2, 6, 11 and 14.

How to do Part 2

1 Talk about the general ideas the photos show. Don't try to describe them in detail.

2 Compare the ideas the two photos show. When you are not sure what the photo shows, speculate (*she seems to be ..., he might be ...* - see **Speculating** on the right).

3 Make sure that you answer the question.

4 Always try to give reasons for your answer.

5 Speak for the complete minute - don't finish early. The examiner will say 'Thank you' when it's time to stop.

6 When it's your partner's turn to talk about the photos, listen but don't say anything yourself. You will be asked a question at the end. You should answer it quite briefly.

Example task: I'd like you to compare and contrast these photographs, and say what you think is enjoyable about communicating in these ways.

What do you think is enjoyable about communicating in these ways?

Referring to the photos

In the first photo*, a girl is ...*

In the second photo*, there are two oldish people who are ...*

In the background*, I can see ...*

In the foreground*, there are ...*

Comparing photos

In the first photo, I can see a girl who looks as if she's chatting on the internet ***whereas / while*** *in the second photo two old people are sitting together on a park bench and gossiping.*

While *the girl seems to be concentrating hard, perhaps because she's writing, the old people seem to be relaxed and enjoying themselves. I think this is because they're together and can see each other.*

I think the girl might be talking to a friend about school work or boyfriends. ***On the other hand****, the old people are probably talking about their grandchildren, or they could be talking about things they did when they were younger.*

Speculating

In the first photo, I can see a girl who ***looks as if*** *she's chatting on the internet whereas / while in the second photo two old people are sitting together on a park bench and gossiping.*

While the girl ***seems*** *to be concentrating hard,* ***perhaps*** *because she's writing, the old people* ***seem to be*** *relaxed and enjoying themselves. I think this is because they're together and can see each other.*

I think *the girl* ***might*** *be talking to a friend about school work or boyfriends. On the other hand, the old people are* ***probably*** *talking about their grandchildren, or they* ***could be*** *talking about things they did when they were younger.*

(For more on speculating, see Unit 10 page 92 and Grammar reference: Modal verbs to express certainty and possibility, page 161; Unit 11 page 104 and Grammar reference: *Look, seem* and *appear*, page 162.)

Part 3

In Part 3 you work together.

- The examiner gives you a page with a number of pictures on it and asks you two questions.
- To deal with the first question, you have to discuss each of the pictures in turn.
- To deal with the second question, you have to discuss and reach a decision.
- You have three minutes to do this.

You studied and practised Part 3 in Units 3, 7, 10 and 15.

How to do Part 3

1. Listen carefully to the questions, although they are also printed next to the pictures to help you.
2. Answer the first question with each picture in turn before you discuss the second question.
3. To start the conversation, you can give a brief opinion about the first picture or make a suggestion and ask your partner what he/she thinks.
4. When your partner says something, react to his/her ideas. Listen to what he/she is saying. Try to make the discussion like a natural conversation. Don't try to dominate the conversation.
5. Manage your time. Spend 1½–2 minutes on the first question and 1–1½ minutes on the second question. Keep the discussion moving by saying things like, 'What about this photo? What do you think?', or 'Shall we move on to the second question?'
6. Don't spend too long talking about one picture.
7. Try to reach a decision on the second question but don't worry too much if you can't agree.
8. If you reach a decision on the second question very quickly, continue by discussing reasons for your decision until the examiner says 'Thank you'.

Example task: I'd like you to imagine that a town wants to attract more visitors and tourists. Here are some of the ideas they are considering. First, talk to each other about how effective these ideas might be. Then decide which two would attract the most tourists.

- **How effective might these ideas be for attracting tourists?**
- **Which two would attract the most tourists?**

Involving your partner

What do you think?

Do you agree (with me)?

What about this picture?

I think ... What about you?

Keeping the discussion moving

What about this picture? What do you think?

Let's move on to the next picture / second question.

Shall we move on to the next picture / second question?

Agreeing

You're right.

That's right.

Yes, and ...

I (quite) agree.

That's true.

(Yes,) that's a good idea.

Disagreeing

I'm not sure. I think ...

Maybe, but ...

I don't really agree. I think ...

Part 4

In Part 4 you continue to work together.

- The examiner asks both of you questions connected with the topic you discussed in Part 3.
- The questions may be about your personal experience *(Have you ever visited a place like this?)*, your tastes *(Would you like to work in a place like this?)* and your opinions *(Why do you think people enjoy visiting places like this?)*.
- You may be asked if you agree with your partner's answer.

Part 4 lasts about four minutes.

You studied and practised Part 4 in Units 4, 8, 12 and 16.

How to do Part 4

1 Listen carefully to the questions. If you don't understand a question, ask the examiner to repeat (*Sorry, could you say that again, please*?).

2 Answer the questions giving a reason or explanation or example.

3 Listen to what your partner is saying because you may be asked to give your opinion on what he/she has said.

4 If you don't know the answer to a question, don't just say '*I don't know.*' Say, '*I don't know a lot about this subject, but I think …*' and then give some ideas.

Example questions

Do you enjoy visiting other towns and cities? Why (not)?

If you could choose, which place in the world would you like to visit? Why?

What things attract visitors to your town?

Some places attract large numbers of tourists. What problems are caused by having too many tourists?

What can people learn by going as tourists to other places?

Do you think it's better if people spend their holidays in their own country or travel to other countries? Why?

Introducing an opinion and giving a reason

I think …

Well, in my opinion … because …

I feel …

I'm not sure. I think …

No, I don't think so …

Introducing an explanation

I mean …

You see …

Giving an example

For example …

For instance …

… such as …

First Certificate model paper from Cambridge ESOL

PAPER 1: READING Part 1

Part 1

You are going to read an article about a woman who writes children's books. For questions **1–8**, choose the answer (**A**, **B**, **C** or **D**) which you think fits best according to the text.

Mark your answers **on the separate answer sheet**.

Jane Hissey, creator of the 'Old Bear' stories

If anyone knows what makes a great children's book, it must be Sussex author and illustrator Jane Hissey. Her 'Old Bear' books have achieved classic status in a variety of formats: books for different ages, audio tapes, calendars and diaries.

I caught up with Jane at her home in the East Sussex countryside and asked her what she thinks is the secret of a classic children's book. 'That's a difficult one. I suppose it's got to be relevant to the child's stage of development – for young children, pictures on a page that are familiar, for older children, an experience. The book should be familiar, but hold some surprises too, in order to maintain the interest. It must inspire and delight, but there is also an element of the matter-of-fact, the things that happen every day.'

Jane was born in Norwich and studied design and illustration at Brighton College, after which she taught art to secondary school students. She married a graphic designer and settled in East Sussex. After the birth of her first child, Owen (who is now 18), she gave up teaching and worked on her own artwork, drawing pictures of teddy bears and designing greeting cards. An editor from a publishing company saw her work and invited Jane to do a children's book. After the birth of her second child, Alison (who is now 14), she set to work.

'Old Bear', the leader of the gang, was Jane's childhood teddy and she still loves him. 'I get the feeling he's writing his own words. I look back at the first book I wrote and realise he's lost a lot of his fur. That's partly because I pin him in front of me in order to draw him. Like the other toys, he gets stuck on little clamps. All the toys have aged more than I show in my drawings; I'm able to keep them looking youthful.'

Over the years, from the first 'Old Bear' book in 1988, her children have made a huge contribution – not least in terms of plot. 'I used to give my children the toys to play with – and they had tea parties and so on. One of my bear characters, 'Little Bear', is the same age as Ralph, my youngest, who's seven now. All the children have been involved and, in years to come, they will realise how much.'

Jane's technique is very interesting. Unlike many other children's illustrators, she works in coloured pencils, which makes her work immediately accessible to children because it's the medium most familiar to them. She likes to draw the original about four times larger than it appears in the book. Because they are eventually reduced in size, the drawings then look more dense, with a deeper texture. 'I build up layers and layers of colour,' she explains, 'so the effect is not wishy-washy. There's a depth of colour and you can see the other colours underneath.' With such a laborious, meticulous method of working, a single book takes a year to write and illustrate. How, I asked her, does this work fit in with the demands of a large family and home? She told me it was a combination of teamwork and good planning. 'My husband is also an illustrator, so we both work from home and we can juggle things so that one of us is always there.'

Despite such phenomenal success in the book world, Jane remains very down-to-earth about her collection of toys. But, she admits she would miss them if she suddenly had no contact with them. 'I hope I'll know when people are getting fed up with the characters. If ever they did, I think I'd go on drawing them for fun. My own children have been very useful to me in my work, but as they are older now, I'll just have to hope that other people's children can inspire me.'

1 According to Jane, a successful children's book

A contains material that is unexpected.
B should offer an escape from everyday life.
C does not lose its attraction as children get older.
D is set in a place which is known to its readers.

2 Jane first became involved in book writing because

A she got in touch with an editor.
B her artwork attracted professional attention.
C her husband encouraged her to try.
D she wrote stories for her own children.

3 What does Jane say about her teddy bear illustrations in paragraph 4?

A They have improved over time.
B She uses real models to work from.
C They have been pinned up around the house.
D She has had difficulty keeping them up-to-date.

4 How did Jane's children assist her in her work?

A by allowing her to concentrate on her work
B by telling her what they thought of her stories
C by suggesting characters for her stories
D by giving her ideas for her stories

5 According to the writer, Jane's books take a long time to produce because

A the pages have to be so large.
B the colouring is a lengthy process.
C she redoes so many of her drawings.
D she colours each page to suit the mood of the story.

6 When Jane says 'we can juggle things' (lines 63–4), she means that she and her husband can

A find someone to look after their children.
B afford to turn down work.
C find space in the home to work.
D organise their daily schedules.

7 How does Jane feel about her future work?

A uncertain
B excited
C encouraged
D depressed

8 What do we learn from the article as a whole about Jane's attitude to her books?

A She is interested in experimenting with different drawing techniques.
B She regards her characters simply as a commercial project.
C She is fond of the toys that she draws regularly.
D She is bored with writing about bears all the time.

PAPER 1: READING Part 2

Part 2

You are going to read an article about sending scientific expeditions to the Moon. Seven sentences have been removed from the article. Choose from the sentences **A–H** the one which fits each gap (**9–15**). There is one extra sentence which you do not need to use.

Mark your answers **on the separate answer sheet**.

Getting back on the Moon

Several decades after the Apollo 11 Moon landing, scientists want another trip.

One of the most dramatic events in human history took place in 1969. Dressed in his space suit and equipped with an oxygen backpack, a walkie-talkie, a camera and a special visor to block out the fierce light of the sun, the astronaut Neil Armstrong stepped from the Eagle lunar module out onto the Moon. He was soon joined by Edwin 'Buzz' Aldrin. The two men collected rock samples and took photographs before returning to the Apollo spacecraft.

After several decades, the excitement surrounding mankind's first visit to another world has not decreased. **9** ______ Moreover, the snapshot of a sapphire-blue Earth, as seen from the Apollo spacecraft, remains a powerful symbol of space exploration.

However, some scientists claim that, despite twelve men having walked on the Moon in six missions between 1969 and 1972, basic questions about it remain unanswered. For example, is there really water there? What is the 'far side' like? How did the Moon come to orbit the Earth? **10** ______ Human beings, they say, would be better at gathering information and samples than unmanned spacecraft.

David Heather, a lunar researcher from London, agrees that such questions could be answered more easily if people were sent up rather than robots. He thinks that people are more intelligent and useful. **11** ______

The researcher, who is studying data from unmanned spacecraft, believes that because scientists have got some sample material from the Moon, most people consider that it is unnecessary to go back there. He insists, however, that a lot of the material we have does not give a good idea of what all parts of the Moon are like. **12** ______ As a result, there are very few pieces of rock from the highland regions and insufficient material from the lunar seas.

13 ______ That is another reason why people like David Heather would like to see more scientists up there, working with more advanced equipment. A lot more could be done today.

There are problems, however, the main one being that it is incredibly expensive to send humans to the Moon. **14** ______ There is only so much money to go round. There would be arguments about the best use of resources between people who want to go to the Moon, people who want to build telescopes on Earth and people who want to build telescopes in space. Each group would argue that their project is the most important and urgent undertaking.

There is another problem to be faced. **15** ______ For example, astronauts on the far side of the Moon, which is invisible to Earth, would be out of contact. A lot of people would oppose manned missions for that reason alone.

A All the Apollo missions had to land near the Moon's equator, so the samples have come from a limited area.

B It is easy to forget, too, that the technology of the early lunar missions was the technology of the 1960s.

C They are supposed to do the kind of tasks that astronauts cannot do.

D The most mysterious areas of the Moon are probably the most dangerous.

E Now, some believe that manned missions should begin again.

F The human footprints on the lunar surface seem as incredible now as they did in the 1960s.

G For that reason, some people might oppose any plans for new missions.

H They can make quick decisions about what they should collect and examine.

PAPER 1: READING Part 3

Part 3

You are going to read a magazine article about four athletes. For questions **16–30**, choose from the athletes (**A–D**). The athletes may be chosen more than once.

Mark your answers **on the separate answer sheet**.

Which athlete

started doing her sport as a way of using up energy?	**16**
thinks she sometimes demands too much of herself?	**17**
has worked as a model?	**18**
sometimes feels too tired to go on?	**19**
took a break from her sport to improve her motivation?	**20**
used to have to combine training for her sport with a job?	**21**
hasn't completely recovered from an old injury?	**22**
feels people's envy is misplaced?	**23**
doesn't avoid any particular type of food?	**24**
knows the time when she can continue in her sport is limited?	**25**
wouldn't consider having a day in the week free of training?	**26**
goes straight from the running track to the pool when she is training?	**27**
says she has a different attitude to her body from non-athletes?	**28**
feels that she was born with certain advantages?	**29**
gave up something time-consuming to concentrate on her sport?	**30**

Top form

Athletes who compete at the highest level in their sport have to work hard to achieve the ideal physical condition.

A

Jessie, 31, is a 100m hurdler.

'People are always commenting on my arms. I think I'm lucky genetically because I had good muscle tone even before I started training. I've actually been earning some extra money recently by posing for some photographers who appreciate the beauty of the strong, fit bodies athletes possess. Obviously, I have to watch what I eat carefully, and as desserts and chocolate are a weakness of mine, it can be a problem! I tore the ligaments in my knee three years ago and since then I've been in constant pain, and have had it operated on four times. But I'm running well at the moment. I train about three to four hours a day, six days a week. I have friends who say they wish they looked like me, but it's hard work to maintain my body in peak condition.'

B

Natasha, 16, is a gymnast.

'My mother got me into gymnastics because I was an over-active child – I was always getting into trouble for standing on my head and leaping around. At the moment, I train up to six hours a day and Sunday is my only day off. I don't worry about my weight or what I eat as my parents do that for me – they think I don't know when to stop. But I do have to keep off peanuts! Anyway, it's more about muscle tone than weight. I don't envy models their bodies because they're a different shape. We're not skinny, we're toned and muscled. Most of us retire at 19 or 20 because you invariably get bigger then. Three years ago, I had a hip injury which put me out of the sport for 18 months and I had to be really committed to get through it. There are days when you're so worn out that you think "I can't do it today", but you must try to work through the exhaustion.'

C

Sophie, 21, is a backstroke swimmer.

'Three years ago, I took three months out because I knew I had to if I was to carry on. I now know that every time I get in the water, it's because I really want to be there. In my time out, I occasionally treated myself to chocolate, which is normally forbidden. I didn't train either, so it was hard when I started swimming again. My body is a tool for me and I don't see it in the way other women view theirs. I was approached by a major chain store once about modelling swimwear, but I wasn't keen on the idea. I train seven days a week, which is tiring, but missing a session is never an option. I swim for two hours in the morning, then spend two hours in the gym before going back to the pool. Now that I have the advantage of financial sponsorship, I can train full-time and no longer have to get up at 4.45 am to swim before going to the office.'

D

Karen, 28, is a modern pentathlete.

'I'm very competitive and I can push myself too far in training. I'm never tempted to miss it, except when I feel ill. A typical day's training is: shooting from 8 am to 9.30 am; running from 10 am to 11 am; swimming from 11 am to midday; riding from 1pm to 3 pm; and then 45 minutes fencing. I snack on bananas to keep up my energy levels, but it's impossible to fit in time to eat and digest anything substantial until the end of the day's work-out. I limit my coffee-drinking because it's bad for me, but I can eat anything really, as long as it's in moderation. I only eat around 2,500 calories a day, which isn't much more than the average woman needs. I was studying to be a vet when I started competing in pentathlons. I was training every day and fitting it in round my coursework, which was exhausting, so eventually one of them had to go. I'm more focused now.'

PAPER 2: WRITING Part 1

Part 1

You **must** answer this question. Write your answer in **120–150** words in an appropriate style on the opposite page.

---

1 You help to organise meetings at your local sports club. You have invited James Wills, an international sports star who is going to visit your area, to give a talk at your club. He has sent you an email accepting your invitation and asking for more information.

Read his email and the notes you have made. Then write an email to him, using **all** your notes.

email

From: James Wills
Sent: 20th April
Subject: Talk at sports club

Thank James — Yes, I'd be very happy to give a talk at your sports club.

During my stay I am free on either 10 June in the morning or 12 June in the evening. Which of these is better for you? — *Say which and why*

Explain — Also please tell me something about your club members, for example their ages and the sports they enjoy.

Finally, can you suggest any topics you would especially like me to talk about? — *Suggest ...*

Looking forward to meeting you.

Regards,

James Wills

Write your **email**. You must use grammatically correct sentences with accurate spelling and punctuation in a style appropriate for the situation.

Part 2

Write an answer to **one** of the questions **2–5** in this part. Write your answer in **120–180** words in an appropriate style.

---

2 You have had a class discussion on the following question:

Which are the most important subjects for young people to study at school and why?

Now your teacher has asked you to write an essay, giving your opinion on this question.

Write your **essay**.

3 You have decided to enter a short story competition. The competition rules say that the story must begin or end with the following sentence:

Suddenly I heard a noise behind me.

Write your **story** for the competition.

4 An international music magazine that you read is looking for reviews with the following title: *'The last CD I bought'*. You decide to write a **review** for the magazine. Describe the music on the CD and say what you think about it. Would you recommend the CD to other people?

Write your **review**.

5 Answer **one** of the following two questions based on **one** of the titles below.

(**a**) *Officially Dead* by Richard Prescott
You see this advertisement in a local newspaper.

> **What makes a good ending to a book?**
> **Articles wanted**
> Some people like a happy ending to a book, others prefer something more real.
> What about you?

Write your **article** about the end of *Officially Dead* and say how you feel about it.

(**b**) *Pride and Prejudice* by Jane Austen
Your English class has been discussing the characters of Jane and Lizzie Bennett. Now your teacher gives you this essay.

How are the characters of Jane and Lizzie different and why is their relationship so strong?

Write your **essay**.

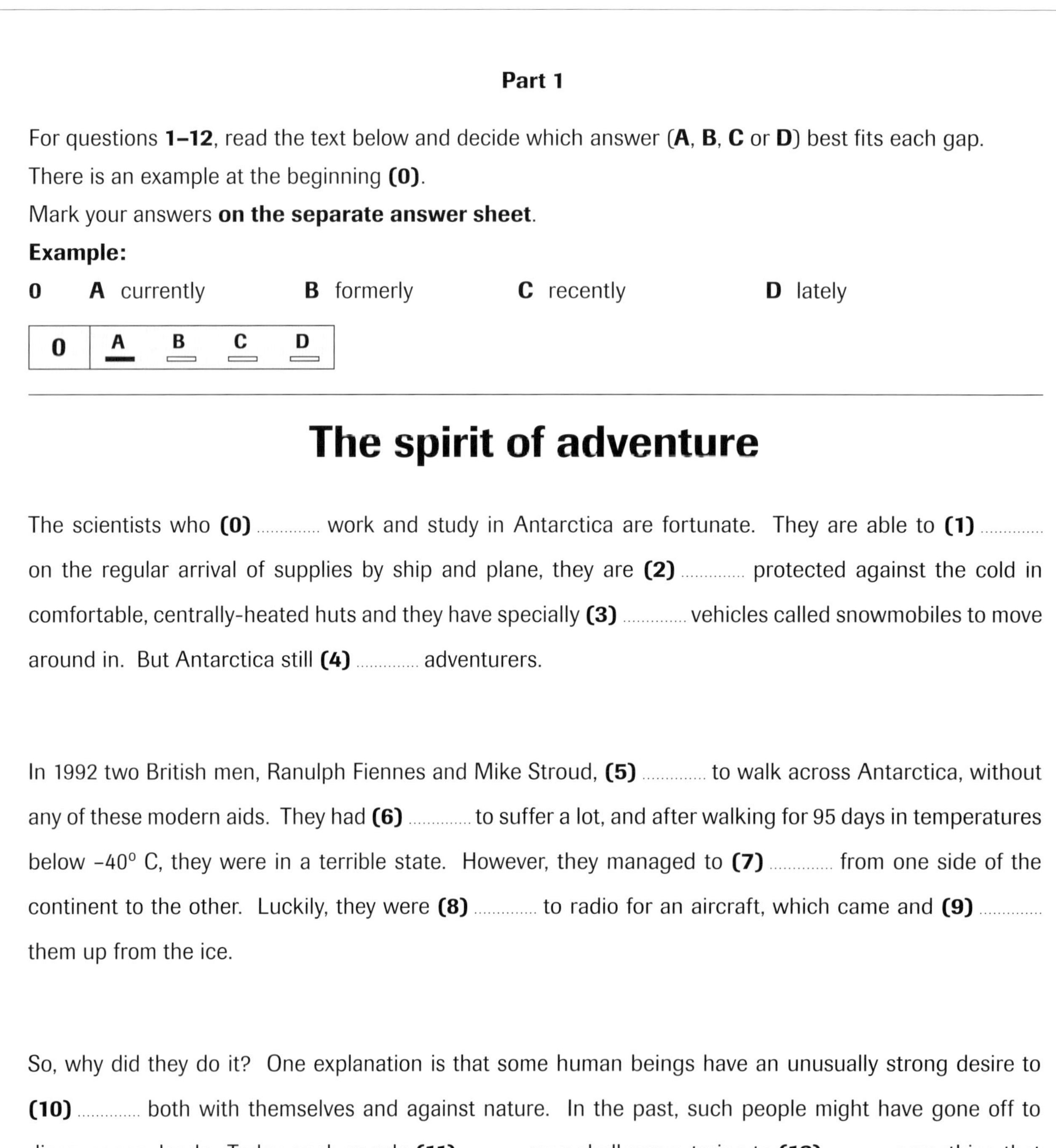

Part 1

For questions **1–12**, read the text below and decide which answer (**A**, **B**, **C** or **D**) best fits each gap. There is an example at the beginning **(0)**.

Mark your answers **on the separate answer sheet**.

Example:

0 **A** currently **B** formerly **C** recently **D** lately

0	A	B	C	D
	▬	▭	▭	▭

The spirit of adventure

The scientists who **(0)** .... work and study in Antarctica are fortunate. They are able to **(1)** .... on the regular arrival of supplies by ship and plane, they are **(2)** .... protected against the cold in comfortable, centrally-heated huts and they have specially **(3)** .... vehicles called snowmobiles to move around in. But Antarctica still **(4)** .... adventurers.

In 1992 two British men, Ranulph Fiennes and Mike Stroud, **(5)** .... to walk across Antarctica, without any of these modern aids. They had **(6)** .... to suffer a lot, and after walking for 95 days in temperatures below $-40°$ C, they were in a terrible state. However, they managed to **(7)** .... from one side of the continent to the other. Luckily, they were **(8)** .... to radio for an aircraft, which came and **(9)** .... them up from the ice.

So, why did they do it? One explanation is that some human beings have an unusually strong desire to **(10)** .... both with themselves and against nature. In the past, such people might have gone off to discover new lands. Today, such people **(11)** .... new challenges, trying to **(12)** .... something that no human being has ever done.

	A	B	C	D
1	**A** live	**B** trust	**C** count	**D** claim
2	**A** accurately	**B** severely	**C** exactly	**D** properly
3	**A** intended	**B** designed	**C** drawn	**D** formed
4	**A** appeals	**B** leads	**C** attracts	**D** catches
5	**A** set out	**B** got away	**C** set up	**D** got by
6	**A** anticipated	**B** waited	**C** predicted	**D** expected
7	**A** reach	**B** cover	**C** cross	**D** arrive
8	**A** adequate	**B** able	**C** capable	**D** efficient
9	**A** put	**B** kept	**C** picked	**D** held
10	**A** compete	**B** attack	**C** oppose	**D** combat
11	**A** search	**B** look	**C** seek	**D** watch
12	**A** win	**B** touch	**C** achieve	**D** make

Part 2

For questions **13–24**, read the text below and think of the word which best fits each gap. Use only one word in each gap. There is an example at the beginning (**0**).

Write your answers **IN CAPITAL LETTERS on the separate answer sheet**.

Example: | 0 | T | H | E | R | E |

The first English dictionaries

Before the publication of the first English dictionaries **(0)** .... was little agreement about how to spell words. It was partly **(13)** .... a result of frustration over the variety of spellings in use **(14)** .... the time that the first English dictionaries were compiled. Schoolmasters **(15)** .... particular were keen to bring some sense to the 'disorders and confusion' in spelling. In 1604 Robert Cowdrey, a schoolmaster, published his *Table Alphabetical*, **(16)** .... is now regarded as the first English dictionary. However, it contained only a few thousand words, far fewer **(17)** .... the number of words found in dictionaries that were available for other European languages. This led to a demand for something much **(18)** .... comprehensive.

The publication in 1755 of Samuel Johnson's *Dictionary of the English Language* is justly regarded as a landmark in the attempt **(19)** .... bring order to a living, evolving language. This two-volume work included around 43,000 words. Many of the words in it **(20)** .... amusingly defined – 'Dull: To make dictionaries is dull work.' It was also remarkable **(21)** .... of its use of 118,000 quotations to illustrate the precise meanings **(22)** .... the words. Johnson's approach was **(23)** .... successful that for many decades his dictionary remained the **(24)** .... widely used English dictionary.

Part 3

For questions **25–34**, read the text below. Use the word given in capitals at the end of some of the lines to form a word that fits in the gap **in the same line.** There is an example at the beginning (**0**).

Write your answers **IN CAPITAL LETTERS on the separate answer sheet.**

Example: | **0** | A | G | R | E | E | M | E | N | T | |

Keeping well

Most people would be in **(0)** .... with the idea, often put	**AGREE**
forward by doctors, that we should avoid taking medicines unnecessarily.	
Even people with only **(25)** .... medical knowledge say that it is not	**LIMIT**
(26) .... to take aspirin, for example, whenever you have a	**ADVISE**
(27) .... or some other minor ailment. It is certainly true that	**HEAD**
people have tended to become very **(28)** .... on pills when in any	**DEPEND**
kind of discomfort, rather than simply waiting for the symptoms to pass.	
Many people would do well to take a different attitude to preventing	
illness. The best way to keep well is to avoid **(29)** .... foods	**HEALTH**
and habits. It is also **(30)** .... to take plenty of exercise, and	**HELP**
we should give **(31)** .... to people of all ages to do this,	**ENCOURAGE**
particularly the very young. If we can educate people at an early	
age to keep fit and to look after themselves **(32)** .... , then the	**CARE**
(33) .... of their having problems in later life will be considerably	**PROBABLE**
reduced. However, no matter how well we look after ourselves and how	
much exercise we do, illness, **(34)** .... , is not always preventable.	**FORTUNATE**

PAPER 3: USE OF ENGLISH Part 4

Part 4

For questions **35–42**, complete the second sentence so that it has a similar meaning to the first sentence, using the word given. **Do not change the word given**. You must use between **two** and **five** words, including the word given. Here is an example (**0**).

Example:

0 A very friendly taxi driver drove us into town.

DRIVEN

We .... a very friendly taxi driver.

The gap can be filled by the words 'were driven into town by', so you write:

Example: | **0** | WERE DRIVEN INTO TOWN BY |

Write **only** the missing words **IN CAPITAL LETTERS on the separate answer sheet**.

---

35 They may ask to see your passport at the border.

REQUESTED

You may .... your passport at the border.

36 I regret not visiting Mexico when I was in California last year.

WISH

I .... Mexico when I was in California last year.

37 I use a dictionary to check any words that I don't know.

UP

If I don't know a word, ... a dictionary.

38 'Have you had enough to eat, Sophie?' Karl asked.

WHETHER

Karl asked .... enough to eat.

39 I didn't know anything about Rosa's problems at work.

UNAWARE

I .... Rosa's problems at work.

40 There are fewer fish in this river than there were three years ago.

AS

There .... fish in this river as there were three years ago.

41 Tomoko's seat at the concert was not close enough for her to see the stage clearly.

AWAY

Tomoko's seat at the concert was .... for her to see the stage clearly.

42 Mr Dunn found the instructions for the video very difficult to understand.

IN

Mr Dunn had great .... instructions for the video.

PAPER 4: LISTENING Part 1

2 3

Part 1

You will hear people talking in eight different situations. For questions **1–8**, choose the best answer (**A**, **B** or **C**).

---

1 On a train, you overhear a man talking on a mobile phone.

Why will he be late?

A because of the bad weather

B because of an unexpected meeting

C because of his car breaking down

2 You overhear a woman in a café telling her friend about her holiday.

What did she do?

A She borrowed a video camera.

B She hired a video camera.

C She bought a video camera.

3 You hear a radio programme about dealing with stress.

What is the woman advising people to do?

A try an unfamiliar activity

B do an energetic activity

C find an interesting activity

4 You overhear two friends talking about a job interview.

How did the young man feel about the question he was asked?

A embarrassed that he didn't have any hobbies

B annoyed at being asked a personal question

C surprised by the way the question was phrased

5 You hear a woman talking about an experience she had when travelling.

What happened?

A She missed a ferry she intended to catch.

B She was given wrong information about ferries.

C All ferries were cancelled that day.

6 You hear a man talking on the radio about a film.

Which aspect of the film did he find confusing?

A the speed of the dialogue

B the development of the plot

C the number of characters

7 You overhear three young people, Jane, Susan and Nick, planning a party.

What is Jane's responsibility?

A decorations

B food and drink

C invitations

8 You hear a woman talking about living on her own.

What does she say about it?

A It's not the first time she has lived alone.

B It gives her plenty of time for housework.

C She prefers sharing with other people.

4

Part 2

You will hear an interview with Ayesha Surrenden, who is responsible for staff in a museum.
For questions **9–18**, complete the sentences.

Working at a museum

According to Ayesha, many visitors come to the museum to see the exhibition in the well-known [**9**] section.

The museum is looking for people to work as what are known as [**10**]

Ayesha says that people who have worked in a [**11**] may have the right experience for this particular job.

The museum would particularly like to employ people who know the [**12**] language.

A person called a [**13**] is in charge of each group of five employees.

Every week, employees have to work for a time at the [**14**] in the museum.

Museum employees wear a uniform which is [**15**] instead of the traditional colours.

At the beginning, employees in this job receive £ [**16**] per year.

Every three weeks, employees can expect to have one [**17**] when they do not have to work.

The museum must receive applications by [**18**] at the latest.

5

Part 3

You will hear five different people talking about their favourite teacher. For questions **19–23**, choose from the list (**A–F**) what each speaker says. Use the letters only once. There is one extra letter which you do not need to use.

A My favourite teacher trained me in skills which are useful in my present job.

Speaker 1 [ ] **19**

B My favourite teacher prevented me from making a mistake.

Speaker 2 [ ] **20**

C My favourite teacher encouraged me to create something original.

Speaker 3 [ ] **21**

D My favourite teacher believed lessons should be amusing.

Speaker 4 [ ] **22**

E My favourite teacher allowed me to break a school rule.

Speaker 5 [ ] **23**

F My favourite teacher wouldn't let me miss any classes.

PAPER 4: LISTENING Part 4

Part 4

You will hear an interview with Peter Jones, who works at an animal hospital. He is talking about how he recently rescued a baby seal. For questions **24–30**, choose the best answer (**A**, **B** or **C**).

24 Peter says that people walking along the beach

A may not notice an injured seal.

B may find injured seals behind rocks.

C may find injured seals near fishing nets.

25 When Peter gets a phone call about an injured seal he always

A goes to investigate the situation personally.

B checks that the animal is in need of assistance.

C asks the caller to check that the animal is still alive.

26 What made it more difficult to rescue the seal called Pippa?

A It was dark.

B She was hiding.

C She was not lying still.

27 Before they moved Pippa, the rescuers

A checked her injuries.

B cleaned her cuts.

C put her in the water.

28 When animals arrive at the hospital they are usually

A uncooperative.

B scared.

C aggressive.

29 Why was Pippa kept alone at first?

A because it made it easier to help her

B in case her condition worsened

C because she refused to let anyone touch her

30 Pippa was not fed fish straightaway because

A she was too sick.

B she was too young.

C she hadn't eaten for some time.

PAPER 5: SPEAKING Part 1

Part 1

3 minutes (5 minutes for groups of three)

Interlocutor

Good morning/afternoon/evening. My name is .... and this is my colleague ....

And your names are?

Can I have your mark sheets, please?

Thank you.

First of all we'd like to know something about you.

- Where are you from (*Candidate A*)?
- And you (*Candidate B*)?

- What do you like about living (*here / name of candidate's home town*)?
- And what about you (*Candidate A/B*)?

Select one or more questions from any of the following categories, as appropriate.

Personal experience

- **Do you enjoy buying presents for people?** .... **(Is it ever difficult to buy for someone?)**
- **What has been the best present you have received recently?** .... **(Who gave it to you?)**

Daily life

- **Is your weekday routine different from your weekend routine?** .... **(In what ways?)**
- **What do you look forward to at the end of the day?**

Media

- **How much TV do you watch?** .... **(What kind of programmes do you not enjoy?)**
- **Do you buy magazines or newspapers regularly?** .... **(Why? / Why not?)**

1 A place to eat
2 Maps

Part 2
4 minutes (6 minutes for groups of three)

Interlocutor In this part of the test, I'm going to give each of you two photographs. I'd like you to talk about your photographs on your own for about a minute, and also to answer a short question about your partner's photographs.

(*Candidate A*), it's your turn first. Here are your photographs. **They show people eating in different places**.

I'd like you to compare the photographs, and say why you think the people are enjoying eating in these places.

All right?

Candidate A ....

1 minute

Interlocutor Thank you.

(*Candidate B*), **which place would you prefer to eat in?**

Candidate B ....

approximately 20 seconds

Interlocutor Thank you.

Now, (*Candidate B*), here are your two photographs. **They show people looking at different kinds of maps.**

I'd like you to compare the photographs, and say **why you think the people are looking at the maps.**

All right?

Candidate B ....

1 minute

Interlocutor Thank you. (Can I have the booklet, please?)

(*Candidate A*), **do you like learning about different places?**

Candidate A ....

approximately 20 seconds

Interlocutor Thank you.

PAPER 5: SPEAKING Part 2

Why are the people enjoying eating in these places?

Why are the people looking at the maps?

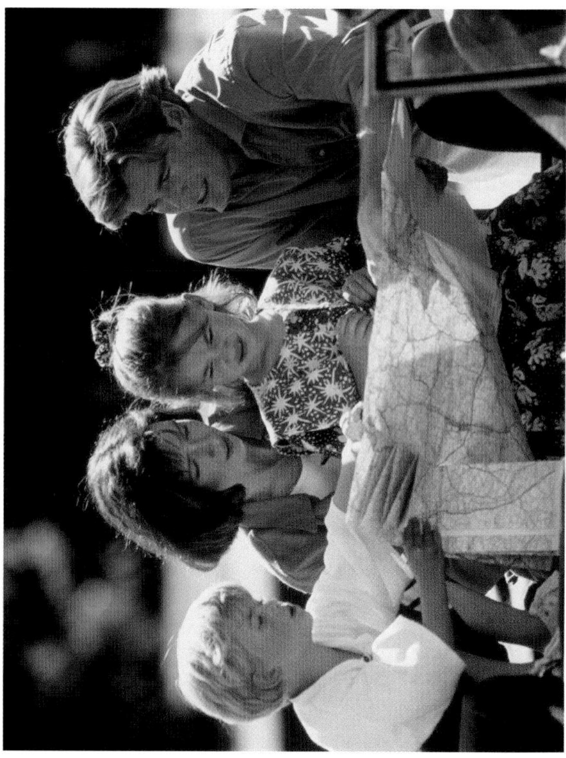

Cycling trip

Parts 3 and 4
7 minutes (9 minutes for groups of three)

Part 3

Interlocutor **Now, I'd like you to talk about something together for about three minutes.** *(4 minutes for groups of three)*

I'd like you to imagine that some friends are planning to go on a two-week cycling trip. Here are some of the things they need to think about before they go.

First, talk to each other about **why they need to think about these things before they go**. Then decide **which two things are the most important for their trip to be successful**.

All right?

Candidates *3 minutes (4 minutes for groups of three)* ....

Interlocutor Thank you. (Can I have the booklet, please?)

Part 4

Interlocutor *Select any of the following questions as appropriate:*

- **Would you go on a cycling trip?**
- **If you have to do something important, how do you make sure that you don't forget to do it?**
- **Some people say you can learn a lot from travelling to other countries. Do you agree?**
- **Do you think it's a good idea to go back to the same place for holidays or is it better to go somewhere different each time?**
- **Should a holiday be relaxing or full of activity?** .... **(Why?)**
- **Is it necessary to spend a lot of money to have a good time?** .... **(Why (not)?)**

Select any of the following prompts as appropriate:

- **What do you think?**
- **Do you agree?**
- **And you?**

Thank you. That is the end of the test.

PAPER 5: SPEAKING Parts 3 and 4

- Why do they need to think about these things before they go?
- Which two things are the most important for their trip to be successful?

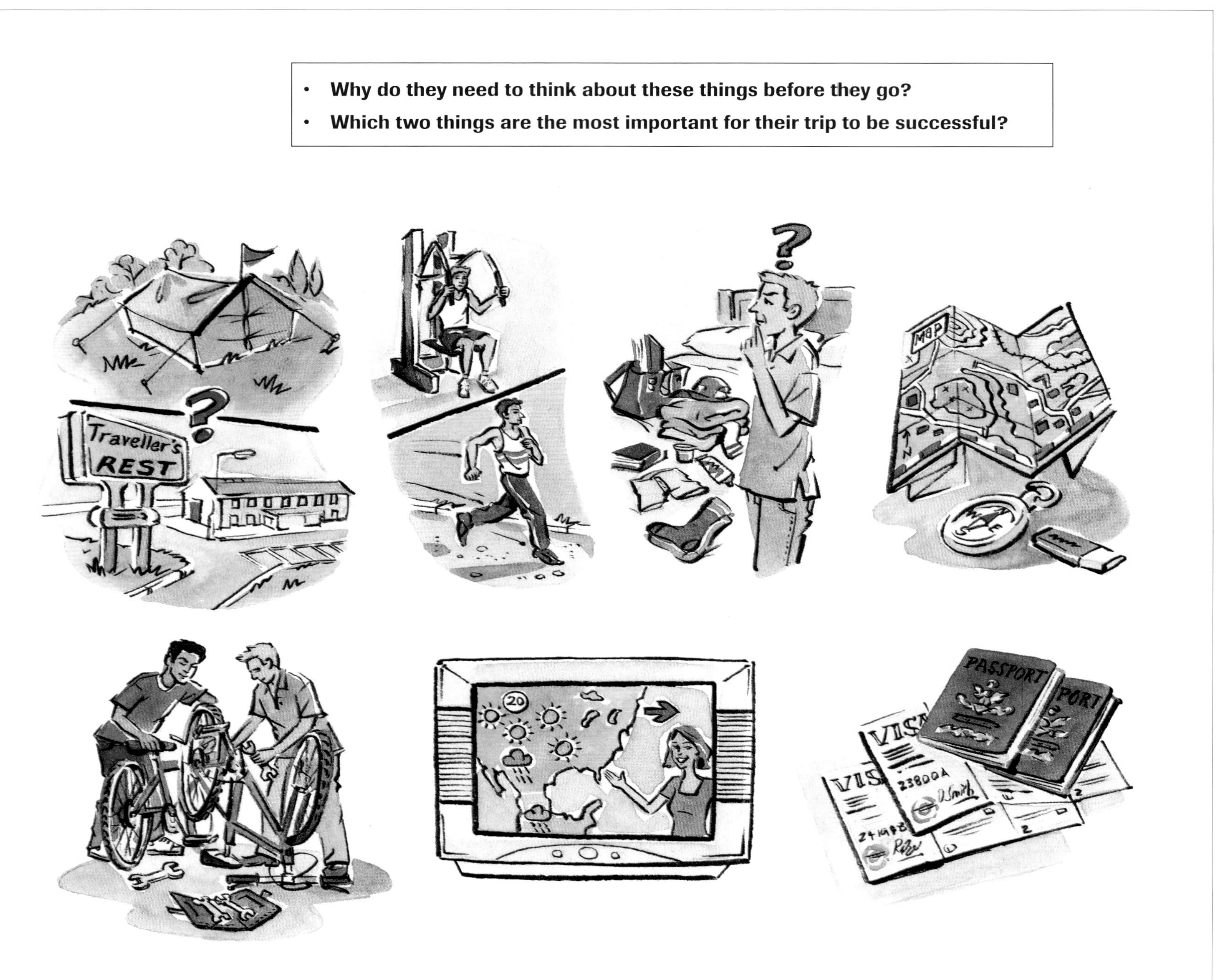

Answer key

Note: You can use contractions to answer the questions, e.g. 'I am working' ⟶ 'I'm working', 'she has done' ⟶ 'she's done', etc.

1 A family affair

Listening Part 1

❷ **Photos:** Patrick 3 Tracey 2 Vicky 4 Kostas 1

Recording script CD1 Track 2

Interviewer: How much do you help around the house, Patrick?

Patrick: Not that much really, but that's because my mum doesn't go out to work any more, so she has more time than she used to. I don't have a lot of free time these days because I'm studying for my exams. I mean, my mum does most of the housework, though I used to help more when I was younger – you know, hang out clothes, lay the table, things like that. She's pretty busy, but even so she usually manages to find a bit of time to give me a hand with my studies – she used to be a maths teacher and she knows I'm a bit nervous about the maths

Q1 exam. But I think she really does it for pleasure – she's really good at explaining things, though sometimes I feel I'd just like to get on with things on my own.

Interviewer: Tracey. How often do you all do things together as a family?

Tracey: Oh, all the time, I mean at least once a week at weekends. You see, we live in this really old house by the sea and we've been working on it all year. In fact, we've just finished doing up the kitchen at the back of the house. It's been great fun because we've all been doing it together and I've been learning a lot about DIY, which is really useful. We've made a lot of mess, of course, which we've had to clear

Q2 up and now we're decorating it, so it's looking nicer and nicer. We had lots of really big arguments about the colour, but in the end everyone agreed with me, so I'm really happy because we're doing things the way I want.

Interviewer: Vicky, do you ever do sports with other people in your family?

Vicky: Well, my dad's a fitness fanatic, so he's always running or cycling or doing something

Q3 energetic. I do sporty things with him now and again, more often in the summer though occasionally at other times of the year as well. He's got a few days' holiday at the moment, so he's probably doing something sporty right now. He's always asking me to go out cycling with him, but now I've got a boyfriend and other things to do, so recently I've been spending more time with him than with my dad.

Interviewer: Do you enjoy family celebrations, Kostas?

Kostas: Not much, to be honest. I just feel they go

Q4 on for too long and I'd prefer to be out doing other things with my friends, not sitting around listening to my uncles and aunts and that. Someone is always standing up and giving a speech or singing a song and I've heard all those songs and speeches so many times that

Q4 I've just lost interest. But I don't get annoyed or anything like that. I mean I just wait for things to end and then I go out with my friends. That's what I really like.

❸ **1** A **2** C **3** B **4** A

❹ 1 How much do you help around the house?
2 How often do you all do things together as a family?
3 Do you (ever) do/play sports with other people in your family?
4 Do you enjoy family celebrations?

Recording script CD1 Track 3

1 How much do you help around the house, Patrick?

2 Tracey. How often do you all do things together as a family?

3 Vicky, do you ever do sports with other people in your family?

4 Do you enjoy family celebrations, Kostas?

❺ *Suggested questions:* Where do you go on family holidays? What do you enjoy doing with your family? How does your family spend the weekends? Which member of your family are you most similar to?

Grammar
Present simple and present continuous

1 **2** present simple **3** present continuous **4** present continuous **5** present simple **6** present continuous **7** present continuous

2 **2** present continuous 6 **3** present continuous 1 **4** present continuous 4 **5** present simple 5 **6** present continuous 3 **7** present continuous 7

3 **2** work **3** am working, am preparing **4** is coming out **5** are always interrupting **6** am watching **7** is coming, are getting **8** does not do, is always bringing

Reading Part 2

1

usually positive	usually negative	could be either
hard-working	critical	quiet
mature	fussy	sensitive
tactful	lazy	strict
polite	nervous	talkative
relaxed	rude	
responsible	tactless	
tidy		

2 critical – uncritical, mature – immature, polite – impolite, responsible – irresponsible, sensitive – insensitive, tidy – untidy

3 hard-working – lazy, tactful – tactless, polite – rude, quiet – talkative, relaxed – strict

6 She has a mostly positive attitude. The article suggests that parents' behaviour causes many of the problems with teenage children.

7 **2** F **3** A **4** C **5** B **6** D **7** G

Grammar
Present perfect simple and continuous

1 1 **1** a, **2** b **2** **1** b, **2** a **3** **1** a, **2** b

2 **2** have asked **3** have cleaned **4** has been playing **5** have passed **6** has only been working **7** have spent **8** have been cooking

Use of English Part 2

1 **2** h **3** d **4** b **5** g **6** f **7** a **8** c

3 The text does not say who should do housework, but implies that it should be shared equally.

4 The four reasons: They say, 'I work long hours', 'my wife's work is less stressful', 'she does it better', and they think their jobs are more important.

6 **1** of **2** doing **3** If/When **4** for **5** that/which **6** so **7** it **8** not **9** mine **10** at **11** is **12** more

Vocabulary
Collocations with *make* and *do*

1 **1** do, doing **2** make, do

2 **1** making, do **2** making **3** doing **4** make, do **5** made **6** make, do

Speaking Part 1

1 **1** Where are you from? – asks for personal information; What do you like about the place where you live? – asks for a personal opinion

2 Where are you from? – can be answered with a short phrase; What do you like about the place where you live? – needs a longer answer

2 Irene: a small town, north of Spain (Llanes); quiet, beaches and countryside, friends

Peter: northern Germany (Bremen); friends, shops, sports centre

Recording script CD1 Track 4

Teacher: So, Irene, where are you from?

Irene: I'm from Llanes. It's a small town near Oviedo on the north coast of Spain.

Teacher: And what do you like about Llanes?

Irene: Well, it's quite a quiet place, especially in the winter, but it has wonderful beaches and beautiful countryside. Also, I have a lot of very good friends living there and we have a really good time when we go out together.

Teacher: And you Peter, where are you from?

Peter: Bremen, in northern Germany.

Teacher: And what do you like about Bremen?

Peter: My friends, the shops, the sports centre …

Teacher: Do you come from a large family?

❸ *Suggested answer:* Irene: she answers in sentences, not single words; she gives a few extra details

Writing Part 1

❶ *Suggested phrases to underline:* … when is the best time of year to visit your country? … meet people our own age (17–18). What's the best way to do this? … what clothes we should bring with us? … would you like to join our group and travel round with us?

❸ **1** Yes **2** *Students' own answers*

❹ *Suggested phrases to underline:* I suggest spending a few days at a school or college. How about coming to mine? It would be a good idea to stay in a youth hostel.

❺ **2** I suggest going to clubs and cafés / cafés and clubs in the evenings.
3 It would be a good idea to contact the youth club in my area.

❻ *Sample answer:* See the model in Exercise 3 in the Student's Book.

2 Leisure and pleasure

Starting off

❶ **1** riding motorbikes **2** window shopping **3** playing computer games **4** clubbing **5** doing aerobics **6** playing chess **7** playing team sports

Reading Part 1

❷ *Suggested answers:* His girlfriend left him for someone with a motorbike; he had enjoyed riding a motorbike when he was six; it would allow him to get to places

❸ **1** B **2** D **3** B **4** C **5** D **6** A **7** C **8** C

Vocabulary
Phrasal verbs

❶ **2** a **3** c **4** b **5** f **6** g **7** d

❷ **2** sum up **3** start up **4** make up **5** goes out with / is going out with **6** taking up **7** shot off

Grammar
Adjectives with *-ed* and *-ing*

❶ **1** thrilled, elated **2** exciting

❷ **2** annoying **3** bored **4** confused **5** embarrassing **6** excited

❸ **2** disappointing **3** interesting **4** worried **5** exhausting **6** amusing

❹ g

Recording script CD1 Track 5

Young woman: The whole experience was amazing actually. I mean, I'd been working really hard, studying, and so I was feeling pretty tired and nervous already, so when my boyfriend suggested I went along with him, I was like shocked like 'No way!' I mean the thought of breaking a bone or something even worse just before an exam was terrifying. But you know he just kept on at me, so for the sake of a bit of peace in the end I said yes. When we were up there in the sky I was just so scared I can't tell you. I just wanted to get out of the plane. I felt trapped, but the only way to do that was to jump, and in fact the jump itself was really exciting. I'd love to do it again. And I didn't break a thing!

❺ **2** tired and nervous **3** shocked **4** terrifying **5** trapped **6** exciting

Listening Part 2

❶ *Suggested answers:*

1 Positive effects
- They encourage people to be more creative.
- They can distract you from your problems.
- Many of the games are very educational.
- They require imagination to play well.
- People learn to concentrate on tasks
- They develop many skills, such as hand and eye coordination.
- They teach people how to solve problems.

2 Criticisms

- Young people play computer games instead of being more creative.
- Video games distract young people from their homework.
- People who play these games have less imagination.
- The games are unsociable activities.
- They encourage young people to be violent.
- They are a waste of time. People should spend their time doing something useful.

❷ *Suggested answers:* **1** adjective/adjective phrase **2** noun/noun phrase **3** comparative adverb/ comparative adjective + noun **4** adjective **5** noun/noun phrase **6** plural noun/noun phrase **7** personal plural noun **8** comparative adjective **9** verb **10** noun/noun phrase

❸ **1** more violent **2** crimes **3** less homework **4** better visual **5** driving skills **6** five objects **7** airport security staff **8** more educational **9** make decisions **10** effort

Recording script CD1 Track 6

Interviewer: And now to video and computer gaming. Many people worry about how these games affect young people and their education. I have in the studio psychologist Sarah Forbes, who has recently written a book about gaming. Sarah, is there any basis behind these worries?

Sarah: Well, people have been suggesting for years that video games and television programmes

Q1 tend to make youngsters more violent, but I'm not sure that these games have really had any negative effect at all. I mean, computer and video games are tremendously popular and the fact that people stay at home playing

Q2 computer games may mean that fewer crimes are being committed. Potential criminals are keeping themselves entertained playing games instead of going out and breaking the law.

Interviewer: So video games are not all bad.

Sarah: Not at all. Of course, you sometimes hear teachers complaining that schoolchildren come to school tired after spending half the

Q3 night gaming and that they do less homework than they used to in the past. And it's true that these days there are lots of things around to distract and entertain young people. But I'm more interested in the positive effects of gaming.

Interviewer: Which are?

Sarah: Well, firstly my research shows that certain

Q4 games give people better visual skills and as a result they are better at managing machines than people who don't play them. Playing computer games seems to be particularly good for old people who react more slowly than young people. When they play computer

Q5 games, their driving skills actually get better.

Interviewer: Interesting. Are there any professions which would benefit from training with computer games?

Sarah: Certainly. We've found that people playing computer games can keep track of as many as

Q6 five objects at any one time on their computer screen. They can also concentrate for longer. So, people who have to spend their working time examining or inspecting things might find their skills improved by playing computer

Q7 games – for example airport security staff might do their job better if they were trained with computer games. They spend hours staring at a screen showing the contents of passengers' luggage as it passes through a machine, looking for illegal items.

Interviewer: That's true. And what about the teachers' criticisms?

Sarah: Well, I think these days there are a lot of interesting things around to distract students from their schoolwork and teachers are finding it harder to compete for their students' attention and enthusiasm. But some educationalists suggest that it's teachers who need to adapt and that computer

Q8 games can be more educational than a lot of the traditional activities that go on in the classroom. Teachers need to see their value.

Interviewer: And that is?

Sarah: Well, games players often spend more than a hundred hours working on a game and trying to dominate its complexities. In doing

Q9 so they gain the ability to make decisions and think more clearly. A hundred hours is a lot of hours and you wouldn't expect your average schoolchild to spend that much time on a school project. By working through these games and eventually winning them, they learn

Q10 how valuable it is to make a sustained effort in their work.

Interviewer: Interesting.

Sarah: Yes, and when looked at from that perspective it's hard to argue that computer games are a waste of time and that young people would be better occupied doing something else.

Grammar

Comparison of adjectives and adverbs

1 **2** and **3** harder / cheapest **4** easiest
5, **6** and **7** more violent / more educational / most successful **8** better **9** less **10** better

2 **2** ~~more cheaper~~ cheaper **3** ~~that~~ than
4 ~~more hardly~~ harder **5** ~~as often than~~ as often as
6 ~~the more enjoyable~~ the most enjoyable
7 ~~the less interesting~~ the least interesting
8 ~~more good~~ better

Use of English Part 4

1 **2** is the most enjoyable **3** one of the easiest
4 not as/so interesting as **5** play tennis so well as
6 is the most hard-working **7** not as/so cheap as
8 more quickly than

Writing Part 2 An article

1 *Suggested answers to underline:* leisure-time activity, How did you get started? Why do you enjoy it so much?

3 **1** **1** D **2** C **3** A **4** B
2 A, C and D
3 A and B

4 **1** satisfying, relaxing, fascinating, complicated
2 creative, useful **3** competent, successful

5 *Sample answer:* See the model in Exercise 3 in the Student's Book.

Vocabulary and grammar review Unit 1

Vocabulary

1 **2** tactless/insensitive **3** fussy **4** talkative/noisy
5 nervous **6** sensitive **7** mature **8** tidy

2 **2** swept **3** doing **4** laid **5** make **6** do

3 **2** make **3** do **4** doing **5** do **6** made **7** made
8 making

Grammar

4 **2** He's doing, he goes **3** is learning
4 I never phone, is always talking, I get
5 are getting **6** isn't coming, he plays

5 **2** have arrived, have been expecting
3 have spent, has turned up
4 have had / have been having, has been telling, has not told, has seen
5 has lost / has been losing, has been feeling

Vocabulary and grammar review Unit 2

Vocabulary

1 **2** started up **3** taking up **4** make up **5** sum up
6 shot off **7** headed off to

Grammar

2 **2** Small towns are ~~more safety~~ *safer* to live in than large cities.
3 Today's the ~~hotest~~ *hottest* day of the year so far.
4 She looks more ~~relax~~ *relaxed* than she did before the exam.
5 Patty is so smart – she's always dressed in the ~~last~~ *latest* fashion!
6 If you study ~~more hardly~~ *harder*, you'll get higher marks.
7 Everest is the ~~higher~~ *highest* mountain in the world.
8 His first day at school was the ~~worse~~ *worst* day of his life.
9 We need to eat ~~more healthier~~ *healthier* food.
10 We should buy this sofa because it's definitely the ~~comfortablest~~ *most comfortable*.

Word formation

3 **2** exhausting **3** bored **4** disappointed
5 annoying **6** interested **7** surprised **8** exciting

3 Happy holidays!

Starting off

1

types of holiday	holiday places	holiday activities
a camping holiday a beach holiday a sightseeing holiday a cruise backpacking	at a campsite at a luxury hotel on a cruise ship at a youth hostel at sea in the mountains in the city centre at the seaside	walking and climbing meeting new people sunbathing relaxing visiting monuments seeing new places

2 **1 Photos: 1** a camping holiday **2** a beach holiday **3** a sightseeing holiday **4** backpacking **5** a cruise
2, 3 and **4** *Students' own answers*

Listening Part 3

1 *Suggested answers:* **A** a sightseeing holiday
B a cruise, backpacking or a camping holiday
C a beach holiday or a cruise
D backpacking or a camping holiday
E backpacking or a camping holiday **F** a cruise

2 **A** good food – delicious meals
B something new – a complete novelty, dangerous – risky
C did very little – sat around
D exercise – physical activity, unspoilt – natural
E friendly – kind
F in style and comfort – in luxury

3 **1** B **2** C **3** D **4** A **5** E

Recording script CD1 Track 7

Interviewer: So, now after that, I'd like to ask each of you a bit more about your holidays. Francesca, what did you particularly like about your holiday?

Francesca: I went on one of those journeys overland to Kenya. Before that I always used to go on family holidays, so really it was a complete novelty for me to be able to go off with a friend and a group of other young people of my own age. I mean, really, on my family holidays we always used to go to the same hotel and lie on the beach and things. This was much more exciting though – going to really strange places and doing lots of things I hadn't done before. But we were well looked after by the driver and the guide so we weren't really doing anything very risky. Otherwise my mum wouldn't have let me go.

Interviewer: Sounds interesting. And what about you, Mike? Why did you choose your particular holiday?

Mike: It was the nightlife we went for really. I went with a couple of my mates, you know, and during the day we just sat around by the pool and were really lazy, unless we made a trip to the beach, which was about twenty minutes away by bus. But after dark we were down at the discos and clubs partying to the small hours.

Interviewer: That sounds like fun! And Sally, what did you like about your holiday?

Sally: My dad used to be a climber and when he was younger, we used to go on climbing holidays together. But this time I went with a couple of my friends, which was great because we were away from the city out in the open air in fabulous natural surroundings. The scenery was amazing, all those big mountain landscapes and we got lots of great photos. And sleeping out under the stars was wonderful. It was a bit tricky at one moment though. We'd just climbed one of the really high peaks and we were on the way down when a storm came. We had to get down quickly or we might have been in trouble. So that was a bit scary. We were carrying pretty big backpacks, so all the physical activity got me quite fit by the end of it.

Interviewer: Sounds a great experience. Now you, Paul. How was your holiday?

Paul: Not my idea of a good time at all, quite honestly. I mean the meals were delicious if you don't mind sitting around with a lot of middle-aged adults in these luxury places. I mean I found it so boring! And my mum and dad dragged me round looking at paintings and sculptures, which I hated. Still there was an upside to it, because that's when I met this Polish girl called Jolanta, while we were walking round one of the museums. She was just as bored as I was, so we left our parents to get on with things and went off for the day together. We had a really great time and we're still in touch.

Interviewer: So, you think you've grown out of family holidays then?

Paul: Pretty much so.

Interviewer: Finally you, Katie. How did you get on?

Katie: It was one of my first non-family holidays too, except for summer camps when I was younger. I went backpacking with some friends round Europe and we took trains and buses everywhere and stayed in these really cheap places with lots of other young people from all over the world who were doing the same sort of thing as us. It was really fun meeting them. I mean, mostly people were so open and kind and wanting to get to know you. I think that's one of the best things about foreign travel – meeting new people. So we've decided to do the same thing again next year.

Interviewer: Fantastic! Now I'd like to ask you all. What do you like about holidays with your friends and what did you use to enjoy about holidays with your families, perhaps when you were younger?

Vocabulary

Journey, trip, travel and *way*

❶ **1** travel **2** journey **3** trip **4** way

❷ **2** way **3** trip **4** trip **5** travel **6** journey **7** trip **8** journey **9** way

Grammar

Past simple, past continuous and *used to*

❶ **2** b **3** d **4** a **5** e

❷ **2** used to do **3** got, jumped, drove **4** used to spend **5** were walking, began **6** used to visit, was

Reading Part 3

❶ *Suggested answers:* Advantages: it's quiet (possibly), you see the countryside, it's safe, you may meet other travellers, trains take you to the city centre, etc. Disadvantages: you may have to wait a long time for trains, they may be delayed, crowded, you may have to stand up, etc.

❷ **2** lost something, beginning
3 with an animal
4 was asked to help solve a problem
5 with people, especially nervous
6 saw wildlife
7 was entertained, by another traveller
8 happy to arrive despite a problem
9 without all the correct documents
10 through an area where few people live
11 didn't mind when the train didn't arrive on time
12 witnessed an illegal activity
13 crowded
14 and **15** obtained food, stopped

❸ **2** C **3** F **4** D **5** G **6** D **7** E **8** F **9** C **10** D **11** E **12** B **13** E **14** A or E **15** A or E

Grammar

Past perfect simple and continuous

❶ **1** b
2 had left
3 In the first sentence, the guard was no longer in the compartment so he didn't hear the alarm; in the second sentence, he hadn't left but was in the process of leaving so he heard the alarm

❸ **2** had never been **3** had organised **4** arrived, had lost **5** recognised, had never spoken **6** had damaged

❹ a – past perfect continuous

❺ **2** had been walking, began
3 had already finished, offered
4 had only been speaking
5 got, had been walking

Use of English Part 3

❶ nature – natural, danger – dangerous, friend – friendly, comfort – comfortable, luxury – luxurious, risk – risky, nerve – nervous, crowd – crowded, disappoint – disappointed/disappointing, care – careful/careless, wonder – wonderful, dust – dusty, memory – memorable, hunger – hungry, enjoy – enjoyable

❷ educate – educational, educated, uneducated; space – spacious; mass – massive; dirt – dirty; use – useful, useless, used; care – careful, careless, caring; thought – thoughtful, thoughtless; accept – acceptable, accepted; mood – moody; emotion – emotional, emotive; change – changeable, unchangeable, changed, unchanged, changing, unchanging; base – basic

3 2 comfortable **3** thoughtful **4** colourful **5** weekly **6** optimistic **7** noisier **8** nervous **9** helpful **10** miraculous

Speaking Part 3

1 *Suggested answers:* End-of-year trips: sightseeing, activity holiday in the mountains, a beach holiday, a cruise, a trip to a theme park, visiting a museum or art gallery

2 Sightseeing holiday: you learn about art, architecture and history, other cultures and visit somewhere different; Activity holiday: you have exciting experiences and adventures, and learn to be independent

Recording script CD1 Track 8

Peter: Shall I start?

Antonia: OK.

Peter: I think this first one is a sightseeing holiday.

Antonia: Yes, that's right.

Peter: How do you think a sightseeing holiday can benefit students?

Antonia: I think you can learn a lot from a holiday like this, you know, about art and architecture and history. Things like that.

Peter: Yes, and also you can visit somewhere very different and learn about other cultures.

Antonia: Right. What about this photo? It's an activity holiday in the mountains, isn't it?

Peter: Yes, this one can give students some exciting experiences and adventures.

Antonia: Yes, and they learn to be more independent because they're away from home and their families.

Peter: And the third photo? What about that?

Antonia: It shows people playing on a beach. How do you think students can benefit from a trip to the beach?

3 2 think **3** What about **4** isn't it **5** that

Writing Part 2 A story

1 *Suggested phrases to underline:* it was a trip I'll never forget; the English-language magazine at your college

2 1 B **2** C **3** E **4** D **5** A

Recording script CD1 Track 9

Presenter: Jean

Jean: Just coming to study here is a really big adventure for me. I always lived at home until a couple of months ago when I came here, so to get away from my family just for a few months is out of this world. I mean I miss them but, well, you know. And it's the first time I've ever been anywhere by air, so for me it's all pretty amazing. Especially as I come from a pretty small village in Scotland.

Presenter: Mark

Mark: I can remember a trip I made when I was quite small – I was probably only about eight years old. Anyway, it was one of the first times I'd travelled anywhere without my mum and dad. I was with the other kids from my class and a trip had been organised to a nearby wildlife park. Well, the bus broke down in the middle of it and while we were all sitting inside waiting for the bus to be repaired two lions came incredibly close to the bus. We kids thought it was terribly funny and all screamed with laughter, but I think some of the teachers were pretty scared actually. We could see them so close up!

Presenter: Maya

Maya: For me it has to be something that happened quite recently. My mother's family comes from India and if you count all my uncles and aunts and cousins there are lots of us. In fact I have family living all over the world in lots of different countries. For example, I have an uncle in Canada and a cousin in Kuwait and so on. You name the place, there's probably some uncle or cousin living there. But this is a time when we all got together – nearly forty of us – for my grandma's 80th birthday at her house. People had made a real effort to get there and we had an unforgettable weekend together.

Presenter: Patrick

Patrick: Oh, I can tell you about a trip we made across the River Plate from Buenos Aires to Montevideo on a rather old ferry when a storm came up. I lived there as a child and I was with some friends from school. We'd been invited to someone's house there for a few days during our summer holidays – that's in December, you know. Anyway, it was very rough and we all got quite ill. Luckily, it all blew over in a few hours, but when we got on dry land again, my legs were shaking.

Presenter: Sarah

Sarah: I can tell you about a magical trip we did when I was quite small. I still remember it because it was like one of those things which makes a big impression on you when you're small. Anyway, we all took a train, my mum and dad, various relations and myself and when we got to the station we walked what seemed a really long way to me. Of course it can't have been very far, but we got to this really nice lake where we had a picnic. Then afterwards we played football together. I'll never forget that day!

❹ **2** had decided **3** had only read **4** had entered
5 had **6** were waiting **7** approached
8 had never felt **9** started **10** managed

❺ **1** Three paragraphs. Paragraph 1: where we were going on the trip and how we were feeling; paragraph 2: the animals we saw; paragraph 3: the puncture and what happened while we waited
2 excited, ancient, noisy, nervous, crowded, fascinating, delighted, thrilled, relieved
3 going to a wildlife park, seeing animals in real life for the first time, the puncture, the monkeys on the bus, his/her classmates' excitement

❻ *Sample answer:* See the model in Exercise 4 in the Student's Book.

4 Food, glorious food

Starting off

1, **2** and **3** *Students' own answers*
4 *Suggested answers:* healthy ways of eating: photos 2, 4; less healthy: photos 1, 3

Reading Part 2

❶ *Suggested answers:* Benefits: learning to do these things, learning about nutrition, becoming independent, health benefits

❷ Students benefit because: they eat what they grow, they eat fresh organic food instead of cheap fast food, they learn about many things connected with what they grow including scientific methods and geography, they learn to cook, they have fun, their attitude to food changes, their diet is healthy which breaks their isolation, they learn to care about each other

❸ *Suggested phrases to highlight or underline:*
D One lesson **E** The problem these projects
F These two projects **G** We in this small space
H Lessons like this one

❹ **2** F **3** G **4** C **5** D **6** A **7** B

Vocabulary

Food, dish and *meal*

❷ **2** meals **3** food **4** dishes **5** meal

❸ **2** ~~meals~~ dishes **3** ~~food~~ dish **4** ~~meal~~ food
5 ~~foods~~ meals **6** ~~food~~ dish **7** ~~dishes~~ meals

Grammar

So and *such*

❶ **2** So **3** such a **4** so **5** such

❷ **a** such – examples 1 and 3 **b** such – example 5
c so – example 4 **d** so – example 2

❸ **2** so **3** such a **4** so **5** such an **6** so

❹ **2** ~~so much~~ such **3** correct **4** ~~so~~ such **5** ~~so~~ such a
6 ~~such~~ such a **7** correct **8** ~~so~~ such

Listening Part 4

❷ Purpose: to save traditional dishes, promote healthier ways of eating and living, improve lifestyles, enjoy variety and difference, educate people about food, improve relationships, make people happier

❸ *Suggested phrases to underline:* **2** What ... is Slow Food **3** the problem with fast food companies
4 main aim ... to improve
5 What is the Salone del Gusto
6 What surprised Valerie **7** Who ... will benefit

Recording script CD1 Track 10

Interviewer: So, Valerie, what is the Slow Food Movement, can you tell us?

Valerie: Yes. The Slow Food Movement is really a reaction to fast food and our fast modern lifestyles. People have been complaining for years about fast food. You know, people eat too many hamburgers, too many pizzas, and too much fast food in general. It's not just that fast food is bad for health. It's also because we're afraid that traditional dishes will

disappear. The Movement itself was
Q1 started by an Italian called Carlo Petrini. He was protesting because a McDonald's had opened near the Spanish Steps – one of the most well-known monuments in the centre of Rome. He felt it was sort of symbolic of the destruction of many valuable traditional things and he was keen to promote healthier ways of eating and living.

Interviewer: So, Slow Food just means healthier food, does it?

Valerie: Not exactly. I think it's more about our lifestyles than anything else. We're always in such a hurry. For many people cooking means rushing into the supermarket, picking up a ready meal and putting it in the microwave. We don't have enough time to take care of ourselves, or enjoy our lives. Slow Food is food that's cooked with care and which we take time to enjoy eating.
Q2 That essentially is what it is: excellent, natural, tasty food that we appreciate.

Interviewer: Fast food companies advertise that their food is healthy as well. How would you answer that?

Valerie: I wouldn't deny it. It may well be true. For me, and for a lot of Slow Fooders, the problem is
Q3 that wherever you sit down for a meal, whether it's in Tokyo, Milan or Cape Town, the food you're given is too similar. It makes eating, and life in general, boring. There's just not enough variety. Traditional food isn't going to be lost completely, but we do want as many people as possible to enjoy it and to take the trouble to look for things which are different.

Interviewer: So, let's see if I've understood you. The Movement's main object is to improve the way we live, is it?

Valerie: Exactly that. It's not just about food. It's about how we live and finding time to enjoy our lives.
Q4 We need to take time to enjoy what's around us.

Interviewer: And what does the Slow Food Movement do to promote its ideas?

Valerie: All sorts of things – it's got a gastronomic university, newsletters, and groups in many different countries. It even has its own trade fair, the Salone del Gusto. Producers of
Q5 traditional food come from all over the world to exhibit their food and meet each other. It includes lots of talks and workshops where people can find out more. It takes place in Italy, so most of the participants are Italian. But
Q6 one of the amazing things is just how many of the visitors are from Britain and how much interest there is in Britain for these sorts of things. I mean the British don't exactly have a reputation for good food, but there they were showing their cheeses and oysters and hams alongside the Italians.

Interviewer: So how, in the end, will this Movement be good for us?

Valerie: Well, as I was saying before, it's not just about avoiding poor quality food. Basically, there are two things we would like to see happen which would generally improve our quality of life.

Firstly, I hope that young people will become better educated about food in general. And while I appreciate that working people may be too busy to cook properly every day I also hope that parents will begin to realise just how important it is to take time over food. And if we can make these two things happen, then I believe we will start to see differences in
Q5 what I think really matters most: the way we live together as families! I think if we sit down together and take time to eat, we'll be relaxed enough to talk to each other more. As a result, relationships will improve and life in general, we hope, will become happier.

Interviewer: Valerie Watson, thank you.

Valerie: Thank you.

4 **1** B **2** C **3** A **4** C **5** A **6** B **7** C

Grammar

Too and *enough*

2 **a** too – example 5 **b** too – examples 1, 2 and 3
c enough – example 7
d enough – examples 4 and 6

3 **1** too many, enough **2** enough **3** enough **4** too
5 too

4 3 ~~money enough~~ enough money
4 ~~enough comfortable~~ comfortable enough
5 ~~too much long~~ (much) too long
6 ~~doing too hard work~~ working too hard / doing too much hard work
7 ~~too much cruel~~ very cruel
8 ~~a sport too difficult~~ a very difficult sport
9 ~~not too much comfortable~~ not very comfortable
10 ~~too much expensive~~ (much) too expensive

Speaking Part 4

1 Magda answers question 3, Miguel answers question 4

3 **1** False **2** True **3** True

Recording script CD1 Track 11

1

Magda: I think it depends what you mean by fast, because if you prepare a salad quickly, that's definitely good for you, but if you eat hamburgers and pizzas and things, that's probably quite unhealthy.

Teacher: And Miguel, what do you think?

Miguel: I think Magda is right, but I'm sure that if you only eat hamburgers sometimes, that's OK. It's when you eat things like hamburgers and pizzas all the time that it can be a bit unhealthy.

Magda: Yes, it's important to have a balanced diet.

Miguel: That's right. And plenty of fruit and vegetables.

Magda: I agree.

2

Miguel: … I think it's a very good thing because we all sit down together and discuss what we've been doing during the day. And we exchange opinions and make plans and it feels very good, because we are spending time together although we are all very busy.

Teacher: And Magda, do you agree?

Magda: Yes, very much so. And also, I think people take more trouble to cook well when they are going to cook for several people than when they are cooking just for themselves, so in fact people eat better.

Use of English Part 1

1 The surroundings, the service, the food, the price

2 **1** C **2** D **3** A **4** B **5** C **6** B **7** A **8** B
9 D **10** A **11** D **12** C

Writing Part 2 A review

1 *Suggested answers:* **2** yes **3** maybe **4** yes **5** no
6 maybe **7** maybe **8** yes **9** yes **10** yes

2 **2** yes – paragraph 1 **3** yes – paragraph 2
4 yes – paragraph 3 **5** no
6 yes – paragraph 2 **7** no **8** yes – paragraph 4
9 yes – paragraph 3
10 no (although the text says 'a short walk from our workplace', the writer does not say where it is located)

3 *Suggested answers:*

the waiters	the interior	the food	the price
friendly informative	airy cosy modern	delicious fresh satisfying tasty wonderful	reasonable

5 *Sample answer:* See the model in Use of English Part 1.

Vocabulary and grammar review Unit 3

Vocabulary

1 **2** trip **3** travel **4** way **5** journey **6** way
7 trip **8** journey

Word formation

2 **2** comfortable **3** disappointed **4** natural
5 hungry **6** crowded **7** noisy **8** unfriendly
9 quieter **10** enjoyable

Grammar

3 **2** I had lost **3** used to travel to work **4** when/while she was (still) studying / while (still) studying
5 had never met **6** used to be more

Vocabulary and grammar review Unit 4

Vocabulary

❶ **2** food / meal **3** dish **4** food **5** dish **6** meal / food **7** meal **8** food

Word formation

❷ **2** convenience **3** healthy **4** organisations **5** encourage **6** balanced **7** disappeared **8** repetitive **9** choice **10** easily

Grammar

❸ **2** slowly enough for us to **3** was so full / crowded (that) **4** such delicious food (that) **5** cook well enough **6** such a long time / so much time

5 Studying abroad

Starting off

❶ **2** b **3** f **4** g **5** d **6** e **7** a **8** c

Listening Part 1

❶ **2** a **3** g **4** h **5** i **6** c **7** d **8** e **9** b

❷ *Suggested phrases to underline:*
2 Who caused the problem
3 What does she like most **4** the main benefit
5 Why is he talking

❸ **1** C **2** C **3** B **4** A **5** A

Recording script CD1 Track 12

1

Will: Actually, at the beginning of term I was a bit lost. You know, I felt that most of the other students knew a lot more about the subject than I did. Listening to them, I got the idea that some of them felt the course was a bit of a waste of time. In my case, I was having problems not just with the language but also with the ideas. But I managed to get over all that and I'm happy to say that the course has lived up to expectations and I've made a lot of progress. I mean, we've got an exam next week which I should be feeling a bit anxious about but in fact I'm feeling pretty confident. *Q1*

2

Mike: Hi, Helena. You're not looking too happy.

Helena: I'm not! Do you know what's happened? We were given an assignment by our course tutor at the beginning of the month and I did lots of research for it in the library, made lots of notes and so on. Anyway, this girl, Valerie, who is on the same course as me came round to my flat one day for coffee and while she was there, my mother phoned. I was out of the room for about half an hour and during that time she must have copied all my notes! I was really embarrassed when I found out about what she'd done. It was during a tutorial and when my tutor gave me my mark for the assignment, he said it looked very like an essay Valerie had handed in the week before. I can tell you I was furious, there was nothing I could say. *Q2*

3

Hitoshi: So, what are you doing here in Japan?

Maggie: I'm learning Japanese at a language school. I go to classes for just two hours a day, which is good because I learn Japanese from Japanese teachers, and then I'm free to practise it during the rest of the day.

Hitoshi: That sounds a good idea.

Maggie: It is. You see they also organise lots of other things for you to take part in after you've finished your language lesson. There are clubs you can join if you're interested and they really are the best part. For example, I'm also doing a karate course taught in Japanese which is great fun. I'm learning something completely different in the language I'm studying and I'm getting to know lots of Japanese people. *Q3*

Hitoshi: Fantastic!

Maggie: Yes, if you speak a bit of the language, it's much easier to make friends.

4

Sandra: I'm not sure whether I'll study abroad. I've been thinking of going to an Italian university and studying international business for a year. The trouble is partly that if I went, it might make it more difficult for me to get a good degree when I come home. On the other hand, I think the opportunity to live abroad for a year would make it a once-in-a-lifetime experience.

Q4	If I lived in Italy, I'd learn about how Italians live and think. The trouble is I'd have to leave the friends I've got and probably live on my own, and I'm not sure if I'm ready for that.

5

Peter: *Q5*	Now, just a few words, especially for new students. First, you're expected to attend all your tutorials once a week and do the assignments which your tutors give you. If for any reason you can't make it to a tutorial, try to let your tutor know. If your tutor has to cancel a tutorial or put it off, he or she'll try to tell you the week beforehand. Also, please remember that this course is largely practical and you have to do one piece of original research during the year. You're allowed to do it in groups, and if you work with other students, you'll probably find it easier. Your tutors will organise you into groups and suggest research unless you prefer working alone.

Vocabulary

Find out, get to know, know, learn, teach and *study*; *attend, join, take part* and *assist*

❶ **2** found out **3** learn **4** learn **5** taught **6** getting to know **7** take part in **8** join **9** attend

❸ **2** got to know **3** study **4** learnt **5** find out **6** know **7** taught **8** assist **9** joined **10** taken part in

Grammar

Zero, first and second conditionals

❶ **1** c **2** b **3** a **4** b **5** a **6** a

❷ **2** f **3** j **4** g **5** a **6** e **7** c **8** d **9** i (or f) **10** b

Use of English Part 3

❶ **2** confidence **3** understanding **4** improvement **5** behaviour **6** advice **7** assistant (assistance) **8** knowledge

❷ **2** entertain **3** feel **4** achieve **5** investigate **6** obey **7** prefer **8** sense

❸ **1** knowledge **2** appreciation **3** interesting **4** difficulty **5** enjoyable **6** communication **7** basic **8** improvement **9** assistance **10** confidence

Reading Part 3

❶ *Suggested problems:* Strange food, finding somewhere to live, making friends, finding one's way around, not understanding the language

❷ *Suggested phrases to underline:*
- **2** made good progress with a foreign language
- **3** entertained by a teacher
- **4** wanted to spend less time studying
- **5** overcame ... initial difficulties
- **6** appreciated meeting people ... different countries
- **7** discouraged ... by problems
- **8** felt homesick
- **9** communicating with other students difficult
- **10** unique experience
- **11** more attractive to future employers
- **12** surprised by the country
- **13** learnt a lot about people
- **14** and **15** practical working experience

❸ *Suggested answers:* **a** 2, 9 **b** 5, 8, (9) **c** 1, 2, 3, 6, 10, 11, 13, (14/15) **d** 4, 5, 7, 8, 9 **e** 3, 6, 8, 9, 12, 13, 14/15

❹ **2** E **3** B **4** D **5** A **6** C **7** E **8** A **9** A **10** D **11** E **12** D **13** B **14** B/C **15** B/C

Speaking Part 1

❷ **1** biology – he likes science, he wants to study medicine, he has an excellent teacher
2 in her job – she wants to work in business and travel

Recording script CD1 Track 13

Teacher:	Nikolai, which is your favourite subject at school?
Nikolai:	I find biology very interesting. That's because I enjoy all science subjects a lot and if I can get good enough marks in my final exams, I'll study medicine when I go to university. Also, my biology teacher is an excellent teacher, so she makes the subject more ... more enjoyable.
Teacher:	And you, Magda, how do you think you'll use English in the future?
Magda:	Well, it'll help me to find a job, and if my work involves travelling, I'm sure I'll need to speak English. I'd like to work in business, and I think English is essential for that.
Teacher:	Thank you. Nikolai, can you remember your first day at school?

3 1 F 2 T 3 T

Writing Part 1

2 1 Two months 2 English
3 Pia wants to go to the mountains because she went to Vancouver two years ago
4 She can make friends and speak English

3 *Spelling mistakes*: ~~corses~~ courses
~~begining~~ beginning ~~wich~~ which
~~excelent~~ excellent ~~preffer~~ prefer
~~experence~~ experience
~~accomodation~~ accommodation
~~becaus~~ because ~~oportunity~~ opportunity
~~foward~~ forward

4 2 True 3 True 4 False 5 False

5 1 Can you tell me how much it costs to rent a flat?
2 I would like to know what qualification I would get at the end of the course.
3 Do you know how far the college is from the city centre?
4 I'd like to know if/whether I will have to do a lot of homework.
5 Can you tell me if/whether the college has sports facilities?

6 *Sample answer:*

Dear Caroline,

Thanks for your email suggesting a summer camp in Australia. Of course I'd love to come. Can you tell me what dates the camp is, so that I can put them in my diary? Also, if possible, I'd like to know how much it will cost because I'll probably have to start saving right away.

As a matter of interest, do you know what subjects are taught? I'd be really interested in studying English because I always need to improve it, and perhaps another subject such as drama or performing arts. I think that I'd really get to know people and make friends by doing that.

I like your idea of travelling together afterwards. I'd prefer to go to the Great Barrier Reef because I love the sea and I really enjoy diving.

What a great way to spend the summer! I look forward to seeing you then.

All the best,

6 The planet in danger

Starting off

1 1 exhaust fumes from cars and lorries
2 construction work
3 industrial pollution
4 endangered species / threats to wildlife
5 destruction of rainforests
6 rising sea levels
7 water problems
8 climate change

Reading Part 2

2 The gorillas were eating, playing, feeding their children; they watched the tourists, listened to the guide and disappeared into the forest

3 3 He, his hairy sleepy friends, back home
4 Despite the climb, watchful
5 Caleb had been doing this for ten years, he still loved the job
6 Then, as the vegetation cleared
7 We followed him along a little path
8 No one felt afraid

4 2 C 3 B 4 H 5 E 6 D 7 F 8 A

Vocabulary

Look, see, watch, listen and *hear*

1 2 listened 3 watched 4 see, looking

2 2 watching 3 hear 4 looking at 5 see
6 watching 7 listening to 8 hear

Listening Part 2

1 *Suggested answers:* To make land for farming, to sell the wood, to exploit oil and other resources; to preserve habitats, species and ways of life; forest fires

2 *Suggested answers:* 1 a time / noun phrase
2 verb – learn (?) 3 adjective
4 verb + *-ing* / verb phrase
5 noun – receptionist, guide (?) 6 noun
7 percentage
8 comparative adjective – hotter (?) 9 a place
10 noun / verb + *-ing*

❸ **1** summer vacation **2** educate visitors **3** relevant work **4** maintaining paths **5** guide **6** farming (land) **7** seventy % / 70% / per cent **8** warmer **9** (living) in zoos **10** buying furniture

Recording script CD1 Track 14

Interviewer: So, here I am at the Anona Biological Reserve in Costa Rica and I'm talking to Sylvia Welling, who's a volunteer here. Sylvia, how did you come to work on this project?

Sylvia: Well, it's quite a long story. I'm studying biochemistry at university back in England and I heard about this project from another student on the course. I'm just doing this in my

Q1 summer vacation, so really I've only been here for a few weeks – since the beginning of July in fact. I'll probably be here till the end of September, then I have to go back to university.

Interviewer: So, what's your role here? Are you here to protect the rainforest?

Sylvia: No, not at all. This one's already protected. No trees are being cut down here. It's a really interesting and beautiful place as a matter of fact. It's full of rare animals and plants and it's incredibly peaceful. The main object of the

Q2 project I'm on is to educate visitors and show them how special this place is. At the same time, I'm learning a lot about it too. Hopefully I'm going to work as a researcher when I finish my degree, so it seemed a good idea to come here while I had the chance.

Interviewer: So you're actually here to learn rather than work?

Sylvia: Well, yes, partly, but as I was just saying

Q3 I really came here to get some relevant work experience. I mean I want to be able to show future employers that I've been doing something connected with biochemistry in my free time. And also I hope in my own small way that I'm doing something useful.

Interviewer: So what's your job here?

Sylvia: I do whatever I'm asked to do. We spend

Q4 part of our time maintaining paths through the forest so that visitors can walk around it without getting lost and without doing much damage. It means I have a great time visiting really remote parts of the forest where the only things you hear are things like animals, the wind in the trees, and the rain. And it rains quite a lot here, believe me!

Interviewer: So you know the forest quite well by now, do you?

Sylvia: I'm getting to know it better and better

Q5 because I also spend time acting as a guide for people who come to see the forest. I take them on a walk and point out special trees and animals and explain a bit of how the place works to them. Then hopefully they go home with a feeling of how wonderful and important rainforests are.

Interviewer: And what do you see as the main dangers facing rainforests now and in the future?

Sylvia: The main problem is that in other parts of the world forests like these are being cut down or

Q6 burnt to create more farming land. As a result, plants and wildlife are becoming endangered or dying out. If things continue like this, by

Q7 the year 2050, 70 per cent of the world's rainforests will have disappeared. I think that's pretty worrying.

Interviewer: It is.

Sylvia: And it's going to have really drastic consequences for the rest of the planet. I mean, forests absorb carbon and this prevents global warming. If we carry on cutting down forests, climate change will become even more extreme, making the

Q8 world warmer and leading to rising sea levels, and so on.

Interviewer: But Sylvia, in spite of all these worries, what are the pleasures of coming to a place like this?

Sylvia: For me, one of the greatest pleasures is seeing all the animals that live here, the frogs and birds and monkeys and insects and all the other creatures which are threatened with extinction. You know, the danger is that in forty or fifty years' time these animals will only

Q9 be living in zoos. They just won't exist in the wild and that will be a real shame.

Interviewer: And what can visitors like myself do when we get home?

Sylvia: Well, you could look closely before buying

Q10 furniture – make sure it isn't made of wood taken from the rainforests. And also tell your friends about these wonderful places and how important it is to protect them.

Interviewer: Sylvia Welling. Thank you.

Grammar
Ways of expressing the future

❶ & ❷

name of tense	example(s)	uses
future simple	won't exist	d
future continuous	will only be living	b
future perfect	will have disappeared	a
'going to' future	it's going to have I'm going to work	c e

❸ **2** I'm going to take part in **3** We're going to spend **4** will have risen **5** she's going to study **6** will change **7** will remember us **8** It's going to make

Use of English Part 1

❷ Car fumes, aerosols and aeroplanes (air pollution); Earth getting darker, reduce the growth of some crops, oceans cooler, less rain forms, changing weather patterns

❸ **1** B **2** A **3** D **4** D **5** A **6** C **7** A **8** B **9** D **10** A **11** C **12** B

Vocabulary
Prevent, *avoid* and *protect*; *reach*, *arrive* and *get (to)*

❶ **1** prevent **2** arrived

❷ **2** reach / get to **3** gets/arrives **4** prevents **5** arrived **6** avoid **7** protect

Speaking Part 2

❶ First photo: countryside, natural surroundings, picking up rubbish, litter; second photo: pollution, exhaust fumes, noise, public transport

❷ picking up rubbish, countryside, litter, pollution

Recording script CD1 Track 15

Teacher: In this part of the test, I'm going to give each of you two photographs. I'd like you to talk about your photographs on your own for about a minute, and also to answer a short question about your partner's photographs.

Magda, it's your turn first. Here are your photographs. They show people doing things to protect the environment. I'd like you to compare the photographs, and say how important these activities are for protecting the environment. All right?

Magda: Yes. Well, the first picture shows two young people who are picking up rubbish from the countryside. I think they're probably doing it at the weekend, and they're picking up plastic bags and other litter. In the other picture we can see a man going to work by bicycle, not by car. I think both these ways of protecting the environment are important. In the first picture I suppose they're cleaning up a mess made by other people, but it's also important to avoid causing pollution ourselves, and I think that's what's happening in the second photo.

If we don't protect the environment the world may soon become too hot and unpleasant and many animals and plants will disappear and become extinct.

Teacher: Thank you.

❸ Magda uses these phrases: The first picture shows …, I think they're probably …, In the other picture we can see …, In the first picture, I suppose …, It's important to …, I think that's what's happening in the second photo …

Writing Part 2 An essay

❶ *Suggested phrases to underline:* giving your opinion, Our children will live in a worse environment than we do

❻ **2** this reason **3** The first **4** result **5** The second aspect **6** Consequently **7** In my opinion **8** Unless we do so

❼

expressing consequences	introducing your opinion	organising ideas logically
Consequently As a result Because of this For this reason	In my opinion I believe I feel I think	The first is Finally Firstly In addition Lastly The second (aspect) is

❾ *Sample answer:*

Scientists have given many warnings about the effects of human activity on the environment and I believe that unless we take drastic action, it is very likely that there will be dramatic changes in the environment over the next 50 years.

I think there will be three major changes. Firstly, as a result of air pollution, global temperatures will rise and this will lead to drier, hotter summers and warmer winters. A further consequence may be more frequent natural disasters such as floods and hurricanes.

The second change will be a rise in sea levels. This will mean that people living near the coast will lose their homes and have to move to new areas.

Finally, we are destroying so many natural habitats such as rainforests that many species of animals and plants will become extinct. Consequently, the world will lose a lot of its diversity.

I believe that unless we take urgent action to prevent these things from happening, the future for the environment will be disastrous and future generations will criticise us for the damage we have done.

Vocabulary and grammar review Unit 5

Vocabulary

❶

1 r	e	2 s	e	3 a	r	c	h	
		u		s				
		b		s				
		j		i				
		e		g				
		c		n		4 m		
		t		m		a		5 t
			6 d	e	g	r	e	e
				n		k		r
		7 n	o	t	e	s		m

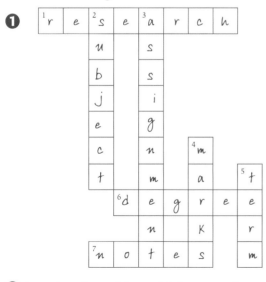

❷ **2** study **3** teaching **4** join, get to know **5** attend **6** take part in

Word formation

❸

verb	noun
obey	obedience
practise	practice
prefer	preference
achieve	achievement
understand	understanding
know	knowledge
qualify	qualification

Grammar

❹ **2** study abroad, you will become / you'll become **3** she would not attend / wouldn't attend **4** look after my book **5** knew the answer, I would / I'd **6** he was not so tired / wasn't so tired

Vocabulary and grammar review Unit 6

Vocabulary

❶ **2** destruction **3** pollution **4** habitats **5** extinct **6** warming **7** change **8** acid **9** rising

❷ **1** B **2** D **3** A **4** B **5** C

Grammar

❸ **2** will probably be **3** will have changed **4** will be living **5** will play **6** will be doing **7** is going to be **8** will be **9** won't have cooked **10** will help

7 My first job

Starting off

❶ **1** bank cashier **2** call centre worker **3** waiter/ waitress **4** hospital porter **5** hotel receptionist **6** teacher

Listening Part 3

1 Speaker 1: **D** hospital porter, positive
Speaker 2: **E** hotel receptionist, positive
Speaker 3: **A** bank cashier, negative
Speaker 4: **B** call centre worker, positive
Speaker 5: **F** teacher, positive

Recording script CD1 Track 16

Speaker 1: My first job was when I was a student. I worked part-time in a hospital and had to fetch patients and wheel them to different hospital departments for treatment. I'm not sure if you can still get jobs like that if you're a student. Anyway, it was hard physical work, you know, lifting people and helping them into wheelchairs and pushing them, but I think I'd expected that. The thing I found most fascinating was chatting to the patients I had to collect. I got to know some of them quite well and you know, we'd talk about all sorts of things. They'd done all kinds of different and unusual things in their lives, so they often had plenty of interesting stories to tell. I think I learnt a lot from them in fact.

Speaker 2: I got my first job as an assistant receptionist in a hotel when I was just eighteen. I didn't have much self-confidence to start with because I was quite shy as a teenager, but I was really happy with the job because I thought it was a great opportunity to get some work experience. Anyway they gave me lots of responsibility quite early on so I learned to do all sorts of things which you need for almost any job, really practical things like dealing with people, answering the phone correctly, maintaining the hotel database. And on some occasions I was left on my own as the only person in charge of the whole of this enormous hotel. Doing that successfully certainly built up my self-confidence, I can tell you.

Speaker 3: Well, this wasn't my first job, but it was what I'd call my first serious job, I mean not just a job for a month or two as a student. I worked behind the counter in a bank and I got the job just after leaving university. I applied for it because I thought at the time that it would be a good way to get to work in finance. Unfortunately, I soon found that that wasn't necessarily true and that's why I eventually left. Before starting, I'd expected the work to be quite routine until I was given more responsibility, but in fact it was very challenging right from the beginning and needed a lot of concentration, especially while I was learning the job.

Speaker 4: It wasn't a very well-paid job, but then first jobs often aren't. I worked in a call centre for a large computer company. I had to answer the phone when customers rang in with their queries or complaints or whatever. Sometimes all they wanted was some information, but they often rang in with a real problem which I had to help them sort out. You see, I already had computer skills because I'd studied computer technology at college. I felt at the time that I was doing something really useful because there were all these people phoning in with urgent problems to do with their computers. Usually just a few simple instructions over the phone were enough, and customers were very grateful, so it could be quite satisfying in fact.

Speaker 5: My first job? Can you believe it? I did it for nearly fifteen years. I started when I was fresh out of university and I worked at the same school until just about a year ago.

I have to say though that I found teaching fun and challenging. It's a job where you're doing something serious but at the same time having lots of laughs. Students prefer it if you have a sense of humour and say something funny from time to time, you know, make a joke. On the other hand, I always had a great deal of homework to correct in the evenings and I hated that. I found it was just a chore, so the job did have a few drawbacks. Now I'm headteacher of another school just down the road, but that's another story …

2 *Suggested phrases to underline:* **B** surprisingly hard work **C** people I met interesting **D** opportunity to achieve my ambitions **E** learning useful skills **F** enjoyed some parts of the job more than others

3 **1** C **2** E **3** B **4** A **5** F

Vocabulary

Work or *job*; *possibility*, *occasion* or *opportunity*; *fun* or *funny*

1 **2** job **3** job, jobs **4** opportunity **5** occasions **6** fun **7** funny

❷ **2** fun **3** possibility **4** occasions **5** opportunity **6** job **7** work **8** jobs

Grammar

Countable and uncountable nouns

❶ **2** Countable **3** Uncountable **4** Uncountable **5** countable **6** countable **7** uncountable

❷

countable	uncountable
accident	accommodation
bed	advice
bus	damage
dish	equipment
hotel	food
instrument	furniture
meal	homework
service	information
suggestion	knowledge
suitcase	luggage
task	news
tool	software
	transport

❸ **2** ~~an advice~~ *some / a piece of / a bit of advice*
3 ~~a work~~ *work / a job* **4** correct
5 ~~accommodations~~ *accommodation* **6** correct
7 ~~furnitures~~ *furniture*
8 ~~many damages~~ *much damage*

❹ **2** number **3** piece/bit **4** piece/bit **5** deal

Reading Part 1

❷ **1** She was a waitress. **2** She cooked cakes and puddings.

❸ *Suggested phrases to underline:*

1. None of us had ever worked in a hotel before
2. I worked as a waitress at breakfast and dinner. This gave me the middle of the day free for studying
3. impressive chef's hat and a terrifying ability to lose his temper and get violent
4. my cold expression used to change into a charming smile
5. The guests, staring with pleasure at the view, I enjoyed getting on well with the people at each table. In the evenings it was funny how differently people behaved; they talked with louder, less friendly voices, and did not always return my smile
6. However, that all changed when Dad created a special role for me which improved my status considerably. I started by making simple cakes for guests' picnics and soon progressed to more elaborate cakes for afternoon teas. This led to a nightly event known as Lucy's Sweet Trolley.
7. Most of them were of my own invention, I had cooked them all myself, and some were undeniably strange

❹ **1** C **2** A **3** B **4** D **5** B **6** C **7** D **8** B

Grammar

Articles

❶ **2** c **3** f **4** d **5** e **6** a

❷ **2** an **3** the **4** – **5** a **6** a **7** – **8** the **9** the **10** – **11** the **12** a

❸ **2** ~~my age~~ the age **3** town ~~the~~ next year
4 useful information on *the* internet
5 parking in *the* city centre
6 are *the* most effective **7** ~~The money~~ Money
8 listening to ~~the~~ music; on *the* radio
9 ~~the~~ foreign cities; ~~the~~ shopping
10 having *a* wonderful time
11 ~~a~~ plenty of spare time at ~~this~~ *the* moment; have ~~a~~ dinner **12** ~~an~~ accommodation

Speaking Part 3

❶ They do these (✓): **1, 3, 4, 6**
They don't do these (✗): **2, 5, 7**

Recording script CD1 Track 17

Teacher: Now, I'd like you to talk about something together for about three minutes.

I'd like you to imagine that your college has invited some people with glamorous and exciting jobs to come and talk to students. They are jobs which many people dream of having.

First, talk to each other about why people dream of doing these jobs. Then decide which two jobs would be the most interesting to hear about. All right?

Irene: So, why do you think people dream of being footballers, or sports stars?

Miguel: Perhaps people think that it's a job where they'll earn lots of money and become famous.

Irene: Yes, and it's easier than other jobs because you don't have to study.

Miguel: No, but you do have to train a lot and be talented.

Irene: That's true. Now, what about this next one? What do you think?

Miguel: The TV reporter? That must be quite exciting, don't you think?

Irene: Yes, because you're reporting the news and you're on television. I think that's quite attractive. What about you? Do you agree?

Miguel: Sure. And this job. Being an actor …

Irene: It's quite creative, don't you think?

Miguel: Yes, it is. I wouldn't mind being an actor! I mean, you're in the theatre, so it's glamorous, and people come to watch you, so you can become quite famous.

Irene: Yes. Lots of people dream of becoming famous, don't they?

Miguel: Possibly. I'm not sure. I think that actually people want to do something which they enjoy more than do something which makes them famous.

Irene: I think you're right. And this job teaching skiing is a good example. I think it's glamorous because you are being paid to do something which most people can only do on holiday.

Miguel: And you can ski all winter.

Irene: And have a good social life as well.

Miguel: That's true. What about this one, being a photographer?

Irene: Well, I suppose it's fun because you're doing something creative and that's always better than doing something which is just routine.

Miguel: Maybe, but you probably travel a lot too.

Irene: Yes, and it would be lovely to have a job where you can travel.

Miguel: Like the pilot in this picture.

Irene: Yes. And flying big planes around the world is probably quite exciting as well. You have lots of responsibility.

Miguel: You're right. Shall we move on to the second question?

Irene: OK.

Miguel: I think all these jobs would be interesting to hear about.

Irene: Really? I'm not sure … I wouldn't be interested in listening to a talk by a ski instructor.

Miguel: Yes, but all jobs have something of interest.

Irene: That's true, but I think if I had to choose, I'd be more interested in listening to a television reporter talking about her job.

Miguel: Why's that?

Irene: Well, TV reporters talk to people who are in the news and they witness important events.

Miguel: Maybe, but I think footballers and actors would also be very interesting to listen to because they do things that other people find entertaining. And they earn a lot of money! What do you think?

Irene: Well, perhaps we should have a footballer or an actor and a TV reporter and that way we'll have a balance.

Miguel: I think that's a good idea. Perhaps an actor, then, don't you think? That would be more interesting for everyone.

Irene: I think you're right, because football usually interests boys more than girls, doesn't it?

Miguel: Yes. So the TV reporter and the actor, then?

Irene: Fine.

Teacher: Thank you.

2

suggesting ideas	asking your partner's opinion	agreeing	disagreeing
Perhaps people think that if they do this job, they'll … People may/ might think a job like this is …	What about you? Do you agree? What do you think? … don't you think? Why's that?	Yes, and … I think you're right. Sure. That's true.	I'm not sure. I think … No, but … Maybe … Possibly …

Use of English Part 2

❷ It gives young people experience they need; the jobs are all rewarding and interesting; volunteers learn organisation and communication skills; they gain experience working in a team environment; they gain self-confidence and this helps when applying for jobs; they become responsible for themselves; it gets young people ready for life

❸ & ❹

1 the **2** spend **3** there **4** do **5** well **6** a
7 deal **8** for **9** or **10** what **11** other **12** such

Writing Part 1

❹ *Suggested phrases to underline:* I have seen your advertisement, I am writing to apply for, I am interested in doing this job because, This will give me the opportunity to, Could you please tell me, I look forward to hearing from you, Yours sincerely

❺ *Sample answer:*

Dear Mr Reid,

I am writing to apply for a job as a sports supervisor at the International Camp, which I have seen advertised on the internet.

I am a 17-year-old student from Estonia, where I am in my final year at secondary school. I am a keen sportsman. I am a member of my school's basketball team and local junior tennis champion. I enjoy organising sports for children and I hope to work as a physical education teacher in the future.

I am interested in doing this job because I would like to gain some work experience as a sports supervisor. I would also like to have the opportunity to travel around Scotland afterwards.

Could you please tell me how much time off I would have if I was given the job?

I look forward to hearing from you.

Yours sincerely,

8 High adventure

Starting off

❶ **2** cross-country running **3** canoeing/kayaking **4** karate **5** athletics **6** windsurfing **7** paragliding

❷ mountain biking, canoeing/kayaking, paragliding, windsurfing

❸ *Some possible answers:* skiing, hiking, abseiling, mountaineering, snowboarding, bungee jumping, hot-air ballooning, heli-skiing + those in the book

Reading Part 2

❶ *Suggested answers:* mountain biking, cross-country running, canoeing/kayaking

❷ **1** C **2** A **3** B **4** C

Recording script CD1 Track 18

Interviewer: So, Gary, just for our listeners who may not be familiar with adventure racing, what is it?

Gary: Adventure racing is a sport which has been around since the early 1990s and it's one of the toughest races you can imagine. Unlike marathons, where the winner is the individual runner who crosses the finishing line first, *Q1* in adventure races the winners are the first team to get over the finishing line all together at the same time. Teams are made up of four to six people, depending on the race, and they must all finish.

Interviewer: In what other ways is adventure racing different?

Gary: Well, these races combine a mixture of different activities or sports – running, kayaking or canoeing, climbing and cycling to name just some of them. They take place over courses which need all these skills. Occasionally, they're organised in cities – there's a famous one which takes place in *Q2* Chicago – but the majority are held in the mountains or desert areas, places where there aren't too many roads or inhabitants, so competitors are really isolated and on their own.

Interviewer: And how long do they last?

Gary: A long time – from 24 hours up to ten days, or even more. Competitors have to carry everything they need with them, all their food and drink, and if they run out they'll go hungry

Q3 or thirsty. And on long races often the greatest difficulty is staying awake, because there are no fixed times for breaks and teams tend to race for as many hours as possible.

Interviewer: I hear that professional athletes are getting interested in the sport too.

Gary: That's right. Many top sports people find adventure racing makes an interesting change because, rather than competing as individuals

Q4 as they've done all their lives, they have to work in a team and help each other and they often find this very exciting and motivating.

Interviewer: Gary Peters, thank you.

Gary: Thank you.

4 No, they had to abandon the race before the finish.

5 **2** H **3** D **4** E **5** G **6** C **7** A **8** B

Grammar

Infinitive and verb + *-ing*

1 **2** f **3** g **4** b and i **5** b and i **6** i **7** d **8** a **9** c **10** h **11** a

2 **2** to go **3** to hold **4** Training **5** to get **6** injuring **7** running **8** pushing

3 **2** to learn **3** doing **4** taking part in

4 **2** ~~to learn~~ learning **3** ~~to wear~~ wearing **4** correct **5** ~~introduce~~ to introduce **6** ~~meeting~~ to meet **7** correct **8** ~~to get~~ getting

Listening Part 4

2 *Suggested phrases to underline:* **2** choose, in France **3** advantage of learning, sand dune **4** spend the first morning **5** how, receive instructions **6** when you land, it feels like **7** best reason

3 **1** A **2** C **3** B **4** A **5** B **6** A **7** C

Recording script CD1 Track 19

Interviewer: So, Andrew, what made you want to go on a paragliding course? It sounds like an extremely risky thing to want to do, even for a journalist like yourself.

Andrew: Well, I thought it was risky too. I mean, as a sports journalist, I spend my time watching people doing different sports and I've done a fair number of them myself. It's one of the qualifications for the job I suppose. Anyway, a few years ago I was actually on holiday in Switzerland and I was playing golf with a

Q1 couple of friends when I looked up and saw these people floating in the air above me. I thought to myself, I'd like to have a go at that. It looks fun

Interviewer: So you went on a course in France, I believe.

Andrew: That's right. I'd actually tried to go on a paragliding course in England a few years ago. I'd even paid the course fee – about £350 – but every time I went down to do the course it was either too windy or it was raining. You can't fly when your paraglider is wet, you see. So I found that I could go to this rather wonderful place, called the Dune du Pyla on the coast in south-west France. It's actually the highest sand dune in Europe – and they run courses there. I had to pay a bit more than it would have cost in Britain, especially with the extra cost of getting there, but it was

Q2 a really nice place and since sunshine was almost guaranteed I went for it.

Interviewer: Great! And can you tell me, are there any advantages to jumping off a sand dune? I imagine it's rather less dangerous than jumping off a mountain, isn't it?

Andrew: Well, it isn't so high – only about 150 metres, in fact – but of course it's quite dangerous to fall even from 20 metres, so whether you're paragliding from a mountain or from a sand dune doesn't necessarily make much difference. And of course you're strongly advised not to land in the sea. They say that if you do, it'll be almost impossible to rescue you. On the other hand, especially for a beginner,

Q3 landing on a beach or the side of a sand dune is relatively soft and comfortable.

Interviewer: And what's the main difficulty for a beginner? I imagine it's taking off and landing.

Andrew: The major problem for a complete beginner like myself is actually learning to hold your

Q4 paraglider up into the air correctly – you know, so that both sides open correctly without even beginning to fly. They only allow you to run off the edge and fly when you've mastered that technique. In fact I spent my first morning just practising how to do it and it's quite tricky, I can tell you. It makes you feel a bit silly when you see other people happily flying around below you – or above you!

Interviewer: And when you actually start flying, how does your instructor give you instructions? Does he fly along beside you?

Andrew: No, it sounds a nice idea, and I'd have loved to have someone up there beside me to make me feel safer. My instructor, Chantalle, stayed on the ground in fact and she talked to me

Q5 through a microphone. I had a radio and an earphone, so I could listen to her instructions and do what she said. All very quiet and calm. No shouting at all.

Interviewer: And is landing a problem?

Andrew: Surprisingly not. I was expecting something rather violent, you know like falling off a horse, but it was an amazingly soft landing – the sand

Q6 cushions you a bit – and it didn't really feel any more violent than hopping off a two-foot-high wall. I'd say it's much safer than horse riding altogether.

Interviewer: But is it safe, in fact?

Andrew: They say it is. I mean there are a couple of serious accidents every year. But then that's probably true of most sports, including apparently quiet and earthbound sports like

Q7 golf. What I really like about it though is the silence. I mean even animals don't notice you till your shadow passes over them. It's wonderful. You get a tremendous sense of freedom, beautiful views, sensations you've never had before.

Interviewer: Andrew, thank you.

Andrew: Thank you.

4 *Suggested answers:* According to insurance companies the most dangerous sport on the list is motorcycle racing. Less dangerous are paragliding and climbing. The least dangerous are snowboarding and scuba diving, though they are still dangerous.

Use of English Part 4

1 **1** B **2** A

2 **1** (in order / so as) to get ready **2** are not allowed to touch

3 & **4**

1 taking part in **2** more expensive to hire
3 to give her a ring/call **4** is not so/as safe
5 to lose his temper

Speaking Part 4

1 *Suggested answers:* **Antonia**: No, because not keen on sports – should be allowed – adults to supervise; normal sports equally beneficial
Magda: Young people yes, old people more – to keep fitter – but often too busy

2

introducing an opinion	adding an explanation	introducing an example
I believe … I'm not sure. I think … No, I don't think so because …	I mean … You see …	for instance … such as …

Recording script CD1 Track 20

Teacher: Antonia, do you think young people should be encouraged to do adventure sports?

Antonia: Encouraged? No, I don't think so because I'm not very keen on sports, especially ones which might be dangerous. I think young people should be allowed to do them if they really want to, of course, but with experts to supervise them to make sure they're safe. Adventure sports are OK for people who enjoy excitement and danger, but people like me can benefit just as much from taking exercise in the normal way, for instance playing tennis or running.

Teacher: Thank you. Magda, do you think that people generally do enough sport nowadays?

Magda: I'm not sure. I think young people in my country do quite a lot of sport, but perhaps older people should do more sport to keep fitter. I mean, older people are often too busy to do much sport because they're busy with other things such as their jobs and looking after their families and so on, but I believe doing sport keeps you feeling younger and healthier, so they should be encouraged to do so.

Writing Part 2 A report

1 2 I **3** I **4** F **5** I **6** F

2 2 I **3** F **4** F **5** F **6** F **7** I

3 **2a** F **2b** I **3a** I **3b** F **4a** I **4b** F **5a** F **5b** I **6a** I **6b** F

4 *Suggested phrases to underline:* types of sporting activities, how doing these activities would benefit young people

5 **1** The town council **2** formal – because the report is for the town council **3** and **4** *Students' own answers*

7 **2** a number of **3** young people **4** outline **5** the benefits of **6** activities **7** is situated **8** enjoy **9** Activities on the coast could include **10** organise **11** Similarly **12** a local mountaineering club could be employed **13** benefit **14** encouraging **15** they would become **16** I recommend **17** enjoyable **18** develop

8 **1** yes **2** four – from the headings **3** to introduce the subject **4** five **5** four **6** to summarise and recommend **7** formal

9 *Sample answer:*

Adventure Sports at Caxton Sports Club

Introduction
The purpose of this report is to suggest what adventure sports young people in the area would enjoy doing and to outline the benefits of doing these sports.

Which adventure sports?
I asked my friends and a number of other young people living in this area which sports they would like to try if the sports club gave them the opportunity. The most popular suggestions were skiing in the winter, and windsurfing and climbing in the summer. A number of people suggested doing other sports such as paragliding and sailing, but in general these were not so popular.

Benefits
The main benefits of these sports for young people are that they will have adventures and new experiences, as well as enjoying themselves. At the same time they will make new friends and learn responsibility and independence.

Conclusion
I recommend that the sports club should provide skiing, windsurfing and climbing activities at weekends and during holiday periods, depending on the season. I am certain that providing these sports will attract large numbers of young people to the club.

Vocabulary and grammar review Unit 7

Vocabulary

1 **2** work **3** job **4** occasion **5** fun **6** opportunity **7** funny **8** possibility

Grammar

2 **2** there were no rooms **3** luggage **4** equipment **5** advice **6** transport **7** facts **8** knowledge **9** information **10** food **11** meals she cooks are **12** work **13** jobs **14** furniture **15** It is

3 **2** bit/piece **3** bit/piece **4** bit/piece **5** number

4 **2** a **3** the **4** a **5** – **6** a **7** – **8** a **9** the **10** a **11** a **12** – **13** a **14** an **15** the **16** the **17** the **18** the **19** an **20** –

Vocabulary and grammar review Unit 8

Word formation

1 **2** patience **3** Unfortunately **4** training **5** simply **6** actually **7** tired **8** uncomfortable **9** realistic **10** valuable

Grammar

❷ **2** to get **3** to invite **4** changing **5** to have **6** stealing **7** to finish **8** to become **9** working **10** asking **11** working **12** spending

❸ **2** aren't allowed to go **3** to avoid getting **4** can't bear windsurfing **5** you mind turning **6** invited Ana to play **7** you risk having **8** no point (in) going

9 Star performances

Listening Part 2

❶ *Suggested answers:* **1** a relation, a person, noun **2** a feeling, adjective **3** piece of clothing or means of transport, noun **4** noun **5** verb phrase – studying? **6** a place, noun **7** personal noun describing an occupation **8** number/type **9** adjective **10** noun

❷ **1** aunt **2** too nervous **3** hired car **4** tie **5** watching quiz shows **6** the green room **7** university teacher **8** general knowledge **9** charming/friendly **10** (big) television/TV

Recording script CD1 Track 21

Dan: So Julie, have you ever been on TV?

Julie: No, but my dad was years ago. What happened was that a TV producer walked in to my grandmother's shop and asked her if she'd let my aunt take part in this quiz show called The Big Question. *Q1*

He'd seen her working in the shop and I suppose he thought she'd look good on TV. Anyway, when she was asked, she said no. She said she was afraid she'd get too nervous and be unable to speak when they asked her questions! My elder sister, who was only eleven at the time, told her she should go because it was the chance of a lifetime, but she wouldn't change her mind. *Q2*

Dan: So then what happened?

Julie: Well, at that moment my dad walked in, overheard the argument and said that if she didn't want to go, he'd be happy to go himself. Anyway, the producer agreed and a couple of weeks later my father took a hired car – ours was very old and he didn't trust it – and drove to the TV studios. I don't think he trusted the trains to arrive on time either. *Q3*

Dan: So he risked getting caught in the traffic instead!

Julie: That's right. Anyway, when he got there, he'd got his suit but he realised that he hadn't remembered to bring a tie, so he asked the producer if he could borrow one. *Q4*

Dan: And did he study at all for the show, you know by reading encyclopedias and so on?

Julie: Not at all! I don't think we even had an encyclopedia in the house. He told me later that the only thing he'd done was spend a few evenings watching quiz shows on TV so he'd know what to expect. My dad is not one of those people who's in the habit of studying really. *Q5*

Dan: And who were the other competitors? Were they people like him?

Julie: Well, what he told me was that before the show he waited with the other participants in a place called 'The Green Room', where they chatted to each other and were given something to eat and drink. Anyway, he said he was quite impressed because the other two competitors were both quite smartly dressed and looked very academic. In fact one of them was a university teacher. The other wasn't though; he turned out to be a bus driver. *Q6* *Q7*

Dan: And what sort of questions did they have to answer?

Julie: As far as I remember all the questions they had to answer were on general knowledge. Nothing specialist if you see what I mean, but I still think my dad felt quite lucky to be able to answer his, because he managed to beat both the other contestants. *Q8*

Dan: Fantastic! And what was the presenter like? Was he, you know, aggressive or anything?

Julie: No, he wasn't – at least during the programme he wasn't. My dad said that he was really charming. But, as soon as the show had ended, he stopped being friendly and left without talking to any of the contestants again. Sounds a bit strange, doesn't it? *Q9*

Dan: It does. Anyway, did your father win a lot of money and become a millionaire or something?

Julie: *Q10*	No! He didn't become a millionaire, but he did win a few prizes – there was a big television, I remember, and a big fluffy elephant, which he gave to me. They were pretty impressive prizes for us then, so we were all very happy. I kept the elephant for years, till I was at least 16, but then it went to a jumble sale.
Dan:	And would you like to take part in a quiz show?
Julie:	I'd love to. I'm hooked on them and I'm always phoning in to try and win some of the prize money! No luck so far though.
Dan:	Well, keep trying!

Grammar
Reported speech 1

❶ **1** a **2** b

❷ **2** had missed **3** would book **4** you **5** today **6** before **7** last **8** following **9** tomorrow **10** there

❸ **2** she would get/come back **3** would arrive on/in **4** wasn't allowed to borrow **5** (had) made several mistakes **6** had found the play

Reading Part 3

❷ *Suggested phrases to underline:*

2 learnt a lot from people already working
3 other people's suggestions improves their acting
4 underline the whole question
5 planned to enter a different profession
6 underline the whole question
7 prefers, theatre
8 underline the whole question
9 necessary to travel to find work
10 unnecessary to leave Scotland to find work
11 worried about performing in front of some important people
12 happy to work outside Scotland
13 motivated, well known
14 train, somewhere else
15 underline the whole question

❸ **1** E **2** D **3** E **4** B **5** C **6** A **7** C **8** A **9** C **10** A **11** A **12** D **13** B **14** D **15** B

Vocabulary
Play, performance and *acting*; *audience, public* and *spectators*; *scene* and *stage*

❶ **2** performance **3** acting **4** stage **5** an audience

❷ **2** play **3** acting **4** performance **5** audience **6** scene **7** stage **8** spectators

Use of English Part 1

❷ Becoming wealthy without qualifications, doing whatever you want

❸ **1** A **2** D **3** B **4** B **5** A **6** C **7** A **8** B **9** C **10** C **11** D **12** B

Speaking Part 1

❶ & ❷

2 listening **3** watching **4** watch **5** going **6** seeing **7** watching **8** watching **9** to go **10** watching

❸

likes	dislikes	neither likes nor dislikes
I really enjoy I'd rather I love I prefer	I can't stand I'm not too keen on I'm not too interested in I really hate	I don't mind

Recording script CD1 Track 22

Teacher:	Antonia, do you watch much television?
Antonia:	Yes, quite a lot. I think I watch TV about two hours a day.
Teacher:	What sorts of programmes do you like most?
Antonia: *Q1*	I really enjoy watching quiz programmes, you know, the ones where they ask you like general knowledge questions about history, sports, things like that. I think you learn quite a lot from them.
Teacher:	And are there any TV programmes you avoid watching?
Antonia:	Sorry, could you repeat the question, please?
Teacher:	Yes. Are there any TV programmes you avoid watching?

Antonia: *Q2* Well, I can't stand listening to the news and programmes like that because I find it so depressing, and I'm not too keen on

Q3 + Q4 watching cartoons. I'd rather watch real actors acting, you know, especially when I'm watching films or series.

Teacher: And Peter, what do you like doing when you go out in the evenings?

Peter: *Q5 + Q6* I love going to the theatre and seeing plays. I like seeing alive performances, sorry live performances. I think the theatre is very exciting and I'd like to be an actor.

Teacher: And which do you think is better: watching a film on TV or going to the cinema?

Peter: *Q7* I prefer watching films in the cinema, because I think they're more entertaining when there's an audience, and there's a better atmosphere. If you watch films on TV, you don't pay so much attention and there are advertisements.

Teacher: Thank you. Miguel, do you watch much television?

Miguel: *Q8* Not much. I don't mind watching music programmes, but I'm not too interested in

Q9 television in general. I prefer to go out with my friends in the evening.

Teacher: And are there any TV programmes you avoid watching?

Miguel: Sorry?

Teacher: Are there any TV programmes you avoid watching?

Miguel: *Q10* Yes, I really hate watching series about doctors and hospitals because I think the plots and the characters are very unrealistic. But in fact I don't watch much television at all …

5 1 Sorry, could you repeat the question, please?
2 Yes – he said sorry and corrected himself
3 Sorry?

Writing Part 2 An article

1 *Suggested phrases to underline:* college magazine; Where do you prefer to see films: in the cinema or at home on TV or DVD?; article

3 The writer prefers the cinema.

4 **1** paragraph 3 **2** paragraph 2 **3** paragraph 1

5 **1** Despite **2** Although **3** However

6 **2** Despite **3** However **4** despite **5** However **6** although

8 *Sample answer:*

Dreams of fame?

Many young people want to be famous because they think this is an easy way to be successful. They believe that their lives will have an extra meaning and that they will be making a difference in the world. In addition to this, they will have rich and exciting lifestyles.

However, I think that these ambitions may be a distraction from studying seriously and working hard, especially as only a small number of highly talented people can really become famous in the end and these people have to live with a lot of disadvantages. For example, they are under a lot of pressure because they are always being watched. If they make a mistake, this immediately appears in the media. Despite being famous, many celebrities are not happy.

I would prefer to be successful in my profession and respected by the people I work with, but not so well known. Although this means working hard to build a solid professional career, you can then benefit from a comfortable and interesting lifestyle without the disadvantages of being famous.

10 Secrets of the mind

Starting off

1 **2** a **3** b **4** g **5** d **6** e **7** h **8** f **9** j **10** i

Reading Part 1

1 The writer thinks happiness comes from: earning enough money to live comfortably; having a challenging job and/or pursuing an absorbing hobby; from concentrating hard on something

2 **1** C **2** B **3** D

3 **4** D **5** A **6** A **7** B **8** A

Vocabulary

Stay, spend and *pass*; *make, cause* and *have*

❶ **2** caused **3** spent **4** spent **5** stay

❷ **2** pass **3** stay **4** have **5** spend **6** spent **7** causing **8** makes/made **9** have **10** make/made

Listening Part 1

❷ *Suggested answers:* **1 A** intonation
1 B body language, appearance, gestures
1 C actual words **2 A** character
2 B people we like **2 C** things in common, hobbies

❸ **1 B 2 C** *Words and phrases used*: appearance, intonation, actual words, things in common, character

Recording script CD2 Track 2

Presenter: One. You hear an expert on a television programme giving advice about meeting people for the first time. What has the most impact?

A how you speak
B how you look
C what you say

Interviewer: In the studio tonight we have Dr Richard Bazey, a psychologist. Doctor Bazey, we all know just how important it is to make a good impression on someone we're meeting for the first time. What can we do to make sure the meeting goes really well?

Dr Bazey: Well, this is interesting. People generally think that it's words that count and they may spend quite a lot of time thinking about how they're going to start the conversation. However, that's not the case at all; the fact is that
Q1 before we've even opened our mouths people have already decided what they think of us just from our appearance alone. Then after that they don't listen to what we're saying so much as how we're saying it – you know, our intonation, the tone of our voice. Only seven per cent of first impressions are based on the actual words we hear. So, dressing carefully is probably time well spent!

Presenter: Two. You hear a man and a woman talking about successful marriages. What does the man think is the most important factor in a successful marriage?

A similar personalities
B similar interests
C the same friends

Mandy: So, Rob, congratulations! Still happily married after 25 years! What's the secret?

Rob: No secret, really. A bit of give and take and consideration for each other. I mean even if we don't like all of each other's friends at least we put up with them and don't show it. We don't
Q2 take each other for granted, and we have lots of things in common – I'd say that's vital – things we like doing together. Not that we're too alike character-wise. I mean, I'm rather outgoing and dominating and I tend to go to extremes, while Liz is more sensitive and cautious. But that probably helps because I think we complement each other quite well.

❹ **3** A **4** B **5** C **6** A **7** C **8** B

Recording script CD2 Track 3

Presenter: Three. You hear a radio programme in which a psychologist is talking about intelligence. What does she say is improving?

A our ability to do certain tests
B our intelligence
C our performance in exams

Psychologist: Psychology is quite a young science, which means psychologists aren't too sure how our minds are changing, or whether in fact we're becoming more intelligent. It's quite difficult to show that our intelligence is actually
Q3 increasing even if we tend to get higher marks on intelligence tests than our fathers and grandfathers did. This could be caused by the fact that we eat really well and have lots of educational opportunities. Surprising, perhaps, because school results don't really seem to be improving – in fact there have been quite a few complaints in the newspapers just recently about educational standards …

Presenter: Four. You overhear a student telling a friend about a project on what makes people happy. What does he say makes people happiest?

A becoming rich
B getting married
C having children

Jess: Hi, Mike. How's your project going? Have you learnt anything interesting from it?

Mike: It's going pretty well actually – and I've come across one or two facts which will probably surprise you.

Jess: Really? Such as?

Mike: Well, for example, lottery winners are often no happier a year later than they were before they won …

Jess: So all that great excitement is really temporary then.

Mike: So it seems.

Jess: And what else have you come up with?

Mike: Well, you know how we're always hearing jokes and things with husbands and wives complaining about each other? Well, in fact it

Q4 turns out that married people are generally a lot happier than before they got married.

Jess: Really?

Mike: Yes, and another thing …

Jess: What's that?

Mike: Well, you know how delighted everyone gets when they have kids?

Jess: Yes.

Mike: Well, it just doesn't seem to last. I found that generally people with children are no happier than people who haven't got any kids at all.

Jess: That's sad, isn't it?

Mike: It is.

Presenter: Five. You overhear a man talking about things which frighten people. What frightens him?

A flying
B heights
C lifts

Man: Oh yeah, you know, I'll do anything to avoid them.

Woman: Including walking up seven or eight flights of stairs?

Man: *Q5* Oh, yes. Or more. I mean, however high the building is, I won't go in them. It does mean that I sometimes arrive at places a bit breathless, but then the exercise isn't a bad thing either.

Woman: Do you know how you got this phobia, this thing which frightens you so much?

Man: I think it must be because I got trapped in one when I was a child and there was a power cut. I can't have been alone in it for more than ten minutes, but it seemed like an hour. It may sound silly to you because I know they're really safe. It's quite irrational, but there you are. I suppose I should get treatment for it – hypnosis or something – but I really can't face that either.

Woman: Well, see you up there in about ten minutes then … breathless!

Presenter: Six. You hear a girl talking to a friend about her dreams. What does she dream?

A She's flying.
B She's falling.
C She's running.

Friend: Do you have recurring dreams – you know, one of those dreams which repeats itself from time to time?

Girl: *Q6* Occasionally, yes, I'm with my mum or my brother and I suddenly take off and go floating above them and I always think, 'This is dangerous, you're going to fall, you're going to fall!' But I never do – and the scenery is fantastic – it's very exhilarating.

Friend: And do you think dreams have any meaning?

Girl: Well, I've heard that when you fall in your dreams it's because you may feel you've failed in some way, or you might just be afraid of failure. And the ones where you're running to get away from someone are because something or someone could be threatening you in your real life.

Friend: And what about flying dreams?

Girl: I don't know. Do you have any ideas about that?

Friend: You must have a secret ambition to become a pilot!

Presenter: Seven. You overhear two students talking about a friend. Why do they think she is stressed?

A She hasn't been sleeping well.
B She's been working too hard.
C She's been having problems with a relationship.

Rob:	Cathy's been behaving a bit strangely lately, hasn't she? I mean she's been very quiet and not talking much.
Ellie:	Yes, she looks pretty stressed out and I guess it's been giving her bad nights.
Rob:	She certainly looks as if she needs a bit more sleep. What's the problem, do you know? Is it to do with her exams or something?
Ellie:	Well, she had a maths exam last week, so she must have studied hard for it. But she's always been pretty hard-working, so she can't have got stressed by it. Anyway, she finds maths easy.
Rob: *Q7*	Lucky her! I suppose she may have had a row with her boyfriend – he can be a bit difficult sometimes, don't you think?
Ellie:	Yeah, it must be something like that. Now you come to mention it, I haven't seen him around recently. Perhaps we'd better ask her about him.
Rob:	And try and cheer her up.
Presenter:	Eight. You hear a man and a woman talking about the man's free-time activities. What do they show about his personality? A He's friendly and sociable. B He's shy and prefers being alone. C He's creative and adventurous.
Man:	I was reading an article in a newspaper the other day about how important it is to do sports and hobbies.
Woman:	Why's that?
Man:	Because they say so much about you; more, according to the writer, than what you've studied at university or what you've done in your job.
Woman:	Really?
Man: *Q8*	Yes. For example, if you play a team sport, it shows that you're probably quite an outgoing sort of person, someone who likes to be with other people. On the other hand if, like me, you do something solitary, for instance reading or painting, it probably shows the opposite, you know, that you're not too comfortable with other people.
Woman:	Or you're happy with your own company.
Man:	That's right. Then again, people who travel a lot are likely to enjoy taking risks and be quite inventive if you see what I mean.
Woman:	But you're the stay-at-home type.
Man:	Yes. That's me!

Grammar

Modals to express certainty and possibility

1 **1** **2** can't **3**, **4** and **5** may, might, could
2 The underlined verbs refer to the present.

2 *Possible answers:* **2** She can't be going shopping **3** She might be French **4** She could be famous. **5** She must be at the opening of a new film. **6** She may be about 30.

3 **2** ~~mustn't be tired~~ can't be tired
3 ~~can have~~ may/might/could have
4 correct **5** ~~can't~~ must

4 **1** must have **2** can't have **3** may have

5 **2** must be **3** must have had / must have been having **4** may/might/could have had to, may/might/could have stopped **5** can't be **6** may/might/could rain **7** may/might/could have left **8** may/might/could go / be going

Use of English Part 4

2 had spoken to Maria the
3 reminded him to lock
4 did not feel well / was not feeling well
5 despite the loud music **6** can't have been
7 may have found **8** did you spend writing

Speaking Part 3

2 *Suggested answers:* **painter**: creative, hard-working, solitary, thoughtful **climber**: adventurous, good at working with other people, well-organised **referee**: responsible, good at working with other people, interested in other people, well-organised **choir-singer**: creative, sociable, good at working with other people, friendly **reader**: solitary, thoughtful **visitor to old people's home**: caring, friendly, responsible, interested in other people, sociable, unselfish, thoughtful **person chatting in café**: friendly, interested in other people, sociable, easy-going

4 **2** yes **3** no **4** yes **5** yes

Recording script CD2 Track 4

Teacher: I want you to imagine that a social club for young people in your town is looking for someone to organise activities in the evenings and at weekends.

The pictures show some of the people who have applied for the job doing their favourite free-time activity. First, talk together about what sort of personality you think each of these people has. Then decide which two might be best for the job.

All right?

Irene: Well, I think the woman in this picture must be quite creative because she's painting a picture …

Miguel: Yes, but it's quite a solitary activity, so she can't be very sociable, although she may be more sociable when she's doing other things and probably quite hard-working. What about the person in this picture?

Recording script CD2 Track 5

Teacher: I want you to imagine that a social club for young people in your town is looking for someone to organise activities in the evenings and at weekends.
The pictures show some of the people who have applied for the job doing their favourite free-time activity. First, talk together about what sort of personality you think each of these people has. Then decide which two might be best for the job.

All right?

Writing Part 2 A story

❸ *Spelling errors:* ~~marvelous~~ marvellous, ~~experence~~ experience, ~~The~~ They, ~~confortable~~ comfortable, ~~fell~~ felt, airplane (American spelling) aeroplane (British spelling), ~~trough~~ through, ~~waitting~~ waiting, ~~exiting~~ exciting, ~~especial~~ special

❼ *Sample answer:*

I will always remember my sixteenth birthday as something special and I still feel excited when I think how I met Leila again after so many years.

My parents had arranged for us all to go to a restaurant for dinner to celebrate. At the next table there were two grown-ups and a beautiful girl with dark hair and wide brown eyes. My mother looked at them and immediately recognised them as friends of hers from years ago. Then I recognised Leila. She had been my best friend at primary school but when she was ten she and her family had moved to another town. Now they were back!

My parents quickly suggested that we should all sit together at the same table and have dinner together. Leila and I sat next to each other and talked and talked. It was as if we had never been separated. She told me that they had come back to my town to live.

It was a wonderful, surprising reunion and that one meeting made it a day I'll never forget.

Vocabulary and grammar review Unit 9

Vocabulary

❶ **1** C **2** B **3** A **4** C **5** A **6** D

❷ **2** despite / in spite of **3** While/Whereas **4** Despite / In spite of **5** However **6** while/whereas **7** although / even though **8** while/whereas

Grammar

❸ **2** the tickets were expensive **3** despite not feeling **4** even though her salary is **5** she had spent all/the afternoon **6** would call at/after the

Vocabulary and grammar review Unit 10

Vocabulary

❶ **2** well-organised **3** adventurous **4** thoughtful **5** responsible **6** creative **7** easy-going **8** sociable

❷ **2** have **3** causes **4** pass **5** had **6** made **7** spent **8** caused

Grammar

❸ **2** can't have turned **3** may not have heard **4** could have left **5** might answer **6** might have forgotten **7** can't have forgotten **8** might see

11 Spend, spend, spend!

Starting off

❶ **2** fashion boutique **3** delicatessen **4** supermarket **5** market stall **6** bookshop

Listening Part 4

❶ *Some suggested answers:* Advantages: many shops in one place, easy parking, places to relax, protected from the heat, cold rain, etc., safe Disadvantages: crowded, noisy, may be expensive, may need a car to reach them

❷ Advantages Will Payne mentions: access (underground station and motorway), good shops, good quality, caters for every taste including people who don't want to shop, family fun, safe and crime free, luxurious surroundings, reduce family conflicts

❸ & ❹

1 B **2** C **3** B **4** A **5** A **6** B **7** C

Recording script CD2 Track 6

Interviewer: Where would you expect to find a shopping centre? We used to think the most convenient place was in the city centre. Then they started building them among green fields where everyone could go by car and park easily. But a

Q1 new one, Redsands Park, has taken over some abandoned industrial land on the edge of the city and is pulling in eager shoppers from all over town. Will Payne, you're the chief architect of Redsands Park, why here?

Will Payne: Principally for the access. We could have put the shopping centre out in the country and we did give it serious consideration, but the area

Q2 we've chosen has got its own underground station and it's also close to the motorway, so it's not hard to get here either by car or public transport. What surprised us though were the protests from local people. We'd expected to be able to get permission easily because we'd be bringing jobs and business to the area. In fact, people worried that there'd be more traffic noise, fumes, more crime and that sort of thing, so getting permission took quite a long time. We were able to get it in the end though, as you can see.

Interviewer: Sure. And judging by the milling crowds of people, I can see the place is a great success. What's drawing them all in, do you think?

Will Payne: Well, surveys of our customers show that people aren't just coming to shop, they're coming to spend the day. Lots of the best stores have branches here, so it's not particularly cheap, but people know they can

Q3 get quality and there's something here for everyone. It caters for every taste including people who'd rather not shop at all but would prefer to see a film or go to the gym instead. Families can have fun in the same place without having to hang around with each other.

Interviewer: The interior really is astonishing. From where I'm standing I can see trees, plants and fountains in the malls. There are cafés, relaxing music and even a free fashion show in one of the halls. Where did the inspiration for all this come from, Will?

Will Payne: A visit to the United States. I went there a number of years ago and visited a couple of malls in San Francisco and Seattle. I was really taken by their appearance. Of course these places offer safe, crime-free shopping, but the

Q4 truth is they're a bit like palaces. People can spend the day there surrounded by expensive things without having to pay a penny. People treat you well and you only have to pay for what you buy.

Interviewer: So, Will, can you explain to me, why is the combination of shopping and other activities so successful?

Will Payne: Well, when we started planning Redsands, we discovered that around half of normal family shopping expeditions end with a family argument, and we wanted to avoid that. We want people to have a seriously good time.

Interviewer: Why is it that families argue so much when they're shopping?

Will Payne: Because they're spending the day together

Q5 and probably not all of them enjoy shopping, or at least they don't enjoy shopping for the same things. When they're at home they can each go off on their own and do what they really enjoy doing separately.

Interviewer: And how does Redsands cater for this?

Will Payne: By organising shops, cafés and other establishments into groups. This means that families can still be fairly close to each other even though they're doing different things. So
Q6 mum can wander into the clothes shop if that's what she wants to do, while dad can pop into the computer shop next door and the kids can go to a game shop or a music shop. They're all nearby and they can find each other easily. We've found this cuts down on a lot of family rows and makes Redsands a great day out for everyone.

Interviewer: And what of the future, Will?

Will Payne: Well, we're now looking at ways of making shopping less tiring. You know, a day at the shops wears people out and we considered a number of ideas. Carrying shopping around is very tiring and we looked at ways to avoid that. We thought of hiring out small electrically-driven cars to shoppers, but we came up against problems of space – there just isn't enough room. We also thought about those moving walkways like the ones you see at airports where people have to walk long distances. We decided against them however, because they'd involve a major redesign of the whole centre. What we've actually come up with is a new technology where you buy what you want and then just leave it in the shop. That way you don't need to carry your heavy shopping around with you all day. When
Q7 you want to go home, our computer system automatically sends everything you've bought to your exit point, and you pick it up there.

Interviewer: Remarkable. Will Payne, thank you.

Will Payne: My pleasure.

Vocabulary
Phrasal verbs

❶ **2** a **3** g **4** h **5** d **6** c **7** f **8** e **9** i **10** b

❷ **2** cut down on **3** pop into **4** caters for **5** hanging around **6** wore us out **7** pulling in **8** taken over **9** come up against **10** pick up

Grammar
Modals expressing ability

❶ **2** c **3** a **4** b

❷ **2** couldn't sleep **3** could **4** Can you **5** could have been **6** were able to do

❸ **2** ~~could~~ was able to / ~~that I could~~ to be able to **3** ~~can~~ could **4** ~~could~~ can **5** ~~can~~ could **6** ~~could~~ were able to **7** correct **8** ~~could~~ can

Use of English Part 2

❷ Women: take time to search for the right item at the right price, shopping is a leisure activity, they enjoy looking at things Men: know what they want and go directly to buy it, they don't compare prices and they spend 10% more than women Reasons: our origins as hunters and gatherers

❸ **1** when **2** like **3** until **4** as **5** hand **6** what **7** it **8** result/consequence **9** on **10** according **11** not **12** that/which

Grammar
As and *like*

❶ **1** a **2** b

❷ **2** as **3** as **4** like **5** as **6** as, as **7** as **8** like **9** as, as **10** as

Reading Part 1

❶ **2** f **3** a **4** e **5** d **6** c

❸ He asks for help because his daughter has used his credit card without permission, she's asking for more and more money, she gets angry when she doesn't get it, he feels she has the wrong attitude to money. He can deal with the problem by giving her an allowance and making her responsible for how she spends it, by making her work for extra money.

❹ **1** B **2** B **3** A **4** C **5** C **6** D **7** A **8** D

Speaking Part 2

1 **2** a **3** b **4** e **5** d **6** c

Recording script CD2 Track 7

Teacher: In this part of the test, I'm going to give each of you two photographs.
I'd like you to talk about your photographs on your own for about a minute, and also to answer a short question about your partner's photographs.

Magda, it's your turn first. Here are your photographs. They show people shopping. I'd like you to compare the photographs, and say what you think the people are feeling.

Magda: Well, both photos show people shopping. In the first photo there are two girls, they're teenagers and they look as if they're shopping for music; I mean, they're buying CDs. They seem to be having a good time and they both look quite happy. In the other photo there's a couple, a man and a woman, who are looking, I mean, they're doing the shopping in a supermarket. In contrast with the young people, they don't appear to be so happy. The man looks rather tired and he's concentrating quite hard, looking for something. On the other hand the two girls seem quite relaxed and they look as if they're having fun.

Teacher: Thank you.

Magda: I imagine that the man and the woman are doing the shopping as a weekly chore, but it's not for pleasure, not for fun.

Teacher: Thank you. Peter, what sort of shopping do you like doing?

Peter: Oh, I quite enjoy shopping for clothes. I'm not too keen on going to supermarkets though and doing the routine shopping.

Teacher: Thank you.

2 in contrast, on the other hand

3 *Suggested answers:*
He looks quite tired.
He seems to be searching for something.
He doesn't appear to be enjoying himself.

Writing Part 2 A report

1 *Suggested phrases to underline:* improving the classrooms, students' social activities, director of your college, report describing the benefits of both ideas, which one you think should be chosen and why

2 **1** the director of your college **2** formal
3 benefits of both ideas, which should be chosen and why

3 **2** spent **3** make **4** contains **5** find **6** benefit **7** improve **8** participate **9** reduce **10** recommend

4 **1** The writer recommends new furniture and an air-conditioning system
2 He/She can look at the section headings and find what he/she needs
3 Yes
4 The *Introduction* states the purpose of the report, *The classrooms* talks about the need for improvements, *Social activities* about the effect of the money on these, *Recommendation* makes a recommendation for spending the money and gives a reason
5 The present tense to talk about the present situation and the conditional to talk about the effects if the money were spent in the ways suggested
6 No – it uses a formal style, as appropriate in a report

5 **2** spending **3** buy **4** to equip

8 *Suggested phrases to underline:* large amount of money available to spend on improving the neighbourhood where you live, town council, making recommendations

Sample answer:

Improvements to the Palmar District

Introduction
The aim of this report is to suggest how the town council can spend the money which it has available for improving this district.

The streets
The Palmar District is an old part of the city with narrow streets and pavements. Because the pavements are so narrow, it is difficult for pedestrians to walk together or pass each other without stepping into the road, which can be dangerous. Also, many of the streets are badly lit at night, which means that it can be quite frightening to walk there.

The traffic
Unfortunately, the district has a lot of traffic, which makes it very noisy and polluted. Also there is very little space available for residents to park their cars.

Recommendations
It would be a good idea to make some of the main streets for pedestrians only, with wider pavements. I also suggest that the council should provide good street lights and build a car park for residents. Finally, I recommend that the council should build a ring road so that traffic does not have to enter the neighbourhood.

12 Staying healthy

Starting off

1 & **2**

2 workout **3** infection **4** get over **5** check-up **6** treatment **7** illness **8** intake **9** putting on

Recording script CD2 Track 8

Speaker 1: I think I'm pretty healthy. I mean I have a lovely
life. I've been retired now for nearly 20 years,
no financial problems and here I am, in my 80s,
Q1 still quite active – I mean I go shopping, visit
my friends and go to the cinema when I want
to. What more can you ask for?

Speaker 2: I really do believe in a healthy mind in a healthy
body, so I get up pretty early, about 6.30. I do
Q2 an hour's workout in the morning before going
to college, and in the evening I usually have
time for a couple of hours' sport, so I really
think I'm very fit.

Speaker 3: Me healthy? I should think so. Of course, I
Q3 do get the occasional cold or other infection.
You really can't avoid them in my job being a
Q4 doctor, but I get over them pretty quickly and
they don't usually stop me going to work. I've
never been stopped from doing anything I
want to do because of an illness.

Speaker 4: I take my health pretty seriously. I think you
have to. I go to the doctor regularly once a
Q5 year for a check-up. Once or twice I've needed
Q6 treatment for something she's found, but I
think I can expect to live for quite a long time.

Speaker 5: I'm just a naturally happy, relaxed person and
I think that's a large part of the secret of good
health. I never go to the doctor and in fact I
don't even know my doctor's name. I'm lucky,
Q7 I've never had a day's illness in my life.

Speaker 6: I'm healthy, but then I take care of myself. I'm
very careful about what I eat – very little meat,
Q8 a high daily intake of fresh fruit and vegetables
Q9 – and I'm careful about not putting on weight,
so I take a moderate amount of exercise as
well. You know what they say: everything in
moderation!

Reading Part 2

2 Students no longer misbehave, fight, drop litter, attack teachers; there's no longer any vandalism; instead of getting final marks 11% below the national average, their marks are 5% above

4 *Suggested phrases to underline:*
B It is certainly true (that our eating habits have dramatically changed)
C exactly this relationship **D** The next step was
E It soon became evident, in this school
F They, some of them **G** Today he
H While he was there

5 **1** F **2** H **3** G **4** D **5** A **6** B **7** C

Vocabulary
Parts of the body

1 **2** chin **3** neck **4** shoulder **5** back **6** chest **7** elbow **8** wrist **9** hip **10** thigh **11** knee **12** heel

Grammar
Relative pronouns and relative clauses

1 **2** who/that **3** which/that **4** whose **5** where

2 **2** non-defining **3** defining **4** defining **5** non-defining **6** defining

3 **3**, **4** and **6**

4 **3** and **4**

5 **2** Frank has a brother ~~his~~ *whose* wife is in hospital with a broken leg.
3 She's a student of yoga, ~~that~~ *which* is done by thousands of people in this country.

4 Can I read that essay which you wrote ~~it~~ last week?
5 Mandy supports the football team which ~~it~~ won the league last year.
6 I'm afraid I can't understand ~~that~~ *what* you are saying.
7 Aziz lives in a large house which ~~it~~ has a view of the sea.
8 Gaby's friends, who you met ~~them~~ this morning, are going to the beach this afternoon if you want to come.

6 2 He studied hard for his maths exam, which he found quite easy.
3 The man (who/that) they sold the car to is a taxi driver.
4 Could you give me the newspaper (which/that) you were reading earlier?
5 That white house over there is the house where he was born.
6 Where's the envelope (which/that) I put the money in?
7 Every morning I go running in the park with Patricia, whose brother you know.
8 Karen and Teresa, whose dog we're looking after, are on holiday in the Caribbean at the moment.

Listening Part 3

1 2 f 3 h 4 a 5 e 6 d 7 g 8 b

2 diagnose, infection, prescribe, examination, sick note, check-up

3 1 F 2 D 3 C 4 A 5 B

Recording script CD2 Track 9

Speaker 1: Well, I arrived at the surgery at a quarter past eight for an appointment at eight-thirty but in fact I had to wait till nearly half past nine to see him. I felt pretty frustrated because there were only two other patients ahead of me. My problem wasn't too important – I had a sore throat – so I was only in there for five minutes. Anyway my doctor diagnosed that it was only a slight infection. I was expecting him to say that – I mean, I was pretty sure myself that it wasn't very serious. Anyway, he prescribed me some antibiotics, which was fine. But I did find having to wait so long was a bit annoying, especially as he only had to see me so briefly.

Speaker 2: I haven't been feeling very well for some time now and I've been to the doctor several times to find out what's wrong. Anyway, the last time I went my regular doctor was away on holiday and there was a new doctor there. What a difference! My usual doctor doesn't say very much though I suppose he does try to help. But this new doctor was so sympathetic. She asked me all sorts of questions about my medical history and my family background and she took lots of notes. She spent a really long time and sounded so interested that I left her feeling a lot better already. She couldn't diagnose my problem straightaway though, but she did send me off for tests, so I'm hoping we'll find a solution soon.

Speaker 3: I went along to see my doctor the other day because I wasn't feeling very well. I thought I'd got the flu and I needed to stay at home for a few days and not go to work. Anyway, I went to the doctor who gave me a very thorough examination. She then told me I wasn't very ill and refused to give me a sick note. Frankly, I was amazed because I'd been coughing and sneezing all week and feeling quite ill. Anyway, I couldn't change her mind so I had to go back to work the same morning, worst luck!

Speaker 4: My doctor hardly looked at me when I went in. She just asked me a few questions without looking up from her notes. She didn't even examine me. She then wrote me a prescription and said that if the symptoms continued,I should come back the following week. I told her I wanted a proper examination straightaway and I stayed there sitting in my chair. I must say she looked a bit surprised, but then she got up from her desk and came and gave me a good check-up. In the end she apologised and said she'd been on duty all night in the local hospital.

Speaker 5: I went to my doctor complaining of neck pains and I was there for what seemed like hours. She took a long time over it and gave me a very complete check-up. She looked at my neck, asked about my medical history and my daily routine. Then she told me that the problem was probably caused by stress. She said that what I needed was a good rest and my neck would heal itself. She suggested that I was probably suffering from overwork and that with a bit of time off the pain would disappear.

Use of English Part 3

1 1 a **2** b **3** a
4 *mis-*: it means *to do something wrongly*

2 **2** disappoint **3** misuse **4** untie **5** misspell **6** disappeared **7** undress **8** misinformed

3 misunderstood unsatisfied / dissatisfied disrespect mispronounce displeased disobey unlikely misinterpret unhealthy unhappy impossible incapable incorrect unaware disappoint disagree incomplete unable (*disable* is a verb) impatient

4 **1** announcement **2** stressful **3** security **4** occasionally **5** unexpected **6** height **7** flights **8** agreement **9** assistance **10** unnecessary

Speaking Part 4

2 **1** e **2** f **3** b **4** c

3 Candidate 1: not important if health good, perhaps young people and people over 50

Candidate 2: more time to relax by taking more exercise, doing sport

Candidate 3: exercise, right food, not smoke

Candidate 4: in some lessons – social problems, smoking, what to eat – but not a formal programme

Recording script CD2 Track 10

Candidate 1: It depends on the circumstances. I think that if you feel your health is good generally, I don't think it's too important. Perhaps young children should go regularly and older people, say, over the age of 50, but I don't think it's really necessary for people my age.

Candidate 2: I'd like to have more time to relax. I think being relaxed and not stressed is important for health. And I think the best way to be more relaxed is by taking more exercise, perhaps by doing more sport. I think if I did that I'd have a healthier lifestyle.

Candidate 3: Well, I think it's important to take plenty of exercise and to eat the right food. I mean, you should eat plenty of vegetables and fruit. Also, you shouldn't smoke because all the doctors say that's bad for your health.

Candidate 4: I'm not sure. I think perhaps they do in some lessons, perhaps those lessons where students discuss social problems and how to deal with them, things like smoking and what to eat, but I don't think they do usually, I mean, as part of a formal programme.

Writing Part 2 An essay

3 **1** lots / plenty **2** what **3** which **4** able **5** they **6** it **7** more **8** at **9** there **10** so

4 **1** paragraph 2 **2** paragraph 1
3 to summarise the essential argument of the essay
4 For instance, we know that smoking is dangerous, which is something our grandparents didn't realise. For example, at work most people spend long hours sitting in front of computers, and in their free time they watch television or play computer games
5 Relative clauses: what is necessary for a healthy lifestyle, which is something our grandparents didn't realise, who live in rich countries, which allow them to take all the exercise they need (two relative clauses), which keep us fit

7 Marina B Saleem F Claire E Paul C Vicky A

Recording script CD2 Track 11

Presenter: Marina

Marina: I know it's supposed to be bad for you, although I feel fine and I don't notice it affecting my health in any way. I mean it doesn't prevent me from doing lots of sports, so I'm not really interested in stopping. But I guess I'll have to around 30 when I start thinking about having a family of my own. But that's a long way off still, after all I'm only 17.

Presenter: Saleem

Saleem: My girlfriend was pretty keen for me to give it up. She went on and on at me about how my health would improve, even if, as she said, I wouldn't notice any changes straightaway. She insisted that in a month or so I'd feel much fitter. I haven't given up meat as a question of conscience. I mean I might start eating it again if I change my mind, but I reckon I'll give it six months.

Presenter: Claire

Claire: I hate team games. All that 'Well done, Claire, nice shot' just irritates me. Besides, I've just got so much to do what with my university entrance exams and my part-time job at the hospital. I just think athletics and football and all that are such a bore and a total waste of time! Still, I enjoy a nice long walk in the country when I have the time.

Presenter: Paul

Paul: I like clubbing, discos, going out with my friends and coming home late at night. I also enjoy smoking, eating fast food, riding my motorbike really fast and generally having a good time. So whatever my mum and dad say, I want to carry on. I expect I'll think differently and start taking care of myself when I'm old and responsible, say when I'm 30, but I don't want to be responsible now. Life is far too good!

Presenter: Vicky

Vicky: I reckon I've been putting on weight since I left school, probably because at school we had compulsory sport three afternoons a week and now I'm at university I don't do that, so I guess I should join a sports club – there are plenty going here – and it would probably make me feel good too. So I'll probably do that next term.

8 *Sample answer:*

Young people generally don't pay enough attention to their health and fitness

In my country there is a lot of discussion in the media about the health problems young people have as a result of eating fast food and not taking enough exercise.

There are a number of reasons given why young people are not so careful about their health and fitness. Firstly, computers and television mean people have increasingly sedentary lifestyles. Secondly, young people are so busy these days that they often do not have so much time for sports.

On the other hand, fewer people smoke than in the past, and I know a lot of young people who are very careful to have a balanced healthy diet. Also, a lot of young people have access to plenty of health information and know what they should do to have a healthy lifestyle.

On balance, therefore, I believe that young people generally pay plenty of attention to their health and fitness, although of course we could always pay more.

Vocabulary and grammar review Unit 11

Vocabulary

1

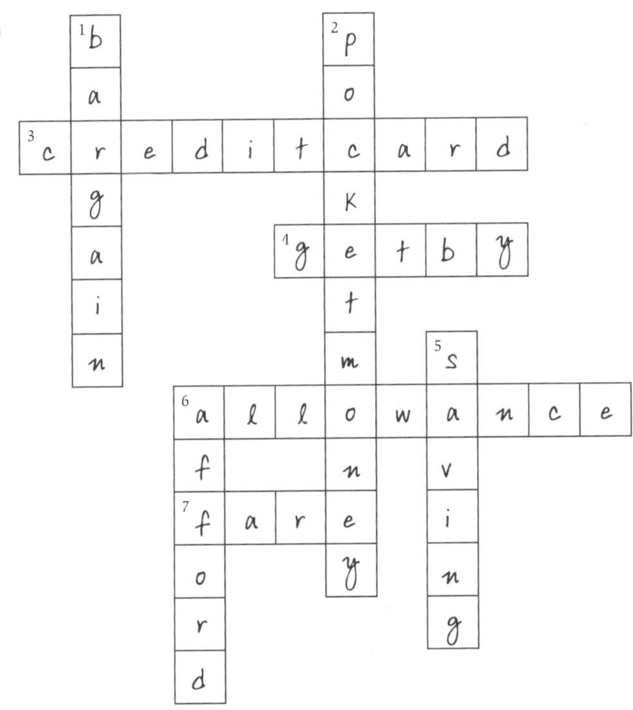

Grammar

2 **2** were able to / could **3** managed to / was able to **4** can/could **5** be able to **6** not been able to **7** was able to / managed to **8** could

3 **2** as **3** as **4** as **5** like **6** as **7** as **8** Like **9** like **10** like

Vocabulary and grammar review Unit 12

Vocabulary

❶ **2** heal **3** treatment **4** infection **5** put on **6** fit **7** prescription **8** cure **9** check-up **10** get over

Word formation

❷ **2** disobey **3** dissatisfied **4** incorrect **5** disappointing **6** unlikely **7** incapable **8** misbehave **9** undo **10** unable

Grammar

❸ **3** when/that **4** where **5** which/that/– **6** whose **7** which/that/– **8** who **9** where **10** why

❹ **2** ~~his~~ whose **3** correct **4** ~~anyone liked~~ anyone who liked **5** ~~that~~ who **6** correct **7** ~~that~~ what **8** ~~her~~ whose

13 Animal kingdom

Starting off

❶ wild animals: **6**; working animals: **1**, **2**, **3**, **4**; pets: **1**, **2**, **5**

❷ provide us with company: **2** and **5**; entertain us: **1**, **5**, **6;** provide us with food: **3** and perhaps **4**; participate in sport: **1**; are used for transport: **4**; help us in other ways: **2**

Listening Part 1

❶ **1** eight **2** different subjects **3** twice **4** read and hear

❷ **1** C **2** B **3** C **4** C **5** B **6** B **7** A **8** A

Recording script CD2 Track 12

Presenter: One. You overhear a woman talking about different animals. Which animal would she let her family have?

A a cat
B a dog
C a horse

1st woman: Aren't you a good boy? Good boy! Lovely dog.

2nd woman: Yes, isn't he?

1st woman: Very well behaved. What's he called?

2nd woman: He's called Bandy. Good boy!

1st woman: Good boy, Bandy! My husband is always saying he wishes he had a dog to go for walks with. He says it would keep burglars away as well, as we live in the country.

2nd woman: So do you think you'll get one?

1st woman: I don't know. It's a bit of a commitment. I mean, you've got to feed them and take them with you when you go on holiday, that sort of thing. Then my daughter, Patsy, would like a horse. She says we could keep it in the field behind us.

2nd woman: But that's a commitment too.

1st woman: I know, which is why I hesitate, but it would give Patsy something to do, an interest, you know, and get her out in the fresh air …

2nd woman: What about a cat?

1st woman: They don't do anything for me really. I think if *Q1* we had an animal, I'd go for the horse, but I'm not wildly enthusiastic, quite honestly. You've got to think of the expense, as well.

2nd woman: Yes, I can see that.

Presenter: Two. You hear part of a television programme about zebras. What does the presenter say about their appearance?

A All members of a family of zebras have the same stripes.
B Zebras can recognise each other by their stripes.
C Male and female zebras have similar stripes.

Man: Of course, seen as a vast herd, every zebra looks alike. During their migration, all the stripes moving in the bright African sun form a confusing pattern which helps to protect the zebras from lions and other predators. But while they look exactly the same to you and *Q2* me, each individual zebra in fact has a unique pattern of stripes and these different stripes help other members of their family to know who they are. Not only that, male zebras have wider, darker, more shiny stripes than their females, although at a distance and in a mass they may all look the same. It's also worth remembering that different species of zebra have different types of stripe.

Presenter: Three. You overhear a woman talking about the birds which come to her garden. How does she feel about them?

A She enjoys watching them.
B She finds them annoying.
C She worries about them.

Man: Lovely here in the park, isn't it?

Woman: Yes. Do you know what I saw in the garden this morning?

Man: What?

Woman: A flock of long-tailed tits. They came to the plum tree and seemed to be eating insects off the tree, greenfly probably.

Man: That's good.

Woman: Yes. We get quite a variety of birds at this time of year. I always hope the cats don't get them. There are an awful lot of cats in our neighbourhood and I hate the idea of them catching birds.

Q3

Man: Yes.

Presenter: Four. You overhear part of a conversation in which two men are talking about dogs. What do they say about them?

A They are good company.
B They are good at protecting property.
C They shouldn't live in cities.

1st man: Have you still got your dog?

2nd man: Yes, yes, but he's a bit of a nuisance frankly.

1st man: Really, why's that?

2nd man: He's just pretty useless, quite honestly. You think your dog is going to warn you about burglars, but mine only seems to bark when there are other dogs around. I suppose people imagine they'll be safer with a dog in the house, but I doubt if they really are. Mine just barks all night, which annoys the neighbours.

1st man: And keeps you awake I suppose.

2nd man: That's right. I certainly don't enjoy having him in the house. I think I'd be happier having a dog if I lived in the country where I could take it for long walks, but living here in the city centre it's just not very practical.

Q4

1st man: Yes, I know what you mean. I think it's a mistake to have them here too, especially big ones like yours.

Presenter: Five. You hear a woman giving part of a lecture about animal rights. What does she say about zoos?

A They are no longer necessary in modern times.
B They should be closely supervised.
C They should only be for endangered species.

Woman: It would I think be ignorant to suggest that zoos no longer serve a useful purpose. The fact is that many of them do quite valuable work conserving rare species. What I do think, and I'm sure you'd agree with me here, is that those old-fashioned zoos which were designed and built in the nineteenth-century just don't give animals enough space. There's no feeling that animals are in a natural habitat. Those zoos should all be closed and banned, while the more modern zoos need to be strictly inspected to make sure that the animals are kept in the best conditions possible.

Q5

Presenter: Six. You hear a young woman talking about some animals she worked with. How did she feel when she was with them?

A frightened
B relaxed
C strange

Girl: Last summer, you see, I went to help on a wildlife conservation project in Africa and I was asked to look after these young lions which had lost their mother. It's curious, because I'd expected to feel quite nervous – I mean, they're dangerous animals, aren't they? In fact, after I'd spent a few days feeding them and playing with them we had a very easy, comfortable relationship. I had to be a bit careful, because they could be quite rough when playing with each other, but I never felt they were going to attack me. You wouldn't expect that with young lions, would you?

Q6

Presenter: Seven. You hear part of a radio programme in which a man talks about how he was attacked by a hippopotamus. What does he say about hippos?

A They are one of the most dangerous animals in Africa.
B They often attack people for no reason.
C They're usually very timid animals.

Man: You'd think that hippos are quite easy to run away from with their big barrel-like bodies and shortish legs, but they can move surprisingly fast. I was on holiday in South Africa and walking along a river bank when suddenly there was a crashing noise in the grass beside me and a hippo rushed at me. Fortunately, I was able to leap to one side and run. If I hadn't reacted quickly, the hippo would have killed me, for sure!

Later, at the hotel, I was told how they get nervous if someone walks between them and the river, which is their natural habitat.

Q7 Apparently more people are killed by hippos in Africa every year than by any other animal. And for that reason: they get between them and the water.

Presenter: Eight. You hear a woman talking to her husband. Why is she talking to him?

A to make a suggestion
B to make a complaint
C to remind him of something

Woman: Brian …

Man: Yes?

Woman: You remember you were asking me what we should do with the children over the holidays?

Man: Yes?

Woman: *Q8* Well, I've been looking in the paper and it's given me an idea. Why don't we take them to the circus? That's something we haven't done for a few years and there's one coming to this area next week.

Man: Well, it's an idea. Do you think they'll enjoy it? I mean the last time we went to a circus a couple of years ago, it wasn't exactly fun, was it?

Woman: I think that's because they had all those acts with tired-looking animals and things, you remember. I think if they'd had more acrobats, we'd have enjoyed the circus more. Anyway, this one's different. It might be much better.

Man: OK, well let's ask the children if they'd be interested in going. What's the circus called by the way?

Woman: Let's see … here it is. It's called Giffords Circus.

Man: Oh yes, I've read about them. Apparently they're pretty good according to what I read.

Vocabulary
Named and *called*

❶ called, called

❷ **1** both *call* and *name* **2** *call* **3** *call*

❸ **2** ~~named~~ called **3** correct **4** ~~named~~ called

Grammar
Third conditional

❶ **1** True **2** False **3** True

❷ **1** b **2** a **3** b **4** a **5** b **6** a **7** a

❸ **2** would have had **3** would have bitten
4 had been **5** hadn't been
6 had paid / had been paying
7 wouldn't have made **8** wouldn't have heard

Reading Part 3

❶ Photos: elephant, shark, scorpion, polar bear, pelican *Most dangerous:* any of the first four *Least dangerous:* pelican

❷ **1** b / c **2** b **3** a / b / c **4** c **5** b **6** a / b / c **7** b **8** c **9** b / c **10** a / b **11** a **12** b **13** b **14** b **15** c

❸ **1** C **2** E **3** D **4** B **5** A **6** A **7** C **8** C **9** E **10** D **11** E **12** A **13** B **14** B **15** C

Use of English Part 1

❷ **1** 12 **2** 15 **3** the text quickly **4** after **5** the alternatives **6** you have finished **7** all the questions

❸ horses

❹ **1** A **2** C **3** D **4** B **5** B **6** D **7** A **8** D **9** C **10** B **11** A **12** C

Grammar
Wish, if only and *hope*

❶ **1** a, b and d **2** a and d **3** b
4 past tense and *would* + infinitive **5** c
6 past perfect **7** e and f **8** present simple

❷ **2** ~~wish~~ hope **3** correct **4** ~~wish~~ hope
5 correct **6** ~~wish~~ hope **7** correct **8** ~~wish~~ hope

❸ **2** I had studied harder
3 would make less / would not make so much
4 hadn't cancelled **5** wish you had met

Speaking Part 1

1 1 yourself, your life and your interests
2 answer giving reasons and examples if possible
3 about three minutes

3 *Suggested answers:* Student 1 a, b Student 2 b, c Student 3 a, c

Recording script CD2 Track 13

Teacher: Do you have any pets or animals at home?

Student 1: No, but my aunt has a white cat and I wish I had one too, but my mother is not too keen on animals.

Teacher: Do you enjoy visiting zoos?

Student 2: Yes, occasionally. We have a very large modern zoo in my city where I go about once a year when we have visitors. I don't like those small old zoos with animals in cages.

Teacher: Do you enjoy watching programmes about animals on television?

Student 3: Yes, I find it relaxing and also it educates you about wildlife, so I think we become more careful about protecting the environment.

Writing Part 2 A letter

1 **1** four **2** 120–180 words
3 a letter, a review, a report, a story, an essay or an article
4 about 40 minutes for this part

2 1 where to go, what to see and the best way of getting around to see countryside, scenery and wildlife
2 *Students' own answers*
3 informal style – it's a letter to a friend – she has written to you in an informal style

3 1 I'm very glad to hear that you're thinking of visiting my country this summer
2 yes – advice about visiting Asturias, what to see while there, and hiring a car
3 yes – he adds information
4 quite informal

4 **1** I'd advise you to go to Asturias **2** You should visit the 'Picos de Europa' **3** If I were you, I'd hire a car to get around **4** The best idea would be to hire it online **5** Make sure that you take warm clothes and a raincoat

6 *Sample answer:* See the model letter in Exercise 3.

14 House space

Starting off

1 1 e – a housing estate
2 f – a houseboat
3 c – a block of flats with several storeys
4 b – a country cottage
5 a – a castle
6 d – a townhouse

Reading Part 1

2 **1** eight **2** 20
3 the text quickly before reading the questions
4 after **5** must

3 *Suggested answers:* It seems like a palace, it's elegant, it's conveniently situated close to the Grand Canal, the district is interesting

4 **1** B **2** C **3** B **4** A **5** C **6** D **7** D **8** A

Vocabulary

Space, place, room, area, location and *square*

1 **2** square **3** location **4** area

2 **2** room **3** space **4** location
5 area **6** space **7** square
8 area **9** space **10** room

Listening Part 2

2 **1** F – it has ten questions **2** F – you will need between one and three words **3** T **4** T
5 F – you should read and try to predict the type of information and type of words you need
6 T

3 **2** probably a noun **3** a person **4** name of a room
5 probably a verb + *-ing*
6 another type of room
7 another type of building
8 swimming pool, or other facility **9** a noun
10 an adverb

4 **1** seven / 7 years **2** (very) strange experiences
3 mother-in-law **4** the library
5 (standing) behind
6 bedroom **7** battle
8 tennis court **9** blood
10 at weekends / part-time

Recording script CD2 Track 14

Interviewer: Now I'm standing outside the rather unusual house of crime-writer Jeff Bowen. It's large and very old and has views of some of the most beautiful countryside in the west of England. Jeff, how long have you been living here?

Jeff: *Q1* We've been here for about seven years now. We came here from Hollywood, where I'd been working on a film script. We house-hunted for about six months and couldn't find anything we really liked. Then finally we saw this place and my wife just fell in love with it immediately, so we bought it.

Interviewer: I believe it's rather unusual, isn't it? Can you tell us about that?

Jeff: Sure. You know, I'm fairly convinced that this house is haunted by ghosts and I'm not joking. *Q2* A lot of people have had some very strange experiences here.

Interviewer: Such as?

Jeff: Well, a few months ago, we were having a family party in the house. We'd just had lunch and were relaxing with coffee when my *Q3* mother-in-law went white as a sheet and dropped her coffee cup. I asked her what the matter was, thinking she'd been taken ill or something. She said she'd just seen a group of men dressed up as medieval soldiers go past the window. We ran outside to look but there was nobody there. But she could describe their appearance in quite a lot of detail, so she wasn't just making it up.

Interviewer: Rather alarming I should think.

Jeff: And that's not all. A week or two later quite a different visitor, a friend of mine from London *Q4* was reading in the library when a desk began to move. Apparently it floated from one side of the room to the other and then back again. He sat watching it, too frightened to move.

Interviewer: Have you personally had any experience of supernatural phenomena?

Jeff: Nothing as direct as the things I've just mentioned. Just a feeling really; when I'm in my study working, I've occasionally felt the hair on the back of my neck stand on end as if there's *Q5* someone standing behind me. When I've turned round, there's been no one there, but as you can imagine it doesn't help my work concentration.

Interviewer: So what have you done about this?

Jeff: First I decided to change my workplace. I got *Q6* the builders in and I had a bedroom turned into a study. I hoped I'd be able to work in there without being interrupted by these uninvited visitors! Then I called in a specialist in supernatural phenomena, someone I'd met while I was working on films and I had the whole house checked.

Interviewer: What did they come up with?

Jeff: She didn't come up with anything very firm, but she checked the local history records and discovered that the house is actually located *Q7* somewhere where a battle took place nine hundred years ago, so there could be quite a few dead people buried here.

Interviewer: Really?

Jeff: Yes, and interestingly, a few months ago I was *Q8* having the tennis court built in the garden. Anyway, one of the workmen, a lad of about 19, was on his own here one morning when he felt someone was watching him. He had the sort of feeling I had when working in my study. When he turned round, he saw something which literally made his hair stand on end: there was a man in ancient clothes standing *Q9* there with a white shirt covered in blood. The lad shouted and the man just disappeared.

Interviewer: But none of this discourages you from living here?

Jeff: Not at all. I don't feel physically threatened. Anyway, I'm in London a lot of the week and *Q10* we mostly come here at weekends, so I only feel haunted part-time!

Interviewer: Jeff, tell me about the house itself. Apart from its spirit life, what other features attracted you to it?

Grammar

Causative *have*

❶ He had a bedroom converted into a study and a tennis court built.

❷ **1** b
2 a – I did it myself;
b – I asked someone else to do it for me

❸ builders

4 2 had a tooth pulled out **3** having the house painted **4** have it cut down **5** have it extended **6** has all his meals delivered

Use of English Part 2

2 1 12 **2** grammar **3** general idea **4** before and after **5** every question **6** the completed text

4 1 as **2** spite **3** since **4** than **5** who **6** takes **7** out **8** should/must **9** to **10** been **11** there **12** enough

Speaking Part 2

1 1 T **2** F – two photos **3** T **4** T

Grammar

Expressing obligation and permission

1 *Suggested answers:* Advantages: you hear lots of real English, practise English, get to know new culture, gain confidence; Disadvantages: strange food, possible cultural misunderstandings, it may be difficult to say what you really feel, it may be difficult to fit into a strange family

2 1 a I have to; b I can't, they won't let me; c I can, They let me **2** b

3 1 Marcos: D **2** Lidia: E **3** Ana: C **4** Erich: B **5** Claudia: A

Recording script CD2 Track 15

Claudia: So, what's your host family like, Marcos? Are they friendly?

Marcos: They're great fun, especially the mother. She's always cracking jokes and suggesting interesting things to do. And she's got a couple of daughters my age who don't stop laughing! The house is always full of their friends too, so it's like a permanent party, and that's great for my social life. The only drawback is that I can't stay out too late because they all have to be up early the next morning. I don't have to do anything around the house, or things like that – though I do help from time to time, just to fit in and make things easier for them. What about you, Lidia? *(Q1)*

Lidia: You sound really lucky with your family, Marcos. Mind you, I haven't got any complaints, but my family certainly isn't such fun as yours. I mean, they didn't let me invite a couple of friends to dinner the other day. They told me it just wasn't convenient and I can see that's not being unreasonable – I mean, it is their house after all. And anyway, it's not always like that – for example, the other day when I wanted to go down to the seaside for the day they actually lent me their car. I thought that was really nice of them and very trusting. I mean, I've only just passed my test! Are you living with a nice family, Ana? *(Q2)*

Ana: Well, we have our ups and downs. The other day my landlady told me off because I'd got home a bit late and missed the family dinner. Apparently I was supposed to phone to say I wasn't coming. Then when I went to see if there was anything left over in the fridge, I got into trouble again. She told me I couldn't just help myself to things without asking her first. *(Q3)*

Marcos: So, what did you do? Walk out?

Ana: No, I apologised for being late and explained that I had to finish some project work at university. She calmed down and said 'Never mind,' and then she helped me to cook myself a really nice meal. So we were all friends again.

Erich: Quite right. Still, all your families sound really nice to me.

Ana: And isn't yours, Erich?

Erich: Well, they're all right I suppose. Not very tidy, which is one thing I would complain about. I'm not the tidiest person myself, but I think they're just taking advantage of homestay students by saying that anyone staying in their home must do their share round the house. You know, like clearing up a bit, doing a bit of the hoovering, a bit of the cooking. I needn't clean the bathroom or do any shopping, fortunately, because I wouldn't have the time. But I doubt if they'd let me have my friends in for dinner or anything like that. Not like you, Claudia. *(Q4)*

Claudia: Well, I'm lucky. Ana, you've been round for dinner and so has Erich. I had to buy the food and cook it of course and they don't allow me to have a real party, but a couple of friends is OK. And they join in too which makes it really interesting because we have, I don't know like a sort of international evening. It's quite good *(Q5)*

	fun. And I cook traditional Sicilian food which makes a change for everyone.
Marcos:	It sounds as if we're all quite lucky then. Not like a friend of mine who went back to Chile last year …

4 1 Marcos 2 Claudia 3 Claudia 4 Ana 5 Lidia 6 Erich

5

present	
obligation	I must I'm supposed to I have to
prohibition	I can't I'm not allowed to They won't let me They don't allow me to
permission	I can They let me
no obligation	I don't have to I needn't
past	
obligation	I had to I was supposed to
prohibition	They didn't let me

6 2 do not have to 3 am supposed to take 4 are not allowed (to go) 5 to let Celia borrow

Writing Part 2 An article

1 a 6 b 4 c 1 d 3 e 2 f 5 g 7

4 1 readers of the college magazine, i.e. other students, teachers, etc. 2 informal 3 conditional – it asks you to imagine your ideal home 4 the type of house, its location and features of the house 5 for example, by surprising the reader, by saying interesting things about yourself

5 1 *Students' own answers*
2 Yes – location Paris or Vienna; conveniently close to theatres, art galleries, and shops; sort of house: small, stylish, modern flat; features: cosy bedroom, well-equipped kitchen, balcony, etc.

6 2 from 3 where 4 who 5 own 6 what 7 of 8 have 9 much 10 If

7 2 T 3 F 4 T (he/she would like to live alone and make his/her own decisions, he/she enjoys theatre, art, music and reading, he/she wants an active social life) 5 T 6 F – he/she lives in a small suburban house

8 *Sample answer:* See the model answer in Exercise 5.

Vocabulary and grammar review Unit 13

Vocabulary

1 2 called 3 called / named 4 named 5 called

Grammar

2 2 c – If Chris hadn't picked up the cactus, the scorpion wouldn't have stung him.
3 d – If Zebedee hadn't provoked the pelican, it wouldn't have attacked him.
4 a – If Craig hadn't reached the shore, he would have died.
5 e – If no one had heard the polar bear, it might have attacked them without warning.

3 2 was/were 3 would have had / could have had 4 wouldn't make 5 lived 6 would have heard 7 hasn't missed / didn't miss 8 would speak 9 would have been 10 wasn't 11 change / are going to change / will change 12 had studied

4 *Suggested answers:*
You should take it for walks twice a day.
Make sure that you take it to the vet for vaccinations.
The best idea would be to train it to behave properly.
I'd advise you to give it baths from time to time.
If I were you, I wouldn't let it bark at night.

Vocabulary and grammar review Unit 14

Vocabulary

1 **2** room **3** place **4** location **5** area **6** place **7** space **8** square

Grammar

2 **2** supposed **3** let **4** can't **5** had **6** needn't **7** have **8** Can **9** must **10** couldn't

3 **2** you had your hair **3** have a tennis court built **4** you have the car checked **5** had the tree cut down **6** have to do **7** are supposed to pay **8** are not allowed to speak

15 Fiesta!

Starting off

1 **2** dress up **3** perform **4** march **5** commemorate **6** hold **7** play/perform **8** gather round **9** let off **10** wearing

2 Photos: **1** fireworks **2** traditional costumes, traditional dances **3** street party **4** parade, band **5** disguises **6** street performers, street theatre

3 **1** and **2** *Students' own answers*
3 The photos were taken in: **1** Sydney, Australia **2** Brittany, France **3** Britain **4** USA **5** Venice, Italy **6** Britain

Listening Part 4

2 **1** interview **2** seven **3** underline, different words **4** general ideas

3 **1** C **2** A **3** B **4** A **5** B **6** A **7** C

Recording script CD2 Track 16

Interviewer: Today South Live visits the Winchester Hat Fair, an extravaganza of processions, fireworks and street theatre with performers from as far away as Australia and Brazil. And we're talking to a veteran performer at the Hat Fair, Mighty Max, who's come all the way from Canada once again. Max, why is the festival called the Hat Fair?

Max: Well, I've been told the fair was only started in 1976, as a way of encouraging street performers like myself. It's not like there was one of those great old English traditions like hat-making here in the eighteenth century or anything. A lot of people come to the fair wearing funny hats because it's called the Hat
Q1 Fair, but that wasn't its origins. It was always supposed to be about street theatre, and typically a hat is passed around so that people like me can earn a living. That's in fact where the name comes from.

Interviewer: Now, you've been coming here for a number of years. Why do you keep coming back?

Max: I just love performing here. There are artists like myself from all over the world who come here year after year and we get to know each other and stuff. But what makes the Hat Fair
Q2 unique is the people who come to watch. You know, people from this part of the country are usually a bit reserved and shy in public, but during the Hat Fair all that seems to change. They let their hair down and get involved in the acts. They really seem to love it when they're being laughed at by other members of the audience. It's amazing and great fun for the entertainers as well.

Interviewer: So, how did you get involved in street theatre in the first place?

Max: Well, as a kid I was always fascinated by the circus and dreamt of being a circus performer. I actually went to quite a famous circus school in Canada when I was a teenager and I was taught juggling and acrobatics there. My father was dead against it and didn't want me to have anything to do with the circus, but he paid for the classes on the condition that I went to university and got myself what he called a proper education. It was ironic really because
Q3 if I hadn't gone to university I might never have got into street theatre. You see, every vacation

I used to travel and I found I could pay for my trips by doing street theatre. That's how I came to the Hat Fair for the first time about ten years ago. I've never had any other job.

Interviewer: Fantastic! And how do you explain your popularity as a street performer? I mean, your act has been attracting tremendous crowds here in Winchester.

Max: Well, you've seen it. It's a combination of high class acrobatics which are performed without safety equipment and some quite risky stunts. So it gives the audience a thrill. But what I think really gets them into it is that I get them involved and I make them laugh. There's a lot of clowning in my act which builds a sort of two-way communication with the audience. They love it. And that's what makes street theatre in general so good. Your audience pay you according to how much they like you. The better your act, the more you get. And if it's no good at all, then you get nothing.

Q4

Q5

Interviewer: An instant comment on the quality of your work, in other words.

Max: That's right.

Interviewer: And what are the problems that street performers come up against?

Max: A good question. In a place like Winchester, not many. We're each given a place and a time to perform. As you've seen I attract pretty large crowds and I need plenty of space for jumping around and so on, so narrow streets are no good. Here we're given the main shopping street, which is fine. In other places, if you haven't got permission, you'll get moved on by the police. But I always make sure that I have the right permits. It's just not worth it otherwise. Probably the main difficulty in places like Britain and Canada is actually things like rain or snow. I mean, people just won't stand around watching you if they're going to get cold and wet doing it, will they?

Q6

Interviewer: I imagine not. But what about Winchester? Has the Hat Fair put the town on the map, so to speak? I mean does it attract a lot of visitors from outside?

Max: I'm not the best person to ask that question to. I'm just a street entertainer. I get the impression that the people who come to the Hat Fair tend to be people from the area rather than visitors from outside. What Winchester gets is an amusing party – something they can do which isn't work. It's just plain fun. You know, they gather in the streets and parks and all have a laugh together, either at the performers or at each other. And it's all so good-natured. They unwind and forget about the other pressures in their lives.

Q7

Interviewer: Mighty Max, thank you and I hope the rest of the fair goes well for you.

Max: Thank you.

4 *Suggested answers:* Some residents may find it annoying, it interrupts traffic, it may encourage pickpockets and thieving, it may be dangerous, etc.

Grammar

The passive

1 *Phrases to underline:*
b is passed round **c** they're being laughed at
d was taught **e** we're given, you'll get moved on

2 *Suggested answers:* **2** a **3** b, d, first passive in e
4 a, b, d, first passive in e

3 **2** My wallet has been stolen!
3 You won't be able to ring me while my mobile is being repaired.
4 Have you heard? I've been given a place on the course!
5 If you'd interrupted the meeting, you would have been arrested.

4 People go out in the open air in the early morning; they eat traditional foods; young men swim in the Nile

5 **2** as **3** been **4** to **5** is **6** being **7** by
8 have **9** doing
10 were (Note: *fish* can be singular or plural, depending on the context.)

6 **1** a
2 A large number of contemporary Egyptian traditions are said to have their origins in very ancient times. For example, offerings of fish are believed to have been made to the ancient gods …

7 2 It is said that a large number of contemporary Egyptian traditions have their origins in very ancient times.
3 Five thousand people are reported to have joined in the festivities.
4 Our festival is said to have the best fireworks in the world.

8 2 expected to be chosen 3 said that the festival is 4 is thought to be 5 is considered to be

Reading Part 2

2 1 F – there are seven questions and no example
2 T 3 T 4 T
5 F – be flexible and change your mind if you find a better place for a sentence
6 F – read it again to check it reads logically

3 *Suggested phrases to underline:* The owner of a nearby vegetable stall provided the perfect weapons; In the main square; When we awoke … the next day; people poured into the town for the fight; From there they went …; Water poured from the rooftops; Nor could I look at or eat another tomato

4 1 H 2 C 3 F 4 G 5 A 6 B 7 D

Use of English Part 3

1 1 owner 2 tourists 3 firemen

2 2 artist 3 performer 4 collector
5 creator 6 participant 7 musician
8 politician 9 fisherman 10 cyclist

3 *Suggested answers:* waiter, swimmer, biologist, typist, director, conductor, policeman, postman

4 1 10
2 Read the whole text quickly before answering the questions
3 what type of word (adjective, noun, verb, etc.) you need
4 Make sure you have spelled the word correctly
5 read the completed text again

5 1 exciting 2 arrangements 3 activities
4 participants 5 impossible 6 visitors
7 disorganised 8 traditional 9 usually
10 impressive

Speaking Part 3

1 1 graduating 2 a sporting triumph
3 a new house 4 good exam results
5 an engagement 6 the first car 7 a new baby

2 a party with friends, a party with family, a meal, a holiday, buying furniture, going to a restaurant, buying something nice, e.g. new clothes, going for a (long) drive

Recording script CD2 Track 17

Teacher: Now, I'd like you to talk about something together for three minutes. Here are some important moments in people's lives. First talk to each other about what would be the best way of celebrating each of these occasions. Then decide which two you would be happiest to celebrate. All right?

Nikolai: Well, I think there are two ways of celebrating graduating from university: you have to have a party with your friends who are graduating at the same time and another party with your family. Don't you agree, Antonia?

Antonia: A party with your friends, yes, maybe. I think that the event – I'm not sure what it's called in English – the event when you graduate …

Nikolai: The ceremony?

Antonia: Yes, the graduation ceremony is enough for the family – with perhaps a meal afterwards.

Nikolai: You could be right.

Antonia: And for someone winning an important race, in other words a sporting triumph, I'm not sure. I guess another party would be fine, wouldn't it?

Nikolai: Yes, or perhaps I'd suggest a holiday somewhere really nice.

Antonia: A holiday?

Nikolai: Yes, because you work really hard to achieve a sporting triumph and I think you'd probably deserve one.

Antonia: I think that's a really good idea. How do you think people should celebrate buying a new house?

Nikolai: Well, people usually have a party don't they, so that people can see where they live.

Antonia: It's parties for everything, isn't it? Maybe in this case I'd celebrate by going out and buying a nice piece of furniture to put in the house.

Nikolai: Good idea – and then you could invite your friends to come and help paint the house!

Antonia: When you pass your First Certificate, will you hold another party?

Nikolai: Maybe. I think it depends on how I'm feeling. I might just go out to a restaurant with a friend to celebrate that one.

Antonia: Me too. And I might also go and buy myself something nice …

Nikolai: As a reward.

Antonia: Yes, some new clothes or something, you know, because I've studied so hard.

Nikolai: Yes.

Antonia: And getting engaged is really a moment to have a party with your family and friends together.

Nikolai: And your fiancé's family and friends as well.

Antonia: What about being given a new car?

Nikolai: That would be wonderful. I'd celebrate by going for a long drive in it.

Antonia: Me too, and with the music turned up really loud!

Nikolai: Yes. Shall we move on to the second question?

Antonia: OK. I think for me the thing I'd be most happy to celebrate would be getting a new car at the moment.

Nikolai: Really? Why's that?

Antonia: Because I'm tired of walking and using public transport. A new car would give me a lot of freedom. What about you?

Nikolai: I'd say graduating from university because then I can start looking for a job and once I have a job I can do other things like buy a car or buy a house, or …

Antonia: Or even get married.

Nikolai: Or get married if I can find the right person!

Teacher: Thank you.

❹ **2** F **3** T **4** T **5** F **6** T **7** T

❺ **2** could **3** suggest **4** idea **5** case **6** depends **7** move

❻ **2** Shall we move on to …
3 Perhaps I'd suggest …, Maybe in this case …
4 You could be right **5** I think it depends on …

❼ **1** F – you do it with a partner
2 F – you have about three minutes **3** T **4** T
5 T **6** F – try to discuss all of them **7** T

Writing Part 1

❶ **1** There is one question you must do **2** 120–150 words **3** a letter or an email **4** You must deal with four specific points in the task **5** 40 minutes

❷ **1** Sam, an English-speaking friend **2** informal
3 Things you must deal with: saying the dates of the festival, describing the festival, inviting Sam to visit, agreeing to visit the festival together
4 *Students' own answers*

❸ ~~bout~~ about, ~~exiting~~ exciting, ~~wich~~ which, ~~begining~~ beginning, ~~were~~ where, ~~especial~~ special, ~~trough~~ through, ~~cloths~~ clothes, ~~their~~ there, ~~preffer~~ prefer, ~~confortable~~ comfortable, ~~becaus~~ because, ~~now~~ know, ~~an~~ and, ~~froward~~ forward

❹ *Sample answer:* See the model email in Exercise 3.

16 Machine age

Starting off

❶ **2** MP3 player **3** webcam **4** digital camera
5 DVD player **6** mobile phone **7** SatNav
8 digital TV

❷ **2** find **3** date **4** give **5** do **6** save **7** wherever
8 take, store

❸ *Suggested answers:* digital camera: to take good photos easily and store them on my computer
digital TV: to keep up to date with what's going on and to give me more choice of what I watch
DVD player: to give me more choice of what I watch
laptop: to help me do my homework, to save time and effort and to keep in touch with friends
mobile phone: to keep in touch with friends
MP3 player: to listen to music wherever I want
SatNav: to find my way
webcam: to keep in touch with friends and to keep up to date with what's going on

Reading Part 3

❷ **1** F – there are 15 questions **2** T
3 F – read the questions carefully before the text(s)
4 T, or think carefully about what they mean
5 F – 20 minutes **6** F – answer every question

❸ **1** C **2** D **3** A **4** A **5** E **6** A **7** D **8** B **9** E **10** E **11** B **12** D / E **13** D / E **14** C / D **15** C / D

Vocabulary

Check, supervise and *control*

❶ **2** control **3** check **4** supervise **5** control

❷ **1** b **2** c **3** a

❸ **2** supervise **3** check **4** supervise **5** control **6** check

Grammar

Linking words: *when, if, in case, even if, even though* and *whether*

❶ **2** ~~if~~ when **3** correct **4** ~~when~~ if **5** correct **6** ~~when~~ if

❷ **2** ~~even if~~ even though **3** ~~even if~~ even though **4** correct **5** ~~Even if~~ Even though **6** ~~even though~~ even if

❸ **2** if **3** in case **4** in case **5** in case **6** if

❹ **2** when **3** if / when / even if **4** in case **5** even though **6** in case **7** if

Listening Part 3

❷ **1** five speakers, six alternatives
2 read and <u>underline</u> the main idea in each alternative
3 the main idea of what each speaker is saying

❸ **1** C **2** F **3** E **4** D **5** B

Recording script CD2 Track 18

Speaker 1: My parents aren't really at home with computers at all. They use one for doing the accounts – they run a small business – but they often forget to check their email, for example. I told them that they'd build up their business no end if they set up a website. They thought this was so sophisticated that they'd need a lot of new equipment in order to do this. <u>My dad had this idea that we should go shopping for some really powerful machine for me to run the website from</u> and I must say I was pretty tempted. But I had to admit we could do the whole thing with the stuff we've got at the moment. I missed a big opportunity to take advantage of my parents there, didn't I?

Speaker 2: Well, I have to do a lot of my homework using the internet, you know, to research things and so on, so my computer is usually switched on when I'm studying anyway. And last term in our class we had to do quite a few group projects which meant having to chat a lot with each other while we were doing them. When my parents saw me, they got the idea into their heads that I wasn't studying properly. <u>They told me to cut down on the chat</u>. They just don't have any idea how good computers can be for working together. Anyway, I got good marks in my end-of-term exams, which showed them.

Speaker 3: I love computers and if I could, I'd spend most of my free time doing things with them. I mean, I don't just use them for chatting with friends or surfing the internet or things like that. Actually, what I really like is designing things on the computer. I've got a really powerful one which my mum and dad bought me when I passed my exams and I'd like to study design in the future. <u>Anyway my dad found these classes you could do in the summer holidays and said if I was really interested I should go to them and learn to do things properly instead of teaching myself</u>. And my mum even offered to pay for them! They're great!

Speaker 4: My parents have the idea that computers are some sort of magic and that I'm some sort of genius just because I can handle them. You know, I can do lots of things which they just haven't learnt to do. When they went to one of those parent–teacher evenings at school last month, I heard them saying, 'But she's marvellous on the computer!' – you know how parents talk – and I saw the teachers looking at them with one of those patient looks teachers have when listening to parents. You could see they were probably thinking, 'Yeah, just like all the others' and 'Pity about her maths'!

Speaker 5: Well, we've only got one PC in my house and I use it a lot for chatting with my mates. I've got friends all over the world in lots of different countries. The trouble is that both my dad and my mum are hooked on this really crumby computer game. Anyway, I get home from school before they get home from work, so I get to the computer before them. This leads to no end of rows. You know, they ask me when I'm going to log off and give them a chance to use it, and haven't I got anything better to do, and isn't it about time I gave a hand with the housework, and so on. It's really funny actually because you can see they're just itching to get on the computer themselves!

4 *Suggested answers:*

1 students can use the internet for research; they can easily share their work with other students; they can work on projects together from their homes; they can store and edit their work easily; they can add graphics and other features to their work and present it in a way which looks smart; they can cooperate with students in other colleges and other countries, etc.

2 they learn research skills, typing skills, creativity, design skills, coordination; they may write more to their friends using email or chat, etc.

Grammar

Reported speech 2: reporting verbs

reporting verb + infinitive	offered to help
reporting verb + object + infinitive	advised me to go told me to send
reporting verb + preposition + noun or verb + *-ing*	complained about (not) having
reporting verb + verb + *-ing*	suggested buying
reporting verb + *(that)* + sentence	said they were

2 **2** of lying **3** to buy **4** for breaking **5** to go **6** to visit **7** to help **8** to buy **9** to visit **10** installing **11** to buy **12** to use

3 *Including answers to Exercise 1:*

reporting verb + infinitive	offered to help agreed to buy offered to help promised to visit
reporting verb + object + infinitive	advised me to go told me to send asked me to go invited me to visit persuaded his mother to buy remind you to buy warned me (not) to use
reporting verb + preposition + noun or verb + *-ing*	complained about (not) having accused (Brian) of lying apologised for breaking
reporting verb + verb + *-ing*	suggested buying admitted stealing recommend installing
reporting verb + *(that)* + sentence	said they were

4 2 suggested going swimming that / suggested they went swimming that
3 told me to turn off / told me to switch off
4 reminded Natasha to post
5 of not taking any
6 to do her best

Speaking Part 4

1 **1** 4 minutes **2** the same theme as Speaking Part 3 **3** may be asked the same questions or different questions **4** your opinion plus an explanation, reason or example **5** listen carefully, may have to

2 Tell me about a machine or gadget you couldn't live without. Why (not)?

Recording script CD2 Track 19

Teacher: Irene

Irene: That's quite a hard question to answer because there are several things which really for me are necessities. If I had to choose, perhaps it would be my mobile phone. I find this really essential because it keeps me in touch with my friends and my family and I can find out where they are and what they're doing at any time. And also if I have any problems or an emergency I can always call someone for help, so for me it would be my mobile phone.

Teacher: Miguel

Miguel: I'm not too sure because I'm using different machines all day long and for almost everything I do. For example, I think I'd find life really difficult without my car to get around in. And I couldn't do any work without my computer. I mean I do everything on the computer. On the other hand, I love listening to the radio and I get all my news from there, so that's another thing I don't think I could give up.

3 **Irene:** mobile phone – to keep in touch with friends and family, to get help with problems or in an emergency
Miguel: several things: car to get around in, computer for work, radio to listen to news

4 **1** Irene **2** Miguel **3** both Irene and Miguel **4** both candidates give good answers

5 They used phrases 1 and 2.

Use of English Part 4

1 **1** eight **2** five **3** word **4** Contractions **5** change **6** vocabulary **7** same **8** number **9** given

2 **1** her homework on her own **2** didn't mean to dial **3** are expected to rise **4** to have got lost **5** had the system installed by **6** wouldn't have broken out **7** can't have borrowed **8** Don would cut down

Writing Part 2
A review

1 **1** *Students' own answers*
2 type of gadget, why you bought it, if it meets your requirements, if you would recommend it to other people **3** *Students' own answers*

2 Yes

3 *Sample answer:* See the model answer in Exercise 2.

Vocabulary and grammar review Unit 15

Word formation

1 **2** scientist **3** singer **4** chemist **5** magician **6** geologist **7** manager **8** electrician **9** assistant **10** postman

2 **2** safety **3** amazement **4** repetition **5** existence **6** truth **7** height **8** addition **9** difference **10** inventions

Grammar

3 **2** was broken into by **3** were/are reported to have **4** has not been serviced for/in **5** is said to be living **6** the cakes had been eaten

Vocabulary and grammar review Unit 16

Vocabulary

1 2 controlling 3 supervised 4 checking 5 supervising 6 check

Grammar

2 2 whether/if 3 if 4 even though 5 in case 6 even if 7 when 8 even if 9 in case 10 even though

3
2 Mark of being the one who caused the accident / of causing the accident
3 to Maria for not ringing her
4 me to go/come skiing with her
5 to do the photocopies for Trish
6 (me) that she would give me all the money back at the end of the month / to give me all the money back at the end of the month
7 visiting the Musée d'Orsay while they were in Paris / that they visited the Musée d'Orsay while they were in Paris
8 me to buy some eggs while I was out
9 her to walk very carefully because the path was slippery
10 the thieves to drop their guns and put their hands on their heads

Writing reference

Part 1

Exercise 1

1
 1 suggest either 5th or 7th November to speak to students
 2 give her some ideas about what aspects of her work students would find most interesting
 3 tell her a DVD player would be better for showing the short film
 4 give number and age range of audience

2 a formal style (similar to the email in the task)

3 aspects of her work students would find most interesting, number and age range of audience

Exercise 2

1 talk about the police's work in fighting crime and how they go about it and about career opportunities in the police force; audience: 100 people aged between 16 and 18 and a few teachers

2 formal

Part 2

Letters

Exercise 1

1 An English friend, Pat

2 what a typical family in your country is like and how family life is changing

3 project, different countries

Exercise 2

1 families close, spend time together, help each other, get together at weekends, young people live with parents until 25 or 30, get married in 30s, have children quite late, just one or two children

2 women now work, men take more responsibility in home, people richer, moving to larger houses in suburbs

Reports

Exercise 1

1 formal – it's for your teacher

2 formal style; yes

Stories

Exercise 1

1 When I got up that morning, I thought it would be just another ordinary day ...

2 starting with the words

3 other students at the school

Exercise 2

2 no – you should use a range of past tenses to make the story more dramatic

3 yes – it makes the story more interesting to read

4 yes

5 maybe

6 yes

7 maybe

Exercise 3

1 yes

2 no

3 yes

4 yes

5 no

6 yes (surprised, shocked, frightened)

7 yes

Reviews

Exercise 1

1 what it's about, why we would all enjoy it

2 everyone would enjoy, film or book

3 readers of your school's English-language magazine, i.e. other students; in the magazine

Exercise 2

1 first and second paragraphs

2 third paragraph

Articles

Exercise 1

2 d **3** e **4** h **5** c **6** b **7** a **8** i **9** f

Exercise 2

Para 1: c Para 2: b Para 3: a Para 4: d

Essays

Exercise 1

1 Your teacher

2 giving your opinions, All young people should continue at school or college until at least the age of 18

Exercise 2

Para 1: Introduction: the situation in my country now

Para 2: Points in favour:

1 *difficult for 16 yr olds to find work* + reason *jobs more specialised and technical*

2 *stay at school* + reason *more opportunities in future*

Para 3: Points against:

1 *some students – school difficult/boring* + reason *prefer earning money*

2 *cause problems for other students* + reason *not motivated*

Para 4: My opinion(s) *stay at school – practical/ technical subjects* + reason(s) *leave too soon – miss opportunities*

Speaking reference

Part 1

Exercise 1

2 f **3** d **4** i **5** g **6** c **7** e **8** j **9** a **10** h

First Certificate model paper from Cambridge ESOL

Paper 1 Reading

Part 1

1 A **2** B **3** B **4** D **5** B **6** D **7** A **8** C

Part 2

9 F **10** E **11** H **12** A **13** B **14** G **15** D

Part 3

16 B **17** D **18** A **19** B **20** C **21** C **22** A

23 A **24** D **25** B **26** C **27** D **28** C **29** A **30** D

Paper 2 Writing

Part 1

Question 1

CONTENT
Email should include all the points in the notes.

- Thank James for accepting the invitation.
- Say which of the two given dates is preferred (not necessary to say why).
- Give some information about the sports club members (not necessarily their ages or the sports they enjoy).
- Suggest one or more topics which James could talk about.

ORGANISATION AND COHESION
Clear organisation of ideas, with suitable paragraphing, linking and opening/closing formulae as appropriate to the task.

RANGE
Language relating to the functions above.
Vocabulary relating to sport and sports people.

APPROPRIACY OF REGISTER AND FORMAT
Standard English appropriate to the situation and target reader, observing grammar and spelling conventions.

TARGET READER
Would be informed.

Question 2

ESSAY

CONTENT
Essay should state which subject(s) candidate thinks are most important for young people to study at school. It is acceptable to say that all subjects are equally important/unimportant.

ORGANISATION AND COHESION
Clear organisation of ideas with suitable paragraphing and linking.

RANGE
Language of describing, explaining and expressing opinion.
Vocabulary relating to subjects studied at school.

APPROPRIACY OF REGISTER AND FORMAT
Consistent register suitable to the situation and target reader.

TARGET READER
Would be informed.

Question 3

STORY

CONTENT
Story should continue from the prompt sentence.

ORGANISATION AND COHESION
Storyline should be clear. Paragraphing could be minimal.

RANGE
Narrative tenses. Vocabulary appropriate to the chosen topic of story.

APPROPRIACY OF REGISTER AND FORMAT
Consistent register suitable to the story.

TARGET READER
Would be able to follow the storyline.

Question 4

REVIEW

CONTENT
Review should:

- describe the music on the CD
- explain what the candidate thinks about it
- say whether candidate would recommend it to others.

ORGANISATION AND COHESION
Clear organisation of ideas, with suitable paragraphing and linking.

RANGE
Language of describing, explaining and giving opinion.

APPROPRIACY OF REGISTER AND FORMAT
Consistent register suitable to the situation and target reader.

TARGET READER
Would be informed.

Question 5a

SET TEXT

CONTENT
Article should give opinions about the ending of the book, explaining how the candidate feels about it.

ORGANISATION AND COHESION
Clear organisation of ideas, with suitable paragraphing and linking.

RANGE
Language of giving opinion and expressing feelings.
Vocabulary relating to how the story ends.

APPROPRIACY OF REGISTER AND FORMAT
Consistent register suitable to the situation and target reader.

TARGET READER
Would be informed.

Question 5b

SET TEXT

CONTENT
Essay should describe how the characters of Jane and Lizzie Bennett are different and explain why their relationship is strong.

ORGANISATION AND COHESION
Clear organisation of ideas, with suitable paragraphing and linking.

RANGE
Language of describing, explaining and giving opinion.
Vocabulary relating to character and relationships.

APPROPRIACY OF REGISTER AND FORMAT
Consistent register suitable to the situation and target reader.

TARGET READER
Would be informed.

Paper 3 Use of English

Part 1

1 C **2** D **3** B **4** C **5** A **6** D **7** C **8** B **9** C **10** A **11** C **12** C

Part 2

13 as **14** at **15** in **16** which **17** than **18** more **19** to **20** were/are **21** because **22** of **23** so **24** most

Part 3

25 limited **26** advisable **27** headache **28** dependent **29** unhealthy **30** helpful **31** encouragement **32** carefully **33** probability **34** unfortunately

Part 4

35 be **requested** to show (them)/produce
36 **wish** (that) I had/'d visited
37 I look/check it **up** in
38 **whether** she/Sophie had had OR her/Sophie **whether** she had had
39 was (completely/totally) **unaware** of
40 are not/aren't **as** many
41 too far **away**
42 difficulty/difficulties **in** understanding the

Paper 4 Listening

Part 1

1 B **2** A **3** C **4** C **5** A **6** B **7** C **8** A

Part 2

9 natural history **10** Room Managers / room managers **11** hotel (for example) **12** Japanese **13** Team Leader / team leader **14** information desk **15** orange **16** 11,200 / eleven thousand two hundred **17** weekend (off/free) **18** 15(th) December / (the) fifteenth of December / December 15(th)

Part 3

19 E **20** C **21** A **22** F **23** D

Part 4

24 A **25** B **26** C **27** A **28** B **29** A **30** B

Model paper

Recording script CD3 Track 2

This is the Cambridge First Certificate in English Listening Test.

I'm going to give you the instructions for this test.

I'll introduce each part of the test and give you time to look at the questions.

At the start of each piece you'll hear this sound:

***

You'll hear each piece twice.

Remember, while you're listening, write your answers on the question paper.

You'll have 5 minutes at the end of the test to copy your answers onto the separate answer sheet.

There will now be a pause. Please ask any questions now, because you must not speak during the test.

PART 1 CD3 Track 3

Now open your question paper and look at Part 1.

You'll hear people talking in eight different situations. For questions 1–8 choose the best answer, A, B or C.

One.

On a train, you overhear a man talking on a mobile phone. Why will he be late?

A because of the bad weather
B because of an unexpected meeting
C because of his car breaking down

***

Did I say I'd be there by seven? ... Well, there's been a change of plan. I'm on the train now, but I can't come straight to you because I've got to call in at the office and see someone about a company car ... I'm sorry, I know it'll make me late, but this evening's the only time he's available. I'll meet you at the restaurant ... Yes, I know it's raining, but get a taxi there and go straight inside. Then you won't get wet.

***

TAPE REPEAT

Two.

You overhear a woman in a café telling her friend about her holiday.

What did she do?

A She borrowed a video camera.
B She hired a video camera.
C She bought a video camera.

***

Man: So, did you enjoy the holiday, though?

Woman: Yes, it was fantastic. You'll have to come round one evening and watch the video Jeff made. It's really good.

Man: I didn't know you had a video camera.

Woman: No, well we've been planning to get one for years, but they're still really expensive and what with Jeff only working part-time, we just couldn't afford it. Then we thought of just renting one for the fortnight, but then in the end my neighbour said we could have hers, as she didn't need it for a while. It cost us quite a lot, actually, because she gave us an enormous shopping list of things she wanted from Spain and we couldn't charge her for them really, in the circumstances. But at least we got the camera.

***

TAPE REPEAT

Three.

You hear a radio programme about dealing with stress.

What is the woman advising people to do?

A try an unfamiliar activity
B do an energetic activity
C find an interesting activity

***

I had a very stressful job and it was very difficult to relax until I found something that completely involved me and where I could try hard to see an improvement. I had two small children, and no time for myself. I tried reading various self-help books but one day a friend suggested Latin American dance classes – I used to go to classes at university ... Now I go as often as I can, and I love it. My dancing has got better – and I've got much fitter too. But it doesn't matter what you do – my friend goes to book-binding classes in the room next door!

***

TAPE REPEAT

Four.

You overhear two friends talking about a job interview.

How did the young man feel about the question he was asked?

A embarrassed that he didn't have any hobbies
B annoyed at being asked a personal question
C surprised by the way the question was phrased

***

Paul: You know that interview I went for at the bank.

Anna: Yeah?

Paul: Well, they asked me what my hobbies were.

Anna: Oh, you're joking! But that's just so predictable. Whatever did you say?

Paul: Well, I told them. People don't call them hobbies any more. I mean, listening to music's not a hobby unless you're crazy about one band or something, and playing football at the weekend, you know, that's more a way of life. No, I told them that they should ask people about their interests.

Anna: Exactly. So, did you get the job?

Paul: No, I didn't actually.

***

TAPE REPEAT

Five.

You hear a woman talking about an experience she had when travelling.

What happened?

A She missed a ferry she intended to catch.
B She was given wrong information about ferries.
C All ferries were cancelled that day.

***

We had such a mess up trying to get back from Ireland. We were on the west coast and we were supposed to come back from Rosslare, the port in the south. And when we got there they'd cancelled the ferry. Brilliant. And the next one wasn't going until something like 9 o'clock that night so they told us we should drive up to Dublin and get another ferry from there. There was one at 4 o'clock. So we raced up the coast and arrived just in time to see it disappearing out of the harbour.

***

TAPE REPEAT

Six.

You hear a man talking on the radio about a film.

Which aspect of the film did he find confusing?

A the speed of the dialogue
B the development of the plot
C the number of characters

***

The problem with thrillers like this is that you spend most of the film wondering what's going on and if you miss a few lines of dialogue at the beginning you'll probably never catch up. It's only right at the end that it starts to make sense. So you actually enjoy it after you've seen it rather than at the time. The film jumps from one part of the world to another, which doesn't help, and several of the main actors look very similar which was really a mistake.

***

TAPE REPEAT

Seven.

You overhear three young people, Jane, Susan and Nick, planning a party.

What is Jane's responsibility?

A decorations
B food and drink
C invitations

***

Jane: Hi, Nick. Hi, Susan.

Nick: Hello, Jane. Hey, what have you got there?

Jane: Decorations.

Nick: Oh, I thought that was my job and you were sending out the ...

Jane: Yes, sorry, Nick. I saw them and liked them. Do you like them?

Nick: Well ...

Susan: They're lovely, Jane.

Jane: Thanks, Susan. So, how's the food and drink going?

Susan: Oh, fine. Lots of ideas. I'll manage very well, I think.

Nick: At least Susan is making progress.

Jane: Hang on. You're the only one who's still got it all to do.

Nick: Decorations aren't so easy as invitations, Jane.

Jane: Maybe, but you don't know the trouble I took over them.

***

TAPE REPEAT

Eight.

You hear a woman talking about living on her own.

What does she say about it?

A It's not the first time she has lived alone.
B It gives her plenty of time for housework.
C She prefers sharing with other people.

***

I lived on my own when I was twenty-six and hated it. I was scared and lonely. So I went back to sharing a flat but it was a nightmare, I felt I was in someone else's house. Now I wouldn't dream of living with someone else. I love the freedom I have, to stay up till 6 am if I want to and leave the washing-up. But the only downside is the worry of something going wrong, like the washing machine breaking down, because I've got to deal with it.

***

TAPE REPEAT

That's the end of Part 1.

PART 2 CD3 Track 4

Now turn to Part 2.

You'll hear an interview with Ayesha Surrenden, who is responsible for staff in a museum. For questions 9–18, complete the sentences.

You now have forty-five seconds in which to look at Part 2.

***

Interviewer: Hi, I'm Brad Taylor and this is the job-finder programme, where we look at job opportunities for young people in the region. This week, I'm joined by Ayesha Surrenden, who's the personnel manager at the City Museum. Ayesha, welcome.

Ayesha: Hi.

Interviewer: Now, it's a pretty big place the museum, isn't it?

Ayesha: Oh, yes, there's all sorts of things on display from paintings, obviously, through sculpture, costume, ceramics, a bit of everything. And we get people from all over the world coming to view the exhibitions in the natural history section, which is really famous. It would take days to see everything properly.

Interviewer: So there are lots of job opportunities?

Ayesha: That's right. At the moment, the museum is looking for more people to work as what are called Room Managers. Now these are not the people who put up the works of art and keep them clean, but they are more than just the old-fashioned security guards that you used to get in museums. These people are there to offer a friendly service to visitors in each room, as well as keeping an eye on the exhibits.

Interviewer: So you have to know a bit about art?

Ayesha: If you have an interest in art, that's good, but it's certainly not a requirement for the job, and you don't need to have worked in a gallery or museum before either. What's much more important is to have some sort of experience in dealing with the public, maybe working in a hotel for example. Because you'll be handling questions from members of the public, especially foreign visitors.

Interviewer: So languages are important?

Ayesha: Yes, any European language would be useful. Lots of people know some French or Spanish these days, but we would be specially keen to hear from anyone who's studied Japanese. We've got Chinese and Russian speakers on the staff, and we can make sure these people are on duty if we know we have a group coming.

Interviewer: So it's quite a varied job?

Ayesha: Yes, you'll be given a specific area of the museum to look after as part of a group of five people under a Team Leader, and you'll be expected to make sure that everything is running smoothly within that area. You could find yourself looking after a party of overseas schoolchildren or approaching people to ask them to observe the gallery's rules, such as not touching the art works. And, to add variety, you'll spend some time each week working at the information desk in the museum as what we call a 'meeter and greeter'. Then there's a restaurant and a shop in the building too. So you could be called on to help out in those places if there's a problem. And you'll look good too: all gallery assistants are provided with a very smart uniform, not the traditional black or brown type either, but an orange one. It was designed specially for us by a leading fashion house.

Interviewer: And is the job well paid?

Ayesha: Basic pay starts at £11,200 annually, but this can rise to £14,500 with experience, and there's also a staff canteen with very low prices. Because the gallery is open seven days a week, twelve hours a day, you work on shift, although you are guaranteed every third weekend off, and you get paid extra for working on national holidays, which is sometimes necessary. And another good thing is that all staff also receive a leisure card offering free entrance to most other galleries and museums in the country.

Interviewer: Right, that can't be bad. So how do you apply?

Ayesha: Well, anyone interested should call or write in for an application form. The office is actually closed from 20th December until 2nd January – it's our annual holiday – so the closing date for applications is 15th December and a series of interviews will be held on 8th January.

Interviewer: Ayesha, thank you.

Ayesha: Thanks, Brad.

Now you'll hear Part 2 again.

***

TAPE REPEAT

That' s the end of Part 2.

PART 3 CD3 Track 5

Now turn to Part 3.

You'll hear five different people talking about their favourite teacher. For questions 19–23, choose from the list A–F what each speaker says. Use the letters only once. There is one extra letter which you do not need to use.

You now have thirty seconds in which to look at Part 3.

***

Speaker 1: The school I went to was a very old-fashioned one so our teachers were quite strict and were always forbidding us to do things. I liked the Latin teacher best because she was incredibly enthusiastic about her subject and I always enjoyed her lessons and tried not to make too many mistakes. I remember studying Virgil's *Aeneid* with her, but we didn't read certain parts about Dido and Aeneas's love affair – they were considered unsuitable for young girls! It seems funny now. In the library, there was a locked cupboard and only teachers were ever supposed to read the books inside it. One day, I felt incredibly worldly-wise when the Latin teacher let me explore its contents.

Speaker 2: Today I make my living writing music, and when I was at school it was the only subject I was interested in. But because I was bad at other school subjects the music teacher believed I was hopeless at that too and never encouraged me. He even wrote to my parents that I was 'a below average student'! Luckily, Mr Hayes, the English teacher, who I liked better than the others, recognised my enthusiasm for music, although he knew little about the subject himself, and persuaded me to write my own musical compositions and play them in our drama classes – I loved that and felt I was making progress. I'm sure I would have gone on to music college after I finished school anyway, but those classes really gave me confidence.

Speaker 3: Mrs Winter was my favourite teacher although I never had lessons from her at school. When my parents wouldn't allow me to apply for a place at drama school, she persuaded them to change their minds. She read through the more amusing scenes from *Romeo and Juliet* with me in her sitting room. It wasn't fun though. I had to give a short performance before I could be accepted at drama school. Mrs Winter's standards were terribly high and, however hard I tried, she always said I could do it better! And when I'm performing on stage today, I still make use of things I learnt from her.

Speaker 4: When I was younger, I used to be a keen swimmer and once I was nearly chosen for a place in my country's Olympic team. My swimming coach, who was the teacher I liked more than any other, also happened to be my father! The difficult thing about having Dad as a coach was that I could never get out of a training session. Even when I broke a finger, he encouraged me into the pool with my hand in a plastic bag and made me practise my leg movements! It was laughable really. Eventually I got bored with swimming but Dad was determined to make a champion out of me. He's still disappointed that I gave it up.

Speaker 5: My teachers probably hated having me in their class. I was always playing tricks on them and trying to get the other kids into trouble. A girl once burst into tears in an English class, saying I was ruining her education by being so noisy! And if I didn't like a teacher I just missed their lessons. But I always went to Miss Ford's classes because she didn't mind us having a laugh sometimes. In between the jokes, we got a lot of serious work done without realising it. Her method of teaching opened up the world of study for me and I'd definitely call her my favourite teacher.

Now you'll hear Part 3 again.

***

TAPE REPEAT

That's the end of Part 3.

PART 4 CD3 Track 6

Now turn to Part 4.

You'll hear an interview with Peter Jones, who works at an animal hospital. He's talking about how he recently rescued a baby seal. For questions 24–30, choose the best answer, A, B or C.

You now have one minute in which to look at Part 4.

***

Interviewer: Peter Jones works for an organisation that rescues sick or injured animals who normally live in the sea. He told me about how he found his latest patient, a baby seal, called Pippa.

Peter: I expect you know that seals feed on fish.

Interviewer: Mmm.

Peter: When they're babies, they can get into trouble really easily. If they're out to sea, for example, they can get caught in fishing nets, and fishermen sometimes bring them in to us.

Interviewer: Right.

Peter: But if they're close to the shore and they're injured, they usually come out of the sea themselves and then lie on the beach. They look rather like a large rock and unfortunately, people often walk right past them.

Interviewer: How did you find out about the seal you rescued recently?

Peter: She's called Pippa ... that's what we named her ... We got a phone call and when we got the call I did what we always do first. I asked the caller some questions to make sure that she was really injured ... sometimes you get calls about baby seals and when we arrive to collect them, we find out that they're simply asleep on the beach.

Interviewer: So there's nothing wrong with them at all ...

Peter: Exactly. But I could tell from this conversation that Pippa had been in a fight – probably with another baby seal, and I needed to collect her quickly because she was still moving.

Interviewer: What do you mean?

Peter: Well, there are things that can make a rescue operation difficult and this is one of them … by the time you've got all the equipment ready and got there, you go to the spot where you think the seal'll be and, of course, it isn't any more. When we arrived at the beach we had to follow the marks she'd made in the sand in order to find her. We were lucky that it wasn't dark and it was a pretty small area of beach.

Interviewer: So did you transport her in a special way?

Peter: There are certain things that we had to do first … before we picked her up … we looked at her cuts and took her temperature to check for any fever. We thought she might have been injured for some hours and be thirsty, so we gave her some water as well. Then we took her to our animal hospital where we checked her for any illness that might be dangerous to other sea animals.

Interviewer: How do animals react to being taken into a hospital – you must get a bit of resistance!

Peter: I think people expect us to get hurt. They think the animals are going to try and attack us or something. Occasionally, I've had a bit of a struggle to pick an animal up or get it to go where I want it to, but generally it's the opposite … they're shaking with fear and we have to reassure them that we aren't going to hurt them.

Interviewer: Was Pippa like that?

Peter: Yes, and what we do on arriving at the hospital, and it's the same with any animal, we always put them in an area by themselves to start with as this seems to make them calmer. Pippa actually had quite an affectionate personality but we do have to be careful – if you put animals together straight away they can bite each other or something. We can also get close to them and treat them more easily. Pippa wasn't that badly injured so …

Interviewer: Just some cuts and bruises?

Peter: Yes, we checked her every four hours and she was soon ready to move into the 'general' area of the hospital. Pippa was only a two-week-old pup so we started by feeding her milk and then we moved her on to fish around five to seven days after that, which is the normal time … about three weeks old. Pippa was quite thin when we first got her but she soon put on weight and made a quick recovery.

Interviewer: Well, I'm sure we're all glad to hear that …

Now you'll hear Part 4 again.

***

TAPE REPEAT

That's the end of Part 4.

There will now be a pause of five minutes for you to copy your answers onto the separate answer sheet. Be sure to follow the numbering of all the questions. I'll remind you when there is one minute left, so that you are sure to finish in time.

You have one more minute left.

That's the end of the test. Please stop now. Your supervisor will now collect all the question papers and answer sheets.

Acknowledgements

I'd like to give my warmest thanks to the editors for their help, advice, guidance, enthusiasm, feedback and ideas throughout the project: Susan Ashcroft and Nicholas White for their painstaking and detailed input; Niki Donnelly and Sara Bennett for their organisation and support; Alison Silver for her expertise, advice, encouragement, enthusiasm and meticulous hard work; Sophie Clarke (production controller), Michelle Simpson (permissions controller), Hilary Fletcher (picture researcher), John Green (audio producer), Tim Woolf (audio editor) and Ruth Carim (proofreader). Special thanks also to the design team at Wild Apple Design.

My thanks also to my students at the British Council, Valencia, from 2006 to 2007, who good-humouredly worked through and trialled materials, pointed out faults and suggested improvements.

Very special thanks to my family, Paz, Esteban, and Elena, for all their help and encouragement.

I dedicate this book to Paz with love and admiration for her courage through difficult times and her huge enthusiasm and support.

Thanks also to: Juan Barrios and Jenny Aquino for photo 3 on page 8, Olga Stankova for photo 4 on page 8 of her husband, Lubor Stanek and daughter Pavla Stankova, Elena and Esteban Brook-Hart and Bianca Selva for photo 1 on page 129.

Guy Brook-Hart
Valencia, Spain, January 2008

The author and publishers are grateful to the following for reviewing the material: Alison Silver, UK; Jane Coates, Italy; Nick Witherick, UK; Kevin Rutherford, Poland, Laura Matthews, UK; Christine Barton, Greece; Petrina Cliff, UK; Gill Hamilton, Spain; Rosalie Kerr, UK; Alison Maillard, France; Anne Weber, Switzerland; Fiona Dunbar, Spain; Rosemary Richey, Germany; Simon Vicary, Italy; Tonie de Silva, Mexico.

Development of this publication has made use of the Cambridge International Corpus (CIC). The CIC is a computerised database of contemporary spoken and written English which currently stands at over one billion words. It includes British English, American English and other varieties of English. It also includes the Cambridge Learner Corpus, developed in collaboration with the University of Cambridge ESOL Examinations. Cambridge University Press has built up the CIC to provide evidence about language use that helps to produce better language teaching materials.

The authors and publishers acknowledge the following sources of copyright material and are grateful for the permissions granted. While every effort has been made, it has not always been possible to identify the sources of all the material used, or to trace all copyright holders. If any omissions are brought to our notice, we will be happy to include the appropriate acknowledgements on reprinting.

Cambridge University Press for the entries from Cambridge Advanced Learner's Dictionary. Used by permission of Cambridge University Press; p. 7 Cambridge ESOL for the FCE content and overview. Reproduced with kind permission of Cambridge ESOL; pp. 10–11 Telegraph Media Group Limited for the adapted article 'How to live with teenagers' by Rachel Carlyle, The Daily Telegraph 27 July 2005, pp. 34–35 adapted article 'Learning about food' by Rose Prince, The Daily Telegraph 16 September 2006, p.120 adapted article 'My sister's circus' by Clover Stroud, The Daily Telegraph 6 July 2005. Reproduced by permission of the Telegraph Media Group Limited; p. 13 adapted article 'Who should do the housework' by Sharon Bexley, The Daily Mail 9 April 2002; pp. 16–17 Little Brown Book Group Limited and Peters Fraser & Dunlop for the adapted text 'My first bike' from Long Way Round by Ewan McGregor and Charley Boorman. Copyright © Long Way Round Limited 2004. Used by permission of Peters Fraser & Dunlop and Little Brown Book Group Limited; p. 37 Slow Food for the Slow Food logo; p. 40 Manchester Evening News for the adapted article 'Moso Moso' by Kyla, Manchester Evening News 17 August 2005. Used by permission of Manchester Evening News; pp. 52–53 Guardian News & Media Limited for the adapted text 'A close encounter in Africa' by Tim Adams, The Observer 22 January 2006, p. 128 adapted article 'Living on a Houseboat' by Tamsin Blanchard, The Observer 10 June 2001. Copyright Guardian News & Media Limited 2007; p. 56 The Press Association for the adapted text 'Earth getting darker as sunlight decreases', The Daily Mail 7 July 2005. Copyright The Press Association; p. 65 Lucy Irvine for the heavily adapted text 'Lucy's first job' from Runaway. Copyright © Lucy Irvine 1987. Used by kind permission of Lucy Irvine; p. 71 Adventure Sports Journal for the adapted text 'Are you ready for an adventure race?' by Rebecca Rusch Adventure Sports Journal 2006. Used by permission of Adventure Sports Journal. pp. 82–83 The Scotsman Publications Limited for the adapted text 'Five young actors' by Adrian Mather, The Evening News 29 March 2006. Used by permission of the Scotsman Publications Limited; p. 84 The Independent for the adapted text 'Young people dream of fame' by Sarah Cassidy, The Independent 13 January 2006. Copyright © Independent Newspapers; pp. 88–89 Mihaly Csikszentmihalyi for the text 'The secrets of happiness', The Times 19 September 2005. Used by kind permission of Mihaly Csikszentmihalyi; p. 102 Andrew Graham for the adapted article 'Help! My daughter's used my credit cards!' The Observer 30 October 2005. Used by kind permission of Andrew Graham; p. 107 Ode Magazine for the adapted text 'Problem school changes diet' by Marco Visscher, Ode Magazine Issue 26. Used by permission of Ode Magazine; pp. 119–120 NI Syndication for the adapted article 'Surviving an animal attack' The Sunday Times 23 April 2006, p. 184 adapted text 'Getting back on the Moon' by Anjan Ajuja, The Times 14 July 1999. Copyright © NI Syndication; p. 125 Curtis Brown Group Ltd for the adapted text 'My new home in Venice, 1733' from Lucifer's Shadow by David Hewson. Copyright © David Hewson 2001; p. 138 Attitude Travel for the adapted text 'The tomato fight fiesta' from' La Tomatina Festival' by Michelle O'Connor on www.attitudetravel.com; p. 143 Nick Clayton for the adapted article 'New Products Review' from The Scotsman. Used by kind permission of Nick Clayton www.nickclayton.com; p. 182 adapted text 'Jane Hissey, creator of the "Old Bear" Stories' by Victoria Kingston, Sussex Life December 1998.

Key: l = Left, r = Right. t = Top, bk = Background, b = Bottom, c = Centre, u = Upper, w = Lower, f = Far.

For permission to reproduce photographs: Action Plus/Neil Tingle p. 16 (7); Alamy p. 123, /© Alibi Productions p. 32 (tl), /© Jon Arnold Images Ltd p. 124 (5), /© Machteld Baljet & Marcel Hoevenaars p. 118 (b), /© David Ball p. 32 (cl), /© Patricia Belo/BrazilPhotos p. 55 (t), /© Oote Boe Photography p. 32 (br), /© Mark Boulton p. 52 (7), 73, /© Bubbles Photolibrary p. 104 (Student A r), /© Dominic Burke p. 70 (2), /© Gary Cook p. 55 (uc), /© Danita Delimont p. 98 (1), /© Elmtree Images p. 124 (3), /© Andrew Fox p. 124 (4), /© Chuck Franklin p. 120, /© David R. Frazier Photolibrary, Inc. p. 52 (2), 67 (cr), /© Stephen Frink Collection p. 118 (tr), /© Simon Grosset p. 10 (r), /© Angela Hampton Picture Library p. 34 (3), /© Robert Harding Picture Library Ltd p. 26 (1), 98 (5), /© Gavin Hellier p. 68 (bc), /© Tim Hill p. 34, 35, /© Images of Africa Photobank p. 116 (6), /© ImageState p. 44 (b), /© ISP Photography p. 129 (Student B t), /© Rainer Jahns p. 76, /© Scott Kemper p. 70 (6), /© Paul King p. 61 (1), /© Art Kowalsky p. 128, /© Stan Kujawa p. 124 (2), /© Chris McLennan p. 67 (r), /© Lisa Moore p. 118 (cr), /© Jeff Morgan technology p. 62 (2), /© Jeff Morgan built environment p. 124 (1), /© Renee Morris p. 33, /© Louise Murray p. 58 (tr), /© David Noble Photography p. 52 (6), /© Chuck Pefley p. 180 (tr), /© Photofusion Picture Library p. 51 (1), 109 (b), /© Powered by Light/Alan Spencer p. 70 (7), /© Paul Rapson p. 179 (l), /© Frances Roberts p. 104 (Students A l), /© Helene Rogers p. 62 (5), /© Philip Scalia p. 134 (2), /© Norbert Schaefer p. 179 (r), /© Alex Segre p. 58 (bl), /© South West Images Scotland p. 116 (1), /© Homer Sykes p. 134 (6), /© Paul Thompson Images p. 180 (tl), /© Vario Images GmbH & Co.KG p. 111, /© Janine Wiedel Photolibrary p. 180 (cr), /© Worldwide Picture Library p. 32 (cr), /© David Young-Wolff p. 16 (2), 88 (bl); ©BAA Limited p. 20 (b); ©BBC p. 80 (tl, tr, br); Anthony Blake Photo Library/©Anthony Blake p. 65; The Grand Canal near the Rialto Bridge, Venice, c.1730 (oil on canvas), Canaletto, (Giovanni Antonio Canal) (1697-1768) / Museum of Fine Arts, Houston, Texas, USA, Robert Lee Blaffer Memorial Collection / The Bridgeman Art Library p. 125; ©Guy Brook-Hart p. 8 (3, 4), 104 (Student B r), 129 (Student A t), 135; Corbis p. 146 (bl), /© Georges Antoni/Hemis p. 51, /© Atlantide Phototravel p. 36 (cl), /© Bloomimage p. 113 (tl), /© Fabian Cevallos/Sygma p. 68 (tr), /© Mike Chew p. 22 (Pair B r), /© Comstock Select p. 58 (br), /© Dean Conger p. 83, /© W. Perry Conway p. 55 (b), /© Philip James Corwin p. 134 (4), /© Jim Craigmyle p. 106 (bcr), /© Jay Dickman p. 180 (bl), /© Kevin Dodge p. 11 (bottom), 49 (tr, br), 146 (tr), /© Vallon Fabrice/Sygma p. 80 (bl), /© Michele Falzone/JAI p. 26 (2), /© Randy Faris p. 36 (bl), /© Najlah Feanny p. 107, /© Waltraud Grubitzsch/dpa p. 44 (lc), /© David P. Hall p.12 (r), /© Paul Hardy p. 26 (3), /© Hoberman Collection p. 28, /© Jack Hollingsworth p. 146 (br), /© Robert Landau p. 104 (Student B l), /© David Madison/NewSport p. 70 (4), /© Ludovic Maisant p. 131, /© Lawrence Manning p. 16 (4), 68 (tc), /© Tim McGuire p. 126 (l), /© Wally McNamee p. 180 (br), /© Meeke/zefa p. 146 (tl), /© Gideon Mendel p. 36 (r), /© moodboard p. 146 (cl), /© Roy Morsch/zefa p. 106 (tcr), /© Marijan Murat/dpa p. 116 (4), /© Gabe Palmer p. 58 (tl), /© Michelle Pedone/zefa p. 113 (cr), /© Photolibrary.com/Flirt p. 116 (3), /© J.Riou/Photocuisine p. 36 (tl), /© Franck Robichon/epa p. 52 (3), /© Schlegelmilch p. 68 (br), /© Ariel Skelley p. 22 (Pair B l), 67 (fr), /© Paul Steel p. 134 (1), /© George Steinmetz p. 55 (c), /© Tom Stewart p. 44 (uc), /© Thinkstock p. 49 (tl), 49 (bl), /© M. Thomsen/zefa p. 109 (t), /© Adam Woolfitt/Robert Harding World Imagery p. 129 (Student B b), /© Scott Van Dyke/Beateworks p. 98 (2); ©CUP/Gareth Boden p. 44 (t); ©CUP/Trevor Clifford p. 142; ©Edifice p. 124 (6); Reproduced with permission of www.ego-lifestyle.com p. 143 (bl); Getty Images/AFP p. 38, /AFP/Jose Jordan p. 137, /Altrendo Images p. 62 (6), 106 (br), 116 (2), /Allsport Concepts/Mike Powell p. 67 (fl), /Bongarts/Martin Rose p. 70 (1), /Gallo Images/Manus van Dyk p. 118 (tl), /Getty Images News/Stephen Ferry p. 52 (5), /Guang Niu p. 70 (3), /Andy Lyons p. 70 (5), /Mark Mainz p. 98 (6), /Photodisc/Jack Hollingsworth p.8 (1), /Photodisc/SW Productions p.16 (1), /Photographer's Choice/Carlos Davila p. 106 (l), /Photographer's Choice/Ron & Patty Thomas p. 50, /Photonica/Christopher Bissell p. 88 (tr), /Photonica/PicturePress p.12 (l), /Photonica/Loretta Ray p 8 (2), /Riser/Pigeon Productions SA p. 129 (Student A b), /Stock4B/Jan Greune p. 71, /Stone/Martin Chaffer p. 204 (bl), /Stone/Joe Cornish p. 77, /Stone/Peter Correz p. 204 (tr), /Stone/Daniel J Cox p. 52 (4), /Stone/Britt Erlanson p. 19 (r), /Stone/Blasius Erlinger p. 104 (l), /Stone/Aaron Farley p. 62 (3), /Stone/John Giustina p. 52 (8), /Stone/JFB p. 106 (tr), /Stone/LaCoppola-Meier p. 106 (cl), /Stone/David Madison p. 68 (tl), /Stone/Hans Neleman p. 22 (Pair A t), /Stone/Marc Romanelli p. 16 (5), /Stone/Pete Seaward p. 26 (5), /Stone/Chad Slattery p. 32 (bl), /Stone/Siri Stafford p. 102, /Taxi/DreamPictures p.11 (t), /Taxi/Ken Chernus p. 32 (tr), /Taxi/Holly Harris p. 26 (4), /Taxi/Philip Lee Harvey p. 88 (br), /Taxi/Michael Krasowitz p. 67 (l), /Taxi/David Leahy p. 22 (Pair A b), /Taxi/Muntz p. 16 (6), /Taxi/Justin Pumfrey p. 16 (3), /Taxi/Jerome Tisne p. 34 (2), /Taxi/Adrian Weinbrecht p. 34 (4), /Taxi/Yellow Dof Productions p. 88 (tl), /Time & Life Pictures p. 126 (r), /UpperCut Images/Michael Grecco p. 92, /Tim Whitby/WireImage p. 17 (r), /Kevin Winter p. 84 (l); The Kobal Collection/Lucasfilm/20th Century Fox/Hamshere, Keith p. 17 (l); Masterfile/©Albert Normandin p. 204 (br); www.mayang.com/teaxtures p. 16 (bk), 31, 117, 119, 127; Moso Moso http://www.mosomoso.co.uk/ p. 40; Nabaztag by Violet (and eventually: the First Internet Connected Rabbit). www.nabaztag.com p. 143 (tl); NASA Goddard Space Flight Centre Image by Reto Stöckli: http://visibleearth.nasa.gov/view_rec.php?id=2429 p. 56, 57; NHPA/Andy Rouse p. 118 (cr); PA Photos/Martin Rickett/PA Archive p. 134 (3); Photofusion/©Guy Bell p. 62 (4), /©Vehbi Koca p. 67 (cl); Photolibrary.com/Flirt/Corbis p. 15, /Foodpix p. 98 (3), /Robert Harding Picture Library Ltd p. 180 (bc), /Japack Photo Library p. 116 (5), /Jtb Photo Communications Inc p. 134 (5), /Nonstock, Inc. p.10 (l), /Photononstop p. 34 (1); 2007 Punchstock/Digital Vision p. 68 (bl); Rex Features/Sonny Meddle p. 180 (tc), /Masatoshi Okauchi p. 84 (r); ©Slow Food p. 37; Still Pictures/©BIOS Ruoso Cyril p. 53, /©Thomas Kelly p. 55 (wc); Superstock/©age fotostock p 47, 49 (cl), 98 (4), 104 (c), 113 (bl, tr, br), 204 (tl); Reproduced with permission of www.verifyandlocate.com p. 143 (br); World Religions Photo Library/Christine Osbourne p. 136; Reproduced with permission of www.x-biking.com p. 143 (cl).

We have been unable to trace the copyright holder for the image on page 143 (tr) and would be grateful for any information to enable us to do so.

Illustrations: Mark Draisey p. 19, 21, 48, 90, 91, 145.
Gary Wing p. 30, 94, 101, 108, 127, 140, 200, 206

Cover design by Wild Apple Design Ltd

Designed and typeset by Wild Apple Design Ltd